Public Policy

Public Policy

A New Introduction

Christoph Knill
and
Jale Tosun

First published 2012 by
PALGRAVE MACMILLAN

Palgrave Macmillan in the UK is an imprint of Macmillan Publishers Limited, registered in England, company number 785998, of Houndmills, Basingstoke, Hampshire RG21 6XS.

Palgrave Macmillan in the US is a division of St Martin's Press LLC, 175 Fifth Avenue, New York, NY 10010.

Palgrave Macmillan is the global academic imprint of the above companies and has companies and representatives throughout the world.

Palgrave® and Macmillan® are registered trademarks in the United States, the United Kingdom, Europe and other countries

ISBN 978-0-230-27838-7   hardback
ISBN 978-0-230-27839-4   paperback

This book is printed on paper suitable for recycling and made from fully managed and sustained forest sources. Logging, pulping and manufacturing processes are expected to conform to the environmental regulations of the country of origin.

A catalogue record for this book is available from the British Library.

A catalog record for this book is available from the Library of Congress.

10 9 8 7 6 5 4 3 2 1
21 20 19 18 17 16 15 14 13 12

Printed and bound in Great Britain by CPI Antony Rowe, Chippenham and Eastbourne

Contents

List of Illustrative Material

Tables

Figures

Boxes

Preface

The study of public policy has made impressive progress over the course of the past thirty years or so. There has been a steady expansion of sophisticated theories and insightful empirical studies based on different methods. Thus, it is not too daring to state that public policy analysis has developed into one of the most productive areas of political science. In this book, we give a comprehensive overview of the most essential analytical concepts, theories and state-of-the-art tools of public policy analysis. While it is our primary objective to familiarize readers with these topics, equally we wish to invoke curiosity for analysing interesting developments in public policies. We believe that empirical observations made in real-life situations provide the most promising starting-points for research, and what we offer in this book are the tools for a theory-led analysis. Public policies all over the world are full of visions and promises. At the same time, there are inherent tensions in public policies and there exist problems that seem to be unsolvable. How do policy-makers cope with this? Are there differences in public policies and how are they made across countries, policy sectors and over time? These are the key research questions guiding this book.

To realize this project we received much help, and this we wish to acknowledge. We thank Steven Kennedy at Palgrave Macmillan, for encouraging us to write this book; he has been very supportive during the entire writing process. We thank Helen Caunce at Palgrave Macmillan for sharing her ideas with us in order to make the book more accessible to readers and Keith Povey (with Nick Fox) for efficient editorial assistance. We also express our gratitude to three anonymous reviewers for their comments and suggestions, that, without question, helped to improve the quality of the book. While we benefited from the feedback of all reviewers, we are particularly grateful to one of them who went through the manuscript sentence by sentence, annotated it and made numerous thought-provoking comments and demonstrated a very comprehensive knowledge of the topic. In addition, this book was helped by suggestions from Radha Jagannathan and Frank Fischer as well as discussions with our students at the University of Konstanz. Alexander Dietrich, Christian Rubba, Moritz Schirmböck and Pascal Simon deserve credit for helping us to finalize the manuscript. It goes without saying that we alone are responsible for all remaining errors or omissions.

CHRISTOPH KNILL
JALE TOSUN

List of Abbreviations

ASEAN	Association of Southeast Asian Nations
EU	European Union
FAO	Food and Agriculture Organization
GATT	General Agreement on Tariffs and Trade
IMF	International Monetary Fund
NAFTA	North American Free Trade Agreement
NATO	North Atlantic Treaty Organization
NATO (scheme)	Nodality, Authority, Treasure, Organization
NGOs	non-governmental organizations
OECD	Organisation for Economic Co-operation and Development
OSCE	Organization for Security and Co-operation in Europe
PPP	purchasing power parity
UN	United Nations
UNEP	United Nations Environmental Programme
UNICEF	United Nations Children's Fund
UPU	Universal Postal Union
WHO	World Health Organization
WTO	World Trade Organization

Acknowledgements

The author and publishers would like to thank the following who have kindly given permission for the use of copyright material:

Tables 2.1 and 2.2, which originally appeared in 'Types of Policies' from chapter 20 'Policy Making' by Christoph Knill and Jale Tosun in D. Caramani (ed.), *Comparative Politics*. By permission of Oxford University Press.

Table 7.2, which originally appeared as figure 7.5 in M. Howlett, M. Ramesh and A. Perl, *Studying Public Policy: Policy Cycles and Policy Subsystems*, 3rd edn © Oxford University Press Canada 2009. Reprinted by permission of the publisher.

Table 11.1, which originally appeared as table 1 in *Politische Vierteljahresschrift*, 51(3), 2010 © Springer SBM.

Table 11.2, which originally appeared as table 1 in the *Journal of European Public Policy* (October 2005, p. 768) © Routledge.

Every effort has been made to contact all the copyright-holders, but if any have been inadvertently omitted the publishers will be pleased to make the necessary arrangement at the earliest opportunity.

Chapter 1

Introduction

Public policies are omnipresent in our daily lives. Newspapers, the television, and the internet provide a constant supply of information on the making of public policies from the regulation of genetic engineering or blood alcohol limits for the operation of a vehicle to the financing of infrastructure projects like new roads or the level of income tax. Being indirectly confronted with policy decisions through media coverage is one thing, but almost every aspect of our daily life is to some extent directly regulated through public policy decisions of which we are often entirely unaware.

To illustrate this point, let us take a look at the daily routine of an average university student. Taking the bus to campus and back home after the classes have finished is governed by local traffic policy. The responsible local authority may decide the number of buses to be employed, their schedules, the routes of the individual lines and ticket prices, or, in a privatized system, may regulate bus companies' activities. At the university, the credits needed to be able to graduate, the possibility to study abroad through exchange programmes such as the Erasmus programme, and the level of tuition fees are central issues of higher education policy. Should a student get sick, health policies determine the costs and quality of the medical services. After graduation, former students applying for jobs will be affected by labour and income tax policy. In the event of economic recession individuals may also have to apply for unemployment benefits – a central area of social policy. These examples show that virtually nobody can escape the consequences of public policies in whichever country they live.

Consequently, learning more about the making of public policies must be seen as an important complement to all other themes addressed by the discipline of political science. Ranging much more broadly than just analysing political institutions, government behaviour, political parties, interest groups, or elections, the study of public policies concerns the whole process of public decision-making (John 2006).

The study of public policies seeks to understand the production and effects of public actions. Students of public policy are interested in the processes and decisions that define the outputs of a political system, such as higher education policies, social services, environmental regulations, the administration of the health system, or the organization of a police force. But policy research also highlights the broader effects resulting

1

from such policy decisions. To what extent do environmental regulations result in environmental quality improvements? What are the effects of budget cuts in the university system on educational performance? To what extent do changes in the organization of the public health system affect health levels?

If policy outputs and policy effects are the core topics of public policy, their study generally focuses on two fundamental issues: policy variation and policy change (see John 2003). Policy variation refers to the explanation of differences between public policies across sectors and countries. To what extent does policy-making differ in relation to say health policies compared to environmental or transport policies, and how can these differences be explained? And which factors account for similarities and differences in public policies between countries? Returning to our previous example on higher education policy, one might wonder why in one country there are tuition fees for university students and in others not. As we will see in Chapter 2, there is an ongoing debate in the literature as to whether and to what extent the shape of public policies is affected by sector- or country-specific factors (see Table 1.1).

With regard to policy change, the central focus is on the explanation of stability and change. Often, public policies remain highly stable over time, although their functionality and effectiveness have constantly been questioned, as has been the case, for instance, for the agricultural policy of the European Union (EU) since the early 1980s. How can we explain the sometimes surprising stickiness and stability of public policies? At the same time, policies can be subject to swift and fundamental transformations. Why do stable periods of decision-making sometimes give way to flux and unpredictability? In responding to these questions, public

Table 1.1   *Basic research topics of public policy analysis*

Analytical dimension	Policy sectors	Countries	Time
Basic research question	Explanation of policy variation/similarity across sectors.	Explanation of policy variation/similarity across countries.	Explanation of policy change/ stability over time.
Potential combinations	• Explanation of policy variation/similarity across sectors and countries; assessment of relative effect of sectoral versus national factors. • Explanation of change in cross-national and/or cross-sectoral policy variation over time; assessment of policy convergence versus policy divergence or persistence of existing differences.		

policy analysis often adopts a comparative research perspective and examines policy changes not only over time, but also across countries and different policy sectors (such as environmental or social policy). In this context, one particular area of interest is whether cross-country variations in public policies remain stable or conversely become more or less pronounced over the course of time. For example, the internationalization of certain issues such as environmental protection has resulted in an increasing cross-national similarity of policy arrangements (Holzinger *et al.* 2008a, 2008b).

It is the objective of this book to introduce the major analytical concepts, theories and state of the art tools of public policy analysis. In so doing, this book is designed to reach well beyond a mere description of public policies and the political processes producing them. It aims to invoke curiosity for analysing 'empirical puzzles' on the basis of compelling theoretical considerations, sound research designs and informative data.

This book takes a broadly positivist approach, seeking to explain variation and change in public policies on the basis of different frameworks and theories, with a particular emphasis on the resources, interests, norms, interrelationships and constraints of the involved actors (King *et al.* 1994; for a discussion see Keating 2009). While following this line of scientific reasoning, we acknowledge that this approach is not unchallenged in the literature. In particular, postpositivist or constructivist approaches to the study of public policy emphasize the complexity of social and empirical reality and the need to situate empirical inquiry in a broader interpretive framework. They question classical concepts of objectivity and proof and argue instead that the scientific interpretation of empirical evidence is strongly affected by the historical, political and social context in which scholars are located (see, e.g., Fischer 2003, 2006). However, we adopt a positivist approach here because in our view it is most suitable for attaining descriptive knowledge of the real world and therefore for shedding light on causal mechanisms.

This chapter provides an entrée to the study of policy-making in three steps. First, we need to get a basic understanding of the nature of the subject under study. What is a public policy and how can it be defined? Second, we outline the central analytical questions that have to be addressed in order to learn more about the processes, structures and problems characterizing the making of public policies. The chapter ends with an overview of the book's structure.

What is a public policy?

In political science, we generally find that there are three major subject areas that cut across the different subdisciplines: polity, politics and policy. While polity refers to the institutional structures characterizing a political system, the study of politics concentrates on political processes, such as party political cleavages. The analysis of public policy, by contrast, puts the content of policies centre stage. Rather than focusing on institutions or processes, the research interest is on the analysis of the outputs of a political system, i.e. the decisions, measures, programmes, strategies and courses of action adopted by the government or the legislature.

Polity, politics and policy

The focus on public policies, however, does not imply that polity and politics are not taken into account. On the contrary, these dimensions play an important role in explaining policy change as well as policy differences across countries. So, an important question of public policy analysis concerns the policy implications of a country's political institutions (its polities). Do polities have a crucial impact on policy-making? Which polities perform better? Likewise, the decision-making processes (politics) in a country are important for public policy choices. In this regard, a prominent argument is that countries reveal distinctive policy styles, i.e. more or less stable patterns that characterize the policy process (politics), which in turn affect the nature and design of their policies (Richardson 1982). By reversing this assumed causal relationship, Theodore Lowi (1964) developed his classical distinction of different policy types, arguing that different policy areas tend to be characterized by different politics which involve more or less conflicting interactions between political actors. So, even if our analytical focus is on the study of public policy, the polity and politics dimensions play an important role either as factors explaining public policies or as phenomena that are determined by policy types.

Elements of a public policy

Having introduced the linkages between polity, politics and policies, we still have to clarify what the term 'public policy' actually means. In the scholarly literature, there is a general consensus that a public policy can be defined as a course of action (or non-action) taken by a government or legislature with regard to a particular issue. Although this definition is very broad, it emphasizes two constitutive elements. First, public policies refer to actions of public actors (typically governments), although societal actors might to some extent be involved or participate in public decision-making. Second, governmental actions are focused on a specific issue, implying that the scope of activities is restricted to addressing a certain aspect or problem (such as air pollution control, animal protection, internet content or the liberalization of the telecommunications sector).

Although this general definition seems straightforward, there is, however, considerable variance in its concrete specification. With regard to public actions, for example, some authors insist that the presence of a policy requires the adoption of a larger number of related legislative and administrative activities (see Knoepfel *et al.* 2007: 24). Other scholars adopt a narrower definition and consider single governmental decisions or legal acts as public policies. This perspective has been prominent in the study of changes to welfare state expenditure (for an overview, see Green-Pedersen 2007). In this book, we will argue that the extent to which the presence of a public policy requires only one or a system of interrelated actions strongly depends on the issue at hand. Sometimes one single legal act might be very encompassing and entail a broad range of different activities, while in other constellations it might only constitute one out of several important elements of a public policy. It is hence not possible to specify generally a threshold number of courses of action as defining a 'public policy'.

In addition, we find different conceptions with regard to the nature of public policies as issue related. On the one hand, such policies are seen as governmental activities made in response to given societal or political problems. In other words, policy-making is conceived as a problem-solving activity (Lasswell 1956; Birkland 2010: 7–11). On the other hand, policy-making can be regarded as a means of exerting power by one social group over another (Knoepfel *et al.* 2007: 21–2). According to this perspective, the existence and particular design of policies are intended to protect the interests of certain groups, while disadvantaging others. For example, studies of political clientelism deal with this aspect, i.e. the distribution of selective benefits to individuals or clearly defined groups in exchange for political support (see Kitschelt and Wilkinson 2007). It is certainly true that 'all governments . . . give greater weight to the preferences of those citizens with more political power than to the preferences of those with less political power" (Miller 2004: 20). However, this does not mean that public policies represent ends in themselves. While the design of a given public policy might reflect the differential power resources of social groups, this need not call into question the need for a specific problem to exist or to be perceived in order for the policy-making process to be initiated. As a consequence, the problem-solving and power perspectives on public policy-making seem in practice to be compatible with each other.

Differences in scope: sectors, targets and instruments

So far, we have gained a basic understanding of the central elements that constitute a public policy. However, this still leaves us with a broad range of activities that might constitute public policies. This can be illustrated by the fact that the term 'policy' is used for activities of very different scope.

First, it is often used to cover a whole range of different measures in a certain sector, such as environmental policy, social policy, economic policy or fiscal policy. Used this way, the term grasps more than one legal act or political programme that belongs to the whole range of legal and administrative activities that are related to a particular distinctive policy field.

Second, a similar approach is used to describe public activities in policy subfields. In most instances, it is possible to classify the public activities in a field along certain subthemes that cover functionally related measures. With regard to environmental policy, for example, subsectors refer to water policy, clean air policy, climate change policy and waste policy. In social policy, examples of subsectors include pension policy, unemployment policy and child benefits.

Third, even within policy subfields, distinctive policy issues or targets can be identified. Taking clean air policy as an example, such targets include industrial discharges of different pollutants, urban air quality and car exhaust emissions. Hence a legal act – even if it is a markedly specific one – can address more than one policy target. For example, the 2004 Brazilian biosafety law is a broad-ranging piece of legislation that regulates all biotechnology activities in the country. The production of genetically manipulated soybeans represents one of many policy targets tackled by this law. Another is human cloning for reproductive purposes, which is banned under this law.

A fourth – and the least abstract – usage of the term refers to its connection with regulatory instruments. While policy targets refer to what a legal act regulates, policy instruments define how they are regulated. For example, one of the main tasks of immigration policy is to regulate which individuals may legally enter a country. The most common instrument is the establishment of a preference system based on quotas, targets or a ceiling, which allocates a number of visas to certain groups of immigrants. Another – and clearly much stricter – instrument would be an official ban on immigration (Adolino and Blake 2011: 103–4).

So we conceive of public policy in this book as a term that can refer to different phenomena, from the whole range of legal and administrative activities in a given policy field or subfield to concrete policy targets or – even more specifically – distinctive instruments. With this approach we will seek to attain a clearer description of the empirical phenomena under study. Reforms of child benefits, for instance, tend to be discussed in the media as if they could constitute a specific public policy. In reality, however, they represent only a single policy instrument. In a similar vein, smoking bans represent only one of many other instruments (such as the imposition of a tobacco tax) utilized by tobacco control policies.

Conversely, these two instruments relate to the corresponding policy target 'limiting tobacco consumption'.

Analytical perspectives on the policy-making process

So far, we have approached public policies from a merely substantive perspective, focusing on the central components that define a public policy. In this section, we adopt a procedural perspective on public policies and take a closer look at the specific phenomena characterizing the policy-making process. First, we will briefly present the different theoretical perspectives on the evolution of public policies. We will then distinguish the different stages of the policy process, which entail distinct research questions and which hence might serve as a basic analytical starting point for studying public policies.

Basic theoretical perspectives on public policies: rational process design, muddling through or just chance?

In the literature we find different attempts at analysing how public policies typically evolve or should evolve. While the rationalist approach defines an ideal conception of how policies should develop, the incrementalist perspective provides an explanation for the fact that in reality this ideal is hardly ever reached. A more radical view is the one advanced by the 'garbage can' model, which emphasizes that public policies often reveal the opposite pattern to that envisaged by rationalist models (Cohen *et al.* 1972).

The rationalist approach conceives of policy-making as a process of problem-solving. Rather than seeking to explain the policy process, this approach prescribes an ideal conception of how policy-making should be organized and evolve in order to achieve optimal solutions to the underlying policy problems. Hence it entails a normative (how policies should evolve) rather than a positive perspective (how policy can be explained) on policy-making. This question of how optimally to develop public policies was at the heart of Lasswell's (1956) thinking. He argued that ideally the policy process should be based on different steps that follow a logical sequence: intelligence (collection and processing of all relevant knowledge and information), promotion (identification and support of selected alternatives), prescription (imposition of a binding decision), invocation (policy enforcement), termination (abrogation of policy), and appraisal (evaluation of policy effects against the backdrop of initial objectives and intentions).

This prescription of how policies should be made was soon brought into question by its overly ambitious view of rational decision-making.

The theory of incrementalism explicitly rejected the idea of public policy being made on the basis of a fully rational decision-making process (Hayes 2006: 19). It originates in Lindblom's (1959) path-breaking article 'The Science of Muddling through' and was further formalized by Hirschman and Lindblom (1962), Braybrooke and Lindblom (1963) and Lindblom (1965). Public policy is regarded as the political result of the interaction of various actors possessing different types of information. These actors need to make concessions and therefore policy-makers primarily concentrate on aspects that are less controversial and more technical. This process of 'partisan mutual adjustment' can only lead to one outcome: incremental policy change. Empirically, the basic aim of incrementalism – i.e. incremental policy change – has often been tested by using budgetary data (see Wildavsky 1964; Berry 1990; Breunig *et al.* 2010).

Rather than an ideal, it purports to be a realistic description of how policy-makers arrive at their decisions. This implies that policy-makers act within the context of limited information, the cognitive restrictions of their minds, and the finite amount of time available for policy-making – all of which is largely congruent with the concept of 'bounded rationality' put forward by Simon (1955, 1957) and Cyert and March (1963). As a consequence, decision-makers apply their rationality only after having greatly simplified the choices available, turning them into 'satisficers' who seek a satisfactory solution rather than the optimal one: 'policy making is serial and remedial in that it focuses heavily on remedial measures that happen to be at hand rather than addressing itself to a more comprehensive set of goals and alternative policies' (Rajagopalan and Rasheed 1995: 291). In this way, policy-makers are not confronted with uncertain consequences which may result from more radical reforms.

While incrementalism still presumes that policy-making is characterized by an – albeit bounded – rational process in which solutions are developed in response to existing problems, the garbage can model (Cohen *et al.* 1972) questions even these less strict rationality assumptions and disconnects problems, solutions and decision-makers from each other. In contrast to the rationalist and incrementalist perspectives, decisions do not follow an orderly process from problem to solution, but are the outcomes of several relatively independent streams of events, namely problems, solutions, choice opportunities and participants.

In contrast to the conventional view that problems trigger decision-making processes, the garbage can model assumes that usually the involved actors within an organization go through the 'garbage' first and look for a suitable fix, i.e. the 'solution'. Hence solutions exist and develop independently of problems. The actors involved may have pre-existing ideas about possible solutions – they may be attracted to specific ones and volunteer to be their advocates. In many instances, solutions are prepared without knowledge of the problems they might have to solve. Organizations thus tend to produce many solutions which are later discarded due to a lack of appropriate problems. The independence of the problem and solution stream is further enhanced by the fact that participants may differ between the two streams: the actors involved in the development of solutions might be different from those who discuss the definition of the respective policy problems. Finally, the extent to which an existing solution might actually be linked to a problem is affected by whether or not a choice of opportunities exists, i.e. occasions when organizations are expected or perceive to be expected to produce a decision.

Stages of the policy process

So far, we have seen that the policy process can be approached from varying analytical angles that entail highly different assumptions with regard to the sequencing of policy-making. In the following it is not our objective to discuss the strengths and weaknesses of the different approaches or to rank them in light of their analytical relevance. Rather we ask if and to what extent it is analytically useful to distinguish between different stages of the policy process – notwithstanding the ambiguous picture that emerges from the previous theoretical discussion.

In the literature, the most common approach is the distinction of different policy stages that can be integrated into a process model: the famous 'policy cycle'. This models the policy process as a series of political activities, which basically consists of the following phases: (1) problem definition and agenda-setting; (2) policy formulation and adoption; (3) implementation; and (4) evaluation (with the potential consequence of policy termination or reformulation).

In many cases, the policy cycle model is interpreted as a sequential development, hence following closely the idea underlying the rationalist approach. Accordingly, the policy process starts with the identification of a societal problem and its placement on the government's agenda. Subsequently, various policy proposals are formulated, from which one will be adopted by the decision-makers. In the next stage, the adopted policy is enacted, before finally its impacts are evaluated. This last stage leads straight back to the first, indicating that the policy cycle is continuous and unending.

In view of the previous theoretical discussion it is not surprising that the idea of a cyclical model based on a sequence of policy stages has been criticized. In particular, it has been emphasized that the model hardly corresponds to empirical reality, as the different stages might often overlap (see, e.g., Colebatch 2006; Jann and Wegrich 2007: 43–5). For instance, a reformulation of policies might occur during the implementation stage; or some phases might be skipped – policies are not always subject to a systematic evaluation. Notwithstanding this criticism, the cycle model is employed as a standard approach for structuring the theories and concepts of public policy-making.

In this book, we will depart from the classical cycle approach by not assuming a sequential model of the policy process, apart from the fact that current policy decisions are not independent of decisions taken before and that policies under discussion today may have 'knock-on effects' leading to further policies tomorrow (Newton and van Deth 2010: 266). In line with many other authors (see, e.g., Fischer *et al.* 2007; Knoepfel *et al.* 2007; Hill 2009; Howlett *et al.* 2009; Anderson 2010; Birkland 2010), we consider it more useful to conceive of the different policy stages as potential analytical lenses on the policy-making process. Depending on the specific lens, we focus on distinctive questions and apply distinctive concepts and theories in order to explain observed patterns. If we focus on implementation, our major goal is to analyse and explain the extent to which we can observe deviations from the original policy goals. Looking at policy adoption, by contrast, the central objective is to explain adoption or non-adoption and in the case of policy formulation we want to account for the specific design of a policy. In other words, we consider the distinction of different stages as a heuristic tool that helps us to investigate the process of policy-making from different analytical angles (see Table 1.2).

Table 1.2   *Policy stages and related research topics*

Problem definition and agenda-setting	Policy formulation and adoption	Implementation	Evaluation
• Why do perceptions and definitions of policy problems change over time/vary across countries?	• How do policy decisions come about?	• Why do certain policies fail?	• How can policy effects (outcomes and impacts) be measured?
• Why are certain problems ignored while others are placed on the agenda?	• How can policy outputs be explained?	• Which factors account for the variance in policy implementation?	• Which factors explain variation in policy effects?

Studying public policy: approach and structure of this book

The study of public policy refers to the analysis of the contents, causes and conditions as well as the outcomes and impacts of governmental activities. It constitutes a highly diverse and dynamic research area. As emphasized above, it is nevertheless possible to identify dominant themes which guide the study of public policy, that is the explanation of policy variation and policy change across countries and policy sectors. These themes form the basic background for this book. At the same time, however, it is obvious that policy variation and change can be studied from very different perspectives, focusing, for instance, on the different elements of public policies or on the causal effects of different factors (such as socio-economic conditions, political and institutional factors, or international influences). Hence, even if we identify overarching research themes, there is still a need for additional analytical considerations that help to structure the analysis of public policy.

In this book, we differentiate between three analytical steps. First, we familiarize the reader with the basic analytical tools, concepts and theories that form the background for the study of public policy. In Chapter 2, we address key issues relating to the nature of public policy. In this context, several research questions are addressed. They include, first of all, the classical question about whether and to what extent it is possible analytically to distinguish different policy types. Second, a long-standing debate centres on the topic of policy styles. Is it possible to identify country- or sector-specific process patterns that characterize the making of public policies? Which factors account for differences in policy styles across countries or sectors?

In Chapter 3, we shift our focus to the central actors and institutions that are involved in the development, formulation, execution and evaluation of public policies. As already emphasized, public policies are affected by many factors, including in particular polity (the institutional context in which policies are developed and implemented) and politics (the interests of the involved public and societal actors and the cleavages and relationships between them). In order to shed more light on potential interlinkages between polity, politics and policy, we discuss the institutions and actors that are most central for understanding the making and shaping of public policies.

Chapter 4 provides an overview of general theories that are applied in order to explain policy variation and policy change. What are the central explanatory factors that are of relevance in this regard? In the literature, varying approaches can be identified. They include structural explanations (in which socio-economic structures and the pressure of problems constitute the basic explanatory variables); interest group models (emphasizing the crucial role of the power and resources of societal interests); political economy accounts involving self-interested, vote-seeking politicians and budget-maximizing bureaucrats; models focusing on the ideological and programmatic differences between political parties; and institutional theories (in which major explanatory relevance is attached to the policy implications of a country's political institutions).

Having gained an understanding of the basics of public policy analysis, we shift the focus to the second analytic step: the specific analysis of the central stages of the policy process. So, different actors might be involved to different degrees during the stages of problem definition, agenda-setting, policy formulation and adoption, implementation, and evaluation – implying that constellations of strategic interaction as well as institutional rules affecting strategic opportunities and constraints for the involved actors will vary. If and to what extent theoretical models and explanatory approaches need to take account and be adjusted in the light of these aspects is an important research topic. This is further enhanced by the fact that the distinction of different stages typically goes hand in hand with different research questions that are addressed. For example, with regard to problem definition, the focus is on the factors that account for why a certain problem is perceived in a certain way. For agenda-setting, by contrast, we are interested in the reasons that explain why a certain problem is placed on the political agenda when others are not. With regard to policy adoption, the major focus is on the explanation of the specific policy design that is selected; while for the implementation stage, scholarly attention shifts to the analysis of the potential deviations from the original policy objectives and the underlying reasons for these shifts. Policy evaluation is about the effects of public policies.

Chapters 5 to 8 take up the phases of the policy cycle. Chapter 5 addresses the phase of problem definition and agenda-setting. The second phase of the policy cycle (decision-making) is explored in Chapter 6. Decision-making consists of two related concepts – policy formulation and policy adoption – which we will discuss at length. Of these two processes, policy adoption is more concerned with institutional arrangements, whereas policy formulation focuses more explicitly on the various forms of political power. Chapter 7 addresses the implementation of policies that have passed the adoption process. We outline why at the implementation stage bureaucrats might deviate from the goals originally formulated by policy-makers and we discuss how the likelihood of 'bureaucratic drift' can be effectively reduced. Once we have clarified how public policies come about, in Chapter 8 we shift our attention to policy evaluation.

In the third analytical step, we shift from a stage-centred analysis of the policy process to a study of the key topics of public policy that cut across different policy stages. In Chapter 9 we consider the topic of governance – a term that has been much developed since the early 1990s. Governance typically refers to the distinctive analytical perspective on policy-making that emphasizes the sharing – sometimes even blurring – of competencies between public and private actors. It cuts across the policy stages model by focusing on the exchange relationships between public and private actors when they are confronted with political problems. By explicitly emphasizing the potential problem-solving contributions of private actors and the potential restrictions for public problem-solving capacities as a result of growing international and domestic-level interdependence, the governance perspective shifts the analytical focus from a purely state-centred perspective to one which deals with the patterns of state–society relations.

In Chapter 10 we take account of the fact that the development and implementation of national policies is increasingly overlapped by similar activities at the international level: the public policies which exist beyond the nation state. There are many reasons that favour the development of joint policies at the international level. At the same time, however, both the adoption and implementation of international policies are characterized by specific challenges that are increasingly addressed by scholars of public policy.

In Chapter 11, the focus is on the analysis of policy change and policy convergence. The study of policy change is a demanding one. Areas of policy change investigated by public policy scholars have included welfare state retrenchment and race-to-the-bottom scenarios in the fields of environmental protection and labour standards. Policy change is closely related to the concept of cross-national policy convergence. Convergence research investigates whether public policies in various countries become increasingly similar over time.

Finally, in Chapter 12 we summarize the main characteristics of policy-making on the basis of the explanations we have given in the course of this book. In addition, we point to potential avenues for improving the state of the art.

Chapter 2

The Nature of Public Policies

Reader's guide

Public policies are omnipresent in our daily lives and relate to many diverse areas, including defence, education, environmental protection, health care, unemployment benefits, motorway construction, monetary issues and taxes. For analytical purposes, however, it is useful to think of ways of assigning public policies into specific groups as this allows us to make more general statements. The objective of this chapter is to introduce and discuss criteria employed in the policy-analytical literature for categorizing public policies. The most widely applied instrument for achieving this refers to the construction of typologies, though the actual idea underlying these typologies is that specific groups of public policies entail equally specific patterns of policy-making. Thus, conceiving of these typologies as tools for descriptively categorizing public policies would not do them justice. We will suggest alternative approaches to categorizing public policies, which include considerations about how they bring about changes in the behaviour of those that the policy is aimed at and how they shed light on different policy dimensions. While typologies represent simple analytical frameworks, the term 'dimensions' concerns the different aspects of a public policy which can refer to the stage of its development or its contents. We will also introduce the concept of policy styles, which is about ways in which governments make and implement public policies: a perspective which further underscores the fact that the nature of public policies cannot be fully understood without paying attention to politics. More generally, the topics addressed in this chapter represent the key issues of 'classical' public policy analysis and serve as the basis for the subsequent explanations as providing a better understanding of what public policies are and how their particular characteristics might influence the process in which they are made.

As outlined in Chapter 1, political science is mainly concerned with three major analytical dimensions: polities, politics and policies. Polities are the institutional arrangements characterizing a political system. Politics refer to the patterns of the policy-making process, involving various types of actors and their interactions. (Public) policies refer to the output of a political system as it is realized in practice, including the laws, regulations, decisions, plans, programmes and strategies that follow a particular purpose: they are designed to achieve defined goals and present solutions to societal problems.

These specifications of what constitutes a public policy still leave us with an immense field of governmental actions. A public policy can as much relate to the minutiae of unemployment benefits and the requirements of air pollution control as to the legalization of drugs or the government's decision to use daylight saving time. To grasp the nature of public policies, identifying nominal policy types is hardly sufficient. We are still left with many different dimensions that define the specific content of a policy. For example, a policy aiming to limit air pollution might be composed of many varying measures, usually referred to as policy instruments, such as maximum permissible limits for all possible pollutants emitted into the air by mobile sources, e.g. passenger cars, stationary sources or production plants. Even if described in an identical manner, such as 'clean air policy', public policies are likely to differ with regard to their design from one jurisdiction to another. So how could we possibly make generalizable statements about clean air policy?

Given the huge variety of different policies, many attempts have been made to classify policies on the basis of predefined analytical criteria. The latter include the characteristics of the policy-making process (policy styles), the effects of a policy with regard to the allocation of costs and benefits concerning the relevant actors, or the way in which a policy seeks to affect the behaviour of individuals in concert with certain policy objectives.

Typologies of public policies

The policy-analytical literature has strongly relied on typologies for classifying different types of public policies. Most essentially, a typology allows for grouping entities by similarity. Initial attempts at classification followed rather obvious lines of similarity in descriptive terms, such as nominal typologies based on the subject matter, e.g. environmental policy, social policy, economic policy or agricultural policy. Other nominal modes of classification are based on time period (e.g. post-war policy), ideology (e.g. conservative policy) or institutions (e.g. regional policy, local policy, European policy) (McCool 1995: 175). With the maturation of public policy analysis, typologies have increasingly emphasized a similarity in terms of analytical considerations. In this section, we present the most influential analytical classifications of public policies. Each of these classifications adopts a different analytical lens, stressing either the possibility that public policies can be grouped with regard to their implications for the politics dimension or how they affect the behaviour of the target group.

Classification by implications for politics

The classical approaches to the study of public policy have often used typologies as 'analytical shortcuts' for the underlying decision-making processes. In this context, the two most influential typologies have been put forward by Theodore J. Lowi (1964, 1972) and James Q. Wilson (1989, 1995).

Lowi's policy typology
The classification proposed by Lowi (1964, 1972) corresponds to long recognized differences among public policies and their making, leading to the famous causal statement that 'policies determine politics'. The categorization consists of (1) distributive policies relating to measures which affect the distribution of resources from the government to particular recipients; (2) redistributive policies which are based on the transfer of resources from one societal group to another; (3) regulatory policies which specify conditions and constraints for individual or collective behaviour; and (4) constituent policies which create or modify the state's institutions.

Of these four policy types, the politics of constituent policy is expected to attract the lowest degree of public attention as only the top political stratum tends to be concerned. Distributive policies are characterized by the use of public funds to assist particular societal groups. Those who benefit usually do not directly compete with one another. The costs are assigned to the general public (i.e. all taxpayers) rather than a specific group (Anderson 2010: 9–17). In this way, distributive policies appear to create only winners and no specific group of losers. As a consequence, the policy process should reflect a rather consensual pattern as the potential for conflicts between winners and losers is very limited.

Regulatory policies define rules for human behaviour rather than entailing financial transfers. However, they can still strongly affect the distribution of costs and benefits between societal actors. For instance, market regulation abolishing monopolist structures and introducing fierce competition will entail benefits for consumers but higher costs for companies. However, the degree of political conflict can vary in the area of regulatory policies.

For redistributive policies, by contrast, such conflicts are much more likely, as they involve the reallocation of costs and benefits between different societal groups. A typical cleavage in this regard refers to resource reallocations between rich and poor people (e.g. by introducing progressive taxation or income-based benefits). Another cleavage underlying redistribution might be observed between younger and older generations (e.g. a pension scheme in which the contributions of younger people are used to pay the pensions of retired people). Any change in the pension level or the contribution level might influence the allocation of costs and benefits between these groups, hence often inducing a highly conflictual political process characterized by the broad mobilization of societal actors (see Table 2.1).

While initially compelling, on closer inspection the clarity of the typology dissolves and conceptual ambiguities among the policy types can be identified, which Lowi himself also acknowledged (1964: 690; see also Greenberg *et al.* 1977; Heckathorn and Maser 1990; Hayes 2007). Most importantly, the typology is not based on clear-cut analytical distinctions. While the distinction between redistributive and distributive policies is based on different policy effects, i.e. the (re)distribution of resources, Lowi emphasizes the regulation of human behaviour as the central criterion of the regulatory policy type. This creates the false

Table 2.1 *Lowi's policy typology*

Type of policy	Definition	Examples
Regulatory policies	Policies specifying conditions and constraints for individual and collective behaviour	Environmental protection; migration policy; consumer protection
Distributive policies	Policies distributing new (state) resources	Farm subsidies; local infrastructure such as highways and schools
Redistributive policies	Policies modifying the distribution of existing resources	Welfare; land reform; progressive taxation
Constituent policies	Policies creating or modifying the state's institutions	Changes of procedural rules of parliaments; creation of new agencies

Sources: Based on Lowi (1972: 300) and Knill and Tosun (2011).

impression that regulatory policies have no distributive or redistributive effects (see also Birkland 2010: 215). As for constituent policies, the analytical focus shifts again to the subject matter of a certain policy, in this case the polity.

There are also some problems that specifically relate to the distinction between redistributive and distributive policies. First and most importantly, it seems hardly possible *ex ante* to define a policy as distributive or redistributive. This can be traced to the fact that this classification depends on the individual perceptions of the actors concerned: the allocation of transfers to a certain group might trigger strong opposition, even though the money is taken from the general budget; or taxpayers may mobilize against such transfers if they fear future tax increases. In other words, in many instances the classification of a policy as distributive or redistributive can only be achieved *ex post*. Second, governments might try to influence the perception by societal actors of the costs and benefits by strategically labelling a policy as distributive notwithstanding its redistributive effects. Third, the perception of a policy as distributive or redistributive might vary over time. When there are high austerity pressures and high unemployment, and hence fewer pension insurance contributors, any increase in contribution levels is more likely to be perceived as redistributive activity, as would be the case during an economic boom. Finally, we should emphasize that the effects of a policy can hardly be considered as the only factor influencing patterns of policy-making. In addition to the policy type, many other variables – such as institutional arrangements, the party system or general relationships between state and society – might have an impact on policy-making processes. We may conclude that it is not just policies that determine politics.

Another issue that has been raised in this context is whether the typology is indeed complete. A case in point is the recent discussion on the extent to which 'morality policy' can be considered as an additional policy type, hence supplementing Lowi's distinctions. This particular policy, inter alia, comprises 'abortion, capital punishment, legalized gambling, homosexual rights, pornography [and] physician-assisted suicide' (Mooney 1999: 675). It is argued that the distinctive feature of morality policies is that they entail the regulation of conflicts amongst social values. This feature makes this policy type distinct from policies of distribution and redistribution or social and economic regulation where political processes are dominated by conflicts over tangible resources (see Meier 1994; Mooney 1999). These issues may also by no means be regarded as similar to constituent policies.

Even though morality policies from Lowi's perspective could still be viewed as regulatory policy, it is argued in the literature that such policies should be conceived as an additional policy type, as one particularly

---

BOX 2.1   Politics of same-sex marriage

An example of morality policies is the legalization of same-sex marriage. In the last few years, there have been highly controversial debates as to whether or not marriage between two persons of the same biological sex should be recognized. These debates have involved arguments based on civil rights, political, social, moral and religious considerations. In fact, in many countries gay people are still confronted with discrimination and cannot live in a way that corresponds with their sexual orientation. Since the early 2000s, however, ten countries and various other jurisdictions have begun legally formalizing same-sex marriages: Argentina, Belgium, Canada, Iceland, the Netherlands, Norway, Portugal, Spain, South Africa and Sweden. In addition, such marriages are performed in the US states of Massachusetts, Connecticut, Iowa, Vermont, New Hampshire, the District of Columbia and most recently in New York. Homosexual couples can also get married in Mexico City. Many other – predominantly European – states legally recognize same-sex partnerships in the form of civil unions, registered partnerships or unregistered cohabitation.

Following Lowi's typology, the legalization of same-sex marriage would correspond to regulatory policy as it specifies the conditions for individual behaviour. The policy-making process in most countries, however, has been more characterized by high degrees of conflict, the involvement of powerful interest groups such as churches, and numerous instances of failed policy proposals due to unfeasible compromises. Hence, in terms of politics, there is here a proximity to redistributive policies, though it should be noted that the intensity of political conflict is unusual for this policy type. In Canada, for example, which legalized same-sex marriage nationwide with the enactment of the Civil Marriage Act in 2005, numerous bills tabled in parliament between 1997 and 2004 did not pass the first reading due to the elevated degree of conflict and the impossibility of reaching a compromise. Similarly, in Argentina which liberalized same-sex marriages in 2010 there was an intense battle of words between the government and the Roman Catholic Church, which organized large protests in the tens of thousands. These characteristics of the process of legalizing same-sex marriage demonstrate potential limitations of Lowi's typology.

---

prone to political salience, societal mobilization, controversial political debate, the responsiveness of politicians to public opinion, political conflict dominated by value-based rather than rational-egoistic orientations, and taboos. All this should lead to a very specific form of politics, i.e. morality politics, which can hardly be expected to result in comprise as the subject of political debate concerns conflicts amongst fundamental values (Meier 1994; Mooney 1999, 2001; Patton 2007).

Wilson's policy typology
Who benefits from a policy? Who has to carry its costs? These questions underlie the alternative approach to classification developed by Wilson

(1989, 1995), who rejects ambiguous policy types and distinguishes instead between policies on the basis of whether the related costs and benefits are either widely distributed or narrowly concentrated. Each of the four possible combinations yields different implications for policy-making.

When both costs and benefits of a certain policy are widely distributed, a government may encounter no or only minor opposition, indicating 'majoritarian politics' as the likely outcome, with policy-makers following very closely the preferences of the electorate when making their decisions. An example of majoritarian politics is universal health care, as it spreads both benefits and costs across relatively large segments of the population (Oliver 2006: 211). This type of politics involves the basic ideological beliefs of the political actors and therefore legislative debates are very important for a visible expression of the respective view on the issue concerned. In a similar vein, interest groups are involved in the policy-making process, which use multiple avenues to express their preferences and win support for them.

When, by contrast, both costs and benefits of a certain policy are concentrated, a government may be confronted with opposition from rival interest groups, signalling 'interest group politics'. In this case, the expectation is that policy decisions will be strongly affected by the positions and resources of relevant interest associations. Where there are clear winners and clear losers, the level of conflict is high and the outcome of any single proposal is highly unpredictable – which should give way to incrementalism: the making of minimal adjustments to existing policy arrangements. An example of interest group politics is the negotiation of free trade agreements with a country that is more favoured either by exporting industries or by importing industries. Another area that is often associated with interest group politics is agriculture. For example, decisions concerning hormone-treated beef are likely to cause controversy as there are concentrated costs and benefits for the farmers involved (see Bernauer and Caduff 2004).

On the other hand, if costs are concentrated and benefits diffuse, a government may encounter opposition from dominant interest groups. In this case, 'entrepreneurial politics' are the probable outcome: that policy change requires the presence of 'political entrepreneurs' who are willing to develop and put through political proposals despite strong societal resistance. Opportunities for entrepreneurial politics usually come with special events, e.g. natural disasters. Tang and Tang (1999: 352–3), for instance, regard the organization of nation-wide demonstrations against nuclear power by environmental groups in Taiwan as an example of entrepreneurial politics as they aimed to introduce environmental policy that would promote the benefits of the general public.

The fourth and final scenario consists of a situation in which costs are diffuse and benefits concentrated. In such a case, governments are likely

Table 2.2 *Wilson's typology*

Costs	Benefits	
	Concentrated	**Diffuse**
Concentrated	Interest group politics ('zero sum game')	Entrepreneurial politics
Diffuse	Clientelistic politics	Majoritarian politics

Sources: Based on Wilson (1989) and Knill and Tosun (2011).

to be confronted with a relevant interest group that is favourable to their reform endeavours, indicating that 'clientelistic politics' is the likely outcome. This type of politics suggests the most politically feasible environment for policy change as it offers relatively concentrated benefits, e.g. assistance to an identifiable group of citizens, while imposing only diffuse costs across other groups and taxpayers (Oliver 2006: 209). Examples of clientelistic politics are health programmes that benefit special groups or agricultural price supports. Clientistic politics mostly take place behind the scenes and are the result of a consensus between political actors and interest groups which allows both sides to pursue their respective interests (see Table 2.2).

As compared to Lowi's typology, the approach by Wilson is analytically more compelling since it is more precise about the characteristics of policy-making and the actors involved in it. Another advantage is that it is more dynamic, since formulating a particular policy may shift from one type of politics to another. For example, in its very early stage environmental policy may be regarded as entrepreneurial politics, since at this point in time those who are regulated still represent a small group. With the proliferation of environmental policy, however, the corresponding debate moves from entrepreneurial to majoritarian politics. The shift causes changes in the policy-making arenas, the actors involved and the methods of politics. Yet, it should be noted that Wilson did not intend this typology to predict outcomes and therefore it does not substitute for proper theorizing.

Classification by governance principles and instruments

A second approach to classifying public policies is based on underlying governance principles and instruments. As we will discuss in detail in Chapter 9, governance is about the political steering of public and private actors (Héritier 2002). Accordingly, governance instruments specify the means or techniques by which governments seek to achieve their policy goals (such as emission limits for environmental pollutants), whereas governance principles refer to specific classes or groups of governance instruments (Vedung 1998: 21; Hood and Margetts 2007: 2). The analytical and political relevance of governance principles and instruments constitutes the central focus of various classification attempts in the literature (e.g. Hood 1986; Peters and van Nispen 1998; Knill and Lenschow 2000; Salamon 2002; Bemelmans-Videc *et al*. 2003; Eladis *et al*. 2005; Holzinger *et al*. 2006; Hood and Margetts 2007; Goetz 2008).

While many typologies apply a highly differentiated scheme, ending up with long lists of different instruments (see, for an overview, Vedung 1998; Salamon 2002), the NATO scheme developed by Hood (1986; see also Hood and Margetts 2007) represents a more parsimonious approach. It classifies governance principles on the basis of four central resources of government, namely **N**odality, **A**uthority, **T**reasure and **O**rganization (NATO). These resources of government illustrate the different ways 'to get people to do things that they might not otherwise do; or it enables people to do things that they might not have done otherwise' (Schneider and Ingram 1990: 513).

Nodality
This refers to the central role governments enjoy with regard to the use and distribution of information within political systems. Governments constitute large institutions involved in a wide range of activities and therefore they have more expertise and information than most other societal actors (O'Toole and Meier 1999: 511; O'Toole 2007: 218–21). This property of being at the centre gives rise to nodality, placing governments in a strategic position from which to spread information to society and to detect information. Typical examples of policy instruments based on this resource are the publication of data and information, education, advice, recommendation and persuasion (Vedung 1998: 33). These instruments are typically based upon an indirect governance logic that attempts to change the beliefs and perceptions of public and private actors, hence changing individual or collective behaviour in order to achieve political objectives. The most commonly observed type of tool is the government information campaign. This includes such campaigns as that to encourage citizens to receive vaccination against certain diseases (e.g. seasonal flu). Another type of this tool relates to communication activities aimed at changing producer behaviour by providing consumers with product and production process information. A well-known example is ecolabelling for food and other consumer products. Ecolabels are intended to make it easy for consumers to take environmental concerns into account when shopping as they certify compliance with a set of minimum requirements.

The advantage of nodality tools lies in the relatively low cost of their application and implementation; their weakness lies in their often limited and uncertain effectiveness. Following Howlett (2009a: 31), many scholars argue that these tools are restricted to policies that do not require complete compliance in order to be effective and that only apply when government and public interests coincide so that government appeals are likely to be favourably received. Though they also appear to be appropriate in relatively short-term crisis situations (e.g. flu epidemics), this is the case only when it is otherwise difficult to impose sanctions and where the issue in question can be reduced to the level of advertising slogans. As a consequence, nodality instruments in reality are often combined with other tools.

Authority

This is defined by the use of the law as the central resource for governmental intervention. Authority implies the legitimacy of legal or official power and gives to the government the ability to force societal actors to follow legal rules. Typical instruments applied in this context are command-and-control instruments, demanding, forbidding, guaranteeing and judging whether the authoritative rule may or may not be followed by negative sanctions. Authority as a principle of governance is hence characterized by what Lowi (1964, 1972) called regulatory policies. The central characteristic of these policies is to achieve directly behavioural changes by altering the legal conditions in which public and private actors operate. Authority-based instruments change the strategic opportunities and constraints for the involved actors (Knill and Lehmkuhl 2002a).

Authority-based policy can take many forms. The most common is certainly that of so-called command-and-control regulation. Here the government hierarchically prescribes requirements that must be fulfilled by the regulatees, with failures to comply usually involving penalties. In addition to this interventionist approach, the formulation and implementation of authority-based policies might occur in more cooperative forms, entailing a more or less far-reaching participation by, and delegation of power to, private actors. These patterns might be characterized by forms of regulated self-regulation, where governmental activity is restricted to setting-up a broad framework for private self-regulation (Knill and Lehmkuhl 2002b). An example is the regulation of illegal and harmful content on the internet, which in many countries is based on regulatory frameworks for the self-regulation of internet providers (Akdeniz 2008).

A further important distinction is made between economic regulation and social regulation. While for economic regulation the focus is on the conditions specifying the access to and operation within markets (such as cartel regulations, price regulations, taxes and licensing requirements), social regulation is concerned with the reduction and avoidance of negative effects that emerge from economic market activities. Classical fields of social regulation are health and safety at work, environmental pollution or consumer protection (May 2002).

A central advantage of authority-based policies is the high predictability of policy effects, at least if effective implementation of the legal rules is assumed. Regulation may be politically appealing, especially when the public expects quick and committed action on the part of the government (Howlett *et al*. 2009: 120). Furthermore, especially with regard to risky or dangerous sectors (such as nuclear safety), regulation constitutes the most feasible governance option and one that can hardly be substituted with other approaches that rely on effecting voluntary compliance or behavioural change (Holzinger *et al*. 2006). A final advantage of regulation from the perspective of governments is that they have only minor budgetary implications. Potential costs usually have to be carried by those affected by a policy, i.e. the policy addressees.

These advantages, however, come with several problems of authority-based instruments. Firstly, regulation generally entails high costs with regard to controlling and monitoring their proper enforcement. Secondly, it is argued that regulation implies there are no incentives for policy addressees to go beyond legal requirements; so there is no stimulus for innovation (Holzinger *et al*. 2006). Thirdly, there is a danger of regulatory capture, which occurs when a public authority or agency created to act in the public interest instead acts in favour of the commercial or special interests that it has been charged with regulating. Regulatory capture is particularly likely when the design of regulatory rules requires detailed scientific and technical information. As the policy addressees (i.e. the regulated industries) often have a deeper knowledge than the regulating authorities, there is a certain probability that the regulators become dependent upon the regulated, which gives the latter an important leverage in influencing regulatory decisions (Laffont and Tirole 1991; see also Chapter 3).

Treasure
This is based on money, or more precisely the various economic tools of governments. These tools encompass anything that can be freely exchanged, and which may materialize as rewards as well as fines. These kinds of tools are, however, different from authoritative rules in the sense that they are voluntary, i.e. policy addressees are not legally obliged to adopt the measures involved. Typical instruments based on treasure involve positive and negative financial incentives. A prominent form of treasure-based instrument is the grant. Grants are offered to producers in order to stimulate them to produce more of a certain good or service than they would otherwise (such as research grants for universities or grants

for public transportation). Other instruments include tax subsidies (i.e. deductions, special rates or exclusions) in response to a certain activity or behaviour (e.g. energy-saving measures in private households), government loans at an interest rate below the market rate, and financial disincentives (taxes and user charges) (Howlett *et al*. 2009: 125).

The advantage of treasure-based policies is that they are easier to implement than control- and monitoring-intensive regulatory policies. By allowing target groups to devise appropriate responses the provision of financial incentives is generally expected to stimulate innovative behaviour on the side of policy addressees. In addition, in many instances, economic tools are characterized by high levels of political acceptance, as benefits are relatively concentrated on certain societal groups and the costs are dispersed rather widely across all taxpayers (see Wilson's typology above).

The disadvantages associated with these tools, by contrast, refer first of all to the fact that they strongly affect the public budget. This holds true as along as these policies are designed to be distributive rather than redistributive. Second, it is often difficult to calculate the level of incentives in such a way that they actually unfold their expected effects. Third, financial incentives might be redundant, entailing a windfall on the side of the recipients: it might be the case that some of the policy addressees would have pursued these actions anyway (that is, also without governmental stimulation).

Organization
This refers to the reliance on formal organizational structures in order to achieve policy objectives. Instead of relying on information, legal requirements or fiscal incentives or disincentives to influence the behaviour of societal actors, in this case governments directly provide public goods or services (Mayntz 1979). Classic examples include national defence, diplomatic relations, education, or road construction and maintenance. A very prominent form of direct state provision is the establishment of public or state-owned enterprises, including railway companies, telecommunications or electricity suppliers. Although many countries from the 1980s onwards witnessed an overwhelming trend of privatization, indicating a shift from the state as a provider to the state as a regulator of the provision of goods and services (see Majone 1996), the public sector still plays a considerable role as a governing body. This holds true in particular if we consider the huge amount of publicly owned companies that exist at the local level, such as local transportation or electricity and water supply companies. In this context, it should be noted that the existence of publicly owned companies applies to some countries more (e.g. Germany) than to others (e.g. the United Kingdom).

While nodality, authority and treasure are characterized by the governmental activities of either directly or indirectly influencing target group behaviour, organization-based tools lack this intermediary step. Rather, they rest on the direct provision of public goods by the state itself. This approach bears several advantages. In particular, problems of indirect provision are avoided, including political conflicts, long processes of negotiation or ineffective implementation. In many cases, public services or goods (such as railway networks) are provided, although private actors would not regard them as profitable to provide.

But there are also disadvantages associated with organization-based tools. First, public enterprises might lead to inefficient operations because poor performance does not lead to bankruptcy, but is compensated for by the taxpayer. Second, political conflicts can affect the provision of public goods and services, implying that contemporary political needs (emerging from elections, for instance) become more important than serving the public as a whole. There is evidence from Italian politics that more infrastructure expenditures were given to those districts electing the politically more powerful deputies from the governing parties as a reward for their core voters (Golden and Picci 2008). In the public choice literature, such behaviour is discussed under the term 'pork-barrel politics', which essentially refers to spending that benefits the constituents of a politician in return for their political support (see Ferejohn 1974; Cox and McCubbins 1986). Third, principal–agent problems might emerge in the sense that the management of public enterprises, i.e. the agent, can pursue different objectives than its political principals, i.e. the government. In these cases principals are unable to ensure compliance with their goals because of an inability to monitor agency activity and/or sanction non-compliance. Finally, many state-owned companies enjoy a monopolistic position (e.g. in the area of railway transportation or electricity supply), enabling them to pass the costs of their inefficiency on to consumers. To that degree, public monopolies display similar pathologies as do private monopolies (Bovens *et al.* 2001a; see Table 2.3 opposite).

Alternative schemes
While the NATO scheme represents the most widely used policy classification by governance principles, many similar approaches have emerged which focus in more detail on certain characteristics. For example, the categorization of Schneider and Ingram (1990: 514–22) sheds light more explicitly on the behavioural assumptions underlying a particular policy type. Their typology is based on the following categories:

- Authority tools involving statements that grant permission, prohibit or require action under designated circumstances.

Table 2.3   *Policy classification by governance principles*

Governance principle	Nodality	Authority	Treasure	Organization
Basic resource	Information	Law	Money	Structures and capacity
Governance logic	Indirect stimulation of behavioural change through information and persuasion	Direct prescription of behavioural rules	Indirect stimulation of behavioural change through financial incentives	Provision of public good or service by the state or public enterprise
Typical instruments	Information campaigns Suasion Research inquiries	Prohibitions Bans Permits Standards	Taxes User charges Grants Tax deductions	Public companies

Source: Based on Hood and Margetts (2007).

- Incentive tools inducing compliance via negative or positive tangible payoffs.
- Capacity tools involving information, training and resources to enable individuals, groups or agencies to carry out expected activities.
- Symbolic and hortatory tools based on the assumption that people are motivated to take policy-related actions on the basis of their beliefs and values.
- Learning tools promoting the drawing of lessons from experience by the target population and/or the policy-makers. This represents an open-ended process, which might be appropriate when a social problem is recognized but not well understood.

There is obviously a high degree of overlap between this way of categorizing public policies and the NATO scheme. The latter category in particular represents a further development (for similar classification attempts and refinements, see, e.g., Lascoumes and Le Galès 2007; Howlett 2009a).

Key points

❑ Policy typologies vary with the respective analytical criteria used for their classification, such as the effects of public policies on policy-making or the governance principles which motivate them.

❑ Typologies of policy effects have in common a basing of their expectations about whether the policy-making process will be adversarial or consensual on the characteristics of the policy measure in question.

❑ Typologies of governance principles refer to specific groups of policy instruments and shed light on how they might bring about changes in the behaviour of the target group.

Policy dimensions

An alternative way of practically specifying public policies is provided by differentiating between their dimensions. In this context, we can, on the one hand, distinguish between policy dimensions that vary with the stage of development of a policy. On the other hand, policy dimensions refer to the different contents of a policy. These two concepts complement the previous approaches to the extent that they do not aim to provide guidance for grouping public policies that belong to different policy domains, but by highlighting different levels of analysis that apply equally to all policy types. This adds an additional layer to the nature of public policies.

Policy dimensions in the sequence of the policy cycle

While it is well-acknowledged that the different stages of the policy cycle overlap and that the scheme is of more heuristic than analytical value, it does serve as a good starting point for identifying different policy dimensions in the sequential development of a policy. In this regard, there are three dimensions that are usually employed when making reference to a public policy and that involve different analytical concepts that are closely related to the individual stages of the policy cycle:

* policy outputs
* policy outcomes
* policy impacts

Policy outputs are the direct result of the decision-making process which usually involves the adoption of a certain programme, law or regulation. They are defined by the content of a public policy, as it is fixed in legal or administrative documents, and can encompass both substantive and procedural aspects (Anderson 2010: 8–9). Substantive outputs, for instance, refer to the specification of claims, prohibitions, bans or service levels. Examples are emission limits for environmental pollutants, minimum requirements for obtaining transport licences, authorization conditions for constructing industrial plants, or registration requirements for the production and distribution of chemicals. In short, substantive policy outputs directly allocate advantages or disadvantages (i.e. costs and benefits) to people. Procedural aspects, in contrast, specify rules guiding the interaction between the implementing authorities and the target groups. They define, for instance, the rules governing private access to public documents or the participation of private actors in the implementation process. They may also define deadlines to be observed or possibilities for appeal proceedings. Hence, procedural policy outputs define how something is going to be done or who is going to take action.

Policy outcomes are closely related to the stages of policy implementation and evaluation (see Chapters 7 and 8). Here the focus is on the way policies induce behavioural change on the side of the targeted actors. How do policy addressees respond to a given policy? Do they alter their previous behaviour in line with the objectives of a public policy? For example, a policy that increases taxes on cigarettes affects, and has as its two main target groups, smokers and those who might consider taking up smoking. The outcome of this policy refers to changes in smoking behaviour (i.e. lower consumption) as a consequence of the increased taxes on cigarettes. Another example is given by the prescription of stricter emission control technologies for industry. The outcome of this policy should be that the regulatees modernize their production facilities in order to comply with the requirements of the policy.

Policy impacts focus on the extent to which a policy decision and its subsequent implementation have actually brought about the expected results, indicating that they are mainly assessed at the evaluation stage (see Chapter 8). Did the introduction of emission limits for environmental pollutants actually lead to environmental quality improvements? Did the liberalization of the telecommunications sector actually increase competition? Did the privatization of public enterprises actually increase their profitability? What matters most in this context is that the focus lies not only on the changes in the regulatees' behaviour but on the implications of these changes for achieving the predefined goals of a particular public policy. For example, the political goal of a policy to increase taxes on cigarettes is to reduce smoking-related diseases. In a similar vein, a policy imposing the need to modernize pollution-control equipment effectively aims to improve air quality.

As the concepts of policy outputs, policy outcomes and policy impacts refer to different stages of the policy cycle, they must also be analytically approached by adopting different theoretical lenses and research methods.

Policy content dimensions

Even if we restrict our focus to the analysis of policy outputs or the content of a policy, we are confronted with broad lists of elements that can be distinguished. Dolowitz and Marsh (1996: 349–50), for instance, differentiate between 'policy goals, structure and content, policy instruments or administrative techniques, institutions, ideology, ideas, attitudes and concepts'. A widely accepted typology has been suggested by Hall (1993) who distinguishes between three components of policy outputs: (1) policy paradigms (i.e. the overarching goal that guides a policy in a particular field); (2) policy instruments (i.e. the means used to achieve these goals); and (3) the precise setting or calibration of these instruments.

Hall developed this typology in his analysis of economic policy change in Britain. In this context, so-called first-order changes refer to constellations in which only the calibration of policy instruments is adjusted (instrument settings). Examples of such patterns are the tightening or weakening of environmental emission standards or the increase or decrease of unemployment benefits. Changes in instrument settings typically imply only minor adjustments to existing policies, as they do not entail changes either in policy goals or in policy instruments that are already in place. If a second-order change occurs the type of instrument is affected, implying that new instruments are introduced or existing instruments are abolished or replaced by others. An example is the shift from command-and-control regulation (emission standards, limit values) towards market-oriented instruments (emission trading, eco taxes) that can partially be observed in many European countries (Holzinger *et al.* 2006; Knill and Liefferink 2007).

The most fundamental category of change – i.e. a third-order change – takes place with regard to policy paradigms. These refer to the goals guiding a policy in a particular field, including how the problem at hand should be understood, i.e. in terms of its basic interpretations and perceptions (Hall 1993: 279; Campbell 1998). British environmental policy, for instance, has traditionally been characterized by a paradigm according to which the environment is considered to be well capable of absorbing a certain amount of dangerous substances. The perception was that there were no harmful pollutants but only harmful concentrations of pollutants. Accordingly, policy solutions were selected that entailed a highly flexible approach allowing the regulatory agencies to define regulatory requirements in the light of given pollutant concentrations, scientific evidence about their detrimental impact and the state of environmental degradation at the local level. This paradigm, however, was fundamentally challenged during the 1990s by EU policies that followed the German paradigm of the precautionary principle. According to this approach, pollutant emissions have to be reduced as far as technologically possible, even if there is no scientific proof of their detrimental impact (Knill and Liefferink 2007: 78–9; see also Fairbrass and Jordan 2001).

While this distinction was originally intended to provide an explanation for different forms of policy change, Hall's typology has also become an important analytical tool for assessing the question as to whether it is possible to identify typical policy patterns across countries or policy sectors. In this regard, the scholarly debate has predominantly focused on the dimension of policy instruments. To what extent can we observe typical instrument choices (such as command-and control approaches or market-based instruments) in individual countries? To what extent are such choices, by contrast, affected by the specifically perceived nature of the policy problems in a given policy sector? These are just some of the questions exemplifying the relevance attached to the choice of policy instruments in the literature.

The discussion of the role of policy instruments dates back to the work of Dahl and Lindblom (1953: 6), which recognized that the capacity of modern societies to solve problems crucially depends on the policy instruments chosen. Schneider and Ingram (1990: 522–5) elaborated a theoretical approach to choosing an instrument. They argued that the characteristics of the policy process (e.g. partisanship) and the extent to which a political system is dominated by elites may have an impact on the policy instruments chosen. Furthermore, they show that different historical periods often show a bias towards particular instruments as a result of the underlying rationale in government action.

Similarly, Lascoumes and Le Galès (2007: 10–11) argue that policy instruments are not purely technical, but that they tend to produce original and sometimes unexpected effects. In this regard, they stress three main effects of instrument choice. First, the instrument chosen creates inertial effects, resulting in a resistance to outside pressures such as conflicts of interest between the actors involved in the policy-making process. Second, the instrument chosen produces a specific representation of the issue it is handling. Third, the instrument leads to a particular problematization of the issue. In short, all these approaches emphasize that an insightful study of policy instrumentation should entail considerations related to social relations and the balance of power between actors (see Kassim and Le Galès 2010: 5).

> ### Key points
>
> ❏ Public policies can be assessed on the basis of policy outputs, outcomes and impacts.
>
> ❏ Policy outputs refer to the content of a public policy and are most directly related to the policy-making process. They can be understood as referring to the underlying paradigms, instruments and instrument settings used by the policy concerned.
>
> ❏ Policy outcomes are the effects of a public policy in terms of the changes in the behaviour of the target groups. Questions related to policy outcomes are addressed during the stages of policy implementation and evaluation.
>
> ❏ Policy impacts are the effects of a public policy in terms of problem resolution and are closely related with the stage of policy evaluation.

Policy styles

A third prominent approach in the policy-analytical literature to understanding the nature of public policies has been represented by efforts to identify policy 'styles'. This research perspective is closely related with the classification schemes already presented, since the fundamental idea of policy styles is to establish similarities between different types of policy-making and the ways in which they are made. Another similarity that the concept of policy styles shares with the typologies of Lowi and Wilson is that the main analytical interest centres on the politics dimension and the question of how public policies come about (Feick and Jann 1989).

With regard to public policies, the concept of policy styles refers to the 'standard operating procedures' of governments in the making and implementing of public policies (Richardson *et al.* 1982: 2). Put differently, policy styles relate to durable and systematic approaches to policy problems (Freeman 1985: 474). Such persistent forms of interaction and behavioural patterns should be observed during the formulation and implementation of a policy. That stable patterns of policy implementation can also be seminally addressed by the concept of policy styles is demonstrated by Battaglini and Giraud (2003). The authors show that the implementation of the federal law on unemployment insurance varies considerably across the Swiss cantons. Based on this analysis, they identify four components of implementation styles, including the scope and style of state intervention, coordination and interaction modes of social actors, and the main traits of the regional political culture.

While the term 'policy style' has been used most generally and widely for identifying such process patterns, some authors (in particular Vogel 1986; Vogel and Kagan 2004) refer to similar phenomena as 'styles of regulation'. The findings of this strand of literature equally allow a better understanding of stable policy-making patterns, since 'regulation' just refers to a specific policy type. While styles of regulation concentrate on a specific policy type, the concept of administrative styles developed by Knill (1998, 2001) explicitly focuses on traditional behaviour patterns of a specific player in the political administrative system, namely the public administration (see also Zysman 1994; Howlett 2002).

The concept of national policy styles was first introduced by Gustafsson and Richardson (1979, 1980), Richardson *et al.* (1982) and Richardson and Jordan (1983). As already explained, the central idea of this concept is that politics in countries have some persistent characteristics that predispose them to formulate and implement public policies in certain distinct ways, irrespective of the issue concerned or the policy sector they belong to (Bovens *et al.* 2001b: 15).

According to Richardson *et al.* (1982), there are two dimensions determining national policy styles. The first dimension relates to a government's approach to problem solving, ranging from anticipatory/active to reactive. The second dimension is about a government's relationship to other actors in the policy-making and implementing process, characterized by their inclination either to reach consensus with organized groups or to impose decisions on them. Based on these two axes, four ideal-typical policy styles for (west) European countries are identified: (1) the rationalist consensus style in Germany; (2) the British negotiation style; (3) the French concerting style; and (4) the Dutch negotiation and conflict style.

An alternative typology has been elaborated by van Waarden (1992: 133), which is based on the degree to which interactions between public and private actors are formalized and whether societal interest groups participate in the formulation and implementation of public policies. The combination of high formalization (i.e. strong state) and low participation (i.e. weak strength of societal interests) yields an étatist policy style (i.e. a state-centred model with top-down policy-making and implementation), as could be observed in France. Low formalization and low participation opportunities, by contrast, result in a pluralist policy style, such as associated with the United States. High formalization and high participation options – as provided in Austria, the Netherlands and Sweden – favour social corporatist or meso-corporatist policy patterns, while low formalization and high participation opportunities correspond to clientelism as well as liberal corporatism – as can be found in Switzerland.

The empirical testing of the concept of national policy styles, however, has not provided much support. For example, the comparative volume edited by Richardson (1982) revealed that there is much more similarity in policy-making styles than anticipated. This induced him to conclude that there is indeed a common (west) European policy style. More precisely, the case studies showed that there was a common demise of anticipatory problem solving and a trend towards more consensus-oriented policy-making. The rise of a less hierarchical and consensual style of policy-making was also confirmed by the comparative volume edited by Bovens *et al.* (2001a). Furthermore, this compilation underscores variations in policy styles within countries, which also concurs with more recent empirical studies. Cairney's (2009: 671) analysis of the policy style regarding mental health policy in the United Kingdom suggests that there is 'more than one picture of British styles'.

Despite the fact that the basic claim of Richardson *et al.* (1982) could not be supported empirically, this study, without question, paved the way for subsequent research endeavours. Highly influential in this regard was Vogel's (1986) analysis of national styles of regulation which characterize environmental policy in the United Kingdom and the United States. The study showed that, in the British case, patterns of regulation were characterized by consensual, pragmatic, informal and highly secretive relationships between the regulatory authorities and the industry, whereas the style of regulation in the United States was more adversarial, legalistic, formal and relied more heavily on transparent interactions (see also Knill 1998, 2001; Cairney 2009, 2011).

In view of the inconclusive empirical testing, a focus on sectoral rather than national factors was advocated as a more promising and accurate way of identifying different policy styles (see e.g. Freeman 1985; Rüdig 1987). Apart from this criticism, however, no progress was made in identifying sector-specific policy styles beyond Lowi's early classification. This general statement holds true notwithstanding the contribution of Howlett *et al.* (2009), who distinguish between different policy styles with regard to different stages of the policy cycle. For each stage, they identify different factors of explanatory relevance and also different process patterns. All in all, however, empirical evidence on sectoral policy styles is sparse.

To advance the conceptual debate, we suggest that a promising approach would lie in a more theoretically grounded analysis of potential determinants of policy styles; these factors would include national characteristics as well as characteristics of policy sectors. Depending on the specific practical constellation of these factors, policy styles might reflect either more national or more sectoral peculiarities. In this way, it is conceivable that empirical findings will provide evidence for both country- and sector-specific influences. At the same time, these factors can be divided into variables that are relatively volatile or remain rather

Table 2.4 *Potential determinants of policy styles*

	High stability	Low stability
Country-specific	• Socioeconomic development status	• Economic situation
	• Cultural orientations	• Public opinion
	• Institutional arrangements (polity)	• Government coalition/government change
	• General relationship between state and society	• Current interactions between public and private actors
Sector-specific	• Nature of problem	• Pressure of problem
	• Policy paradigms	• Current experience
	• Policy legacies and path dependencies	• Current policy developments
	• Typical cleavages and conflict	• Current conflicts and bargaining processes

stable over time. Based on such a differentiated approach, we are able to account for the variation and change of policy styles across countries, sectors and time (see Table 2.4).

With regard to national factors, the socio-economic development of a country might influence patterns of policy-making. We can expect more conflictive and adversarial patterns, the less developed a country is. This mainly stems from the restrictions in the resources that can be (re)distributed by means of public policy. The extent to which this structural factor affects patterns of policy-making might at the same time be influenced by the current economic situation. In addition, dominant cultural orientations (e.g. with regard to accepted patterns of governmental intervention and relationships between state and society) might exert an influence on policy styles. These orientations are typically closely linked to the state and legal tradition of a country (Dyson 1980; Knill 2001), but can also be affected by current developments in public attitudes and opinions. Patterns of national policy-making are moreover strongly affected by institutional arrangements which define the strategic opportunities and constraints that public and private actors face during the formulation and implementation of public policies.

These structures, for instance, strongly affect the extent to which policy styles reflect more consensual or more adversarial patterns (Lijphart 1994, 1999). Notwithstanding the stability of these structural aspects, short-term developments, in particular changes in government, might bring about changes in the strategic opportunities of the involved actors. Finally, institutionally entrenched patterns of state–society relationships, such as more corporatist or pluralist patterns, leave their mark on national policy styles (van Waarden 1992, 1995). Again, the effects of these structures might vary as a result of context-specific interactions between public and private actors.

Turning to sector-specific factors, the nature of the policy problem, as well as short-term changes in the pressure of the problem, can have an impact on policy styles. For instance, it makes a difference whether the problem refers to the regulation of risks (such as nuclear plants or genetically modified organisms), of markets, or of social and environmental issues. Depending on the problem type, different actors and conflicts of interest might be involved, implying different policy styles. At the same time, dominant policy paradigms – i.e. dominant perceptions of a problem and ideas of how the problem can be solved – influence which actors might have more or less influence in the policy process.

Previous policy developments (policy legacies) can create path dependencies, as changes in established policy patterns can induce high costs (both economically and in terms of institutional adjustment needs). This point is aptly illustrated by Myles and Pierson (2001), who demonstrate how much old-age pension systems are affected by path-dependent processes. Pensions in most countries correspond to a pay-as-you-go system: current workers pay contributions that finance the previous generation's retirement. Pay-as-you-go systems are highly resistant to radical reform as they generate unfunded pension commitments for the future retirees. Shifting to private pension arrangements would place an untenable burden on current workers as they have to finance the previous generation's retirement while simultaneously saving for their own. Thus, the best predictor of privatization outcomes of pension systems is the size of the unfunded pension commitments already in place. Finally, of course, policy-type cleavages will have an important impact on observable policy styles. This is basically the argument developed by Lowi (1964), who stated that distinctive policy types are characterized by distinctive process patterns.

Key points

❏ The concept of policy styles seeks to identify stable country- or sector-specific patterns of policy-making. This entails that, akin to the typologies presented previously, the politics dimension is of crucial importance.

❏ Empirical studies of policy styles reach contradictory conclusions regarding the empirical relevance of this approach.

❏ A more promising avenue for explaining policy-making is provided by systematically exploring the potential determinants of policy styles, implying an analysis of national and sectoral characteristics.

Conclusions

In this chapter, we have sought to specify the realized nature of public policies by presenting the main policy-analytical approaches to classifying them. The most popular way of structuring the many different types of public policies is based on the elaboration of typologies. In this context, we have distinguished between typologies that are based on policy effects and those that rely on governance principles. A second approach to illustrating what public policies are essentially about is provided by focusing on different analytical dimensions. This step brought the differences between policy outputs, policy outcomes and policy impacts to the fore, as well as Hall's (1993) classification of policy paradigms, policy instruments and instrument settings. Classifying public policies on the basis of their analytical dimensions is indeed different from the previous approach. The concept of policy dimensions emphasizes the importance of the individual stages of the policy cycle that analyses public policies, including as to whether or not they should be studied from a more abstract or more concrete perspective. This perspective does not attempt to generate groups of public policies according to whether they are able to make predictions as to how they affect policy-making or the behaviour of the addressees. Instead, it seeks to make intelligible the notion that in order to explore effectively the nature of public policies one must take into account the different aspects constituting the individual policy measures. This also provides a promising way of being able to make generalizable descriptive or causal statements. Thus, we can now state that focusing on specific policy dimensions can facilitate comparative analysis.

In the third and final step we illustrated the research on policy styles, which again combines considerations about public policies with stable processes of policy-making and implementation. This perspective further corroborated the fact that it is very difficult to assess the nature of public policies without the politics dimension. As a result, we have drawn the overall conclusion that the classical policy-analytical literature has perhaps ironically more to say about the nature of politics than public policies per se. At the same time, however, this indicates that the study of public policy cannot be successful without including the politics and the polity dimensions. Therefore, in what follows we will attempt to refine these approaches.

Web links

www.who.int/research/en/. This is the most comprehensive information resource regarding public health; it gives a good overview of the different governance principles and instruments used in this policy field.

www.oecd-ilibrary.org/statistics. At this website various types of statistical data and policy fact books can be found. We particularly recommend the 'at a glance' series on development aid, education, health and pensions, but the database is very broad.

www.policypointers.org/PolicyAreas/. At this website various think tanks provide access to research and conclusions from their work in various policy fields. It is suitable for gaining a snapshot impression of the attention that think tanks pay to individual policy fields.

www.apsc.gov.au/publications09/smarterpolicy.htm. The Australian government explains various policy instruments and discusses and their strengths and weaknesses.

Further reading

Adolino, J. and C. Blake (2011) *Comparing Public Policies: Issues and Choices in Six Industrialized Countries*. Washington, DC: CQ Press. This book provides a concise overview of decision-making in various national contexts in the fields of immigration, fiscal policy, health care, social, education and environmental policy.

Bovens, M., P.'t Hart and B.G. Peters (eds) (2001) *Success and Failure in Public Governance: A Comparative Analysis*. Cheltenham: Edward Elgar. In this compilation of case studies, the determinants of policy success are addressed. It is worth reading since it explicitly points out the causes and consequences of policy failures – a perspective seldom addressed in policy analysis.

Cram, L. and J.J. Richardson (eds) (2004) *Policy Styles in the European Union*. Routledge: London. This is an insightfully edited volume on how EU policy-making is influenced by the different policy styles of the various institutions, and the departments within those institutions, particularly the Commission.

Knoepfel, P., C. Larrue, F. Varone and M. Hill (2007) *Public Policy Analysis*. Bristol: The Policy Press. A compelling book, which ideally complements the content of this chapter. In this regard, we particularly recommend Chapters 1, 2 and 4.

Moran, M., Rein, M. and R.E. Goodin (eds) (2008) *The Oxford Handbook of Public Policy*. Oxford University Press: Oxford. This book is a very carefully edited and authoritative volume of insightful scholarship on public policy.

Peters, B.G. and J. Pierre (eds) (2006) *Handbook of Public Policy*. Thousand Oaks, CA: Sage. An excellent collection that addresses the characteristics of policy-making, the nature of various policy fields and evaluation research.

Chapter 3

The Context for Policy-Making: Central Institutions and Actors

Reader's guide

Policy choices are affected by both the polity (i.e. the institutional arrangements characterizing a political system) and the politics (i.e. the policy-making process). This chapter provides an overview of the most central institutions and actors participating in the policy-making process and paves the way for the analytical approaches to be presented later. We conceive of institutions as established sets of formal rules that determine the extent to which actors' preferences may be transposed into public policies. We define 'actors' as (groups of) individuals who participate in policy processes and whose preferences will ultimately determine the policy choice. The most central institution of any political system is represented by the constitution and – where this exists – the constitutional court protecting the fundamental principles of government it defines. This is followed by the horizontal division of power between the executive, the legislature and the judiciary as well as the vertical division of power determining whether a state is unitary or federal. This group of fundamental institutions is complemented by the electoral and party system. In addition to national institutions, supranational and intergovernmental institutions are increasingly influential on domestic policy-making. Taking this into account, we outline the main characteristics of two such international organizations: the United Nations (UN) and the World Trade Organization (WTO). We then shift the focus from the institutions to the key policy-making actors, including the executive, the legislature, the judiciary, bureaucracies, political parties, interest groups and experts.

Public policy is determined by many factors. Among the most crucial are a country's polity and its politics. But before we shed light on the underlying causal relationships and the role of additional factors, we first provide a characterization of the main policy-relevant institutions and actors. Of the numerous existing definitions of institutions, we will use a very narrow one in which we conceive of them as sets of legal rules that can be enforced by state actors – they are the 'rules of the political game' (see, e.g., North 1990; Immergut 1992). This stands in marked contrast to other definitions of institutions, most notably with that of sociological institutionalism, which conceives of institutions in very broad terms, incorporating informal cultural practices as well as formal rules (see, e.g., Hall and Taylor 1996). Instead, the institutions we talk about in this chapter are those that correspond to formal organizations, i.e. they are entities with a stable set of rules defining their composition and functioning. We focus on formal rules since we want to (i) show what one intuitively associates with institutions and (ii) illustrate the general context of policy-making – before we present (in Chapter 4) the theoretical arguments that build on wider definitions of institutions.

We conceive of 'actors' as individuals, corporations or other collective entities, who possess policy preferences and the desire to realize them through their participation in the policy-making process (see Scharpf 1997a: 43). For the purposes of this chapter, we will regard institutions as exogenous to actors. In this way, institutions determine the extent to which actors can transform their preferences into public policy (Mayntz and Scharpf 1995; Ingram and Clary 2000). For example, if a policy-maker for whichever reason wishes to promulgate a policy that gives younger workers preference over older workers, most constitutions would effectively prevent such a proposal from becoming law.

However, distinguishing between actors and institutions is not a very straightforward task. Indeed, the actors we present here are predominantly collections of actors (e.g. the executive), which are at the same time formal organizations, i.e. they are constituted through institutional rules (Jackson 2010). For example, the *government as institution* is defined by its formal powers, how it is composed, which procedures exist for its internal decision-making, etc. The *government as collective actor* is composed of persons who have preferences regarding the policy area they are responsible for and which they express in front of the other actors (mostly the legislature) in order to turn their preferences into public policy. Hence, when referring to a government as an actor we are stressing that its role for policy-making stems from its preferences and not its internal organization.

National institutions: defining the rules of the political game

This section introduces the most essential institutions of polities, which have important repercussions on the process and output of policy-making. Over the last four decades institutions at the international level have become more influential. We will discuss these and outline how they may affect the public policies in their respective member states.

Constitutions and constitutional courts

The most essential institution in a political system is its constitution, which is a set of fundamental principles and formal rules according to which a state is governed. In some polities (e.g. New Zealand and the United Kingdom) the constitutions are flexible, meaning that they can be changed by regular majorities in the legislative body. In other polities (e.g. Australia, Canada and the United States) constitutions are rigid and any changes must be approved by super-majorities (i.e. two-thirds or more) (Lijphart 1999: 216–23). The reason for having rigid constitutions is that they cannot easily be modified to deal with short-term political conflicts. High thresholds for change – quorums – ensure that politicians are bound by their own decisions, which should impede governmental encroachment on the rights of individuals and ensure that the provisions of the constitution do not become modified in order to serve the interests of particular governments (for instance by changing the rules for re-election).

Put simply, constitutions define the most basic rules of the game in any political system by structuring and restricting the exercise of government power. In this regard, the constitution determines the centralization of power, that is whether a state is organized in accordance with unitarism (i.e. sovereignty is concentrated at the level of a single central government) or federalism (i.e. sovereignty is shared across several levels of government). For example, the Australian Constitution establishes a federal system of government, in which powers are distributed between a national government (i.e. the Commonwealth) and the six states (i.e. New South Wales, Queensland, South Australia, Tasmania, Victoria and Western Australia). The Australian Constitution also defines that three territories (i.e. the Australian Capital Territory, the Northern Territory and Norfolk Island) have self-government arrangements.

Likewise, constitutions establish the three branches of government and assign them formal rights to make, implement and interpret laws. And yet constitutions do not only outline how a state is organized. They are also crucial for determining procedural rules that are indispensable for making a political system work. For example, constitutions 'lay down legislative procedures; and they tell us how legislative authority is constituted (through elections, for example), and what the legislature can do (through enumerating powers)' (Stone Sweet 2011: 164). Beyond this, constitutions generally limit the exercise of government power in the name of individual rights, e.g. by prohibiting some acts of discrimination. In addition, constitutions may explicitly define public rights (Shane 2008: 193–4). Article 20 of the German Basic Law (an equivalent of a constitution) defines that Germany is a 'social federal state'. This 'social-state principle' compels policy-makers at each level of government to protect the social welfare of the German people (see Figure 3.1).

In most polities, the constitution is protected by a supreme or constitutional court. In some countries, however, constitutional courts are missing and ordinary courts are in charge of fulfilling this task, such as in Denmark. Detecting constitutional violations occurs through judicial review, which mainly occurs in three forms (Stone Sweet 2011: 167–8): abstract reviews, concrete reviews and constitutional complaints. Abstract reviews are made before legislation enters into force (or in some systems after promulgation but before application). The purpose of an abstract review is to check that a legislative bill is compatible with the constitution. In most cases they are initiated by other government institutions, such as a parliamentary minority. Concrete reviews, by contrast, are carried out in accordance with procedures for ordinary litigation and are hence initiated by ordinary judges who activate the process by sending a constitutional question to the constitutional court. The presiding judge will initiate a concrete review if the constitutional question is decisive for determining who wins or loses the case and if there are reasonable doubts about the constitutionality of the legal act in question. The third form, the constitutional complaint, can be directly activated by individuals who can prove that their constitutionally guaranteed rights

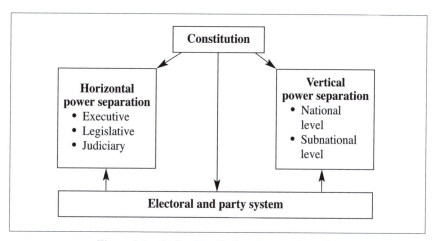

Figure 3.1 *Stylized institutional setup of a polity*

have been violated by a public authority, usually after judicial remedies have been exhausted or are not available.

Division of powers

The functioning of modern states is determined by an old principle that was laid down by the French political philosopher Montesquieu in his famous book *On the Spirit of Laws* (Cohler *et al.* 1989). In this book, Montesquieu argues that the best government would be one in which power was balanced among three groups of officials. By taking 18th-century England as the benchmark, the three branches of government were identified as the executive, the legislature and the judiciary. Often, these three together are referred to as the horizontal division of powers of the state. Of these branches, the executive and the legislature can be conceived as the principal actors in the process of policy-making, although as we have seen the judiciary can in some countries veto public policy in cases where it violates constitutional provisions.

The executive branch is, in principle, in charge of implementing public policy and has the authority to administer the bureaucracy. It corresponds to what people tend to call 'the government'. In real-life politics, however, governments are not only in charge of implementing public policies but are also actively involved in their formulation (see Chapter 6). There are three forms of democratic government: parliamentary, presidential and semi-presidential. In parliamentary systems, the head of government – who can have many different official titles such as prime minister or chancellor – and his or her cabinet (i.e. a collective executive) are derived from and are responsible to the legislature. In a presidential system, the president as the head of government (i.e. a non-collective executive) is directly or indirectly elected by the citizenry and cannot, or can only on very demanding conditions, be removed from office by the legislature. In a semi-presidential system, the government must respond both to the legislative assembly and to an elected president. Typically, these systems are characterized by a president who is elected for a fixed term with some executive powers and a government that serves at the discretion of the legislature.

The legislature (often referred to as 'parliament') is the branch of government endowed with the competency to make legislation. Legislative assemblies have many different names (e.g. House of Commons, Diet, Bundestag, Senate, Congress). In most systems (one such exception would be Estonia) they consist of two houses: a lower and an upper. Generally, the lower house is elected directly and is more influential in terms of policy-making than the upper house. There is, however, a considerable variation across countries in the degree of power exercised by the different houses (see Lijphart 1999: ch. 11; Kreppel 2011).

Box 3.1 Composition of the legislature in South Africa

The parliament of South Africa is composed of two houses: the national assembly and the national council of provinces. The national assembly is the lower house and consists of no fewer than 350 and no more than 400 members. The members of the national assembly are directly elected, which is in line with the procedure of most lower houses in parliamentary systems. The number of seats that a political party has in the national assembly is in proportion to the number of votes it received in an election. The national council of provinces is the upper house. Its purpose is to represent the governments of the nine South African provinces, rather than directly representing the people. Therefore, election to the national council of provinces is indirect: citizens vote for provincial legislatures, and each legislature then nominates a delegation of ten members. The Constitution of the Republic of South Africa sets out the following functions of the parliament:

- passing of legislation
- scrutiny and oversight of executive action
- facilitating public participation and involvement in the legislative and other processes
- participation in, promotion of and oversight of cooperative government
- engagement in international participation (i.e. in regional, continental and international bodies)

In addition, the South African parliament is in charge of promoting the values of human dignity, equality, non-racialism, non-sexism, the supremacy of the Constitution, universal adult suffrage and a multiparty system of democratic government.

The judiciary is composed of the various levels of courts (generally with a supreme or constitutional court as the court of final appeal) that interpret and apply the law and resolve disputes emerging among private and public actors. The judiciary is independent of the other branches of government. In a similar vein, judges should only be influenced by the law and the facts of a case. As the judiciary can affect policy-making through its sentences, in many countries the selection of judges to supreme or constitutional courts is a political process. In the United States, for instance, judges are nominated by the president, who then places his or her ideological stamp on the courts. Whether the candidate is eventually appointed depends on the Senate (O'Connor and Sabato 2009: 350).

In some political systems, the horizontal division of powers is complemented by a vertical division of power between the state as a whole and its geographically defined constituent units. Such political systems are known as federal polities. The core idea of federalism is to help prevent the abuse of power as a considerable share of it is exercised at regional levels (e.g. in states, provinces or regions). In such systems, certain powers are exercised by the federal or general government (shared rule) and other powers by the regional governments of the constituent states (self-rule). In marked contrast, in unitary states, such as Greece or Ireland, there is only one level of government.

Generally, the United States is regarded as the prototype of a federal state, but Australia, Belgium, Canada, Germany and Switzerland – to name but a few – are also federal systems. To be precise, the United States represents one specific model of federalism, i.e. coordinated federalism, where the federal government and regional governments are financially and politically independent from one another within their own spheres of responsibility. The complementary model is cooperative federalism in which the different levels of government interact cooperatively, as is the case in Germany (Loughlin 2011: 205).

It should be noted that unitary states can also experience decentralization, i.e. a transfer of decision-making powers from the federal government to subnational units, which subsequently display a number of 'federal' characteristics (see Hooghe *et al*. 2008). In 1998, the United Kingdom, for instance, launched devolution reforms to transfer powers in areas like education and health to Scotland, Wales and Northern Ireland (see, e.g., Keating *et al*. 2009). From this it follows that decentralization does not necessarily correspond with federalism. Likewise, a unitary state is not synonymous with a centralized state, i.e. a concentration of decision-making powers in the hands of government institutions. Rather, both federal and unitary states can be more or less centralized or decentralized (Lijphart 1999: 186–91). Hence, the difference between federal and unitary states is principally based on the constitutional division of labour between the national and subnational levels of government (Loughlin 2011: 206).

Federalism certainly represents an effective means of mutual control between different elements of government and may produce desirable public policies as decision-makers at the subnational level should have a better understanding of regional problems than in unitary states. Moreover, the variety of different political arenas in federal systems might favour policy innovation and learning. Policies that turned out to be successful in one subnational unit are often emulated by other units – a phenomenon that has been extensively studied in the US context (see Gray 1973; Volden 2006) as well as in Australia (see Painter 1991; Chappell 2001; Hollander and Patapan 2007) and Canada (see Poel 1976; Nykiforuk *et al*. 2008) (for comparative assessments, see Hueglin and Fenna 2006; Gamkhar and Vickers 2010). By the same token, however, the two levels need to seek compromises which can prevent or at least delay (necessary) policy reforms. Problems emerge in particular in constellations in which decisions at the federal level require the consent of the subnational units. This situation often entails the persistence of ineffective policies as long as only one state objects to policy change. Finally, there is an economic aspect to federalism and decentralization: maintaining individual parliaments, governments and administrations at various levels of government is expensive.

More generally, there are hints in the literature that unitary states tend to change policies to a greater extent and more rapidly. Treisman (2000), for instance, shows that unitary states as compared to federal states often change monetary policies more swiftly and radically, moving quickly from high to low inflation-interest rates and vice versa. This finding is not very surprising considering that in unitary states the number of actors whose consent is needed to enable a policy to pass (also known as veto points or veto players; see pp. 91, 135–6) is lower than in federal states, which is likely to increase the speed of policy-making as well as the 'radicalism' of the measures proposed, which can be good or bad depending on the issue concerned and one's point of view.

Electoral institutions and party systems

Elections are one of the most central features of democracies as they legitimize policy-makers and determine who is going to have the greatest political influence for a certain period of time. Electoral institutions vary from one country to another. They include provisions about who can be elected (e.g. age, residency requirements), specifications of election types (e.g. general elections, regional elections, presidential elections), the time that may elapse between elections, and issues of suffrage and compulsory voting. Another important aspect is how votes are transformed into parliamentary seats, which is understood as the electoral 'system'. There are numerous ways in which electoral systems can be categorized. Here we follow Gallagher and Mitchell (2008) and Gallagher (2011), who categorize electoral systems in accordance with the magnitude of the constituencies (i.e. electoral districts) in which seats are allocated to candidates and, inter alia, their proportionality. The two most basic types are majoritarian systems and systems of proportional representation.

Majoritarian systems are usually based on single-member constituencies, in which the strongest party in each constituency wins the seat. This is a very straightforward way of voting: only one candidate can be chosen and the one who receives the highest number of votes is awarded the seat. In some polities, e.g. Australia, this system is in use in a slightly modified version to fill a single seat as the voters can rank-order the different candidates, with their ordering being taken into account when there is no clear overall winner. Another modification (used in French elections, for example) is the two-round system: if no candidate wins a majority of the votes cast, the top-ranked candidates participate in a second election round; whoever wins this is declared the winner.

Proportional representation systems are characterized by multimember constituencies, in which the seats are shared among parties in proportion to the share of votes they have received. The basic idea is to give each party the same share of seats as it won votes, which can be achieved in various ways. In some countries (e.g. the Netherlands) the entire country is regarded as one constituency. Despite the high level of proportionality guaranteed by this system, there is no possibility of choosing local members of parliament – this does, however, favour extremist parties. Therefore, in many countries (e.g. Brazil) there are multiple constituencies within which seats are awarded proportionally. Another refinement is the use of so-called tiers: seats are first assigned in a lower tier (i.e. individual constituencies) and then in a higher tier (i.e. the whole country) to avoid disproportional representation (e.g. Denmark, Germany, New Zealand, Sweden and the Scottish Parliament) (see Gallagher 2011: 184–6).

Electoral institutions are considered to be an important explanatory variable for a wide range of political phenomena. Typically, they have been used to explain party systems. In this regard, Duverger's (1954) very influential book argues that majoritarian electoral systems favour two-party systems, whereas proportional representation leads to multiparty systems (a rare counter-example is provided by India; see Diwakar 2007).

Conversely, the party system has important repercussions on policy-making. Party systems are a concept developed by scholars of comparative political science for categorizing enduring institutional characteristics of the party landscape (see Blondel 1990). More precisely, they describe the system of interaction between multiple parties that are engaged in competition (Sartori 2005: 39). This research perspective has primarily focused on characterizing party systems and determining changes to them over time. Following Caramani (2011: 244–8), we distinguish four types of party systems:

- dominant-party system
- two-party system
- multiparty system
- bipolar system

The first type, dominant-party systems, characterize a situation in which one very large party (with an absolute majority of well above 50 per cent of parliamentary seats) dominates all others over long periods. This is not to say that there is no party competition in these systems, just that no other party has received enough votes to come close to 50 per cent. As a consequence, the dominant party holds a hegemonic position and does not need to enter into coalitions with other parties to form a government.

A well known case of a dominant-party system was Mexico where the Institutional Revolutionary Party was the hegemonic party from the mid-1930s to the late 1990s (see Lehoucq *et al.* 2008).

Two-party systems are characterized by two equally strong parties (with vote shares of 35 to 45 per cent each) which dominate the party system and alternate in holding power. In these systems even a small amount of votes changing from one party to the other can lead to a change of majority, which makes alternations in power fairly frequent. As a result, such systems tend to be very competitive. Since both parties have high vote shares, the winning one is likely to hold the absolute majority of seats and therefore be able to form a single-party government. Yet, there are also often other, smaller parties (i.e. with a very low share of votes) in these systems. According to Caramani (2011: 245), only the United States provides a perfect example of this party system, which is essentially composed of the Democrats and the Republicans (for an overview, see O'Connor and Sabato 2009: ch. 12). Another example would be the United Kingdom until recently, with the Conservative Party and the Labour Party as the dominant political forces and the (for a long time) Liberal Democrat Party as a merely marginal one.

Multiparty systems are the most frequent type of party system, although there is remarkable variation in the number and size of the parties. Relatively small multiparty systems (up to five parties) can be found in Canada, Ireland, Japan (especially in recent times) and Norway. Party systems with more than five parties in parliament exist in Belgium, the Netherlands, Switzerland and Turkey, even though the latter has a 10 per cent threshold for entering parliament. Regardless of the actual number of parties, what multiparty systems have in common is that none of the parties is majoritarian (i.e. holds 50 per cent of the votes or seats), leading to the necessity of forming coalitions. Usually, all of these parties run individually in elections; governmental coalitions are negotiated after the elections. Due to the particular election dynamics and the need to form coalitions, government change rarely takes place through electoral change. Instead, government change is likely to occur by swaps of coalition partners.

The final type is the bipolar party system, which combines elements of multi- and two-party systems. As in multiparty systems there are many parties, of which none is majoritarian, making coalition governments the rule. The major difference, however, is that parties form relatively stable electoral alliances. In most systems, there are two large electoral coalitions running in elections and alternating in power, making electoral competition look like a two-party system. An appropriate example for a bipolar system is Germany, where in usual circumstances two electoral alliances oppose each other. On the one side, there are the Social Democrats and the Green Party; on the other, there is the coalition formed by the Christian Democratic Union and its Bavarian sister party the Christian Social Union as well as the Liberal Party. 'Grand coalitions' consisting of the Christian Democratic Union, the Christian Social Union and the Social Democrats are relatively rare and only formed if there is no other option for forming a government at the national level.

Policy-making can be expected to vary across different party systems. Dominant-party systems should be able to respond immediately to emerging policy problems, whereas the policy-making process can be expected to take longer in multiparty systems due to the need to receive the consent of the other parties for a policy proposal. As in two-party and bipolar systems, policy-making might occur relatively swiftly, but a change in the majority situation could entail drastic changes in existing policy arrangements.

Key points

❏ Constitutions define the most fundamental principles of government in a political system. They are often protected by special courts through means of abstract judicial review, concrete judicial review and constitutional complaints.

❏ Horizontal division of power refers to the three 'classic' branches of government: the executive, the legislature and the judiciary. In some countries, various levels of government are responsible for decision-making. In such cases, the horizontal division of power is complemented by a vertical one.

❏ Electoral systems determine how votes are transformed into seats in legislative assemblies. These can generally be assigned into two categories: majoritarian systems and proportional representation systems.

❏ Electoral systems have repercussions on party systems, which can be categorized accordingly: dominant-party systems, two-party systems, multiparty systems and bipolar systems. These, in turn, are expected to have an impact on how policy-making occurs.

Supranational and intergovernmental institutions: policy-making in a multilevel system

Similar to our understanding of domestic institutions, we conceive of supranational and international institutions as formal organizations. Organizations operating in an international context are classified either as supranational or intergovernmental organizations. A supranational organization has powers that its member states do not have because they have delegated a limited amount of their sovereignty to it. In this way, the supranational organization may enact legislation that pre-empts the laws and regulations of its member states (see Mitchell and Sheargold 2009: 5). In other words, supranational organs can adopt public policies that are binding for their member states. To date, there is only one international organization that corresponds mostly – yet not fully – to these criteria, namely the EU (Kinney 2002; Higgott 2008: 615; Nadakavukaren Schefer 2010: 21; for an overview, see Hix and Høyland 2011).

An intergovernmental organization also consists of member states, but they remain independent and engage in voluntary cooperation and coordination. The crucial aspect is that in this type of organization the member states do not surrender any sovereignty to it. There are many examples of intergovernmental organizations, such as the North Atlantic Treaty Organization (NATO), the International Union for Conservation of Nature, the International Maritime Organization, the International Atomic Energy Agency, the Organisation for Economic Co-operation and Development (OECD) and the Organization of Petroleum Exporting Countries – to name just a few (see Chapter 10).

Here we will limit our presentation to two intergovernmental organizations: the UN and the WTO. The UN is a multifunctional organization with an impressive breadth of tasks and scope of membership. The WTO – together with the World Bank and the International Monetary Fund (IMF), also known as the Bretton Woods institutions – plays an essential role in promoting free trade. At the same time, both of these organizations possess formal legal powers. The UN can take collective security action, whereas the WTO possesses an instrument of formal legal suasion over its member states by means of its dispute settlement mechanism (Higgott 2008: 616). However, in contrast to a supranational organization, the WTO does not have the right to adopt rules that are superior to national law. These rules have no direct effect on domestic actors, unless they are formally transposed into national law.

The United Nations system

The UN was founded in 1945 to maintain international peace and security, develop friendly relations among nations and promote social progress and human rights. Since it comprises a large number of organizations and carries out many different functions, one usually speaks of the UN system. The organization works on many different issues, including disaster relief, refugee protection, sustainable development, the promotion of democracy, gender equality and the advancement of women, economic development, international health, clearing landmines, and expanding food production.

At the centre of this system is the General Assembly, which is the main deliberative organ of the UN and which is composed of representatives of all its 193 member states. The Secretariat supports the activities of the General Assembly and the other UN organizations by carrying out various tasks. The Economic and Social Council is the principal organ which coordinates the economic, social and related work of the UN and its numerous specialized agencies and institutions, such as the Food and Agriculture Organization (FAO), the World Health Organization (WHO), the World Bank Group and the IMF. The International Court of Justice is the chief judicial organ. It settles legal disputes between states and gives advisory opinions to the UN and its specialized agencies. Another important institution is the Security Council: this has primary responsibility for the maintenance of international peace and security (for an overview, see Hanhimaki 2008; Weiss and Daws 2008).

The UN is usually associated with conflict prevention and peace missions as well as humanitarian assistance (see Thakur 2006). There are many other ways in which the UN may affect public policy. This mainly happens through the UN's specialized agencies or funds and programmes such as the United Nations Environment Programme (UNEP) or the United Nations Children's Fund (UNICEF). These organizations can affect public policy in the UN member states through: data gathering and the dissemination of information; the definition of benchmarks and good practice; and financial or other forms of aid. With regard to peace keeping and state building, the UN, of course, has a much more far-reaching impact as it can alter the polity of countries and thus profoundly modify ways of policy-making. More generally, however, the UN's impact on national public policies varies from one UN organization to another as well as across issue areas. Therefore it is not easy to make general statements about its various possible impacts.

Under usual conditions, i.e. if there is no armed conflict or a humanitarian or natural disaster occurring in a country, the numerous UN conventions play a decisive role in shaping public policy in its member states. A particularly well-known instance of this is the Convention on Climate Change, which came into force in 1994. This sets an overall framework for intergovernmental efforts to tackle climate change. Under the Convention, participating governments are expected to:

- gather and share information on greenhouse gas emissions, relevant national policies and best practice for reducing emissions
- develop strategies for lowering greenhouse gas emissions and adapting to expected impacts
- cooperate in preparing for adaptation to the various impacts of climate change

There are many more UN conventions which target, for example, corruption, children's rights, the law of the sea and the rights of persons with disabilities. Signing up to these instruments of international law clearly impacts on national policies that are affected by the issues targeted by the respective conventions and which can entail significant constraints to policy-making. For example, membership of the UN Convention against Torture and Other Cruel, Inhuman or Degrading Treatment or Punishment requires states to take effective measures to prevent torture within their borders. Additionally, it forbids states to return foreign residents or asylum seekers to their home country if there is reason to believe that they will be tortured there.

The World Trade Organization

One of the most important international institutions is the Geneva-based WTO, which is the successor to the General Agreement on Tariffs and Trade (GATT) (Martin 2008). The WTO currently has 153 member states and in this way directly affects well above 90 per cent of total global trade. Its main objective is to reduce or completely eliminate trade barriers in order to facilitate free trade. To this end, it negotiates agreements with its member states, and these define legally binding rules for international trade. The organization is governed by a ministerial conference, which meets every two years, and a general council that is in charge of implementing the ministerial conference's policy decisions and is responsible for day-to-day administration. Additionally, the WTO has a director general, who is appointed by the ministerial conference.

The monitoring of the national trade policies of its member states is the WTO's most fundamental activity. Central to this task is the trade policy review mechanism. All WTO members are subject to review, with the frequency depending on the country's size. Furthermore, the WTO asks its member states to notify it of new or modified trade measures. For example, details of any new anti-dumping legislation, technical standards affecting trade and changes to regulations which impact on commercial services all have to be communicated to the appropriate body of the WTO. As a consequence of the continuous reviewing process and the obligation to communicate relevant modifications of trade policy the WTO has indeed the potential to affect domestic policy arrangements.

Even more important is the impact of the WTO's dispute settlement mechanisms. These help to resolve trade disputes between member states, which usually involve questions about the legality of a particular trade policy or practice (see Grando 2010; Josling 2010). Disputes start with a request for consultations in which the member government bringing the case to the WTO (i.e. the complainant) explains why it objects to the trade policy of the other member state (i.e. the defendant).

Box 3.2   The WTO, tuna and dolphins

The first and best known example of how GATT/WTO rules may affect food production standards in its member states is the 'tuna-dolphin case'. In 1990, the United States banned the import of tuna from Mexico and other Pacific states due to fishing practices that caused many dolphins to die when they were caught with tuna. The legal basis for this decision was the US Marine Mammal Protection Act of 1972, which requires fishermen to use dolphin-safe nets and fixes a ceiling on dolphin mortalities. Mexico challenged the US ban in the dispute resolution system of the GATT and won. The case was taken up again under the WTO system, with the result that the dispute resolution panel confirmed the decision that the United States could not justify the ban, which it then had to lift. In response, the US Department of Commerce created the 'dolphins safe label', which tells the consumers that the catching of this particular tuna product did not involve the deliberate netting or circling of any dolphins. Thus, it is now left to consumers to decide whether to buy the tuna product or not. This means that the WTO ruling induced the US government to replace the command-and-control instrument, i.e. the import ban, by an information-based instrument, i.e. a label providing information about the production process.

The rules determine that the complainant and defendant must engage themselves in consultation activities for 60 days to try and find a solution that satisfies them both and ends the dispute. If these efforts fail, the complainant can request a panel proceeding, i.e. enter formal litigation. The panels vary in their composition and typically comprise two rounds of testimony. At this point, the complainant and defendant can still negotiate a settlement. If this does not happen, the panel issues a final report.

This leads to three possible scenarios. The first is that the final report will be adopted by the WTO. The second is that both the complainant and defendant agree not to adopt the report for whatever reason. The third and most likely scenario is, however, that the complainant or the defendant or both appeal against the panel's report. These appeals are considered by the appellate body, i.e. a standing body of jurists, which then arrives at a final decision. The body scrutinizes the case again by hearing testimony and checking ways in which the panel might have arrived at the wrong conclusion. It can either confirm the entirety or parts of the panel's report or overturn it. If the body decides that the measure in question is inconsistent with the terms of the relevant WTO agreement, the member state concerned will be asked to bring the measure into conformity with that agreement. Mitchell and Sheargold (2009: 18) illustrate this well by making reference to the *Australia – Subsidies Provided to Producers and Exporters of Automotive Leather* dispute. The WTO panel ruled that a subsidy, which had been provided to a private company, had to be repaid in full to the Australian government. Remarkably, this decision had to be implemented even though no domestic legal basis existed to force the company to repay the subsidy as under domestic law it had already been legally granted.

Key points

❏ There are two types of international organizations: supranational and inter-governmental.

❏ Supranational organizations may enact rules that pre-empt the laws and regulations of their member states. To date, there is only one international organization that corresponds to these criteria, namely the EU.

❏ Intergovernmental organizations do not require their member states to surrender any sovereignty; there exist many different types of these kind of organizations.

❏ The UN system is the most encompassing intergovernmental organization in terms of its organizational structure as well as its tasks.

❏ The WTO can equally affect the trade policies of its member states. An effective way of doing this is by reviewing the member states' trade policies and the WTO's dispute settlement mechanism.

❏ Both the UN and the WTO impose limitations on domestic actors' room for manoeuvre, thus affecting national policy choices.

Key actors

Actors are individuals, collectives or corporations involved in the policy-making process, who seek to turn their preferences into public policy. While there can also be influential individual actors, policy-making is usually characterized by collective and corporate actors. Collective actors such as social movements are composed of individuals coordinating their actions; they are dependent on and guided by the preferences of their participants. Corporate actors are also composed of participants, but they 'are typically "top-down" organizations under the control of an "owner" or of a hierarchical leadership representing the owners or beneficiaries' (Scharpf 1997a: 56; see also Engel 2010). In the literature, firms are often conceived as corporate actors.

For understanding how actors might determine policy outputs there are three characteristics to which we must pay attention: their capabilities, perceptions and preferences (Scharpf 1997a: 43). Firstly, actors are characterized by their capabilities, i.e. the action resources at their disposition to influence the policy-making process in a way to make one specific outcome more likely than another. Secondly, actors can be characterized by the way they perceive a particular social problem. Depending on their perception, actors will review potential solutions to the present problem and decide which ones they find most desirable. Thirdly, actors are characterized by their specific preferences, which can be either relatively stable or changeable. In addition, actors can be distinguished according to whether they are public (acting on behalf of the state) or private (acting on behalf of their own preferences).

Public actors

In representative democracies, government is based on elected individuals representing citizens. These elected officials, in turn, appoint additional actors who equally represent the state and are involved in various aspects of policy-making. This section gives an overview of these public actors.

The executive

When we speak of the executive as an actor, we are referring to the people who compose it. In parliamentary and semi-presidential systems, the executive consists of the head of government (prime minister, chancellor) and the ministers who form the cabinet. The number and denomination of ministers varies from country to country, as does the extent to which the head of government dominates the other cabinet members. The relationship between the individual cabinet members and the cabinet as a whole can take two distinct forms. One is the 'principle of collective responsibility' that characterizes Westminster systems. This means that all cabinet members must publicly support decisions made in cabinet, regardless of whether they privately agree with them or not. The other form is represented by the 'principle of ministerial autonomy', which is, for instance, applied in Germany. It gives each cabinet member the freedom and responsibility to supervise departmental operations and prepare legislative proposals without cabinet interference.

As a rule, cabinets must be formed in a way that they can be supported or at least tolerated by a parliamentary majority. Against this backdrop, there are two ways in which the cabinet can be composed: a one-party government or a coalition cabinet. In the first case, one party alone holds the absolute majority in parliament and it is also this party to which the head of government and the cabinet members belong. In the second case, parties must form a coalition in order to enjoy the support of the parliamentary majority. Such coalition cabinets can take three different forms. Firstly, they can form a minimal winning cabinet, implying that the cabinet will include just as many parties as are necessary for gaining control of a majority of parliamentary seats. Secondly, a cabinet can be 'oversized' insofar as it includes more parties than is necessary to provide the government with majority support in the legislature. Thirdly, a cabinet can include fewer parties than is necessary for majority support in the legislature. Such minority cabinets need to be tolerated by the parliament (Lijphart 1999: 90–1). It is clear that a coalition cabinet's leeway in proposing legislation increases with a lowering of the number of parties participating in it. At the same time, however, forming an oversized cabinet can be useful to ensure that controversial policies will be passed in the legislature.

In presidential systems, by contrast, the executive is not drawn from the legislative majority and only needs its support for the president's legislative proposals. Within the executive domain the president is sovereign and decides autonomously the extent to which he or she will rely on the cabinet. Some US presidents, for instance, used their cabinet members either as advisers or for carrying out their orders, but they were never regarded as equal participants (Müller 2011: 145). Therefore, in presidential systems the whole policy-making process is to a much stronger degree characterized by the president's preferences.

The legislature
Legislatures are important actors in policy-making and fulfil three principal tasks (Kreppel 2011: 125–8). Firstly, legislatures provide legitimacy for the political system. In this context, it is important that the members of the legislature facilitate communication between citizens and government. Strongly related to the communication function is representation: citizens expect that their preferences are expressed by 'their' members of the legislature. The representation of these preferences primarily occurs through debating, since legislatures are forums for deliberation (Carey 2008: 431).

Secondly, legislatures have control and oversight functions. Their control rights mainly refer to control over the executive. These tend to be relatively limited in presidential systems as the executive is neither drawn from nor responsible to the legislature. Also in these systems, the policy agenda of the executive is not subject to legislative control. In parliamentary and semi-presidential systems, by contrast, executives are responsible to the legislature for their policy agenda. There is, however, no difference between the regime types regarding the right of legislatures to oversee policy: they possess a variety of tools for monitoring the executive. Committee hearings, hearings in plenary sittings, investigative committees, question times, special inquiries and hearings, interpellations, ombudsmen, and the preparation of reports on specific topics are among the most common tools. They can be used during policy formulation or after the government has enacted a policy and the legislature wants to check whether that policy has been implemented correctly (see Pelizzo and Stapenhurst 2008: 9–13). Another option is the indirect overseeing of the executive by controlling the budgetary process.

The third group of activities refers to what legislatures should, in theory at least, principally do, i.e. legislate. In most political systems, however, it is the executive which tends to dominate the policy-making process (see Chapter 6). Even so, there are still various ways in which legislatures can participate in policy-making. The weakest way to influence public policy is through consultation, i.e. presenting an opinion about a legislative proposal introduced by the executive branch. Another option is to delay the passage of a policy proposal, at times by using the power of a formal veto. In most cases, this will lead to bargaining between the executive and the legislature. While delaying and blocking policy-making represents a 'negative' power, legislatures also possess the 'positive' power of initiating and amending policy proposals. The extent to which this positive power is possible very much depends on the political system that is studied (Kreppel 2011: 128). Generally, however, legislatures tend to be more actively involved in policy-making in presidential systems than in the other two regime types, namely semi-presidential and parliamentary systems.

When conceiving of the legislature as an actor, it is important to note that these functions are not equally carried out by the entirety of the legislature. In parliamentary and semi-presidential systems, the majority of the legislature and the executive form an entity, which drastically reduces the chances of policy-related conflict between them. In marked contrast, in presidential systems there is a clear-cut separation between the president and the congressional majority. As a result, the likelihood of policy-related conflict tends to be higher.

The judiciary
The judiciary is the third branch of government and mainly refers to constitutional courts. For a long time the judiciary was not considered to play an important role in policy-making. This seems to have changed as other political actors have been affected by the policy-modifying power of the judiciary (Adolino and Blake 2011: 71). In this sense, abstract judicial review, for instance, has increasingly been used by parliamentary minorities for strategic reasons (Vanberg 1998). In such cases, the parliamentary minority, also known as the 'opposition', can ask the constitutional court to annul a constitutionally dubious bill introduced or passed in the legislature by the governing party. A resultant negative decision could force the government and/or governing majority in the legislature to modify its policy. In the case of Turkey, for instance, Hazama (1996) argues that the availability of abstract judicial review provides opportunities for the parliamentary opposition to compensate for its legislative weakness.

However, abstract review is not the only way in which constitutional courts can affect public policy: they can become involved in policy-making by declaring a certain piece of legislation to be unconstitutional. Yet, as Stone Sweet (2007: 87–9) explains, there are two ways in which constitutional judges exercise indirect authority over the legislature. The first way is 'self-limitation' and refers to the exercise of self-restraint on the part of the government and its parliamentary majority when it is seeking an annulment by the constitutional court. This is observed when the government and the parliamentary majority take decisions that sacrifice previously held policy objectives in order to lower the probability that a bill will be either referred to the court or found unconstitutional. The second way, 'corrective revision', takes place after a bill has been annulled. It refers to the reworking of a censured text in conformity with the court's decision, so as to secure promulgation.

Constitutional court decisions therefore can have a profound impact on the content and design of public policies. The most important policy-making power of the courts stems from their authority to interpret and apply the constitution and other laws. In this way, they can help to resolve disagreements about abstract goals enshrined in a country's constitution, such as the main characteristics of its economic regime (Dahl 1957: 280). Policy decisions can be subject to judicial review and when they are found to violate constitutional rules decision-makers need to start a new policy process, one involving the elaboration of another policy design and the need to receive broad support for it. For example, the US Supreme Court in 2010 ended a policy banning self-declared homosexuals from serving in the military (known as the 'don't ask, don't tell' policy) by declaring it unconstitutional. The previous policy had prohibited any homosexual or bisexual person from disclosing his or her sexual orientation.

The judiciary can also affect public policies by acting as an agenda-setter (see pp. 113–15). If the key policy-makers, i.e. the legislature and the executive, neglect certain social problems, filing lawsuits can bring this problem on to the policy agenda and force policy-makers to address it appropriately. Indeed litigation has been successfully employed to reduce industry practices that may be harmful to the public health, such as smoking (Daynard *et al.* 2002).

There are also many indirect ways in which the judiciary can influence policy-making. One way is by excluding certain actors from the policy-making process. The Turkish constitutional court, for example, has, in the past, banned a number of political parties (mostly Islamic ones, such as the Welfare Party). By excluding certain actors from the policy process, their preferred policy proposals cannot enter the political arena, and so are unlikely ever to materialize as public policies.

In this context, it should be noted also that the courts can become quite political. Hönnige (2009) shows that judges in France and

Germany have political preferences of their own and that the ideological position of the court is determined by the selection of the pivotal judge. So if a court is mainly staffed by supporters of the government, it is likely to favour the ideological preferences and policy proposals of the government rather than those of the parliamentary minority that is assumed to have opposing preferences.

The bureaucracy

For implementing public policy, the executive relies on the bureaucracy, i.e. the layers of hierarchically appointed officials (Kettl 2008: 371). However, bureaucrats are not only involved in policy implementation but also policy formulation due to their procedural and specialist knowledge. Therefore, it is reasonable to distinguish between the implementing bureaucracy and the ministerial bureaucracy as it is the latter type that might play a role in policy formulation. The important role of the bureaucracy has been particularly emphasized by Max Weber (1947), who attributed to it three main characteristics that he deemed were needed to make it an effective instrument of government:

- *Personnel stability*: the attracting and maintaining of qualified bureaucrats working in a governmental organization, enabled by the provision of suitable career paths.
- *Organization*: organizing bureaucracies by their functional speciality, and assigning their members to units based on the type of work they do. Bureaucracies are marked by a hierarchical authority, with higher-level officials supervising lower-level workers.
- *Procedure*: having a high degree of standardization of decision-making and the application of rules, which is also achieved by management keeping written documents.

There are two ideal-typical systems of how bureaucrats are appointed. With the 'spoils' system, individuals are appointed on the basis of their political loyalty, which they are expected to demonstrate in all aspects of their work. This kind of clientelistic bureaucracy displays a low level of autonomy from elected politicians and results in staff with reduced technical capacities. With the meritocratic system, bureaucrats are appointed because of their expertise and experience – and this form is now adopted in most advanced democracies. Meritocratic bureaucracies are characterized by high degrees of autonomy and technical capacities. In addition to these two extreme forms, there are 'administrative bureaucracies' that have autonomy but low capacity and 'parallel bureaucracies' that have high capacity but low autonomy (Scartascini 2008: 64–5). Weber (1947) acknowledged the fact that bureaucracies – in light of their characteristics – did not just constitute an instrument of the government, but could also exert an autonomous influence on policy formulation and implementation. If and to what extent this is still the case will be discussed in Chapters 6 and 7. In general, we find a broad variance across countries regarding the political autonomy of the bureaucracy (Peters 2010).

Political parties

So far, we have shed light on the elected and appointed officials involved in the process of policy-making. However, the members of legislatures, executives and in some countries the bureaucracy must be recruited from somewhere. This is one task of political parties, which, in seeking to influence government policy, usually nominate their own candidates and try to seat them in political office. According to Katz (2011: 223–5) political parties perform four core tasks:

- coordinating
- conducting electoral campaigns
- structuring competition
- representing

Coordinating involves many different dimensions. Political parties are in charge of coordinating functions in party caucuses (e.g. maintaining discipline; coordination of action of the parliamentary caucus in support of or opposition to the cabinet), organizing the political activity of citizens and linking them with elected officials. Another important field of action is electoral competition. Political parties provide candidates, formulate policy programmes and organize electoral campaigns. This aspect is strongly linked with the recruitment of personnel, which parties do by selecting candidates for elections and/or appointed offices. Finally, parties represent their members within government institutions as well as in society.

More directly with respect to policy-making, the role of political parties is to influence the ideas and beliefs of citizens about public policy and so affect their electoral decisions, which themselves then define the strength of a given party in the legislature and/or the executive. However, since elections in democracies take place on a regular basis, the policies adopted by the political parties will shape the electoral decisions of the citizens (Aldrich 2008: 571; see also Gilardi 2010). The policy options that parties offer citizens vary as they are strongly affected by their fundamental beliefs. These differing ideological views can be used to categorize parties into so-called 'party families' (von Beyme 1985). This notion has since been further developed. For example, Mair and Mudde (1998) identify the following party families, which have certain very general policy orientations (see Gallagher *et al.* 2005: ch. 8; Colomer 2008):

- *Communist parties*: have their ideological roots in Marxism–Leninism and seek to secure a more equitable distribution of income and opportunity in society.
- *Social democratic parties or labour parties*: seek to align capitalism with social justice.
- *Christian democratic parties*: apply Christian principles to public policy. They are often considered conservative on social and moral issues, and moderately market-liberal on fiscal and economic issues.
- *Conservative parties*: are market-liberal without having a religious background.
- *Agrarian parties*: typically combine a commitment to decentralized policy-making and environmental protection as well as maintaining the interests of small businesses.
- *Liberal parties*: a difficult category as they can be centre left, centrist or centre right, depending on the national party system, though they all strongly support civil rights.
- *Left-libertarian parties*: essentially liberal parties supporting some form of income redistribution.
- *Green parties*: foster the principles of environmental protection, social justice, reliance on grassroots democracy and opposition to war.
- *Nationalist parties*: put the well-being of their 'own' people to the fore. Often, their policy agenda is defined by nationalist separation from a state in which they are presently subsumed. Examples of these can be found in Northern Ireland, Scotland and Wales (see Moran 2005: 336); the Basque region; and to an extent in Belgium and northern Italy.
- *Right-wing populist parties*: associated with a political ideology that rejects the existing political consensus and combines economic liberalism and anti-elitism.
- *Racist parties or extreme right-wing parties*: this category comprises parties seeking to attract votes by racist and anti-system statements. (See Ennser 2010).

Private actors

This section concerns so-called 'private actors'. Despite not being elected or appointed by elected officials, they are central to policy-making – on the grounds that they bring valuable information to policy-makers that might eventually guide the way to solving social problems.

Interest groups
Interest groups are organizations that make policy suggestions to governments in order to bring public policies more in line with the interests of their members. In the literature they go by numerous names, such as

lobby groups, interest associations, pressure groups and non-governmental organizations (NGOs). The study of interest groups concerns two major topics, namely how interest groups organize and the ways in which they affect public policy. Regarding organization, Olson's (1965) famous study emphasized the problems typical of collective action. Based on the assumption that individuals are rational and possess perfect information, he contended that joining an interest group is irrational since individuals can enjoy the benefits secured by participants in other interest groups, i.e. by 'free riding'. As a consequence, smaller groups face fewer problems of collective action as they are susceptible to a higher degree of social pressure that reduces the risk of free riding. Concerning the formation of large interest groups that are particularly subject to free riding, Olson argues that only the provision of 'selective' incentives, i.e. a benefit reserved strictly for group members, can stimulate individuals in a latent group to act in a group-oriented way (see also Moe 1981).

Wilson (1974, cited in Werner and Wilson 2008: 351) identifies three reasons for individuals becoming members of interest groups. The first is that they want to enjoy the benefits that are exclusively accessible to members, what Olson calls 'selective incentives'. For example, when joining an automobile club, members benefit from first-hand legal and technical information and support. Wilson's second reason is that individuals join an interest group to pursue their specific goals. A third motivation is that membership can be seen as a (political) statement, e.g. being against the use of nuclear energy.

We can distinguish between private and public interest groups. Private interest groups are organizations that seek to affect policy-making in a way that pursues the special – often economic – preferences of their members. Due to their relatively small size, the homogeneity of their members and the concentration of potential benefits from their activities, private interest groups are on average less likely to face free-riding problems. These groups often come in various forms, representing, for instance, enterprises or professions (e.g. doctors, farmers or teachers). In most cases, however, they are equated with business groups and labour groups (see Dye and Zeigler 2006: 235–9).

Public interest groups, by contrast, may be defined as organizations that seek to pursue goals that are not exclusively limited to their members. They are usually non-profit organizations and lobby for greater government regulation, for example to strengthen public safety. Like private interests groups, public ones come in many forms. The areas in which they are particularly active include environmental issues, peace, human rights, animal rights and gender equality. Generally, they are confronted with larger organizational problems than private interest groups. The large size and the prospect of diffuse benefits make these groups relatively vulnerable to free riding.

In this context, it is important to delineate public interest groups from social movements. Kriesi (2011: 293–4) defines social movements as (1) a group of individuals with a conflictual orientation towards an opposing group; (2) having a collective identity and sharing common beliefs and objectives; and (3) having a repertoire of collective actions. What predominantly distinguishes a social movement from an interest group is that the first is composed of a network of individuals and organized groups of individuals who engage in non-institutionalized coordinated actions to achieve common goals while maintaining their autonomy. Interest groups, by contrast, are more formally constituted and mostly engage in institutionalized actions as they have regular access to different decision-making arenas.

The scope of action of a social movement is also much greater. Social movements target, for example, women's rights, gay rights, peace, anti-nuclear and environmental policies. One of the most famous social movements of the 20th century is the American Civil Rights Movement, which sought to end racial discrimination against African Americans. Interest groups and political parties may be part of a social movement, though the latter cannot be reduced to interest groups or political parties. A case in point is the (global) environmental movement, which encompasses green parties and green interest groups such as Greenpeace (see Leonard 2007 on the green movement in Ireland). In light of these characteristics, Kriesi (2011: 293) argues that social movements cannot be regarded as simply another type of interest group.

How can interest groups affect policy-making? Following Erne (2011: 268–70), there are four ways in which interest groups and policy-makers

---

Box 3.3   Forum 50%: a women's interest group

Despite great progress, in most countries women are still under-represented in political life. Generally, the more important a position, the less likely is the incumbent to be a woman. This trend has also been evident in the post-Communist world since 1989–91. In the Czech Republic, for example, there are still many obstacles against women reaching positions of political leadership. Forum 50% is an interest group that focuses on various issues with respect to the representation of women in decision-making and public life more generally. The group aims to achieve equal representation for women and men in all decision-making positions, both elected and appointed. To reach this goal the group members support all women who want to enter into politics or who are already politically active. It offers workshops for different interested audiences, utilizes the mass media to draw attention to the under-representation of women in public life, and collaborates with various research institutes. It also organizes the competition 'The Women-Friendly Party' for assessing which Czech political party best promotes and follows the policy of equal opportunities for women and men.

interact. The first one is known as inside-lobbying, which is based on personal contacts between interest groups and politicians, and which involves various strategies such as meetings and participation in legislative committees. As a rule, inside-lobbying tends to be more effective when interest groups possess generous resource endowments. This strategy can be complemented by outside-lobbying, namely activities of interest groups taking place outside the actual policy-making arenas. Outside-lobbying includes media activities and campaigning in favour of or against a particular policy.

Some interest groups (predominantly labour and business associations) may try to establish a specific structure for political exchange with policy-makers. The idea of this perspective – which we discuss in detail when introducing the concept of (neo-)corporatism – is that interest groups must be given access to the policy-making process by politicians, who are willing to 'open doors' on the condition that they receive something in exchange. Consequently, not all kinds of interest groups have the same chances of affecting public policy; their success depends on the resources they can exchange which itself is shaped by the institutional context. These resources include, among other things, valuable policy-relevant information, i.e. expert knowledge and a guarantee of achieving social consent over public policies, which is expected to turn policy implementation into an uncontroversial issue (see Bouwen 2004). The flipside to this relationship is that 'regulatory capture' might emerge, i.e. a situation in which interest groups abuse their access to policy-making in order to shape policies in such a way that they serve their private benefits (Stigler 1971; see also pp. 127–8).

The final form in which interest groups can become involved in policy-making has been described by Streeck and Schmitter (1985) as 'private interest government'. This describes a situation in which private interest groups, primarily business representatives, make legally binding decisions, thereby acting as a central function of the state (see Knill and Lehmkuhl 2002b: 50–1). There are, however, few examples of this type of relationship.

Experts

Not all individuals who can provide knowledge and expertise to policy-makers are members of interest groups. We use the term 'expert' for individuals or groups of individuals that can have an impact on policy-making on grounds of the information they supply to policy-makers. In contrast to interest groups, experts do not necessarily pursue any specific policy goal, though they are expected to deliver unbiased knowledge that is required for effective policy-making.

In most cases, experts can be understood as part of 'epistemic communities', i.e. networks of recognized specialists with policy-relevant knowledge in a particular issue area (Haas 1992: 5). However, following this classical definition, we can speak of an epistemic community only where there is a structured network of experts, who share a common interest and task, and possess diverse knowledge – which explains why it is useful for them to collaborate. Some examples of these communities include the World Futures Studies Federation or the Global Facilitation Network for Security Sector Reform. One problem with the notion of epistemic communities, however, is that it concentrates on knowledge elites who possess scientific expertise. Yet, there are many other kinds of knowledge-based actors, such as individual scientists, consultants and practitioners, who can equally help to change policy-makers' ideas about a certain issue (see Head 2008; Howlett 2009b). Ideas, in turn, can be understood as causal beliefs produced by cognitive processes. They posit causal connections, thus providing guides for action (Béland and Cox 2011: 3–4).

In this context, the role of political advisers is particularly interesting as they have become relevant in the formulation of public policy in the many Westminster systems. In New Zealand, for example, a minister's office will typically 'include officials seconded from departments or agencies for which he or she is responsible . . . a Senior Private Secretary responsible for overall office administration, other administrative staff, at least one designated Press Secretary, and one or more "political" ministerial advisors' (Eichbaum and Shaw 2007: 610–11). Usually, political advisers are partisan rather than neutral, which distinguishes them from experts.

The increasing importance of political advisers is sometimes viewed with suspicion (see Maley 2000; Tiernan 2007). According to Eichbaum and Shaw (2008: 338), however, there is too little empirical data available to make reliable statements about how influential political advisers actually are. This does not rule out that there is, in principle, a political dimension to the provision of policy-related information and advice.

Key points

❏ Numerous actors participate in policy-making; they can be categorized into public actors and private actors.

❏ The most central public actors are the executive, the legislature, the judiciary and the bureaucracy. With the general exception of the judiciary and parts of the bureaucracy, these are mostly recruited from political parties with different ideologies. In accordance with these, political parties offer specific policy suggestions, which are subject to evaluation by the electorate.

❏ Interest groups and experts are particularly influential types of private actors.

Conclusions

In this chapter, our main objective has been to familiarize the reader with the main institutions and actors affecting policy-making. We defined institutions in a minimalist way as formal rules determining the extent to which the policy preferences of actors can be transposed into public policies. In shedding light on institutions, we did not limit ourselves to domestic institutions only but also outlined the functioning of the UN and the WTO as two influential intergovernmental organizations.

We defined actors as individuals or groups of individuals forming a collective entity that participate in policy processes and whose preferences can ultimately determine policy choice. We have shown that there are numerous actors participating in policy-making. Yet, we have restricted our presentation to the most essential ones who are involved at each of the various phases of policy-making. Indeed, there are additional actors to which we will turn to in Chapter 4 when discussing the various theoretical concepts of policy-making. Most importantly, however, we have not introduced citizens as a specific category of actor. This stems from the fact that in representative democracies the direct involvement of citizens is restricted to elections and in a few cases to referendums. As a result, citizens' preferences are mediated by the actors presented here.

Web links

http://rulers.org/index.html. This site contains lists of the most important international organizations and provides details about their purposes and scope of membership.

www.uia.be/links. Numerous international associations are listed here.

www.politicsresources.net. This site locates some helpful resources relevant to the study of politics and government.

www.wto.org. First-hand information about the WTO plus a variety of resources, ranging from statistics to publications and a glossary of economy-related terms.

www.ipu.org/english/parlweb.htm. This site provides links to all national parliaments.

www.cses.org. This is the site of the Comparative Study of Electoral Systems programme, which addresses almost every aspect of elections. The data centre is particularly useful.

http://aceproject.org/main/english/es. A very detailed overview of electoral systems around the globe.

www.un.org. Presents the United Nations system; particularly recommended is the section 'UN at a glance'.

Further reading

Lijphart, A. (1999) *Patterns of Democracy: Government Forms and Performance in Thirty-Six Countries*. New Haven: Yale University Press. One of the most influential books on comparing political institutions.

Newton, K. and J.W. van Deth (2010) *Foundations of Comparative Politics*. Cambridge: Cambridge University Press. An accessible and comprehensive introduction to comparative politics, which aptly outlines the characteristics of policy actors.

Rhodes, R.A.W., S.A. Binder and B.A. Rockman (eds) (2008) *The Oxford Handbook of Political Institutions*. Oxford: Oxford University Press. This is a compelling collection of a wide range of topics touching upon political institutions.

Selin, H. and S.D. vanDeveer (eds) (2009) *Changing Climates in North American Politics: Institutions, Policymaking, and Multilevel Governance*. Cambridge, MA: MIT Press. A stimulating read of North American policy responses to global climate change with a variety of analytical lenses.

Sinclair, B. (2006) *Party Wars: Polarization and the Politics of National Policy Making*. Norman, OK: University of Oklahoma Press. The book shows how the ideological gulf now separating the two major parties in the United States developed and how partisan competition affects the political process and policy-making.

Van den Bossche, P. (2008) *The Law and Policy of the World Trade Organization: Text, Cases and Materials*. Cambridge: Cambridge University Press. A comprehensive yet straightforward publication covering the WTO's legal rules.

Chapter 4

Theoretical Approaches to Policy-Making

Reader's guide

The objective of this chapter is to provide a basic idea of the processes underlying policy-making. We will present different theoretical perspectives to explain why governments institute, modify and, indeed, terminate public policy. In this regard, structure-based models, institution-based models and interest-based models have received considerable scholarly attention. Structure-based models emphasize the possible policy consequences of enduring macrostructures in societies. In this context, socioeconomic development and divisions between different social groups (cleavages) are important. Institution-based models primarily outline how formal and informal institutional arrangements may influence public policy. Thus, the theoretical perspectives to be presented complement the description of formal institutions that we gave in Chapter 3. Interest-based models, by contrast, emphasize the role of actors and their respective policy preferences. The three theoretical perspectives are complementary as they address various levels of analysis. Structure-based models offer an explanation at the macrolevel, whereas interest-based models are at the microlevel. Institution-based models can relate to both levels, although in most cases they produce mesolevel explanations, i.e. they illuminate how macrolevel pressures shape microlevel activity. While this complementarity of analytical perspectives is desirable for developing a full understanding of policy-making, it also implies that looking at one and the same subject of interest might lead to different conclusions, depending on which theoretical underpinning is chosen – and the appropriateness of this choice depends on the researcher's particular interests.

Policy-making is undoubtedly a complex process – often one factor that stimulates the promulgation of a public policy in one political system does not necessarily lead to the same outcome in another political system. For example, many countries are confronted with demographic changes. In particular, the proportion of senior citizens is growing, creating increased demands for certain public services, such as social care. Despite having common demographic changes, countries have adopted different policies for addressing this problem. Germany, for instance, has established long-term care insurance to cover the costs resulting from elderly persons losing their ability to look after themselves. Another approach, adopted in Scotland, is to introduce free at the point of use personal and nursing care for older people in care homes and in their own homes. But there are also many countries that have not yet adjusted their policy arrangements to deal with the ageing population. Why are some countries more aware of reforming their social care policies than others? Why do the adopted policies diverge across countries? To answer these and similar research questions theoretical considerations are needed – which we will introduce in this chapter.

Key to explanatory success is a simplification of the various processes accompanying the making of one particular policy. This requires leaving out any distracting details and focusing on the essential features of an empirical phenomenon – and this is best attained by relying on theoretical approaches. Essentially, a theory is a set of statements comprising various hypotheses, i.e. the expected causal relationship between a dependent variable (what we want to explain) and an independent variable (the factor that explains something) that may or may not be true. An example of a hypothesis is: if the green party is elected to govern (the independent variable), then environmental policies (the dependent variable) will become more stringent. In the field of public policy analysis there are several theoretical approaches that can explain why some governments are more likely to introduce or modify a public policy than others. It would become very difficult, if not to say impossible, to provide answers to important research questions without the use of theories (Peters 2011: 40). As we will show in the following, there are a number of basic theoretical perspectives that help to give us a simplified idea of what policy-making is like.

Structure-based models

Structure-based models draw attention to the most basic socioeconomic problems present in societies, which provide decision-makers with the incentive to create or modify public policy. In this context, it is important to note that these models concern the structure of the socioeconomy rather than the structure of problems. Here we introduce the socioeconomic school of policy-making as described by Schmidt (1995) and the social cleavage approach put forward by Lipset and Rokkan (1967). Of these two, the first approach directly connects socioeconomic changes in society to policy-making. The cleavage approach, by contrast, outlines a broader range of social problems that are related to policy-making by means of political parties that define their policy positions in accordance with them. Essentially, it represents the foundation of why different political parties exist, namely because they address a lasting division between societal groups on policy problems. The cleavage approach hence represents a complement to the party families presented in Chapter 3.

The socioeconomic school

According to the socioeconomic school, public policy is a response to social and economic developments and problems that a society is confronted with. It is primarily associated with the research of Émile Durkheim, Karl Marx and Adolph Wagner. The first two political philosophers also deserve credit for introducing the concept of socioeconomic stratification – i.e. the unequal distribution of valued goods or holdings in a society, including wealth, status and resources – which has become a central concept in social science. The theoretical arguments to be presented in this section must be clearly seen against the backdrop of industrialization, which to a certain extent created 'modern' societies. 'Industrialization' is generally defined as the modernization process which turns an agrarian society into one in which the production of goods and services predominates. Perhaps the first country to experience industrialization, in the 18th century, was the United Kingdom. This was followed by countries in all continents in the 19th and 20th centuries.

The main argument of this school is that socioeconomic development entails positive and negative changes to an existing society. On one hand, socioeconomic development increases the division of work, leading to higher productivity and economic well-being as well as social and political progress. On the other hand, 'old' institutions such as families cannot fulfil their original functions any more as women, for instance, now too participate in the industrial production process. From these changes emerges the need to create new institutions that are capable of providing new services that in the pre-industrialization period used to be provided by the family. For example, workers in early industrialized societies were exposed to new production processes, including the use of chemical substances and other potentially toxic materials, so that many of them suffered from health problems. In response, the state promulgated legislation that defined certain minimum standards for the protection of workers and set up a social security system covering health care. Thus, the socioeconomic school argues that the objective of public policy is to correct the negative consequences of industrialization. In other words, it is the state's self-interest in maintaining its economic functioning that drives policy-making. A case in point for this argument is provided by South Korea. The country's rapid industrialization in the 1960s and 1970s challenged the pattern of family structure: the extended family was replaced by the nuclear family. This loss of traditional family structure was one reason why the government began to establish a national welfare policy in 1976 (Kim 1990: 419).

This viewpoint entailed two opposing expectations regarding the development of public policy. The first and more common perspective was that as a country grows richer, the need for government activity would diminish, due to there being fewer or less intense socioeconomic problems (Henrekson 1993: 406). The opposing expectation was put forward by the German political economist Adolph Wagner (1893). He formulated the famous 'law of increasing state activity', which linked economic growth to rising public expenditures so as to ensure social services that previously were provided by families (see Lamartina and Zaghini 2011).

Wagner expected the state to increase its involvement for three main reasons. Firstly, in an increasingly complex society, such as the one created by industrialization, there would be a need for protective and regulatory activity to ensure contractual enforcement, which represents a necessary precondition for a functioning economy. Secondly, economic growth would entail that the state can more efficiently provide education and culture than private actors. Thirdly, the state had to take over natural monopolies (e.g. infrastructure such as streets or railways) to increase economic efficiency. If the state were to delegate this activity to private actors, the collective welfare would depend on their preferences, thus posing a risk to the sufficient supply of these goods (see pp. 88–90).

A further development of the socioeconomic school is provided by Wilensky (1975), who argued that public spending – as an indicator of state activity – should uniformly increase in advanced industrialized countries due to their mutual experience of industrialization processes and related social problems. While there is some evidence for Wilensky's 'convergence hypothesis' (see Schmitt and Starke 2011 for social spending), it should be noted that the containment of public – and especially social – spending growth has come to be regarded as a core goal of policy-makers in most advanced industrial countries since the 1980s (see Kittel and Obinger 2003: 20), including the explicit political attempts of the Thatcher government (1979–90) in the United Kingdom and the Reagan administration (1981–89) in the United States, and also in many other states, such as New Zealand (see Pierson 1994; Stephens 2003). All these attempts have, however, been met with varying success. The deliberate decision of governments to reduce the degree of their intervention represents a 'modern' complement to this analytical perspective.

The analytical strength of the socioeconomic school is that it systematically takes into account developments in society for explaining public policy (Schmidt 1995: 578). This establishes a 'functional' understanding of public policy that is capable of explaining a good deal of variation in public policy across countries. While it is very historical in its understanding of stimuli for policy-making, it is still suitable for addressing more recent phenomena in society and the economy. Economic globalization, i.e. the increasing transnational exchange of goods and services, and financial crises of a global scale do indeed bring considerations of the socioeconomic school to the fore. How do governments protect their citizens from the 'new' risk of global financial crises? What are the implications of economic globalization for the scale of state activities? These are some of the questions that could be addressed by relying on the socioeconomic school. We will return to these in Chapter 10 when we introduce the concept of 'regulatory competition' and the corresponding 'race to the bottom' argument.

The cleavage approach

Akin to the socioeconomic school, the cleavage approach is based on the idea that certain enduring socioeconomic problems exist in societies and that affect policy choices by means of creating lasting divisions between social groups (i.e. social cleavages) which possess different perceptions about these problems and the ways of solving them. These social cleavages are important for policy choices in a country as they have been taken up by political parties that offer policy proposals in accordance with those problems that they deem most important.

There are four major social cleavages identified by Lipset and Rokkan (1967) that emerged in the context of the national revolutions in the 19th century and of the industrialization in the 19th and 20th centuries, which created profound and lasting socioeconomic and cultural divisions among social groups. This already suggests that the cleavage approach is a concept that emphasizes historical developments. According to Caramani (2011: 239), there are also two 'modern' cleavages, leading to a total of six social cleavages:

* centre–periphery
* state–church
* rural–urban

- workers–employers
- materialists–post-materialists
- open–closed societies

National revolutions created the division between the centre and the periphery: a division that consists on the one hand of social groups supporting the view that political power and administrative structures in a nation-state should become centralized, and, on the other hand, of social groups which assert their traditional autonomy against such centralizing pressures. Individuals attaching importance to this particular cleavage will either support or oppose policies strengthening the centralization of the state, for instance by means of a centralized use of tax revenues. This cleavage is mainly associated with separatist nationalist parties, which are sometimes also described as 'regionalist' parties.

The state–church cleavage is about social groups seeking to separate secular from religious authority and social groups in favour of preserving the connection between them. Depending on whether they are religious or not, individuals will differ in their views with respect to various policy issues. To give an example: in OECD countries religiosity has a major influence on the strictness of embryo research laws – the Catholic Church being the most influential actor in this particular policy field. The more powerful the Catholic Church is in a country, the more restrictive is the respective embryo research law (Fink 2008). Intuitively, this state–church cleavage is of importance to Christian democratic parties and to a certain extent to conservative and social democratic parties.

The Industrial Revolution created two further structural divisions. First, there is the cleavage between rural and urban societies, i.e. between social groups whose survival depends on traditional activities, and social groups that endeavour to remove traditional constraints in order to foster new economic activities. The rural–urban cleavage yields far more policy implications than one might suspect at first glance. With respect to trade policies, for example, the rural population usually favours trade barriers for protecting national agricultural products, whereas the urban population tends to prefer trade liberalization to enhance their economic well-being (Caramani 2011: 241). Usually, agrarian parties are mostly associated with this cleavage.

The second cleavage to come out of the Industrial Revolution concerns the opposition between 'capital' and 'labour'. On one side, there are the employers who favour a low level of state intervention in the economy, and, on the other side, there are the workers who demand job security and social protection. This cleavage reflects the ideas of the socioeconomic school as it takes into account social changes as a consequence of industrialization. In fact, this division between workers and employers is still present in every modern society and has important implications for policy choices. It is the classic domain of communist parties, social democratic parties and labour parties.

The materialist–post-materialist cleavage describes what priority social groups give to new values. This cleavage is strongly interlinked with Inglehart's (1997) value concepts of materialism and post-materialism. These terms explain the way in which political values rise out of individual needs during the process of socialization, i.e. the learning of how to behave according to cultural norms. Materialist values are the concern of those who have experienced political and economic insecurity, leading them to give priority to political stability and economic strength. Those who have post-materialist values have been exposed to greater security and are oriented towards satisfying other needs. As a result, post-materialists place higher value on ideas such as equality of opportunity, citizen involvement in decision-making at government and community levels (also known as 'direct democracy'), and environmental protection (Braithwaite *et al.* 1996: 1536–7). In modern societies, green parties are predominantly associated with post-materialism.

With national boundaries becoming more and more permeable, an open–closed society cleavage has emerged, in which social groups are either in favour or against the opening of markets. Those who feel disadvantaged by economic globalization favour trade barriers to protect local manufacturing and 'locals-first' policies in the labour market. The economically defensive attitude of these groups is reinforced by anti-immigration stances which stress religious and national values against a multi-ethnic society. Often nationalist parties, right-wing populist parties, racist parties and extreme right parties address this social cleavage (Caramani 2011: 239).

The cleavage approach is important for understanding how party families have formed. The various political parties, in turn, address existing social problems by proposing specific solutions to them, which may eventually become a public policy. In this context, it should be noted that the cleavage approach as outlined here mostly corresponds to the European context. Nevertheless, many of these social cleavages can be found elsewhere. Australian rural policy, for instance, is marked by the rural–urban cleavage (see Botterill 2009). Outside Europe there are other cleavage structures. In Canada, for example, there is a linguistic cleavage between English-speaking and French-speaking Canadians that is likely to influence public policy (see Béland and Lecours 2007; Lambert and Curtis 2008). Irrespective of the exact cleavage structures, what matters is that there are deep and lasting divisions between groups in societies that generate certain political parties that are then involved in the policy-making process and which aim to realize their preferences when proposing public policies.

Key points

❑ There are two elements to structure-based approaches: the socioeconomic school and social cleavages.

❑ The socioeconomic school regards social and economic developments as the main driver of public policy.

❑ The cleavage approach focuses on basic lines of societal conflicts as the main determinants of policy-making. Historical cleavages include conflict between centre and periphery, church and state, rural and urban areas, and employers and workers.

❑ The two newer types of cleavage address the division between materialists and post-materialists and supporters and opponents of an open society.

Institution-based models

In Chapter 3 we introduced the most important formal institutions to provide an overview of the context in which policy-making takes place. In this section, we move beyond the mere description of the characteristics of institutions and introduce theoretical approaches that explain *how* they matter for policy outputs. The different theoretical perspectives all conceive of institutions as the central independent variable for explaining policy-making, which itself represents the dependent variable.

The major difference between institutional approaches is their respective definition of 'institutions'. The 'classic' approaches to institutional analysis rely on a conception of 'institutions' as formal-legal arrangements, similar to the understanding presented in Chapter 3. 'New institutionalism', by contrast, offers more complex or broader notions of institutions and the ways in which they matter for policy-making. Despite being termed 'institutionalist', it should be noted that both approaches explicitly acknowledge the importance of actors. Indeed, the most general way of explaining how institutions affect policy outputs is by stating how it is that they empower and constrain actors (see March and Olsen 2008: 3). In the following section we will illustrate this causal relation.

The classical approach to political institutions

For a long time, classical institutionalist analyses of public policy were based on the formal-legal approach, which emphasizes the role that governmental organizations play. This classic form of institutionalism can be characterized in two ways. Firstly, the basic independent variable is given by the legal rules and procedures in a political system. The different functions of the state, including policy-making, and how they are performed, represent the dependent variable. Secondly, legal rules are regarded as behavioural prescriptions. For example, policy-makers in some nations would not think about formulating legislation with a discriminatory character because they know that the constitution prohibits this.

Against this backdrop, classical institutionalism contends that the functioning of the state not only depends on economic and social conditions but also on the design and effectiveness of political institutions (March and Olsen 1984: 734). A similar perspective is adopted by Arend Lijphart (1999) in his influential book *Patterns of Democracy*. The author scrutinizes the relationship between government forms and policy performance, i.e. how effectively a government can solve a social problem. In so doing, he argues that political systems of advanced democracies in all their complexity can be basically assigned to two competing categories: 'majoritarian' and 'consensus'. Majoritarian democracies typically have majority or plurality electoral systems, only two major political parties, single-party cabinets, effective unicameralism, and a unitary and centralized government. Consensus democracies, by contrast, are characterized by proportional electoral systems, having more than two major parties, coalition cabinets, bicameralism, and decentralized or federal political systems.

Accordingly, the United Kingdom would represent a majoritarian democracy and Switzerland a consensus democracy. Applying the logic of classical institutionalism, British public policy would have to be significantly different from Swiss public policy because of the different institutional arrangements in the two countries (for discussions, see Armingeon 2002; Schmidt 2002; Roller 2005). To be sure, Lijphart's approach somehow parallels the idea about national policy styles, which we introduced in Chapter 2. Lijphart's theoretical argument suggests that policy styles flow from electoral systems and the distribution of power. So, policy styles in countries corresponding to a majoritarian democracy are expected to be different from those consensus democracies as the former produces a concentration of power at the centre and encourages majoritarian, top-down government, whereas the latter diffuses power and encourages the formation of coalitions and the pursuit of consensus (for a discussion, see Cairney 2011).

Another important classical institutionalist analysis is represented by the work of Francis Castles (1998), which analyses variations in public policy by combining political-institutional variables and socioeconomic indicators. The study reveals the existence of four 'families of nations', which differ in respect of policy-making, particularly in the areas of social and economic policy:

- an English speaking family of nations, including Australia, Canada, Ireland, New Zealand, the United Kingdom and the United States
- a Continental family of nations, consisting of Austria, Belgium, France, Germany, Italy and the Netherlands
- a Scandinavian family of nations, consisting of Denmark, Finland, Norway and Sweden
- a southern family of nations, comprising Greece, Portugal and Spain

Again, this analytical approach corresponds with the notion of national policy styles, especially to the extent that political-institutional variables – including a categorization of countries in accordance with Lijphart's concept of majoritarian and consensus democracies – represent an essential component of the theoretical framework. Moreover, it is the assumption that the public policy is the result of stable and family-specific policy-making processes which parallels the concept of national policy styles.

While the core argument put forward by classical institutionalism (that formal-legal institutions matter) seems intuitive, two major points of criticism have been raised. Firstly, it was argued that classical institutionalism would not open the 'black box' between formal institutions and policy choices. Why would a British government allow, for example, the cultivation of genetically modified crops when the Swiss government opposes it? As Schmidt (2002: 160) puts it: 'types of democracy, like other constitutional structures, are both constraints on policy choice and at the same time conditions enabling choice between policy alternatives. However, types of democracy do not determine these choices: nor do they determine their outcomes'. Secondly, political institutions in a country tend to be stable even though public policy is constantly being modified. These and other points of criticism of classical institutionalist approaches have given way to 'new institutionalism'.

The new approaches to political institutions

Strictly speaking, new institutionalism does not constitute a single and coherent body of theory, but comprises many different streams of arguments. Although sharing a basic common assumption, namely that institutions do matter, there are a variety of conceptions of how, why and to what extent institutions make a difference (Knill 2001). Essentially, it contends that institutions matter as they exert an influence on public policy (Thelen and Steinmo 1992: 7). In this regard, they can be independent variables or 'intervening' variables, i.e. have some impact on the relationship between the main independent variables and the dependent variable.

Following Hall and Taylor (1996), three different varieties of new institutionalism can be distinguished: sociological institutionalism, historical institutionalism and rational choice institutionalism. Here we will focus on sociological and historical institutionalism since they represent so-called institution-based approaches, i.e. they attach a determining explanatory role to institutional factors. With rational choice institutions, the actors come to the fore, so we shall discuss this form in the next section on interest-based models.

Sociological institutionalism

At the heart of sociological institutionalism is a very broad understanding of institutions, incorporating symbol systems, cognitive scripts and moral templates that provide meaning to action. Hall and Taylor (1996: 947) argue that this definition abrogates the divide between 'institutions' and 'culture'. Sociological institutionalism has a distinctive understanding of the relationship between institutions and individual action. It stresses the way in which institutions influence behaviour by providing the cognitive concepts and models that are indispensable for action. In this way, the relationship is between institutions, and individual action is thought to be interactive and mutually constitutive.

Central to this perspective is the notion that action is tightly bound up with interpretation, which corresponds to the idea of social constructivism. This means that sociological institutionalists perceive actors as purposive, though purposive action is itself socially constituted in accordance with the 'logic of appropriateness' (March and Olsen 1996: 252). The logic of appropriateness states that individuals make their choices according to what they view as socially valuable. Rules, for example, are followed because they are regarded as the 'right thing' (see Börzel and Risse 2010: 121). Put differently, individuals' actions are determined by their sense of obligation as structured by the 'appropriate' institutional rules and routines rather than by self-interest. This adds another understanding to what institutions are as they are not only regarded as enabling and constraining actors' preferences, but also as influencing the way actors conceive of their preferences in the first place. It is hence by influencing actors' preferences and perceptions that institutions shape a polity and thereby the context in which policy-making occurs.

Furthermore, sociological institutionalism argues that many of the institutional forms and procedures used by modern organizations are culturally specific practices rather than a means to enhance efficiency and effectiveness. On this basis, the research question that sociological institutionalists typically pose is: why do organizations take on specific sets of institutional forms, procedures or symbols? They also stress that organizational practices are prone to diffuse through organizational fields or across nations. In this context, sociological institutionalists are interested, for instance, in explaining the striking similarities between organizational forms and practices. With regard to this latter question, the concept of legitimacy is crucial, for it implies that the main logic of action guiding organizational behaviour is to increase legitimacy in the organizational environment rather than functional efficiency. A consequence of seeking legitimacy is that, when creating new institutions, these will most likely be patterned after existing institutional templates. This is expected to lead to institutional isomorphism, that is the emergence of similar organizational structures. According to DiMaggio and Powell (1991), an organization will engage in institutional isomorphism in response to three types of pressures: coercive, mimetic and normative.

According to coercive isomorphism, organizations adjust their structures and procedures to be in line with those organizations on which they are dependent. However, organizational adjustment to the environment is not only expected to take place as a result of coercive pressures, but it may also occur in constellations of high uncertainty, e.g. in the presence of ambiguous goals or confrontations with new problems. In such constellations organizations are likely to practise mimetic isomorphism by imitating the structures of other organizations which they perceive as particularly successful so as to ensure their legitimacy by emulation. Normative isomorphism is based on similar dominant normative orientations of staff members. In this regard, similar professional backgrounds and the role of professional organizations in spreading mutual understanding of policy problems and solutions are important (for an overview, see Knill and Balint 2008).

Regardless of the type of isomorphism concerned, the central argument is that legitimacy rather than functional efficiency is the main driving force of organizational change. For example, institutional isomorphism can be seen as the main mechanism underlying changes in higher education policies. In the last decade, many countries started to change their higher education policies and the organizational structures of their universities and colleges in order to pattern them after the US or the British model as these are broadly perceived as legitimate (see Dobbins and Knill 2009; Dobbins 2011).

Historical institutionalism
At the core of historical institutionalism is the argument that 'history matters'. More specifically, historical institutionalism emphasizes the

fact that former choices about policies or institutions affect the range of subsequent policy options, inter alia by generating certain ideas about public policy (see Cox 2004). This structuring effect of existing arrangements is conceived as so far-reaching that existing institutions or policies are considered as independent rather than as merely intervening variables in explaining policy choices, which distinguishes historical institutionalism from the other two new institutionalisms. A central emphasis is hence placed on institutional path dependence and policy legacies.

Historical institutionalists point out that for explaining policy choices it is more important to recognize that 'history matters' than to figure out whether path dependency is the result of lock-in effects, the distribution of bargaining power or the institutional reproduction of standard operating procedures (Hall 1986: 19; Thelen and Steinmo 1992: 9). Institutions can be seen as the points of 'critical juncture' (i.e. the adoption of a particular institutional arrangement) in a historical path analysis since political battles are fought inside institutions and over the design of their futures (Steinmo *et al.* 1992). Thus, critical junctures represent *rare* events in the development of an institution. Instead, the normal state of an institution is either one of stability or one of limited adaptive change (Maloney 2000; Capoccia and Kelemen 2007: 367).

Historical institutionalists stress the structuring impact of institutional 'lock-ins', where deviations from the initial path become increasingly costly or difficult as a result of the institutionally structured distribution of power between different actors (North 1990; Pierson 2000, 2004). However, this does not mean that public policy must remain stable. Streeck and Thelen (2005) argue that policy and institutional change takes place, but usually in a gradual manner. This suggests that institutional change is not necessarily the result of a critical juncture: it can also be the result of an incremental process. Therefore, historical-institutionalist analyses have to make sure that they conceive of policy and institutional change as long-term processes (see Pierson 2004: 82).

The puzzles that have typically been addressed by historical institutionalists are mostly empirical, corresponding to questions such as: why was one policy chosen rather than another? (Immergut and Anderson 2008: 351). The concepts of critical junctures and path dependence as the central components of historical institutionalism have been applied to many policy areas, including social welfare policies, constitutional law, budgetary law, regulation of competition in product markets and banking, and the development of regimes or entire regions (Capoccia and Kelemen 2007: 345).

A well-known example of a historical institutionalist approach is given by Esping-Andersen's research (1990). Pursuing the analytical objective of explaining welfare state development, the author (1990: 29) argues that the following three factors are relevant: the mobilization of the working class, class-political action structures and the historical legacy of regime institutionalization. These considerations induce Esping-Andersen to categorize welfare state regimes into three groups: the Anglo-Saxon liberal model, the Scandinavian social democratic model and the Continental conservative model. Following Esping-Andersen, modifications to welfare policy may occur within these three types but they do not cut across them. In other words, it is highly unlikely that the Scandinavian countries will give up their historically developed generous social democratic model and replace it with the less generous Anglo-Saxon liberal one. Rather, they are expected to preserve the essential characteristics of their welfare policy and make only marginal modifications to it.

Key points

❏ Classic institutionalist approaches conceive of institutions in strictly formal terms, i.e. the 'rules' of the political 'game'. This perspective regards policy outcomes as exclusively the result of existing formal political institutions.

❏ Sociological institutionalism defines institutions very widely and argues that they shape actors' perceptions of their preferences, which, in turn, affects their behaviour, so that it becomes based on the logic of appropriateness and/or on legitimacy.

❏ Historical institutionalism emphasizes the structuring impact of institutional lock-ins and path dependence.

Interest-based models

This section introduces the most influential interest-based models. First, we outline the concepts of full and bounded rationality as these represent the behavioural assumptions underlying many interest-based models. Next, we introduce models focusing on the strategic actions of public and private actors. This is followed by a concise presentation of the main characteristics of game theory, which represents a useful device for analysing the interaction of actors. Finally, we will shed light on how institutions can structure the interaction of actors. To this end, rational choice institutionalism will be introduced.

Concepts of rationality

When focusing on actors, it is necessary to decide whether to model them as 'fully' rational or 'boundedly' rational. A rational actor is broadly perceived to make choices about public policy that tend to maximize his or her expected utility. For a choice to be rational, an actor must be faced with alternatives that can be rank-ordered according to some degree of utility or desirability. A rational policy choice requires preferences to display at least two characteristics. First, they should be complete, that is all alternatives must be ranked in order. Second, they should be transitive, implying that if alternative A is preferred to B and alternative B is preferred to C then A must also be preferred to C.

Let us assume that a policy-maker can choose between the following three policy instruments in order to lower the emission of greenhouse gases: (1) expansion of nuclear power generation; (2) imposition of a tax on energy-intensive industries; and (3) offering insulation subsidies for home owners. In real life, there exist many more possible policy instruments, but to illustrate the concepts of completeness and transitivity we will constrain ourselves to these options. A preference order is complete if the policy-maker can place each of these three policy instruments in a rank order. Such a preference order could look as follows. The most preferred policy instrument is the insulation subsidies, followed by the tax on energy-intensive industries, followed by an expansion of nuclear power generation. The preferences are closely related to the respective utility of each instrument, which may as much stem from the likelihood of becoming re-elected as from believing that one policy instrument out-performs the others on account of its superior effectiveness. Now transitivity comes into play since if the subsidies are preferred over the tax then the subsidies must also be preferred over an expansion of nuclear power generation. Only if this condition holds, can a policy-maker's preference order be regarded as rational.

The concept of a fully rational actor is demanding as it rests on the strong assumptions that he or she possesses the best information available and can use it in a way to choose from among all other possible policy options that alternative which is most likely to maximize his or her utility. When looking at the immense number of tasks that policy-makers are confronted with every day, doubts arise as to whether these assumptions are realistic. In response to the dissatisfaction with the assumptions underlying fully rational behaviour, Herbert Simon (1957) developed the concept of bounded rationality (for an overview, see Jones 2001).

Similar to the concept of full rationality, bounded rationality assumes that actors are goal-oriented, though it equally takes into account their cognitive limitations. Most importantly, the amount of information actors can gather and process in a meaningful way is thought to be limited. While the concept of full rationality pays attention to the notation of optimizing, i.e. the selection of the best possible action, bounded rationality mostly relies on the concept of 'satisficing', which describes the situation where people settle on a solution that is satisfactory.

Recalling our previous example about the three possible policy instruments for reducing greenhouse gas emissions, a decision-maker practising satisficing might choose the insulation subsidies simply because this is an instrument that has already been applied in the country's past and/or in other countries, and which produced satisfactory results. Hence, the policy instruments are not rank ordered to meet the criteria of completeness and transitivity – rather the instrument chosen is the one for which information is available concerning the most likely satisfactory outcome.

Strategic choices of actors

As we demonstrated in Chapter 3, there are numerous actors participating in the policy-making process. So, it is impossible to introduce at once all the theoretical approaches that name the relevant policy actors and the ways in which they affect public policy. Rather, we here limit ourselves to outlining briefly some of the most important theoretical approaches for explaining the behaviour of elected officials and bureaucrats on the one hand, and of interest groups as key private actors on the other hand. In so doing, we present theories that are based on the assumption that the actors are fully rational – 'rational choice approaches'. In subsequent chapters, we will also introduce some theories that rest on the assumption of bounded rationality.

Explaining the behaviour of public actors
Rational choice theorists have formulated theories to explain the behaviour of elected officials. Often, individual behaviour is explained on the basis of competitive party behaviour. Strøm (1990) explains that political parties and therefore elected officials can be seen as (1) vote-seeking, (2) office-seeking or (3) policy-seeking. The first model is based on Downs's (1957) work on electoral competition, in which parties maximize their electoral support for the purpose of controlling government. Office-seeking parties want to maximize their control over political office, for instance by acquiring the most influential or prestigious ministries. This theoretical perspective on the intrinsic reward of office is based on the work of Riker (1962). Finally, parties can be policy-

seeking, i.e. they participate in politics in order to further particular policy objectives, often reflecting their underlying ideological positions (Budge and Laver 1986: 485).

When exploring the impact of political parties on public policy, the 'party difference hypothesis' put forward by Hibbs (1977) is of crucial importance. In its original form, the model explains political parties' different views on macroeconomic policies, notably the alleged trade-off between inflation and unemployment. The basic argument is that left-wing parties would solve this trade-off by preferring lower unemployment over inflation, whereas right-wing parties would tend to keep inflation at the lowest possible level. Rational voters should hence support left-wing parties when high unemployment is expected and right-wing parties when high inflation is expected. According to more recent approaches to the partisan theory (see Schmidt 1996), 'parties do matter' for all areas of policy-making. This means that parties compete for votes by offering diverse policy options.

The role of bureaucracy in the policy-making process has most prominently been addressed by Niskanen's (1971) model of a budget-maximizing bureaucracy. It contends that bureaucrats will try to maximize their department's budget in order to increase their salary and prestige. The basic idea is that the government defines a department's budget on the grounds of the quantity of service it supplies. The more services the department supplies, the higher will be its budget. Therefore, the bureaucrat's objective will be to maximize the quantity of services supplied. This can only work due to information asymmetries between the bureaucracy and government. The latter cannot directly observe the level of service output, which gives the bureaucracy a preferential position in this relationship. Further, the dead weight loss of the excessive production of services must never be higher than the government's consumer surplus, otherwise the government would notice irregularities in the bureaucrats' activities. Despite its far-reaching analytical impact, Niskanen's model has also provoked criticism, which has led to the development of alternative models (see also Chapter 6).

One of these alternative approaches is the 'bureau-shaping model' as put forward by Dunleavy (1991). In a nutshell, it argues that senior bureaucrats are most interested in maximizing the status and quality of their work, which is best pursued through bureau-shaping rather than budget maximization. To pursue bureau-shaping, bureaucrats can employ up to five strategies:

1. Refer to internal reorganizations in which the policy-making role of senior bureaucrats is strengthened.
2. Internal work practices can become transformed so as to increase the status of monitoring activities.

3. Bureaucrats can redefine relationships with external partners in order to maximize their control over policy and rid themselves of routine issues.
4. Bureaucrats may compete with other bureaux over the defence of policy oriented responsibilities.
5. The bureau-maximizing actor seeks to transfer to other bodies (such as executive agencies) all functions and tasks which do not fit with their preferred bureau shape (see Marsh *et al.* 2000).

Recall that in Chapter 3 we hinted that bureaucrats might be more than just an instrument of government. Above, we have reinforced this argument by underscoring the fact that bureaucrats also have their own individualistic preferences that they seek to realize in the policy-making process. In other words, despite Weber's (1947) prognosis of a concern for the collective future of government, the preferences of bureaucrats can deviate from those of their political masters and have implications for public policy. We will return to this in subsequent chapters.

Explaining the role of private actors
While elected officials are central for taking policy decisions and bureaucracies are essential for the drafting of public policies and policy implementation, interest groups can also exert considerable influence on policy-making through their specialist knowledge, financial contributions and political campaigns (Howlett *et al.* 2009: 96; see also pp. 62–5). The relative influence of an interest group principally depends on three factors. Firstly, the internal organization matters, which includes factors such as income and organizational characteristics (e.g. sanctioning mechanisms). In this context, the size of membership and the internal cohesion as well as the recruitment of new members are equally relevant factors. Secondly, the very topic on which the interest group works might make a difference as with complex and highly technical issues interest groups possess more leverage over policy-making as the necessary information may not otherwise be provided. Thirdly, the relative influence of an interest group depends on the degree of competition with other interest groups (see Cohen and Richardson 2009; Maloney and van Deth 2010; Newton and van Deth 2010: 170). The intensity of competition in turn is determined by the access of various interest groups to decision-makers, which leads us to the concepts of pluralism, corporatism and neo-corporatism.

The theory of pluralism suggests that in democratic polities power is widely distributed among different groups, creating a 'marketplace' with more or less perfect competition for influence over public policy (Dahl 1958). Pluralism is based on four premises. It assumes: equal access to the policy-making arena between different groups; a fragmentation of the 'marketplace' of interest groups; a competitive process for determining policies; and the neutrality of government. From this it follows that the relative influence of a group is a function of its resources and 'decibel rating' (Hill 2009: 30). In pluralist systems – according to the criteria defined above – such as the United States or the United Kingdom, interest groups are viewed as making a vital contribution to policy-making 'because (1) they provide a more effective voice for citizens who are competing for resources, (2) they reduce the anxiety produced by feelings of powerlessness, and (3) they provide an element of stability' (Dye and Zeigler 2006: 234).

In corporatist polities, the central actors are still organized interests, but the policy-making process is cooperative rather than competitive, and is closed to all but certain privileged interest groups, mainly those representing business and labour (Schmidt 2008: 305; see also Lehmbruch and Schmitter 1982). Following Schmitter's (1977: 9) definition, corporatism is a system of interest intermediation in which the interest groups are organized into single, compulsory, non-competitive and hierarchically ordered categories that have been given a representational monopoly by the state in return for them exercising control over their supporters. An ideal, typical, corporatist system would exhibit :

- a high degree of unionization
- a concentration of labour unions
- a business community dominated by large export-oriented firms
- centralized bargaining of wages
- the existence of work councils in industrial firms and codetermination in important industry sectors
- a centralized state that is involved in the economy. (Siaroff 1999: 176–7)

This basically means that fewer interest groups participate in policy-making, but the ties between them and the decision-makers are institutionalized. Often, these interest groups are incorporated officially into policy-making as members of a committee.

Neo-corporatist polities differ from corporatist ones with respect to the greater constitutional autonomy of the groups involved and the voluntary nature of involvement in policy-making. Neo-corporatism also refers to social arrangements dominated by tripartite bargaining between unions, the private sector (capital) and government (Lehmbruch 1982; Streeck 1982). This model of interest intermediation principally evolved in the post-war period in connection with the increased state intervention in the economy and the growing involvement of the central trade union and employers' associations in economic planning and incomes policy.

Common to both corporatist and neo-corporatist models of interest intermediation is a stable pattern of consultation and cooperation between one or a few dominant interest groups and policy-makers, indicating that public policy is a 'negotiated' outcome between both actor groups (Adolino and Blake 2011: 51). As a result, we do not further distinguish between corporatism and neo-corporatism, but employ the term '(neo-)corporatism' instead. Another reason is that 'corporatism' can have a negative connotation since it has been to an extent associated with semi- or non-democratic regimes, especially in Latin America. Therefore, we have a preference for the term '(neo-)corporatism' to underline that we exclusively focus on democratic forms of interest intermediation.

Understanding the interaction of actors: game theory

So far, we have mainly discussed theoretical approaches that focus on individual actor groups. An exception was the presentation of the concepts of pluralism and (neo-)corporatism, which address the relationship between interest groups and the government. However, to understand policy-making, one cannot only concentrate on the actors in isolation but must pay equal attention to the ways in which they interact with one another. This is necessary as, akin to institutions, the presence of other actor groups can either help or impede policy-makers' interests from becoming directly transposed into public policy. The most general way of theoretically addressing interactions is provided by game theory.

Game theory is a device to analyse decision-making in situations in which two or more rational players interact, and where the outcome depends on the choices made by each. Actors involved in games are referred to as players. Each player in a game faces a choice among two or more possible strategies. A strategy tells the player which actions to take in response to every possible strategy other players might use. A crucial aspect of the specification of a game involves the information that players have when they choose strategies. The simplest games are those in which the players have perfect information, meaning that at every point where each player's strategy tells him or her to take an action, he or she knows everything that has happened in the game up to that point. More realistically, however, players generally have imperfect information about each other's strategy (for an overview, see McCarthy and Meirowitz 2007).

The most famous game of incomplete information is the prisoner's dilemma. This game is representative of an important class of structural situations involving conflict and cooperation among actors. Despite the availability of better outcomes, the suboptimal one is chosen due to a lack of trust in the other player. It is a dilemma since it illustrates how, even when rational actors appreciate the importance of cooperation, they still find themselves trapped in situations where they cannot get to their desired goal through cooperation.

The theory of regulatory competition in environmental policies represents an illustrative example of a prisoner's dilemma. In brief, this theory argues that states have incentives to lower their environmental protection standards in order to attract mobile capital. The idea underlying this reasoning is that environmental protection standards (e.g. the need to meet criteria for industrial emissions into air and water) cause costs to industries that they seek to evade by shifting to another jurisdiction. Assuming that governments are rational actors interested in optimizing their benefits, the theory of regulatory competition predicts that there will be a continued lowering of environmental protection standards across the countries to the level of the least stringent country. This will ultimately result in suboptimal environmental protection standards, simply because the countries do not trust one another, which prevents them from collectively attaining higher standards (see Holzinger 2008).

In political science, the provision of common goods (i.e. goods where one cannot be effectively excluded from using them) is frequently modelled as a prisoner's dilemma. In this regard, the best known pathology is the 'tragedy of the commons' (Hardin 1968; Ostrom 1990), meaning that if there is no regulation of a certain public resource, e.g. a clean environment or public roads, individuals are likely to consume more than their fair share of it. The long-term effect of this free-riding is that at some point in time the amount of public resource will decline, entailing negative consequences for all. In such a case, we are confronted with a so-called negative externality since the cost to society as a whole is greater than the cost to the individual who is paying for it. Again this point can be illustrated by drawing on an example from environmental policy. When pollution crosses borders countries are often reluctant to exercise full control. This happens mostly in the case of air pollution, which never stops at national borders. In the past, countries tried to avoid stricter regulation and the ensuing higher costs on industry by building high stacks or locating plants close to borders. In other words, they externalized their pollution to their neighbouring countries and benefited from free-riding.

More recent work, however, shows how the occurrence of the prisoner's dilemma can be circumvented. In this context, the most influential work has been done by Axelrod and Hamilton (1981) and Axelrod (1984). Based on computer simulations, they show that in repeated games the best strategy is 'tit for tat', implying that you play whatever your opponent played in the previous round. Take for example the current problem of China 'deviating' from the commonly agreed practices of free trade by refusing to purchase Western imports with its export earnings. This hoarding of foreign currencies has a negative impact on the trading partners' economies. To prevent China from hoarding foreign currencies, the trade partners could, in principle, reciprocally restrict Chinese exports (Rosefielde 2011).

Box 4.1   Structure of the prisoner's dilemma

Suppose that the police have arrested two men, whom they know have committed an armed robbery together, but lack enough admissible evidence to get a jury to convict them. They do, however, have enough evidence to send each prisoner away for two years for the theft of the getaway car. The inspector now makes an offer to each prisoner that if he confesses to the robbery – and his partner in crime does not – he will go free, whereas the partner will be sent to prison for ten years. However, if both confess, each will get five years in prison. If neither of the suspects confesses, then each will have to go to prison for two years for the car theft. We can now rank these options with regard to their utility for each of the two suspects. The following numbers in parentheses are used to express each player's pay-offs in the various possible outcomes. Pay-offs are the values assigned to each individual outcome with regard to their desirability: the higher the numerical value of a pay-off, the more a certain outcome is desired. The best option is to go free (3), followed by a two-year stay in prison (2), then a five-year stay (1), and then a ten-year stay (0). The matrix below represents this situation of strategic interaction in the so-called normal form. We refer to the two suspects as player 1 and player 2:

		Player 2	
		Confess	Keep silent
Player 1	Confess	1, 1	3, 0
	Keep silent	0, 3	2, 2

Each cell of the matrix indicates the pay-offs to both players for each combination of actions. Player 1's pay-off appears as the first number and Player 2's as the second. If both players confess each gets a pay-off of 1. If both keep silent, each gets a pay-off of 2. If one player confesses but not his partner, that player gets a pay-off of 3, whereas the partner gets a pay-off of 0. Taking into consideration that one player might always have an incentive to confess, this action represents the best strategy regardless of what the partner does. In more technical terms, this means that confessing beats keeping silent for both players. Both players know this about each other, thus entirely eliminating any temptation to depart from the dominant strategy. This solution represents the so-called Nash equilibrium of the game which is named after the Nobel Laureate John Nash who proposed it.

Actors and institutions: rational choice institutionalism

In the previous section on institution-based models we presented two of the three approaches to new institutionalism, namely sociological and historical institutionalism. Now we add the third, which is based on the notion of actors making rational decisions. Rational choice institutionalism is based on the 'logic of consequentialism' (March and Olsen 1989, 2008): that rational actors engage in strategic interactions using their resources to maximize their utilities on the basis of given, fixed and ordered interests (also known as 'preferences'). In marked contrast to sociological institutionalism, rational choice institutionalism conceives of actors' preferences as exogenously given: the preferences are not affected by institutional factors and not subject to social construction.

According to Hall and Taylor (1996: 945), rational choice institutionalism regards politics as individuals acting to maximize their utility in ways that are likely to produce an outcome that is collectively suboptimal. Typically, what hinders actors from taking a collectively superior course of action is the absence of institutional arrangements that would guarantee complementary behaviour by all concerned. Classic examples of such suboptimal collective action include the prisoner's dilemma and the tragedy of the commons.

Accordingly, rational choice institutionalism is not only about actors and their interests but also about institutions, as they ultimately structure the opportunities for strategic choice and interaction. Existing institutional structures restrict or provide opportunities for policy-making either by affecting the cost–benefit calculations of the actors involved or by defining a certain distribution of powers and resources between them. In this context, the concepts of 'veto points' and 'veto players' are important. A veto point 'is defined as a political arena with the jurisdictional power to veto a government legislative proposal, in which the probability of veto is high' (Immergut 2008: 567). The veto player approach is a further development of the concept of veto points. This approach principally concentrates on the role of veto players for policy-making. Veto players are most essentially defined as any institutional or partisan actor whose agreement is required to adopt a policy proposal (Tsebelis 2002; see also pp. 135–6).

Most importantly, for rational choice institutionalists, institutions affect the strategies of actors in order to get what they want, though they have no impact on the formation of their interests, which are conceived as exogenous to institutional analysis. So rational choice institutionalists focus on interests as the primary, independent explanatory factor: institutions are considered to be a secondary, intervening factor for explaining political outcomes (Shepsle and Weingast 1987; Weingast 1996; Shepsle 2008).

Rational choice institutionalists have also developed a distinctive approach to the problem of explaining how institutions originate (Hall and Taylor 1996: 945). The rules of formal institutions are explained by reference to the way in which they minimize certain costs, such as decision, transaction and information costs. Decision costs are incurred when actors try to come to an agreement, including costs related to bargaining. Transaction costs are incurred after an agreement is reached, involving costs that ensure compliance with contractual agreements. There are also costs incurred by searching for relevant information for decision-making (see Jones and Baumgartner 2005: 151–2). These and other kinds of costs can be reduced by establishing appropriate institutional structures.

Key points

❑ Fully rational behaviour aims to optimize actions, whereas bounded rational behaviour is about finding a satisfactory solution.

❑ Game-theoretic approaches are useful for modelling strategic interactions. The most prominent game-theoretical model is the prisoner's dilemma.

❑ Rational choice institutionalism is based on the 'logic of consequentialism', meaning that rational actors engage in strategic interactions that are structured by institutional arrangements.

Conclusions

The perspectives introduced above are admittedly abstract – though this is intended: they abstract from the real world in an attempt to simplify the processes that underlie policy-making. How can these be applied to the analysis of actual public policy? As an example, take the data on per capita health spending in the 34 member states of the OECD. The country sample includes the most advanced countries as well as emerging countries like Mexico, Chile and Turkey. Many comparative analyses of public policy rely on OECD statistics due to the relative homogeneity of the socioeconomic development of the countries concerned (see, e.g., Gilardi *et al.* 2009).

The most striking observation to be made about Table 4.1 is that there is a remarkable degree of variation in the countries' expenditures on health services. That of the United States in both 2001 and 2008 exceeds those of the other OECD countries by a huge margin. The other extremes are represented by Turkey in 2001 with a per capita spending corresponding to only 8 per cent of US expenditure, and by Mexico in 2008 with a spending equal to about 11 per cent of US expenditure. In light of this

Table 4.1 *Health expenditure in OECD countries*

Country	2001 (PPP$)	2008 (PPP$)	Change in per cent[1] (2001–08)
Australia	2,388	3,445	144
Austria	2,905	4,128	142
Belgium	2,364	3,714	157
Canada	2,732	4,024	147
Chile	655	1,092	167
Czech Republic	1,081	1,839	170
Denmark	2,680	4,052	151
Estonia	521	1,331	255
Finland	1,970	3,158	160
France	2,726	3,809	140
Germany	2,797	3,963	142
Greece	1,754	2,724[2]	155
Hungary	970	1,495	154
Iceland	2,844	3,571	126
Ireland	2,069	3,784	183
Israel	1,881	2,142	114
Italy	2,227	3,059	137
Japan	2,074	2,878	139
Korea	918	1,736	189
Luxembourg	3,182	4,451	140
Mexico	552	892	162
Netherlands	2,554	4,241	166
New Zealand	1,709	2,784	163
Norway	3,265	5,230	160
Poland	642	1,265	197
Portugal	1,714	2,508	146
Slovak Republic	664	1,859	280
Slovenia	1,583	2,451	155
Spain	1,635	2,971	182
Sweden	2,501	3,644	146
Switzerland	3,428	4,930	144
Turkey	423	902	213
United Kingdom	1,996	3,281	164
United States	5,146	7,720	150
OECD mean	2,016	3,090	153

[1] Values are rounded off.
[2] Data for Greece in 2008 is not available; the cell entry shows the data for 2007.

Note: PPP$ = purchasing-power parity (international dollars).

Source: Based on OECD (2011).

empirical observation, how can we explain the cross-country variation in spending patterns?

This question can be evaluated by making reference to various models. The first option is provided by the perspective of societal cleavages and of post-materialism in particular. One possible theoretical expectation could be that the levels in health spending increase as the share of the population with rising incomes and real or perceived health needs increases. Following the logic of classical institutionalist approaches, it could be argued that health expenditures depend on the countries' institutional characteristics. We might adopt Lijphart's (1999) argument and formulate the hypothesis that majoritarian democracies display spending patterns that are different from those of consensus democracies. With interest-based models, the role of private actors appears suitable for explaining cross-country variation. Hence, one argument could be that, in countries where there are powerful interest groups representing the pharmaceutical industry and the medical profession, health spending should be higher. This is particularly true if the system of interest intermediation is (neo-)corporatist and grants health-related interest groups privileged access to policy-makers.

Table 4.1 presents another interesting piece of information regarding health expenditures, that is, the average annual change between 2001 and 2008. The figures tell us that health expenditure in relation to the size of the population increased in all OECD countries, with the mean spending in the entire OECD area in 2008 being 1.5 times higher per head of population than in 2001. However, in Slovakia, Estonia and Turkey health expenditure increased more than 200 per cent between 2001 and 2008. To be sure, these are all countries that had very low spending levels in 2001, and the figure for Turkey in 2008 clearly indicates that the country is still a long way from the mean expenditure level for the OECD area. This latter observation could be explained by making reference to historical institutionalism and the concept of path dependence. It would seem that the Turkish government cannot – or does not wish to – immediately increase health expenditure to the mean OECD level.

One way of explaining these changes in all of these three countries could be that vote-seeking political parties pay more attention to this issue because there is a heightened public demand for better health services and they want to be re-elected. Another possibility is that the governments of these countries are uncertain about how to design their health policies and therefore practise 'mimetic isomorphism', i.e. they follow the example of the countries they regard as legitimate and increase their expenditure to reduce their distance from these models.

There are many further interesting observations that can be made about health expenditure in the OECD countries. There are also many other theoretical perspectives we can apply to formulate theoretical expectations. What is most important in this context is that the theoretical perspectives introduced in this chapter are complementary rather than competing. They allow for the examining of a certain empirical phenomenon from many different angles. This also means there are no objective criteria for judging which perspective produces the 'most correct' explanation. However, while this complementarity is desirable for fully understanding policy-making, it also implies that looking at one and the same subject of interest might lead to different conclusions, depending on the analytical perspective that is taken. Therefore, for the purposes of scientific discussion and the avoiding of unjustified criticism, the theoretical approach chosen for analysis should always be explicitly spelled out.

Web links

www.iterated-prisoners-dilemma.net. This webpage offers an interactive online game of the prisoner's dilemma, consisting of several rounds. The game is useful for demonstrating the effects of repeated interactions and the tit for tat strategy for the evolution of cooperative behaviour.

www.auburn.edu/~johnspm/gloss/. This is the online edition of *A Glossary of Political Economy Terms* by Paul M. Johnson of Auburn University. It provides a good overview of most of the terms introduced in this chapter.

www.oecd.org/document/16/0,3343,en_2649_34631_2085200_1_1_1_1,00.html. On this webpage you have access to a sample of key indicators that can be found in the OECD Health Data 2009 dataset. To retrieve the data you must download an excel file.

www.newinstitutionalism.org. An international platform for scholars and students interested in new institutionalism.

Further reading

Bernhagen, P. (2008) *The Political Power of Business: Structure and Information in Public Policy-Making*. Abingdon: Routledge. A systematic and easily accessible overview of group models with a number of elucidating case studies.

Cairney, P. (2011) *Understanding Public Policy: Theories and Issues*. Basingstoke: Palgrave Macmillan. The book provides an overview of the most important theories in public policy.

Dye, T.R. (2005) *Understanding Public Policy*. Englewood Cliffs, NJ: Prentice Hall. This is a leading book on policy-making that gives a comprehensive presentation of policy-making models.

Fischer, F., G.J. Miller and M.S. Sidney (eds) (2007) *Handbook of Public Policy Analysis: Theory, Politics, and Methods*. Boca Raton, FL: CRC Press. A valuable volume that explores the policy-making process in relation to different theoretical considerations.

Holzinger, K. (2008) *Transnational Common Goods: Strategic Constellations, Collective Action Problems, and Multi-level Provision*. Basingstoke: Palgrave Macmillan. A theoretical examination of strategic interactions and their implications for the provision of common goods.

Mueller, Dennis C. (2003) *Public Choice III*. Cambridge: Cambridge University Press. A thorough overview of the most important topics in the study of public choice. The chapter on bureaucracy is particularly useful.

Chapter 5

Problem Definition and Agenda-Setting

Reader's guide

This chapter addresses the initial moments of the policy-making process, namely problem definition and agenda-setting. Most citizens and organizations possess some concerns – real or perceived – that they believe merit government attention. There are many different ways in which one and the same issue can be defined. Our first goal in this chapter is to show that problem definition is subject to different interpretations and 'social construction'. Although there are many public problems, in the end only a small number of them will be given official attention by legislators and executives. Public problems – which may be real or mere social constructions – that are chosen by decision-makers for further consideration constitute the policy agenda. Our second goal is to outline the dynamics by which ideas, policy proposals and new understandings of problems are formulated. We will learn that the possibility of influencing the agenda is an important source of power since legislative institutions grant an advantage to the 'first movers', i.e. those who address a problem and propose a solution to it first. Several groups of actors compete with one another in order to set the agenda in accordance with their preferences: politicians, the mass media, interest groups and epistemic communities.

How are issues selected for government attention? Why are some issues taken up while others are left unconsidered? Which actors are involved in defining policy problems and bringing them on to the agenda? These are the questions guiding the discussion in this chapter on the first stage of the policy-making process, namely problem definition and agenda-setting. Fundamental to these two processes is a focus on the dynamics by which new ideas and understandings of social problems emerge, thus giving way to policy change. Although problem definition and agenda-setting are in reality closely interlinked, for analytical purposes we will discuss both issues separately.

We will begin with the stage of problem definition. Here we not only show that the way a problem is defined has important repercussions on the subsequent decision process, but that current and differing factors influence the definition process. While this process appears quite intuitive, in many cases conflicts emerge as to how a given issue should be defined and whether it actually needs to be addressed by policy-makers.

We then turn to the stage of agenda-setting. Put simply, this stage is about getting an issue on to the 'agenda'. Here our analysis starts to become problematic as there are many different agendas. However, we can make a basic differentiation between systemic and institutional agendas (Cobb and Elder 1983). The former consists of all issues that are commonly perceived as meriting public attention, whereas the latter is composed of those issues that are clearly of concern to decision-makers. Having defined in more detail the various forms of agendas, we then introduce the theoretical approaches to agenda-setting that can be found in the relevant literature.

In a final step, we shift our analysis to the actors that are involved in the agenda-setting process. This perspective is an important complement to the previous approaches as actors' activities are important for the recognition and framing of issues.

Problem definition: the path to agenda-setting

Problem definition can be understood as a causal story which (1) identifies harm; (2) describes what causes them; (3) assigns blame to those causing them; and (4) claims that the government is responsible for stopping them (Stone 1989: 282). Problem definition is policy consequential, that is, it sets the stage for the other components of the decision-making process, because the way a problem is defined to a certain extent determines the feasible set of policy responses through which the problem can be resolved (Hogwood and Peters 1983; Dery 1984). For instance, it makes a big difference whether unemployment is conceived of as a problem in terms of a lack of education, an economic recession or a lack of willingness to look for a job. Depending on the definition used, solutions might vary considerably, from improving the public funding of the education system, to intervening at a macroeconomic scale to stimulate economic growth, to cutting unemployment benefits in order to motivate individuals to look for a job.

This example illustrates the fact that in most cases there is no 'obvious' conception of a problem. Different actors might have different perceptions of the same empirical phenomenon. In this regard, it generally holds that the actor proposing the first definition of the problem has a strategic advantage, i.e. a first-mover advantage, since subsequent normalizing of a 'deviant' definition will require considerable effort by competing actors. This effort stems from the fact that not only must another and equally persuasive definition of a problem be presented, but also that the first definition needs to be discredited, which its proponents will oppose. All this suggests that problem definition is a highly contested process. Depending on the outcome of this process, we may find highly different policy approaches across countries, even though the objective characteristics of the problem are very similar. However, the definition of a problem is not only affected by the interests and resources of the involved actors, but also by the distinctive characteristics of the problem that render its definition in a certain way more or less likely. In the following we will first take a closer look at the aspects of the process that characterizes problem definition, before we discuss the relevance of the different characteristics that problems can possess.

The process of problem definition

Problem definition is essentially characterized by two features: objective data (e.g. environmental pollution or poverty levels) and the question of if and to what extent these objective criteria are actually acknowledged. To be sure, problem definition is not about a neutral realization of the existence of problems but rather about their 'social construction' (Lindblom and Cohen 1979; Wildavsky 1979; Dery 1984, 2000; Fischer 1993; Bacchi 2009). In fact, a 'problem' might only exist because people think that it exists. Studies of risk regulation, for instance, have revealed that there tends to be a significant difference in how experts assess the existence and severity of a risk (e.g. health and environmental risks related to genetically modified organisms) and the public perception of it (see Kahneman *et al.* 1982; Sunstein 2005). This split has important implications for policy-making since public demand might lead to an initiation of a policy-making process despite the absence of a 'genuine' social problem that needs to be solved.

In situations in which it is uncertain whether or not a social problem really exists, policy-makers may still prefer to address it. There are two main reasons for this. Firstly, even if a certain social problem may seem 'irrational', it can still result in a loss in social welfare. For example, if people are afraid of eating beef treated with growth hormones, this fear should be taken seriously by policy-makers as it could lead to a lowering of beef consumption, which, in turn, reduces the income of farmers (see Chang 2003: 7–8; see also Slovic *et al.* 1982; Fischer 1993; Sunstein 2005) – regardless of whether or not growth hormones are likely to impact on the population's health. Secondly, policy-makers who do not address an issue that is broadly perceived as a social problem run the risk of not being re-elected. That said, governments can equally be responsible for creating such 'problems'. According to Bacchi (2009), unemployment through a lack of education and training, for instance, can be conceived as a government-induced problem, with the solution ready to hand in the form of life-long learning to continue the education and training of adults.

While the previous explanations give the impression that the problems addressed by policy-makers might be inflated, there is also the opposite dimension to problem definition, i.e. that policy-makers refuse to see an issue as a problem that warrants a policy response (Crenson 1971; Lukes 1974). While the United Kingdom, similar to many other states, has experienced poverty and inequality, these have only sporadically been defined as policy problems (Dorey 2005: 11).

How can a social problem – real or perceived – turn into a political problem? Firstly, this can only happen if the social problem can potentially be addressed by public policies (Wildavsky 1979: 42). Earthquakes, for example, do not constitute a political problem as governments cannot affect the likelihood of their occurrence. The picture is different, by contrast, if we focus on disaster management which of course does fall within the realm of public policy. This argument, however, does not eliminate the possibility that there are also political problems that can only be solved temporarily and in an imperfect manner. Rittel and Webber (1973) refer to these as ['wicked' problems;] they entail conflicts that are value based, difficult to define and resist resolution. Environmental policy issues are often regarded as such wicked problems (see Fischer 1993; McBeth *et al.* 2007), but there are certainly many other policy issues with 'no solutions', such as the reform of health care systems or different issues of morality policy.

Secondly, the turning of a social problem into a political problem is characterized by conflict (Schattschneider 1960; Cobb and Elder 1983; Wood and Doan 2003). According to Schattschneider (1960), politics is a means to resolve conflicts about how to govern a community. Thus, the organization of conflict is important and is achieved through the scope (who is involved) and the bias (how the audience is involved) of the conflict. The interplay of these two dimensions determines what happens. Schattschneider deems the scope of conflict to be more decisive for the outcome than the bias and thus a rational policy-maker should address the scope dimension. This can occur through privatization, by restricting the scope of the conflict through trying to keep it out of the public domain (i.e. 'socialization'). In this context, interest groups and – and even more so – political parties play a key role in socializing conflict (see Mileur 1992: 178).

In this regard, Cobb and Coughlin (1998: 417) distinguish between two types of actors. The first is the so-called 'expander' who seeks to publicize the issue to different societal groups in order to get them involved in the policy debate. In this regard, the expander can be regarded as an innovator since he or she brings up an issue that is not currently under consideration by decision-makers. However, the content of this issue will be evaluated by other individuals – 'containers' – who might be adversely affected if this issue enters the agenda stage and eventually becomes a law. These containers try to prevent the expanders from reaching the agenda stage. If they are successful then no action will be taken and the status quo will prevail. Accordingly, we can characterize the problem definition process as a battle between expanders and containers in which the expanders must redefine the issue so that the public, who previously did not care about it, now become concerned. Each of the two groups tries to frame the issue for the public and politicians in a way which makes action or inaction likely, according to their interests – which indicates the importance of public rhetoric (Riker 1986).

However, it is not only persuasion from expanders and containers that matters but also the interpretation of these activities against the background of dominant beliefs. As a result, the status quo of a given social perception can be a powerful force making it difficult to move people away from the prevailing perception of a condition as not being problematic. However, occasionally forces may emerge that produce movement towards a new social perception.

Against this background, Wood and Vedlitz (2007) illustrate how problem definition is affected by both stable and dynamic factors. First, the manner in which an individual defines an issue depends on a set of relatively fixed factors such as values. Second, the more uncertain is the information environment surrounding an issue, the more likely it is that an individual will rely on these established values than on new information that becomes available for defining the issue. Conversely, as individuals possess greater trust in existing information surrounding an issue, the more likely they are to define the issue in a manner consistent with that information rather than redefining it in the light of new evidence. In this context, trust in information increases if, for example, it is supplied by epistemic communities (see pp. 65–6). Third, an information signal of sufficient strength can produce shifts in definitions of specific issues, regardless of the individual's predispositions and knowledge. Information signals pro-

Box 5.1   Media advocacy and smoke-free bars in Australia

Few policy areas have experienced a more profound shift regarding their public perception than smoking. The mass media around the world has been decisive for changing public opinion on smoking and the health risks related to it. However, pro-tobacco groups have also employed the mass media to convince people of their message, such as the Hotels Association in Australia. As Champion and Chapman (2005) show, both groups were highly active in Australian newspapers in expressing their views on smoke-free bars. The tobacco control groups naturally supported smoke-free bars and made clear that this problem had two dimensions, one related to public health and one about working conditions. The Hotels Association, by contrast, stressed the economic costs related to the ban. Accordingly, the two groups tried to achieve a different definition of the 'problem' and the desirability of smoke-free bans. In all likelihood, the economic costs as emphasized by the Hotels Association were not found to be too serious as compared with the health effects – in the meantime all Australian states and territories have banned smoking in enclosed public places and many of them have also explicitly banned smoking in bars.

ducing such redefinitions can relate directly to the issue itself, or they can somehow alter an individual's interpretation of the social forces surrounding the issue. In this context, the mass media plays a key role since it represents the main means of communication and persuasion (Jerit 2006).

For example, the influence of the mass media became particularly apparent with the nuclear emergency that Japan faced in the spring of 2011. Reacting to the comprehensive media coverage of this incident, a global debate about the perils of nuclear power was started. In Germany, for instance, this particular event led to a completely new evaluation of the risks of nuclear power and a social consensus that the phasing out of this energy source should be completed as soon as possible. In many other countries, however, the event did not stimulate similar policy processes.

The characteristics of problems

The definition of a problem is not only affected by the interests and beliefs of different actor coalitions, but also by the specific characteristics of a problem. Again these characteristics are socially constructed. Some attributes of a problem may be highlighted as they lend themselves to a particular solution, while other attributes are downplayed. Such a specific way of presenting problems is commonly referred to as 'framing'. It 'involves the selective use of knowledge and information about a problem and the causal relationships surrounding it, to give it meaning and render it manageable' (Ward *et al.* 2004: 92). Frames are strategically employed by political actors as a key way by which legislators and other policy-makers try to structure a conflict so that they can win (Riker 1986; Stone, 1988; Rochefort and Cobb 1995; Baumgartner *et al.* 2008, 2009a; Baumgartner and Jones 2009).

Rochefort and Cobb (1995: 15–23) have advanced a series of categories which influence how a problem can be framed. The seven categories refer to causality, severity, proximity, crises, incidence, novelty and problem populations. The category of 'causality' deals with the question of which factors or actors have caused a problem in the first place. In many instances, issues of culpability and allocation of blame play an important role in this context. For many problems, however, the underlying causes are not easy to diagnose. The political debate about problem causes can therefore constitute a highly contested area of problem definition. An illustrative example is given by the determinants of state debts and decreasing tax revenues. Usually, excessively low or high tax levels lead to low revenues. Depending on which of these two views is supported the policy proposals will differ substantially.

'Severity' concerns how serious an issue and its consequences are perceived to be. The more a problem can be framed as severe and serious, the more it will capture the attention of decision-makers and the mass media. Often, different actors have different views regarding the severity of a problem, depending on their interest positions. The severity of nuclear accidents, for instance, will be judged very differently by the affected population on the one hand and the power company on the other. This was illustrated by the very different ways in which the Japanese power company TEPCO (the owner of the Fukushima nuclear reactors that experienced partial meltdowns in 2011) described the situation and how the media judged the severity of the emergency. In order to increase the severity perception of an issue, expanders might try to attach the 'crisis' label to an issue, alerting the public to an urgent problem requiring action, while containers would deny that a crisis exists.

In a similar vein, problem proximity might play an important role for mobilizing political support. 'Proximity' implies that the issue is directly or indirectly affecting the personal interests of a broad public. If a problem can be defined in such a way that a broad range of people are potentially affected, the higher are the chances of political mobilization. To increase problem proximity, it is more reasonable to link a cut in the salaries of teachers to a reduction in the quality of education than to highlight the disapproval of this measure by the teachers' union.

'Incidence' refers to the actual prevalence of the problem. How many actors are potentially affected? In this regard, the expanders must show that the problem is of huge scope and causing misery for many people, and argue that the problem is getting worse. Although many societal problems are persistent, their perception as prevalent is likely to change. It is natural to think in terms of thresholds here – up to a given critical value the public's attention to a certain issue is negligible, but once this value has been reached public pressure on policy-makers becomes too strong and they must act. That public pressure can be decisive for the initiation of a policy-making process is illustrated by the following examples. In 1998, the French government stopped its hepatitis B vaccination programme for school children, bowing to public pressure and rampant fears that the vaccine could trigger or exacerbate certain diseases such as multiple sclerosis. Remarkably, there was no scientific evidence to support such an association (Birmingham 1998: 1217).

The Japanese nuclear emergency also illustrates this point. In the last decade, nuclear power has become an increasingly uncontroversial issue since policy-makers constantly assured the public that the technology was safe. Only a few groups in society remained sceptical about its safety. With the events taking place in Japan, the share of people worried about this issue became so critical that policy-makers somehow needed to react to it. On the other hand, some issues might not be defined as problems warranting a policy response due to insufficient public pressure, such as British policy-makers' unwillingness to recommend a daily intake of vitamin D (Vieth *et al.* 2007: 650).

'Novelty' as the sixth category is also an important device for winning attention. Labelling an issue as something new and unprecedented can result in wide media coverage. This was the case with the swine flu pandemic in summer 2009, which was everywhere in the news. Another example is provided by the promotion of nanotechnology in the United States. Lindquist *et al.* (2010) argue that the strategy of the supporters of nanotechnology, by emphasizing its novelty, was an important factor in attracting media attention. However, when using this strategy one has to be careful since issues that have not yet been experienced are difficult to tackle since they lack familiar solutions and therefore policy-makers might refuse to pick them up. Thus, novelty has an ambivalent impact on problem definition.

The seventh and final category concerns the characteristics of a 'problem population'. It deals with how the image of target groups is manipulated by contending parties. The expanders seek to place the target group in a positive light. This can, for instance, be done by portraying the problem population as helpless. To gain public support for the controversial Economic Opportunity Act of 1964, which included various social programmes to promote the health, education and general welfare of the poor, the US government constructed the target population as 'hopeless victims'. With this understanding, the act made sense as one which would provide tools for ending poverty. Thus, a very particular image was created to attain Congressional consent for the act. Consistent

Box 5.2   Sexual harassment as a policy problem

One topic that has certainly become more salient over the last two decades is sexual harassment. In their study, Wood and Doan (2003) examine the declining tolerance of sexual harassment in the United States. Their empirical illustration refers to the case of Judge Clarence Thomas of the US Supreme Court. In 1991, President George Bush nominated Thomas to the Supreme Court. On this occasion, the Senate Judiciary Committee examined charges by a law professor at the University of Oklahoma, Anita Hill, who accused Thomas of sexual harassment. Testimony and debate on the charges were broadcast nationwide on television. Prior to these hearings, widespread social tolerance prevented most individuals from an active and open opposition to sexual harassment. With the hearings emphasizing the costs of sexual harassment and the negative tone of the media coverage following the hearing, individual perceptions of the phenomenon started to change, leading to a new social interpretation of the issue. While the accusation did not prevent Clarence Thomas from receiving a seat in the US Supreme Court, US policy-makers felt that they had to react to the increasing public disapproval of sexual harassment and immediately adopted legislation that resulted in an increased number of charges.

with the views of who the poor are, the goal of the act was framed as giving new hope to the hopeless (see Guetzkow 2010: 175–83). A promising strategy for the containers would have been to emphasize that the poor should not be regarded as 'victims' but as people who took advantage of the possibilities already given to them. These considerations suggest that a helpful way of thinking about political problems is to illuminate how they are linguistically constituted (see Fischer 2003: 46).

By and large, the analysis of the specific characteristics of policy problems represents a promising research strategy. While the categories outlined above already provide a framework for insightful research, the analytical approach of Bacchi (2009) further helps to explain problem definition. This approach stimulates critical thinking about this step of the policy-making process, and is achieved by framing the problems as questions:

- What is the problem to be represented by a specific policy?
- What presuppositions or assumptions underlie this representation of the problem?
- How has this representation of the problem come about?
- What is left unproblematic in this problem representation? Where are the silences? Can the problem be thought about differently?
- What effects are produced by this representation of the problem?
- How has this representation of the problem been produced, disseminated and defended? How could it be questioned, disrupted and replaced?

Key points

❏ The way in which a policy problem is defined is consequential for all subsequent policy stages.

❏ Problem definition is not predominantly about pointing to the existence of an objective issue but is an endogenous construct and thereby the subject of social conflict between supporters and opponents. Each of these groups can employ various devices to increase or reduce the public's attention towards certain problems.

❏ Public attention can be increased or decreased by framing, which can refer to the causality, severity, proximity, crises, incidence, novelty and problem populations for any particular policy problem.

Analytical concepts of agenda-setting

The fact that a certain societal problem is perceived as a problem that needs to be addressed by the government is only a necessary but not a sufficient condition for political action. Not every political problem ends up on the agenda. Policy-making generally occurs in the presence of multiple constraints, e.g. shortages of time and resources. As a consequence, there are always more public problems warranting action than there is space on the so-called agenda. The central research question with regard to the agenda-setting stage hence concerns the conditions that affect whether a public problem actually reaches the policy agenda or not.

To answer this question, varying models have been developed that analyse agenda-setting using different analytical lenses. However, before we enter the theoretical discussion, we will first have a closer look at different agenda types as agenda-setting can refer to quite different phenomena which entail different theoretical explanations and perspectives.

Agenda types

Agenda types are usually defined in accordance with Cobb and Elder's (1983) distinction between the 'systemic agenda' and the 'institutional agenda'. The systemic agenda refers to all societal problems that demand public attention and which form the discussion agenda. Most items on it are general and still lack a precise definition. Systemic agendas exist for all levels of the political system: national, state and local. Some items may appear on multiple systemic agendas, while others will appear on only one.

The institutional agenda contains a set of problems that are up for serious consideration by decision-makers. The institutional agenda is the action agenda, which is more specific and concrete than the systemic agenda. Remarkably, most issues on the institutional agenda are hardly recognized by the general public since they predominantly require a detailed, technical knowledge about the already existing public policy. To be sure, some issues will attract much attention from the general public, but usually the number of highly salient issues is rather limited. Similar to the systemic agenda there is a multitude of institutional agendas referring to the different levels of government – i.e. the national, state and local institutional agendas – and within these levels there is a further distinction among branches – i.e. the legislative, executive, administrative and judicial institutional agendas (Anderson 2010: 90–3). Only if a public problem reaches one or more institutional agenda(s), it will be considered as needing a solution.

Taking into consideration Kingdon's (2003) approach, we further suggest differentiating between the 'drafting agenda' and the 'decision agenda'. The drafting agenda – which Kingdon terms 'governmental agenda' – is a list of subjects that are getting attention within government. As will be shown in Chapter 6, the adoption of a policy in a first step requires the development of policy proposals. The government needs to take a basic decision that a certain policy problem needs to be addressed and start drafting potential measures that relate to the problem. Those issues for which such a decision has been taken constitute the drafting agenda. The decision agenda, by contrast, is based on those issues for which the government has agreed on a draft proposal and hence has decided to put the issue on the agenda of the responsible decision-making body (usually the legislature), which has to take the final decision as to whether or not to adopt the policy.

In the literature there is a major debate about the extent to which the setting and shaping of the decision agenda might affect the chances of policy adoption. It is generally acknowledged that those actors who have the power to influence the decision agenda enjoy a powerful position in the decision-making process (see Anderson 2010: 90–3).

Analytical perspectives on agenda-setting

Analyses of the processes of agenda-setting proceed from very different theoretical angles. Basically, the diverse literature can be grouped into four approaches that focus on different aspects of agenda-setting phenomena and that emphasize: process patterns, power distribution, institutional factors and contingency.

The process perspective

Process-based assessments all focus on general patterns characterizing agenda-setting dynamics. Agenda-setting is hence described and explained from a more abstract perspective by focusing on systemic factors that shape political processes. The most influential descriptive account of agenda-setting processes has been developed by Cobb *et al.* (1976), who differentiate between three generic models: (1) the outside-initiative model; (2) the mobilization model; and (3) the inside-access model.

The outside-initiative model describes a situation in which an individual actor or a group of actors outside the governmental structures initiates an issue for reform which they then seek to expand into the public domain. This can take place through various means: media coverage, public lobbying of politicians or other forms of public action which pressure decision-makers to place the issue on the institutional agenda. In this context, the dynamics of public attention paid to issues are of key relevance.

The mobilization model describes a process of agenda-setting where institutions or political leaders seek to move issues from the systemic to the institutional agenda in order to muster the support needed to attain their objectives. In contrast to the outside-initiative model, the mobilization model takes into account the possibility of top-down agenda-setting as issues are placed on the institutional agenda directly by decision-makers. While there may have been extensive debates about the issue among decision-makers prior to the announcement, the public may have little knowledge of the issue. This process is often triggered by a systems failure or exogenous shocks – also known as 'focusing events' (see Birkland 2006) – followed by the commissioning of a panel of experts. The decision-makers may then formally adopt the experts' recommendations in the decision process. Hence this model takes into account the fact that expert opinions can make an important contribution to constructing agendas. After the initiation of the issue, decision-makers then elucidate it and explain what they seek from the public. Mobilization of the issue within the public domain is necessary in circumstances where the implementation of a policy requires widespread voluntary acceptance. Decision-makers seek to expand an issue from the institutional to the systemic agenda in the same manner as proponents seek to attain a formal agenda under the outside-initiative model.

In contrast to the two previous models, the inside-access model describes a pattern of agenda-setting that seeks to exclude public participation. Under this model, the initiators seek to place an issue on the institutional agenda. If the issue is expanded into the public domain, it is usually limited to a few selectively influential groups who are considered

Box 5.3 Issue attention cycle

What are the characteristics of public perception of 'crises' or 'problems'? This question underlies Downs's (1972) seminal concept of the dynamics of the 'issue attention cycle'. The main argument is that public perception does not reflect real conditions as much as it reflects the operation of a cycle of increasing interest and then of rising boredom with issues. This cycle has five stages, which may vary in duration depending upon the particular issue concerned.

1. The pre-problem stage: some undesirable social conditions exist, but at this stage they only capture the attention of experts or interest groups.
2. Alarmed discovery and euphoric enthusiasm: for certain reasons (e.g. accidents, riots, epidemics) the public becomes alarmed about a particular problem. This discovery of a problem is accompanied with a euphoric enthusiasm about society's ability to solve it within a relatively short time.
3. Realization of the costs of significant progress: the public gradually realizes the high costs of solving the problem. These costs are not only monetary but also refer to sacrifices some groups in the population would need to make.
4. Gradual decline of intense public interest: as more and more people realize the costs and other difficulties in solving the problem, they get discouraged. Some just suppress thinking about it; others become bored by the issue. Additionally, by this time another issue has usually entered the stage of alarmed discovery and euphoric enthusiasm.
5. Post-problem stage: an issue moves to receiving less attention, but as it has gone through the cycle it almost always receives a higher level of attention than in the pre-problem stage. This results from the new institutions and policies that may have been created to help solve it. These entities often persist and can have a long-lasting impact on public attention. Another reason for the higher average level of attention might stem from the success of the institutions and policies in addressing some aspects of the problem.

important to the passage of the policy. So we are mainly confronted with a situation in which the initiators seek a 'private' decision within government, and who are 'insiders' such as a government department or a regulatory agency.

The power distribution perspective

While the process model described above provides an important starting point for assessing how processes of agenda-setting unfold, it cannot explain why certain issues are moved on to the agenda while others are not. To address this, existing theories emphasize in particular the distribution of power between the involved actors.

The origins of research into agenda-setting relate to the pluralism-elitism debate of the 1950s and 1960s. The key aspect of this debate concerned the notion of power, especially its use and distribution in society (see Truman 1951; Schattschneider 1960; Dahl 1961; Polsby 1963).

Regarding agenda-setting, the debate asserted that different groups of actors seek to increase the probability that an issue will receive collective attention by attempting to raise an issue's salience and/or its support. In a similar vein, but from an inverse perspective, Bachrach and Baratz (1962) argued that the political power of decision-makers could be exercised through the banning from the agenda of certain issues, i.e. as 'non-decisions'. In other words, they could use tactics to decrease the probability of agenda inclusion for an issue, thus helping to preserve the status quo (Gerston 2004: 67).

Schattschneider (1960) emphasized that rather than the actors actively participating in agenda-setting it is the wider public domain which is key to understanding politics. In this regard, Schattschneider argued that strategically it is in the best interest of the contestant who is losing a battle over an issue to bring more and more fence-sitters into the conflict, thus socializing them, until the balance of forces changes. Conversely, it is advantageous for the one who is winning to contain the scope of the conflict so as not to upset this favourable balance of power. Hence, issue battles are frequently won or lost over the combatants' success either at getting the public involved or excluding them.

The importance of redefining the presentation of issues is illustrated by Sheingate's (2000) analysis of agricultural retrenchment in the United States and the EU. The author argues that advocates of retrenchment must redefine the issue of agricultural subsidies in a manner that highlights the negative externalities associated with farm policy. Second, they must also exploit opportunities for strategic changes of venue so that policy decisions in agriculture do not rest solely with those who benefit from the status quo. A similar argument is put forward by Daugbjerg and Studsgaard (2005). Their analysis of radical agricultural policy reforms in Sweden and New Zealand in the 1980s and 1990s shows that the redefinition of agricultural policy – from constituting a matter of finding the balance between budgetary costs and farmers' income to considering agricultural policy as a part of macroeconomic policies – was an important factor in venue change and eventually successful reform. In a similar vein, Pralle (2006) illustrates how Canadian anti-pesticide activists mobilized otherwise apathetic members of the public by changing the image of garden pesticides from useful and seemingly harmless to superfluous and dangerous.

An additional insight concerning venue shifting and issue redefinition is presented by Timmermans and Scholten (2006) who deal with the different roles that scientific knowledge can play in shaping policy images. Focusing on immigrant policy and assisted reproductive technology policy in the Netherlands, they show how science and the structural arrangements through which it is produced and disseminated can aid depoliticization – or, on the contrary, fuel emerging policy disputes.

The institution-based perspective

In addition to the ways in which an issue can be mobilized, early theories of agenda-setting also emphasized the role of institutional structures in defining the lines of conflict and the balance of power: 'all forms of political organizations have a bias in favour of the exploitation of some kinds of conflicts and the suppression of others because organization is the mobilization of bias. Some issues are organized into politics while others are organized out' (Schattschneider 1960: 719).

One of the best known theoretical approaches that takes into account institutional arrangements is the 'punctuated equilibrium' framework developed by Baumgartner and Jones (2009) and True *et al.* (2007). Essentially, this framework seeks to explain why political processes are generally characterized by stability and incrementalism, i.e. by minimal adjustments to existing policy arrangements (see Lindblom 1959, 1979), but occasionally produce fundamental shifts (labelled as 'policy punctuations'). According to this approach, both policy stability and change are mostly determined by the presence of policy venues and policy images. Policy venues are institutional arenas in which decision-making takes place. Policy images are the shared views of policy communities concerning the characteristics of a given public problem and the ways of solving it. It is through agenda-setting that policy images become changed. As a rule, this happens when a new policy image is received well by the actors of a new policy venue. What bears the highest potential to affect both policy images and venue promotion is external shock, such as the Japanese nuclear accident in the spring of 2011 or the global credit crunch in 2008–09.

The influence of institutional rules is of particular relevance when it comes to the specification of the decision agenda. The question of who sets this is determined by the institutional rules that characterize the legislative process. Actors who have the power to shape the decision agenda are more likely to have their proposal adopted than those whose influence is basically confined to reacting to policy. This can be traced to the fact that agenda-setters, in anticipation of the preferences of the other actors, can frame a proposal in such a way that it is more likely to be adopted. This aspect was first discovered by Shepsle and Weingast (1987) who showed that institutionally determined differences in agenda-setting power implied that certain committees of the US Congress were more influential than others when it came to getting their proposals accepted.

The contingency perspective

In contrast to models that emphasize the central explanatory role of the distribution of power between the involved actors and institutional arrangements, contingency models conceive of agenda-setting as a process that is affected by chance rather than rational calculation and characteristics of politics. The central argument is that policy-making is basically about the coupling of policy problems and policy solutions that are considered as evolving independently of each other. This view also underscores the arguments presented in the section on problem definition about the social construction of problems by the public as well as policy-makers. On the one hand, within political systems there is a continuous discussion over policy problems and how to define them; on the other hand, at the same time, there is an ongoing debate and development of solutions which take place rather autonomously from the definition of the problem. It can even be the case that solutions are developed for problems that are not yet existing or perceived to be. This is the basic argument of the garbage can model (Cohen *et al.* 1972). These solutions are then in need of problems to which they can be applied.

According to this approach, it is only when pre-existing solutions can be successfully coupled with perceived problems that an issue is put on the agenda. As argued by Kingdon (2003), the extent to which coupling is possible is not only affected by independent streams of problems and proposals, but also by the politics stream. The latter refers to events such as elections, changes in government or the emergence of new social movements. The three independent streams of problems, proposals and politics need to come together at a critical time in order to open up the famous 'policy window', resulting in an issue being put on the agenda. The process of coupling is not considered as something that can be influenced by strategic behaviour, but as a highly contingent phenomenon.

Key points

❏ We can analytically distinguish between different agenda types, including the systemic, the institutional, the drafting and the decision agendas.

❏ The systemic agenda refers to all societal problems that demand public attention and which form the discussion agenda. The institutional agenda, by contrast, contains a set of problems that are up for serious consideration by decision-makers.

❏ The drafting agenda is a list of subjects currently receiving attention within government. The decision agenda is based on those issues for which the government has agreed on a draft proposal and hence has decided to put the issue on the agenda of the responsible decision-making body.

❏ Agenda-setting can be analysed from different theoretical perspectives, including models emphasizing process patterns, the distribution of power, the role of institutions, and contingency.

During the 1970s, for instance, in the United Kingdom several think tanks had advanced proposals to privatize state-owned enterprises. This standard solution was then adopted by a wide a range of enterprises, although not all of them were viewed as needing to adopt this reform, i.e. as having a problem. Nevertheless the adoption of this solution was possible because of changes in the politics stream, i.e. the election of the Conservative Thatcher government in 1979 which had been strongly in favour of market liberalization and the rolling back of the state (Gamble 1988; Zahariadis 1996).

Actors and interests in the agenda-setting process

The theories presented above map out the theoretical state of the art in the agenda-setting literature and contribute to our understanding of the agenda-setting process. Nevertheless, they are still rather abstract and lack precise statements regarding the role that the different groups of actors play in the process. Therefore, we will now reduce the level of abstraction and concentrate in more detail on the following four types of actors that can play a central role in the agenda-setting processes, namely: elected public officials and judges; the bureaucracy; the mass media; and interest groups. In addition, we will highlight how international organizations can help to place certain issues on the policy agenda.

Elected public officials and judges

Elected public officials (e.g. the president, prime minister or chancellor; ministers; members of parliament) are the most obvious agenda builders since their position enables them not only to make decisions about policies, but also to place certain issues on the agenda. The battle for control over legislative agenda-setting is predominantly waged between the executive and legislative branches. However, actual agenda-setting is related to the larger political game in terms of power and intensity of ideological conflict both within and between government and parliament. In this regard, Green-Pedersen's (2006) study of the politicization of the issue of euthanasia in Denmark, the Netherlands and Belgium shows how the possibilities of linking issues to pre-existing conflicts in party systems can determine whether such issues are placed on the agenda.

Notwithstanding a high degree of variation in the rules and practices of agenda building in western European parliaments (Döring 1995), setting the agenda for parliament is the most significant institutional weapon for governments to shape policy results. As argued by Rasch and Tsebelis (2010), governments with significant agenda-setting powers (e.g. France or the United Kingdom) are able to produce the outcomes they prefer, while governments that lack these powers (e.g. Italy or the Netherlands) see their projects being significantly altered by their parliaments. More precisely, this power stems from the fact that in some political systems it is easier for policy-makers in the legislature to accept the government's proposals and demand minor amendments to them than to come up with their own separate proposal, due to the difficulties of attaining a necessary majority for it. As a rule, the executive's agenda-setting powers are more pronounced in political systems in which there is a partisan congruence between the government and the parliamentary majority. However, even in polities characterized by a strong executive, the legislature might to some extent affect the agenda-setting process via parliamentary bills, as shown by Baumgartner *et al.* (2009a) and Bräuninger and Debus (2009).

For elected officials, agenda-setting power might emerge from various tools, such as control over the legislative calendar, the amendment process and the overall timing of the legislative process – and whichever actors control them will largely control the entire policy-making process within a given polity (Kreppel 2009: 185–8). In most cases no single actor controls all aspects of agenda-setting, although there is usually a tendency towards a dominant role for the executive or the legislature, depending on the general character of the political system. So, the greater the degree of centralization of agenda-setting processes, the higher the level of agenda-setting power in the hands of either the legislative majority or the executive (see Tsebelis and Alémán 2005).

In some nations, agenda-setting might result from judicial review of existing legislation, thus awarding judicial institutions the status of agenda-setters. The agenda-setting power of courts comes as no surprise as they are often asked to decide on controversial political issues. The main focus of research on judicial institutions has been the study of the determinants of decision-making. Of course, judges may privately have policy preferences, but they cannot act as independent agents (Gibson 2008: 521). Instead, the expression of their preferences is strictly limited to cases in which they have been authorized to act in accordance with the constitution. Yet, within this scope judges can certainly instigate a political debate about issues that policy-makers have previously dealt with.

The 2010 decision of the German Constitutional Court on the constitutionality of welfare and unemployment benefit levels is a case in point. In the context of the so-called Hartz reforms – named after the head of the responsible commission, Peter Hartz – these benefits had been merged into one scheme and at the same time considerably reduced. Despite ongoing criticism, the issue of the appropriateness of benefit levels had disappeared from the policy agenda. The court, however, ruled that the benefit levels were not in line with constitutional requirements and obliged the legislature to undertake reforms to them. This judgement brought the controversial issue of benefit levels back on to the German policy agenda.

Empirical evidence from the United States illustrates that judges of the Supreme Court are more willing to review public policy and so possibly set the agenda for a new policy-making process when they believe that the new policy output will be closer to their preferences than the status quo. However, these judges tend to deny review when they are in favour of the status quo policy (see Perry 1991; Hammond *et al*. 2005; Black and Owens 2009). From this it follows that policy preferences are a predictor of US Supreme Court agenda-setting.

Bureaucracy

It is well known that bureaucracies have an impact on policy-making during the stages of its formulation and implementation (Hammond 1986). With regard to the first, the power of the bureaucracy not only emerges from its important role in the drafting of policy proposals (see pp. 60–1), but also from its influence on shaping the agenda. Niskanen's (1971) economic model of bureaucratic behaviour assumes that bureaucratic agenda control allows the bureaucrats to impose upon a passive legislature their most preferred alternative. His argument rests on two assumptions. First, the bureaucracy has a virtual monopoly on true supply-cost information. Second, the bureaucracy knows the demand of the legislature for the services it delivers. Based on these assumptions, it is expected that bureaucratic agencies are able to make all-or-nothing offers to the legislature (concerning both the budget and the policy output).

Legislatures, however, might not always be as uninformed as assumed in Niskanen's model: rather, information asymmetries might vary from issue to issue. Accordingly, Eavey and Miller (1984) argue that the imposition of bureaucratic agendas should be replaced by theories of bureaucratic bargaining which emphasize the key structures of the relationship between the bureaucracy and the elected officials. In this context, Schnapp (2000) speaks of bureaucracies as 'stand-in' agenda-setters in situations where politicians do not have the time and/or technical knowledge to set the agenda for all the problems that may arise in a polity (see also Suleiman 1974; Aberbach *et al*. 1981). Here the bureaucracy can stand in, take up problems and advance proposals for their solution, thereby becoming the agenda-setter for a certain policy. In this vein, Kato (1994) shows that bureaucratic agenda-setting was crucial for accomplishing a major tax reform in Japan which entailed the introduction of the value added tax in 1989. Likewise, Page (2003) illustrates for the United Kingdom how important civil servants are for placing issues on the decision agenda and initiating policies. From these empirical findings it follows that the shift of an issue from the drafting to the decision agenda is mostly determined by the preferences of the bureaucratic actors and their ability to exploit the legislative process.

Mass media

Research has started in the field of communication research regarding the role of the mass media in agenda-setting (Cohen 1963; Lippmann 1964; see also Soroka 2002: 7). Both Lippmann and Cohen stress the relevance of the mass media in forming the image of issues. Here the focus has been on the assessment of links between the salience of issues on the media's agenda and those on the systemic agenda. McCombs and Shaw's study (1972) is widely regarded as the first empirical analysis of public agenda-setting. The authors demonstrate a relationship between what survey respondents feel are the most important issues and the coverage these issues are given in primary news sources. Numerous studies have examined the influence of news media coverage on the public's issue priorities. The vast majority of these have indeed found strong correlations between the amount of coverage issues received in the media and the public's level of concern with them (see Rogers *et al.* 1993).

Subsequent research has investigated the relationship between both the mass media and institutional agendas. Walgrave and van Aelst (2006: 99–101; see also Walgrave *et al.* 2008) argue that media coverage is associated with public opinion. Whether the media really affects public opinion or not is less relevant than the fact that political actors believe that it does. Political actors do not primarily react to the media coverage itself but to the presumed public opinion about issues. This implies that they anticipate the expected media impact on the public and build their political strategy on that premise to maximize their electoral benefits in accordance with rational choice logic (see pp. 82–92). Green-Pedersen and Stubager (2010) further explain that media attention to an issue generates attention from political parties when the issue is one that parties have an interest in politicizing in the first place.

Another strand of research systematically relates the agenda-setting power of the mass media with the type of issue concerned. For example, Soroka's (2002) study of agenda-setting in Canada differentiates between prominent, sensational and governmental issues. Prominent issues have concrete effects on citizens such as inflation; they can be experienced without the media providing information about them. Sensational issues are less connected with daily experience but still have tangible effects for most of the population. Often they are marked by dramatic events which draw massive media attention. Examples of sensational issues are the spread of an epidemic and oil spills from grounded tankers. Governmental issues are unobtrusive and often without specific effects on the population (e.g. budgetary policies). Of these three issue types, the media are expected to be most influential in the case of sensational issues. For prominent issues with strong and specific effects, the political effects of the media are expected to be much more modest as people and politicians can rely on their own direct observation. Finally, the impact of the media should be lowest in the case of governmental issues.

Interest groups

Similar to the mass media, the logic underlying the impact of interest groups relates to generating awareness for an issue and striving for public support (Wasieleski 2001). At the same time, interest groups are involved in the process by framing issues and providing elected officials with information (Cobb and Elder 1983; Haider-Markel 1999).

Baumgartner and Jones (2009) present a comprehensive theoretical model relating interest groups to agenda-setting. The authors contend that interest groups help to destroy policy monopolies by means of 'conflict expansion' (Schattschneider 1960). Put differently, a given societal problem must be perceived as such by those who are responsible for policy-making. The politicization of an issue facilitates its inclusion on the policy agenda. To achieve this, the opponents of the prevalent image of the issue must mobilize and increase the scope of the conflict in order to include actors outside of the policy monopoly. If the mobilization efforts are successful they will alter the dominant image of the policy through agenda-setting.

In this regard, Baumgartner *et al.* (2009b) distinguish between three forms of lobbying. The first one is given by inside advocacy, in which information is supplied to those involved in the policy-making process. This can, for instance, happen though (in)formal meetings with civil servants or ministers, contacts with local government authorities, participation in commissions and government advisory committees, contacts with members of parliament or parliamentary committees, and contacts with officials of political parties. The second strategy is outside advocacy, where information is communicated to actors outside the policy-making process, such as through press conferences. The third form refers to grassroots advocacy, entailing the mobilization of the masses.

The extent to which interest groups are able to influence the agenda-setting process depends on various factors. First is their resources, in terms of budget, staff and expertise. These affect if and to what extent interest groups might be able to mobilize public support for an issue. Second, interest group influence is not only a matter of resources, but also a matter of access, i.e. the extent to which such groups are actually consulted by politicians and the bureaucracy. The more that interest groups enjoy an 'insider status', implying close and institutionalized relationships with political and administrative actors, the less they need to rely on mobilization strategies when trying to influence political agenda-setting processes.

International organizations

Increasing economic and political interdependence among nations affects national policy-making (see Braun and Gilardi 2006), including agenda-setting. Majone (2008: 241) explains that this has led to two polar positions on how growing internationalization influences agenda-setting. The 'diminished democracy' thesis argues that international economic integration in particular restricts national policy agendas (see Rodrik 2000). Membership in the WTO, for instance, effectively prevents any issue from reaching the decision agenda that is related to restricting international trade (e.g. by adopting higher import quotas for products from certain countries). The complementary view is that international cooperation provides an opportunity to enrich the national agenda. These views emphasize the importance of transnational communication and policy-oriented learning for modifying agenda-setting processes (see, e.g., Holzinger *et al.* 2008a, 2008b; Meseguer Yebra 2009). For example, the OECD and the EU were decisive for bringing up the idea of innovation policy and placing it on to the political agenda of their member states (Mytelka and Smith 2002).

In this context, Majone (2008: 247) further explains that a notable share of the work of international organizations such as the OECD and the numerous organizations belonging to the UN system explicitly aims to influence agenda-setting in the member states. The WHO, for example, has been influential in bringing vaccination issues on to the

---

Key points

❑ Agenda-setting can occur (i) in a bottom-up manner in which societal actors and the media seek to convince policy-makers to take up a certain issue and (ii) in a top-down manner in which the decision-makers publicize their planned legislative activities.

❑ The central actors in the agenda-setting process are elected public officials, the bureaucracy, the media and interest groups.

❑ The political agenda may also be shaped by international influences by stimulating transnational communication and policy-oriented learning.

political agenda worldwide (see Fedson 2005). Likewise, the Programme for International Student Assessment of the OECD, an internationally standardized assessment of 15-year-olds in schools, brought education issues on to political agendas – especially in those countries that scored unexpectedly low (see Ertl 2006). There are many more examples that could be given here. Altogether, the empirical evidence rather confirms the second view, namely that growing economic and political interdependence among nations helps to bring new or neglected issues on to the political agenda.

Conclusions

In this chapter we have shed light on the stage of policy initiation and examined problem definition and agenda-setting. We have seen that problem definition is about making issues public and turning them into problems that are perceived as important. In general, a social problem may turn into a political problem only if it meets the following three criteria: (1) the issue must receive attention from a large number of people; (2) a sizable number of the population must demand action; and (3) the government must be able to tackle it. Yet, we have also highlighted that problem identification is rarely a mere matter of objective data. Rather, the perception of problems is constructed socially and so there will be a struggle over the definition of problems at various stages.

The perception of the population is, however, not a sufficient condition for policy-makers to include an issue on to their institutional agenda. If and to what extent this is the case is addressed by various analytical approaches to agenda-setting. Models emphasizing process patterns, the distribution of power between the involved actors, institutional factors and contingency have been discussed. Regarding the role of different actors in the agenda-setting process, particular emphasis was placed on elected public officials, judges, the bureaucracy, the mass media and interest groups. We have also highlighted how international organizations might influence domestic political agendas. All in all, the success of agenda-setting depends on the levels of attention, the image of the issue to be brought on to the agenda, and the extent to which conflict can be expanded or contained.

Web links

www.comparativeagendas.org. This is the website of a transnational research project on agenda-setting. It provides links to country-specific research groups as well as publications and data.

www.policyagendas.org. The website of the Policy Agendas Project provides data from various archived sources for tracing changes in the US policy agenda and public policy outcomes. A real value added available here is the supply of graphing and data tools, including corresponding tutorials for using them.

www.agendasetting.com. This site offers some intriguing case studies and announces international conferences on agenda-setting.

www.newspaperarchive.com. This is a very comprehensive online newspaper archive featuring articles from newspapers around the United States and some other countries.

Further reading

Baumgartner, F.R. and B.D. Jones (2009) *Agendas and Instability in American Politics*. Chicago: University of Chicago Press. Recommended reading for everyone working on agenda-setting and policy dynamics.

Birkland, T.A. (2006) *Lessons of Disaster: Policy Change After Catastrophic Events*. Washington, DC: Georgetown University Press. An insightful book that is useful for understanding how governments react to disasters.

Cobb, R.W. and C.D. Elder (1983) *Participation in American Politics: The Dynamics of Agenda-Building*. Baltimore: The Johns Hopkins University Press. This is a systematic introduction to agenda formation.

Kahneman, D., P. Slovic and A. Tversky (eds) (1982) *Judgement Under Uncertainty: Heuristics and Biases*. Cambridge: Cambridge University Press. An illuminating collection that brings together psychology and public policy.

Kingdon, J.W. (2003): *Agendas, Alternatives, and Public Policies*. New York: Harper Collins. Informative reading for undergraduate students and those who wish to gain a more complete picture of policy-making.

McCombs, M. (2004) *Setting the Agenda: The Mass Media and Public Opinion*. Oxford: Polity Press. This book gives an overview of the agenda-setting power of the media in theoretical and empirical terms.

Chapter 6

Decision-Making

Reader's guide

When a specific policy problem has become a part of the institutional agenda, the relevant actors will address it in the course of the decision-making process. This stage consists of two theoretically separable – albeit empirically closely related – actions. The first action concerns the drafting of a legislative proposal, which often involves a debate about the more specific nature of the social problem to be resolved by it. Based on this definition, official and unofficial policy-makers discuss the policy design, which also includes decisions about the instruments to be employed and their specific settings. Central to policy formulation are the executive and the ministerial bureaucracy; the latter in particular often has a dominant position. The way in which the ministerial bureaucracy develops a policy proposal might be affected by external expertise, policy recommendations of international organizations, interest group preferences, partisan ideology and bureaucratic self-interests. The second action related to decision-making refers to the actual adoption of the policy proposal in order to turn it into binding law. At this stage, the number of actors involved diminishes and executive–legislative relations are brought to the fore. Depending on the institutional and procedural characteristics of the country concerned, in the formal adoption process the executive and the legislature can either be on an equal footing or have a relationship in which one dominates the other, bringing us back to the characteristics of polities discussed in Chapter 3. We illustrate how institutional arrangements may affect decision-making processes by referring to Australia, Canada, the United Kingdom and the United States.

When speaking about decision-making, most of us would think of members of parliament debating draft legislation introduced by the government. These parliamentary debates are generally characterized by the evaluation of the government proposal and the discussion of alternative suggestions, often brought in by the opposition, i.e. parliamentary groups of parties holding a minority of seats. Though debates are often long and controversial, alternative proposals are rarely picked up by the majority parties and the government. Rather, these debates serve the objective of sending signals to the electorate that the current minority parties also have policy solutions to offer. Of course, the idea underlying these signals is that with the next elections the electorate will take this information into account and help the minority parties to gain a majority of votes.

As we have already seen in Chapter 2, there is a plethora of policy instruments: their employment varies significantly across individual policy fields. For example, if decision-makers aim to reduce traffic jams, they can choose between several options. First, they could invest in new road construction or the maintenance of existing roads. Second, they could decide to develop a parking guidance system. Third, they could change road users' attitudes about how to use their cars. It might be useful to promote the idea of car sharing or to provide incentives for using public transport more frequently. Fourth, they could charge road fees. Which of these instruments might they propose? Which of the different existing proposals have a realistic chance of being turned into binding law?

These are exactly the questions to be addressed during the stage of decision-making. This not only involves considerations about the technical and/or financial feasibility and effectiveness of each of these options. It is also based on considerations about how the electorate would respond to them. There are almost always some actors that benefit from a certain policy design, while another group is disadvantaged. Policy-makers – who generally seek to become re-elected – have to keep all these points in mind when they develop a policy proposal and seek to take it to adoption.

Which factors determine the design of a certain policy proposal? Why are the chances of a specific policy proposal being adopted higher than for another one? These are the two main research questions lying at the heart of this chapter on decision-making. Technically speaking, decision-making consists of two processes, which are empirically interlinked but which for analytical reasons should be treated separately. The first process is about the drafting of a piece of legislation, whereas the second is represented by its formal adoption. Both of these phases are characterized by procedural and substantial restrictions. Procedural restrictions emerge from the country's respective polities and politics.

Substantial restrictions refer to the policy problems that need to be resolved. In some cases, a problem might simply be so extraordinary or present itself in so many diverse facets that the elaboration of a sound policy is seriously hampered. Examples of such 'wicked' policy problems are the prevention of terrorist attacks and governance in natural disasters (see p. 100).

Along with the government and parliament, the ministerial bureaucracy is a key player at the drafting stage. It may be assisted by experts, interest groups and ideas promoted by international organizations; or the policy proposals set out could be influenced by partisan ideology or the maximizing of self-interest. In some polities or specific legislative situations, e.g. drug policy in some Australian states (see Hall 2003: 30), the public is explicitly encouraged to participate in the formulation of draft legislation within consultation processes.

Once we move to the stage of policy adoption, the number of actors declines, as now only public actors can decide on whether to accept a bill or not. Nevertheless, this stage entails controversial parliamentary debates and a formal voting process in at least one chamber. Often, however, there is also a second chamber that needs to approve of a legislative bill. Depending on the specific institutional characteristics of the country concerned, the need to get a majority in both chambers might lead to delays and additional modifications of the policy proposal. In some countries, e.g. Switzerland (see Frey 1994; Vatter 2000), referendums can be held that ultimately determine whether the legislation is adopted or not. Hence, drafting a bill that effectively solves the policy problem in question and is likely to be adopted by the relevant official actors – and accepted by the public – is a challenging task.

Determinants of policy formulation

In parliamentary systems, the formulation of public policy is mainly carried out by the executive. In presidential systems, by contrast, there is no executive monopoly with respect to the formulation of policies. Instead, legislative committees play a vital role in proposing legislation – however, they also tend to cooperate closely with the ministerial bureaucracy (O'Connor and Sabato 2009: 322), again giving the executive notable discretion over policy proposals (Kreppel 2009: 183). There are, however, also presidential systems, such as Chile's, in which the executive is directly responsible for policy formulation.

The above considerations suggest that the executive is crucial for the stage of policy formulation, though it needs – albeit to various degrees – support from the ministerial bureaucracy (see Aberbach *et al.* 1990).

Recognizing the importance of ministerial bureaucracy for drafting public policy, in this section we will discuss the ways in which bureaucrats form their preferences. All of the factors to be presented can, in principle, also affect legislative actors preparing policy proposals; and in some countries (e.g. Italy) this would represent a more accurate perspective. However, we will frame the explanations in a way to account for the central role of bureaucrats in preparing legislation in many countries (Peters 2010).

Expertise, information and ideas

The first way of thinking about how the ministerial bureaucracy formulates a policy proposal emphasizes the importance of expertise. Bureaucrats typically possess special insights into the relation between programmes and their effects due to their professional training and the fact that in most political systems ministerial bureaucrats do not regularly change their positions and, hence, are able to accumulate expert knowledge over time (Bendor *et al.* 1985: 1041; see also Wildavsky 1979; Hammond 2003; Peters 2010). Several empirical studies demonstrate that bureaucrats do indeed opt for policy designs they believe will produce desirable results (see Eisner *et al.* 2006: 21). It is often implied that policy-relevant expertise stems from inside the bureaucracy. While this is certainly true for procedural knowledge, that is knowledge about how to carry an action out, it is likely that the ministerial bureaucracy's own expertise is enriched by additional information sources to which it has privileged access.

With policy problems becoming increasingly complex (Aberbach *et al.* 1981: 2), it is likely that bureaucrats cannot provide themselves with all the relevant information about a certain social problem. For example, what are the long-term effects of genetically manipulated crops on public health and the environment? This is a question that might be difficult to answer as the issue of genetically manipulated crops is a relatively recent one and therefore knowledge might be absent. In such cases, bureaucrats can rely on information provided by experts such as think tanks, consultancy firms, (political) foundations and scientists, who may be members of epistemic communities (see Stone 2004).

Haas (1992) outlines how experts can influence policy choices. Firstly, they can give advice about the likely results of different courses of actions following a shock or crisis. Secondly, they might help decision-makers to grasp complex interlinkages between issues. Thirdly, they can help to develop fundamental policy principles such as 'workfare', i.e. an alternative model to conventional social welfare systems that became popular in many countries from the 1970s onwards, where recipients must demonstrate certain participation efforts to continue to receive their benefits. Neoliberal think tanks were indeed highly influential in establishing the idea of workfare in Australia, Canada, the United Kingdom and the United States in the late 1970s (Stone 2001: 342). Finally, experts might provide support for choosing among policy alternatives through framing them in accordance with certain norms. In view of these opportunities to affect public policy, (internationally operating) experts have been informing national policy-makers about successful policy ideas adopted elsewhere, thus stimulating processes of 'lesson-drawing' (Rose 1991) and 'policy learning' (see, e.g., Radaelli 1995; Braun and Gilardi 2006; Holzinger *et al.* 2008a, 2008b; Gilardi *et al.* 2009; Meseguer Yebra 2009; Gilardi 2010).

While these arguments clearly underline the many different ways in which experts can affect policy design, it must be noted that the institutionalized participation of experts varies strongly across countries. In some countries (like the United Kingdom) expert actors tend to play an important role in policy drafting, while in many Continental countries the role is limited. In Germany, institutionalized circles of ministerial bureaucrats and scientific advisers formally linked to the government are decisive for policy formulation; this makes it difficult for independent experts to gain access to ministerial bureaucrats (see Knill 1999). Similar findings of a limited role for independent experts are reported for Austria and Denmark (see Lindvall 2009).

International organizations

The proposals of ministerial bureaucrats can also be affected by ideas promoted by international organizations. There are, however, many ways in which such organizations can be influential (see Chapter 10). Firstly, ministerial bureaucrats can voluntarily employ information provided by international organizations. Virtually all these organizations dedicate considerable resources to gathering data and preparing reports on specific policy situations or the presentation of policy recommendations. The air quality guidelines published by the WHO since 1987 represent such a compilation of information. These recommendations are employed by countries all over the world when defining their air quality standards. Many developing countries are in particular grateful to have this source since it spares them from carrying out costly scientific studies. This turns the formulation of clean air policy into a more efficient process. However, the degree to which ministerial bureaucrats in individual countries finally choose to follow these recommendations varies.

The involvement of international organizations in policy drafting can be also of a more coercive character. This is particularly the case when governments turn to organizations such as the IMF or the World Bank for financial help. When these organizations get involved they often make very specific policy recommendations, which the governments have to take into consideration (Dolowitz and Marsh 2000: 11; see also Holzinger and Knill 2005). Generally, the more drastic the financial and/or economic situation of a country, the stronger will be the IMF or the World Bank's influence on the economic and/or financial policy proposals to be implemented by the national ministerial bureaucrats. The World Bank has, for example, had a great impact on economic and financial policy in Argentina after the country became dependent on loans as a consequence of the currency crisis of 2002 (see Teichman 2004). More generally, during the 1990s these same organizations affected policy formulation by vigorously promoting the idea of allowing private sector participation in water and sanitation in Africa, Asia and Latin America. Policy recommendations in these regions in the area of water provision and sanitation correspond with the broader 'neoliberal' reform policies that the IMF and the World Bank encourage (Budds and McGranahan 2003).

Box 6.1   Drafting the Kenyan biosafety law

Biosafety issues focusing on ecology and human health have been receiving burgeoning public and political attention. Most prominently, biosafety legislation defines the rules for the cultivation, manufacture, use, import, export, storage and research of genetically modified organisms such as biotech cotton, maize or soyabeans. The way in which the Kenyan biosafety law was drafted is particularly interesting as a large number of national and international stakeholders participated in the process. According to Karembu *et al.* (2010), at the initial stage of policy drafting in 2001, workshops were held which were attended by members of the Kenyan executive and legislature, universities, NGOs, religious groups, media, different industry branches, farmers' associations, foreign development organizations and UN agencies. Some of the topics discussed were about the merits and demerits of modern biotechnology, the question of how to integrate the law into the existing body of public policy and the government department to be made responsible for regulating biosafety. In 2002, the first draft was finished and circulated among the most relevant stakeholders for comments and input. A more formal discussion of the bill took place in 2003. Although the bill was then, in principle, ready to be presented to the legislature, some fresh problems arose concerning the country's preparedness, which significantly delayed the drafting process. It took until 2005 to finalize the drafting of the bill. At this last stage, the bill was rewritten in order to incorporate all unsettled issues and the experiences that other countries (e.g. Australia, Canada, India, South Africa and the Philippines) had had while regulating for biosafety. Technical and financial support was provided by some industrialized countries to improve further the regulatory and scientific quality of the bill. It then took the Kenyan policymakers until 2009 finally to enact the biosafety law due to unforeseen complications and some particularities of Kenyan politics.

Interest groups

In parliamentary systems the executive branch of government – i.e. the cabinet members plus the ministerial bureaucracy – represents the primary focus of interest groups (Werner and Wilson 2008). This also holds true for presidential systems such as the United States, although in these the relevant congressional committees are also addressed by interest groups. In fact, for a long time US policy-making has been associated with 'iron triangles', consisting of closely knit relationships between the responsible ministerial bureaucracy, congressional committees and interest groups (see Jordan 1981: 96).

There are good reasons for why ministerial bureaucrats are willing to cooperate with interest groups when drafting legislation. The first is that interest groups are able to supply valuable information concerning the effects of a policy to be proposed as well as how it might be received by their members. Accordingly, in addition to the issue-related information provided by experts, interest groups are able to provide information about the 'political' dimension of a law proposal. This turns them into a particularly valuable resource for those drafting legislation. Second, interest groups engage in a two-way information mediation process, which means that they also supply information to their members. In so doing, they can frame policy proposals so as to make their acceptance more or less likely. Consequently, interest groups can, in principle, act as advocates of public policy and thereby help to increase the chances of their implementation and – more generally – the popularity of a government. Grossman and Helpman (2001) further argue that interest groups can attempt to educate the general public. The typical voter lacks the expertise to evaluate alternative policy proposals. For their part, interest groups are willing to serve as educators because by doing so they can shape public opinion in a way that will be beneficial to themselves.

On the other hand, interest groups aim to pursue the objectives of their members and so are likely to present information in a way that it is most instrumental to their members. As a result, administrative actors might not receive information about the entirety of feasible policy alternatives but only about those that correspond to the organizational goals of interest groups. In extreme scenarios involving areas of regulatory policy characterized by high technical and scientific complexity, information asymmetries between interest groups and the bureaucracy can lead to problems of 'regulatory capture' (Stigler 1971; Peltzman 1976). This implies that administrative actors no longer serve the public interest, but advance the private interests of those actors they are charged with regulating. There is, however, evidence in the literature that an interest group's effectiveness at influencing public policy is determined by its ability to establish a reputation as a provider of reliable and complete information (see Grossman and Helpman 2001; Coen 2007). It should also be noted that much lobbying activity is concentrated on only a few issues, while the majority of policy proposals are only addressed by one or a few interest groups (Baumgartner and Leech 2001; Baumgartner *et al*. 2009b).

Depending on the general patterns of interest intermediation, the exchange relationships between the bureaucracy and interest groups might vary considerably. In pluralist systems, the bureaucracy might be confronted with a broad range of different interest groups. This means that the administration can select from very different sources of information. The problem is, however, that in view of rather diverse interest groups it might be difficult for bureaucrats to discern the accuracy of information. In (neo-)corporatist systems, by contrast, the state usually grants representational monopolies to a limited number of associations, hence reducing the number of interest groups that are formally consulted (see pp. 87–8). This more structured approach might bear the disadvantage that the provision of policy-relevant information becomes further reduced if only a limited number of interest groups gain access to the policy-formulation process.

There is another dimension along which the interest groups involved in policy-making in (neo-)corporatist systems can be distinguished, namely the type of exchange relationships they maintain with political actors. More precisely, we can identify 'multipartite' relationships, 'clientela' relationships and 'parantela' relationships. Multipartite structures manifest themselves in various ways. The 'classic' (neo-)corporatist mode of political exchange is tripartite, including unions, employers (i.e. the social partners) and the government. Many studies, however, argue that even in (neo-)corporatist systems there is the tendency that political exchange involves more extensive 'issue networks' (Heclo 1978).

A 'clientela' relationship describes the mode of political exchange within a (neo)-corporatist setting where one single interest group manages to become the key cooperation partner of a ministry (La Palombara 1964; Peters 2010: 181–5). For example, Enjolras and Waldahl (2007) demonstrate that the making of Norwegian sport's policy is in some instances characterized by a clientela relationship between a monopolistic interest group (i.e. the Norwegian Olympic Committee and Confederation of Sports) and the ministerial bureaucracy.

'Parantela' relationships refer to a situation of close ties between an interest group and the government or dominant political party (La Palombara 1964). Interest groups obtain access to administrative decision-making through the willingness of a hegemonic party to intercede on their behalf with the bureaucracy and therefore, in essence, control bureaucratic policy-making. This type of relationship today cannot be found in Europe or North America, but it still exists in some African and Latin American states (Peters 2010: 185–8).

Regardless of the specific form of relationship between government and interest groups, the latter must be regarded as essential for policy-making. For example, when Helen Clark became New Zealand's prime minister following the 1999 election, she adopted a pro-interest-group rhetoric and signalled that she would accept the legitimacy of interest groups and appreciate their support in policy-making. It should also be noted that Clark's approach was intended to 'correct' the previous government's attempts at eliminating interest groups from policy-making. In fact, this decision had created some practical problems for the New Zealand government, especially with regard to the role of interest groups to increase the acceptance of governmental policy among those they represent (Tenbensel 2003: 353). It is particularly this potential to mobilize support for political decisions that turns interest groups into key actors in the policy-making process.

Political preferences stemming from partisan ideology

A way of limiting the range of alternatives when developing policy proposals is to impose an ideological filter corresponding to the party membership of ministerial bureaucrats or that of their political masters. For example, education policy in Germany is a highly politicized issue. With regard to the secondary school system, there are two models: one is to distinguish between three levels of secondary schools, and the other one is to integrate them into a comprehensive school. Generally, members of the Social Democratic Party tend to prefer comprehensive schools, whereas members of the Christian Democratic Union and the Christian Social Union are in favour of the three-tiered structure. In consequence, policy proposals developed by the ministerial bureaucracy under a Social Democratic minister would most certainly entail modifications to the existing comprehensive schools rather than their replacement through the three-tiered model. In other words, ideological considerations may impose restrictions on the policy alternatives that are taken into account by bureaucrats.

However, the effects of party ideology strongly depend upon the extent to which political actors control bureaucrats, that is, how strongly they are politicized. The reason for politicization is that political actors want to ensure that ministerial bureaucrats possessing an informational advantage do not deviate from political guidelines when drafting legislation. Therefore, in the last three decades there has been a tendency towards politicizing bureaucratic actors. Yet, not all political systems are willing to take this particular step.

The British political system, for instance, is characterized by the separation of politics and administration (Campbell and Wilson 1995: 14; see also Sausman and Locke 2004). This separation is not at all obvious, as the role of the British ministerial bureaucracy is essentially a political one. Notwithstanding the emphasis placed on a non-partisan, permanent civil service, the Whitehall model demands not that ministerial bureaucrats be non-political but that they be politically promiscuous (Rose 1987). In fact, many of the classical activities of the ministerial bureaucracy are essentially political as it has always worked in a situation where the need for high technical ability has been low and the demand for politically attuned advice high and frequent (Campbell and Wilson 1995: 29). From this perspective, British ministerial bureaucracy potentially constitutes an independent source of political influence (for a discussion, see Page and Jenkins 2005).

The fact that a politically powerful ministerial bureaucracy has always been an important characteristic of the British political-administrative system does not automatically imply that the degree of this influence is absolute. Thus, the Conservative governments under Margaret Thatcher and John Major demonstrated that political influence is nothing to be taken for granted, but is contingent upon the preferences of political leaders (Knill 1999: 132). It is also underlined by the creation of 'special advisers', who are members of the governing political party and on the civil service payroll.

In contrast to the United Kingdom, the German ministerial bureaucracy is strongly politicized (Schröter 2004: 75). The politicization basically occurs in two ways. First, administrative positions at the very top of the hierarchy, i.e. state secretaries and division heads in the ministries, are filled with so-called 'political civil servants' who have no life-time tenure, but can be temporarily retired (Derlien 1995). A second trend is the increasing party politicization of the ministerial bureaucracy. Mayntz and Derlien (1989: 397) have observed a correlation between membership of the governing party and employment in the federal bureaucracy, which significantly reduces the advancement opportunities for non-party members and those with the wrong party sympathies (for an overview see Knill 2001: 92–5).

In the United States bureaucrats are also appointed for political reasons. Yet, Peters (2004: 127) argues that the politicization of the ministerial bureaucracy in that country is different from the situation in other countries as both Congress and President control the administrative actors. Congressional control in particular ensures that patronage appointments by the executive are low in number and that a functioning merit system is in place.

Pursuit of private interests

It should have become clear by now that bureaucrats possess an information advantage over elected officials, which might allow them to exercise discretion over policy decisions. There are various theoretical approaches that make use of public choice theory (i.e. the economic theory of political choices) to explain the problem of the control of administrative organizations by their political masters and that consider that bureaucratic pathologies have much to do with problems related to information flow (for the most essential approaches, see Parkinson 1958; Tullock 1965; Downs 1967; Niskanen 1971). Theoretical considerations building on sociological institutionalism are unlikely to predict that bureaucrats would necessarily deviate from organizational priorities, but instead they would assert that institutions socialize their members in such ways that they define an institution's goals and values as their own. Thus, it should be noted that the idea of bureaucrats indulging in 'bureau-shaping' or expansionist tendencies is constrained to rational choice theory.

What kinds of pathologies exist? The most important one is that bureaucrats – akin to all other individuals – might aim to increase their income and prestige by climbing up the career ladder and by seeking to realize their private interests when drafting legislation (Müller 2011). The influential work of Dunleavy (1991) contends that senior bureaucrats are more interested in utility maximization through bureau-shaping than budget maximization (Niskanen 1971). Dunleavy contends that senior bureaucrats seek to enhance their functions as policy advisers. In the event of budgetary cuts or other requirements for reorganizations, senior bureaucrats reshape their bureaux into small staff agencies. This strategy ensures organizational survival and allows them to concentrate on their role as policy advisers, which grants them a high status and quality of work.

Against this backdrop, Downs (1967) puts forward an argument that is different from the public choice perspective by stating that the extent to which self-interested bureaucratic behaviour dominates depends on the personality types present in administrative agencies. The author differentiates between five types of bureaucrats who are more or less likely to follow their private interests in preparing legislation. In this sense, 'climbers' and 'conservers' are interested in maximizing or conserving personal power and prestige, which entails that they are relatively likely to pursue their self-interests. 'Zealots', by contrast, are unlikely to be driven by private interests as they are loyal to narrow aspects of the organization's goals, e.g. the specific programme they work for. In a complementary vein, 'advocates' are devoted to the organization's broader policy goals and equally unlikely to pursue their own interests. Finally, there are 'statesmen' who seek to make sure that the organization they belong to follows the public interest, which also reduces the chances of self-interested behaviour.

Although theoretically compelling, one must wonder whether policy decisions are likely to be affected by such reasoning. This question is addressed by Egeberg (1995), who suggests that we should differentiate between 'substantive' policy-making on the one hand and 'administrative' policy-making on the other. The first type is concerned with formulating proposals in the various policy fields, e.g. transport policy. While bureaucrats might have their private preferences regarding the policy proposals to be set out, Egeberg argues that the coupling between a certain policy proposal and its utility for different bureaucrats is rather low. Things are, however, expected to look different with the second type of policy-making, which deals with aspects of the administrative system itself, e.g. the definition of levels of reward for top civil servants. In this case, the coupling between bureaucrats' self-interests and policy choices should be much stronger and thus lead to a situation in which private interests move to the fore. On balance, however, bureaucrats are predominantly engaged in substantive policy-making, thus indicating that there is little risk of self-interested behaviour in regular political business.

The pursuit of self-interests more generally represents a situation in which an agent (here, the bureaucracy) deviates from the guidelines defined by the principal (here, the politicians). Such situations are known as agency problems and the politicization of bureaucracy presented in the previous section aims to minimize this risk of shirking, i.e. the taking of actions that maximize the benefits of the agent while imposing costs on the principal (Huber and Shipan 2002: 84).

Key points

❑ Ministerial bureaucracies are heavily involved in drafting policy.

❑ Ministerial bureaucrats can rely on their own expertise or on ideas put forward by experts. They can also reduce the feasible set of policy options in accordance with certain criteria. One way of doing this is to rely on only that kind of information provided by interest groups. Another way is by using an ideological filter corresponding to that of their political masters.

❑ Bureaucrats can also be perceived to act in an egoistic way when they propose legislation that primarily promotes their own well-being.

Institutional and procedural dimensions of decision-making

In this section we turn to the theoretical approaches to formal policy adoption that, first, clearly distinguish between policy formulation and adoption and, second, underscore the institutional and procedural dimension of policy adoption. Yet, these approaches not only stress the nature of policy-making rules but also the policy actors' preferences (Hammond 2003: 78). In what follows, we shall first outline how policy preferences are formed, second introduce the veto player concept for explaining policy adoption, then present some empirical illustrations to underline the centrality of institutional arrangements for decision-making.

How are policy preferences formed?

Legislation proposed by the executive is subject to discussion on the parliamentary floor(s) and scrutiny in the relevant legislative committees. Depending on the political system, legislative committees can possess high degrees of specialization and expertise and so disagree with a legislative bill introduced by the executive if they deem another policy to be more effective (see Strøm 1995: 65). As a result, legislative actors might ask for (far-reaching) amendments before accepting a bill. Likewise, disagreement with the policy proposal can be based on information supplied by experts.

Arguably more relevant, however, is the collaboration of decision-makers with interest groups (see Austen-Smith and Wright 1992). As already outlined above, the involvement of interest groups in the policy process not only means that they can provide relevant information but also that they are able to ensure acceptance of a policy with their members. In fact, the degree to which an actor is lobbied is a good indicator of his or her policy-shaping power. From this perspective, the increasing attention the European Parliament receives from interest groups clearly signals its growing political influence (see Lehmann 2009). For a long time, the European Parliament was not regarded as a central player in making European policy. Due to the strengthening of its formal decision-making powers, this situation has changed. For example, in 2010 it rejected the introduction of 'traffic light' food labelling. Many observers claimed that this was a direct consequence of the successful lobbying activities of the food industry (see *The Guardian*, 16 June 2010; *The Daily Telegraph*, 16 June 2010).

Hall and Deardorff (2006: 70) argue that the actual impact of interest groups very much depends on the actors' policy predispositions. This means that only if the policy suggestions made by interest groups correspond to the views of politicians are they likely to affect policy decisions.

Consequently, the influence of knowledge-based actors or interest groups is likely to strengthen the views elected officials have already developed. How can one learn about these views? The best indicator is ideology, which in most cases correlates with a politician's party affiliation.

A political actor's mindset as to what the political world ought to be – also known as ideology – is very likely to guide policy choices. For example, a person endorsing the Social Democratic ideology is likely to support the use of government to (re-)distribute private resources in order to equalize economic and political opportunities. Members of parliament with similar world views are very likely to support proposals introduced by the parliamentary party group of the Social Democrats or a government that is composed of them. Further, members of parliament will evaluate any policy proposal brought in through this particular ideological lens and may or may not arrive at the conclusion that it corresponds to their preferences.

In most political systems, members of a legislative group have an almost perfect discipline, so that, for instance, the members of parliament belonging to the majority parties normally vote for any policy proposal made on the floor by the government (see Depauw and Martin 2009). For example, if the Social Democratic party is a member of government, the corresponding legislative group will probably accept proposals advanced by the executive or legislative committees. By the same token, in most systems opposition parties automatically vote against any proposal brought in by the government or the majority parties (see Martin and Vanberg 2005; Bräuninger and Debus 2009). They do this to signal that they can also offer policy alternatives and because agreeing with a government proposal – even if it is a reasonable one – would make it difficult to claim credit for a policy change. As a result, 'agreement may be thwarted by pressures to compete' (Scharpf 1997a: 192). This notion of party competition is central to the stage of policy adoption.

How policy preferences are transformed into actual policies

The second set of factors determining policy adoption is the institutional and procedural arrangements in a given political system. In this context, the concept of veto points has received some scholarly attention (Immergut 1992). Veto points refer to the fact that policy decisions need the agreement of several, constitutionally generated, institutional points (or links) in a chain of decisions. The adoption of legislative proposals depends upon the number and location of opportunities for veto along this decision-making chain. For example, a parliament represents a veto point if it can block the decision of the executive. The logic here is straightforward: the more veto points in a given political system, the more difficult it is to gain approval for a policy proposal. While the veto point perspective already provides an improved understanding of policy adoption, some scholars (e.g. Weaver and Rockman 1993) argue that a more complete explanation would require a tackling of the question as to why veto points are willing to use their formal power in some circumstances and not in others.

This question guides a refinement of the veto point perspective that is almost exclusively associated with the work of George Tsebelis (1995, 2000, 2002). His veto player theory holds that policy adoption can be explained by the institutions governing the decision-making process and the preferences of the actors involved in it, thus following the logic of rational choice institutionalism (see Chapter 4). More precisely, however, the general expectation of this model is policy stability, that is, that it is very difficult to change existing policies.

Veto players are defined as 'individual or collective actors whose agreement is necessary for a change of the status quo' (Tsebelis 2002: 19). There are two types of veto players: institutional and partisan. Institutional players are those established by a country's constitution. So, the executive and the legislature form the key veto players in any political system, though there are additional institutions that can impede the adoption of a policy, for example constitutional courts or referendums. Partisan veto players correspond to a more dynamic concept as they are formed in the course of decision-making. Tsebelis concentrates on partisan veto players whenever possible. For the strictly illustrative purpose of this chapter, however, we will only discuss institutional veto players.

For analysing veto players and their impact on policy adoption, three pieces of information are necessary. Firstly, one has to determine the number of players. It generally holds that greater numbers of veto players reduce the odds of policy adoption. This reasoning becomes quite straightforward if we compare a situation in which a government proposes a legislative bill to either a unicameral parliament or a bicameral parliament. Excluding any considerations about the partisan composition of the parliament, policy adoption should be more likely in the first case as the government would simply need to ensure the approval of one potential veto player instead of two.

Secondly, one has to assess the ideological distance between the actors possessing formal veto power. This dimension generally refers to the veto players' partisan composition and is calculated as the distance on a policy continuum between the most extreme player on the left and the most extreme one on the right. For example, when conceiving of a parliament as a veto player cooperating with a coalition government in a parliamentary system, the ideological distance across the range of policy positions of coalition parties is decisive. The likelihood that the parliamentary majority – which is formed by the coalition parties – agrees with a legislative proposal should increase with lower ideological distance between the individual factions.

Finally, as veto players are often collective actors (e.g. parliamentary factions), it is important to assess how cohesive they are concerning their policy interests. High cohesion implies that, for instance, all members of a parliamentary group have the same policy preferences and hence form a single collective actor with a marked veto potential. In cases of low cohesion in which individual veto players have differing preferences, their veto power can be considered to be lower as they are likely to fail to speak with 'one voice'. Numerous empirical analyses have demonstrated that these three main expectations of veto player theory essentially hold true (for an overview, see Hallerberg 2010). Moreover, the design of the existing policy and the allocation of agenda-setting power may be of importance for the outcome of decision-making (see Ganghof 2011).

Which kind of veto players exist at the stage of decision-making? There is no uniform answer to this question. In cases of minority cabinets, for instance, the cabinet does not have sufficient seats in parliament to change the status quo. Thus, as the cabinet depends on parliamentary support, it may or may not be confronted with the parliamentary majority acting as a veto player, depending on the particular piece of legislation (Ganghof and Bräuninger 2006). In this regard, Green-Pedersen (2001) explains that policy adoption has become a smoother process in Denmark as minority governments have become more open about bargaining and entering agreements with changing legislative groups. In contrast, in semi-presidential and presidential systems, the president is usually a relevant veto player because his or her assent is needed for a bill to become law. Further, constitutional courts can act as powerful veto players (see Hallerberg 2010).

There are cases that are more difficult to predict. For instance, in multiparty governments, each coalition partner can, in principle, be a veto player. However, coalition governments usually emerge as a collective actor and do not veto policy proposals brought in by their coalition partners (Birchfeld and Crepaz 1998). Such behaviour is essentially achieved by 'logrolling', i.e. a situation in which parties give successive decisions different priorities (Crepaz 2002: 174). Logrolling occurs in many legislative assemblies in which two (or more) legislators agree to trade their own vote on one bill to which they attach a lower importance, in exchange for the other's vote on a bill that is much more important them. This practice is particularly common when the legislators are only sporadically controlled by their national party leaders and are seeking to secure votes for bills that concentrate benefits on their home districts while spreading the costs out over taxpayers in the rest of the country. This corresponds with the logic of pork-barrel politics outlined in Chapter 2 in the context of the NATO scheme (see also Ferejohn 1974; Cox and McCubbins 1986).

Similarly, a second legislative chamber is not necessarily a veto player, but can become one if its party composition varies from that of the first chamber, which happens quite often in federal states (see Vatter 2005: 196). Another type of veto player is represented by citizens who give or refuse their consent to a policy proposal in referendums (Hug and Tsebelis 2002). In 2009, the 'anti-smacking law', which would have imposed sanctions on parents smacking their children, was stopped by a New Zealand referendum. In 2011, the residents of the Canadian province of British Columbia used a referendum to stop a new government tax policy, namely the new sales tax. In the same year, Italians rejected the government's plans for nuclear power and water privatization through referendums. These random examples illustrate that in some jurisdictions referendums can be an effective means for stopping policy proposals that are not supported by the public.

To set the implications of the veto player theory into perspective, we point to the theoretical concept of incrementalism which we introduced in Chapter 1 (see Lindblom 1959, 1979). While the veto player theory is based on the concept of rational choice, and incrementalism, in contrast, relies on bounded rationality, the predictions of both theories concerning decision-making are remarkably similar. Both perspectives underline the difficulties in achieving agreement among the relevant actors. Within incrementalism this can only lead to marginal changes in public policy. In a similar vein, the veto player theory emphasizes the likelihood of policy stability.

Key points

❏ During the policy adoption stage, interest groups seek to influence the relevant formal actors to modify a policy proposal so that it fits their preferences better.

❏ The actual impact of interest groups depends on the actors' policy predispositions; only if the policy suggestions made by interest groups somehow correspond to the views of politicians are they likely to affect policy decisions.

❏ Veto players are defined as actors whose agreement is necessary for a change of the status quo.

❏ They can significantly lower the likelihood that a policy proposal brought in by the government will be adopted.

❏ The relationship between the executive and the legislature is central to understanding decision-making. However, this relationship changes substantially from one country to another.

An important means by which incremental policy-making occurs is through the practising of legislative self-restraint by governments. Governments usually have an interest in avoiding complete legislative failure, because, apart from anything else, failure 'looks bad' to the electorate, giving the impression that the government is unable to get its preferred policies through. If a government has to give up too much of its preferred policy position in order to avoid legislative failure, then it might prefer to delay introducing the bill in the first place (Manow and Burkhard 2007). The result will be lowered policy-making activities and relative overall policy stability.

Illustration: decision-making in the United Kingdom, Australia, Canada and the United States

The veto player approach, without question, provides an important tool for institutional analysis. Nevertheless, to understand fully the logic of decision-making, it is useful to look at different polities in more detail. Thus, in this section we illustrate decision-making in the four major English-speaking countries: the United Kingdom, Australia, Canada and the United States. We will see that there is variation with regard to the powers of the executive and the legislature, which has repercussions on how public policy is made. We begin the illustration with the United Kingdom since decision-making structures in Australia and Canada are closely patterned after the British system.

The United Kingdom

The United Kingdom is a parliamentary democracy based on a unitary structure and plurality electoral system that often produces a two-party system (the coalition government in power at the time of writing represents an important exception). The head of the executive is the prime minister and his or her Cabinet. The prime minister takes on a wider range of responsibilities, which cannot be listed in detail here. Most importantly with regard to decision-making, the prime minister 'leads' the government and is also the leader of the majority party, which involves close cooperation with the parliamentary party (Budge *et al.* 2001: 203). This also indicates that the prime minister as the party leader has a specific standing and is likely to influence the party's preferences regarding public policy in a way that corresponds to his or her own preferences. The prime minister and the Cabinet members are responsible for government policies and actions. They are supported by the Cabinet Office that is in charge of structuring government departments, allocating ministerial responsibilities, developing policies and defining the broader legislative programme in parliament. The members of the ministerial bureaucracy working inside the British executive are non-politically appointed and usually do not change when a new government comes in. Due to their long-standing experience, ministerial bureaucrats are very important to ministers for guiding policy decisions. As already mentioned, there are also temporary civil servants – special advisers – who are political appointees and whose loyalties are claimed by the governing party and often particular ministers with whom they have a close relationship.

The British Parliament consists of two Houses: the directly elected lower House of Commons and the upper House of Lords (see Moran 2005: Chapter 10). Of these two, it is mainly the House of Commons that fulfils the 'classical' parliamentary tasks: members can propose new laws – although it should be kept in mind that very few private members' bills will actually get to the stage of legislation – and can scrutinize government policies by asking ministers questions about current issues, known as the ministers' question time, and by written questions. Party unity is high in the House of Commons. Even when Members of Parliament disagree with their party leadership they normally vote with their party for the sake of unity. This underlines once again how important political parties are in some polities.

The British government faces few legal and constitutional restraints. Despite the name 'parliamentary democracy', the parliament plays only a limited role in decision-making in the British Westminster model. Policies are largely determined by the executive and, together with the high degree of party cohesion in the House of Commons and the fact that the majority party and the executive are strongly interlinked with one another, draft legislation introduced by the government is likely to pass with few changes to it. The opposition parties, however, are ideologically different from the majority party and thus affect decision-making through criticizing and opposing government proposals. The opposition parties also put forward their own policy proposals to improve their chances of winning the next election. However, the likelihood that these alternative proposals will be preferred over the government's are low. In parliamentary committees the majority party also holds the committee majority and often controls all committee chairmanships (Strøm 1995: 65). As a result, the British parliament can be seen as a 'policy-modifying body, rather than a policy-making one' (Dorey 2005: 162).

The devolution process that begun in the late 1990s is an important characteristic of the British polity. Under the Scotland Act 1998, the Scottish Parliament can pass acts and the executive can make secondary legislation in areas other than those which are reserved to the Westminster government in London. Health policy, for example, is an important area in which the Scottish government can adopt specific legislation (see Keating 2005; Cairney 2009, 2011). Likewise, Scottish social policy displays some specific traits. It is interesting to note that the prospect of formulating more generous social policy played a key role in nationalist campaigns for devolution and the creation of the Scottish Parliament (Béland and Lecours 2008: 139), although in the end it was created with cross-party support and not by the nationalists.

However, policy-making by the devolved institutions is still de facto constrained by the common security area, common market and common welfare state arrangements throughout the whole of the United Kingdom (see Keating 2005: 33–43). Principally, the Westminster Parliament can legislate in devolved policy areas, but under the Sewel Convention it explicitly needs to be asked by the Scottish Parliament to do so (Leeke *et al*. 2003: 3).

While the policy-making powers of the Scottish legislature and executive must be regarded as far-reaching, devolution is less advanced in Wales and Northern Ireland. Under the Government of Wales Act 1998, powers in devolved areas have been passed to the National Assembly for Wales, which can make delegated or secondary legislation in these areas, though primary legislation for Wales is still made by the Westminster Parliament. However, in some areas there is wide scope for the details of the policy to be made under secondary legislation, allowing the National Assembly for Wales some autonomy. The Northern Ireland Assembly can make primary and delegated legislation in those policy areas which are transferred, such as environment and health policies (Leeke *et al*. 2003: 29).

The devolution process is important to the extent that in devolved policy areas it is now possible to have diverging legislation across the United Kingdom. However, devolution does not affect how the Westminster government drafts and adopts public policies. Rather, the devolution of decision-making powers suggests that in some areas different policies might exist in the United Kingdom due to the different preferences of key policy-makers and/or specific politics (see Keating *et al*. 2009).

Australia

The Australian polity resembles the British Westminster system in many ways. In Australia, as in the United Kingdom, there are two dominant parties: the centre-left Australian Labor Party and the centre-right Liberal Party of Australia. The Australian government – consisting of a prime minister and his or her Cabinet – is drawn from the legislature, and due to this the executive tends to dominate the working of Parliament.

The Australian Federal Parliament is composed of the Senate (upper house) and the House of Representatives (lower house). The House of Representatives performs a function corresponding to the British House of Commons. However, as in the Commons, the opportunities for the House of Representatives to control the government are reduced because the party or coalition of parties forming the government holds a majority of seats.

Unlike the British House of Lords which is mainly appointed, the Senate is composed of elected representatives of each State, with representation being proportional to population. The Senate has virtually the same legislative powers as the House of Representatives. In the literature it is argued that the Australian Senate has become the 'House of Review' (Mulgan 1996), which scrutinizes the government. This results from the system of proportional representation, which often leads to a balance of power among the political parties in the Senate. There are some examples of cases in which the government has been involved in long negotiations with a few Senators over policy proposals that they did not want to pass through parliament (Maddison and Denniss 2009: 27). Consequently, government tends to adjust policy proposals so that they will receive the Senate's consent. In so doing, the government often seeks the support of a 'neutral' party, e.g. the Australian Democrats, in the Senate; that is, minor parties which are not in the House of Representatives and are therefore not opposition parties in the narrow sense of the term (Ganghof and Bräuniger 2006).

The Senate is one of the key features of the federal system in Australia. The second key feature is a division of powers and responsibilities between the federal government and the state governments. While there are specific powers granted to the federal government, most are concurrent and can be exercised by both the Commonwealth and the States. The States are the entities that mostly provide public services and the regulations experienced by citizens. Since both levels of government possess policy-making powers, the Australian High Court fulfils an important task in settling disagreements about which government has power over particular issues.

Judicial review represents the third key feature of Australian federalism (Parkin and Summers 2006: 52–3). Summers (2006: 138) contends that, on balance, the effect of judicial review has been to increase the power of the Commonwealth at the expense of the States, especially with regard to financial issues. Notwithstanding these shifts in power, the States retain their power to make public policy on a wide range of issues such as education and health services.

Thus, for understanding decision-making in Australia, it is important to investigate processes at both levels of government. On the one hand, this entails that the political constellations in each single State are of interest for explaining policy outputs; on the other hand, the interplay of the two levels is worth studying in detail, especially when some or all State governments have policy preferences that diverge from those of the Federal government. It should be kept in mind that the Senate as a veto player directly results from the country's federal polity, which represents a marked contrast to the decision-making situation in the United Kingdom.

Canada

A Westminster-style polity coexisting with federalism are also the main characteristics of Canada. When appointing ministers to a Cabinet, i.e. the supreme policy-making body, the Canadian prime minister usually selects at least one per province. The ministers forming the Cabinet make policy decisions together and are collectively responsible for them. As in the United Kingdom, the lower chamber is the House of Commons, where seats are distributed roughly in proportion to the population of each province and territory. The Senate consists of 105 members appointed by the governor general, i.e. the representative of the Canadian monarch, on the advice of the prime minister. Seats are assigned on a regional basis. On paper, the Canadian Senate has a veto power. In reality, however, most analysts argue that it is reluctant to use this power due to its lack of democratic legitimacy (see Russell 2001); hence it rarely rejects bills passed by the directly elected House of Commons.

Compared to the United Kingdom and Australia, there is a higher number of political parties. In the current legislature, five are represented in the House of Commons: the Conservative Party (right wing), the New Democratic Party (left wing), the Liberal Party (centre left), the Bloc Québécois (nationalist) and the Green Party. Especially in recent years, party discipline in the House of Commons has been very strictly enforced (see Penner *et al.* 2006: 1008), which obviously affects policy-making because majority parties have an advantage over those holding only a minority of seats. Further, there have been several minority governments, which have had to rely on the support of other parties to stay in power. Concerning policy-making, minority governments are likely to engage in incremental policy change as they need to gain the consent of the other parties. This situation represents another major difference vis-à-vis the United Kingdom.

In Canada, federalism is constitutionally entrenched against unilateral modification by either level of government. In addition, limits on the authority of both the federal and the provincial governments are judicially enforceable. 'It is difficult to overstate the complexity of Canadian federalism and its supporting policy institutions in such a huge, regionally and linguistically diverse country, with provinces and territories of starkly different fiscal, population and land bases' (Howlett and Lindquist 2004: 234). Executive federalism has long been considered the defining characteristic of Canadian intergovernmental relations, i.e. relations dominated by the executives of the different governments within the federal system (Watts 1989: 3), and in recent years it has been increasingly informed by a set of practices known as 'collaborative federalism', which is characterized by a co-determination of broad national policies. While co-determination in the Canadian context generally involves the two orders of government working together as equals, it can also entail provincial and territorial governments taking their own initiative – acting collectively in the absence of the federal government – to formulate national policy (Cameron and Simeon 2002).

By and large, policy-making in Canada is characterized by the absence of a veto power being exerted by the provinces as the Senate usually does not reject policy proposals that have been passed by the House of Commons. Nevertheless, policy adoption can become complicated if the government is a minority one, dependent on the support of the other parties, as this may require giving up preferred policy positions.

The United States

Legislative decision-making in the United States is highly structured by the strong degree of federalism on the one hand and by the dualism between the president and Congress on the other. Despite the fact that the office of the president – who serves as the head of state and the executive, as the commander-in-chief of the military and who nominates judges for the Supreme Court – is seen as the most important in the world, many of the president's decisions need the approval of both houses of Congress, i.e. the House of Representatives (the lower house) and the Senate (the upper house). More generally, US politics is characterized by a very well-developed system of checks and balances, which gives each of the branches of government – the legislative, the executive and the judiciary – some degree of oversight and control over the actions of the others.

At the national level, the power of the president is limited with regard to the process of legislative decision-making. First, he or she cannot introduce a law proposal in both houses of Congress directly: he or she needs a member of the House of Representative or the Senate to insert a bill. As a result of the institutional relevance of the legislature in the US system, legislative committees are strongly specialized and possess high expertise in a wide range of areas (Strøm 1995: 65). Congress rather than the president and his or her ministers are the targets of interest group activities (Werner and Wilson 2008). However, each law adopted by Congress has to be signed by the president. If he or she refuses to sign a bill approved by the majority in the House of Representatives and the Senate, the proposal goes back to both houses of Congress. Only if the president's veto is overridden by a two-thirds majority, inside both the Senate and the House of Representatives, can a bill rejected by the president become law (O'Connor and Sabato 2009: 258–62). Another interesting observation in this regard is that the US Cabinet, which consists of so-called secretaries (i.e. heads of executive departments) who assist the president in executing laws and making decisions, is only an informal institution, which again distinguishes the US political system from the ones presented previously.

This clarifies that in terms of legislative decision-making not only do the policy preferences and thus the partisan affiliation of the president matter, but also the partisan composition of both houses of Congress and the degree of majority possessed by the two main parties – i.e. the Republicans and Democrats. Although there also exist some other political parties, the electoral system in which the political party that receives more votes wins the election – known as the 'winner-takes-all system' – favours their concentration. Moreover, it should be kept in mind that US political parties are more loosely organized and that there is more intra-party variation concerning policy positions as compared to the ideologically cohesive political parties in other countries. However, party politics matter in the US and this becomes most apparent in decision-making in Congress, which has far-reaching competences regarding budgetary issues.

In contrast to the four-year term of the president, the complete House of Representatives and one-third of the Senate face re-election every second year. During 'mid-term' elections, voters tend to vote for the candidates of the party that does not control the presidency at that time. As was the case after the 2010 elections for Congress, so-called 'mid-term loss' (Gaines and Crombez 2004) often results in majorities for the opposition parties in at least one chamber of Congress. These patterns of divided government can result in legislative gridlock between the executive and the legislature, which often results in policy compromises between both partisan camps and, therefore, in moderate policies being adopted.

Key points

❏ The British executive is particularly powerful due to its two-party system and the high degree of party coherence.

❏ In Australia, the Senate, which is composed of the representatives of each state, can force the government to modify its policy proposal before agreeing to give its consent to it.

❏ In Canada, the Senate is a weak player, with federalism unlikely to complicate policy-making at the national levels. Policy adoption can, however, require the government to give up policy positions if it is a minority government relying on the support of other parties.

❏ In the United States the number and power of veto players is much higher. On the whole, this makes policy adoption more complicated, often leading to substantial modification between the initial policy proposal and the form of law that is adopted in the end.

Conclusions

Which factors determine the design of a policy proposal? When does a policy proposal more easily gain adoption? These have been the research questions guiding this chapter. In response to the first question, we note that in parliamentary systems the (initial) design of a policy proposal is mostly determined by the executive, comprising both the cabinet and the ministerial bureaucracy. While cabinet members are important for placing a certain issue on the policy agenda, it is the ministerial bureaucracy that develops the actual proposal. In presidential systems, however, legislation is introduced by the legislature, entailing that the ministerial bureaucracy and the responsible legislative committees have to cooperate to a greater degree than is the case in parliamentary systems.

The actual design of a policy proposal depends on the preferences of competent actors. This can result from their own expertise, information supplied by experts, international organizations and/or interest groups. Further, with regard to the dominance of ministerial bureaucrats in drafting legislation in parliamentary systems, we have stressed that they might, in principle, deviate from political guidelines and propose legislation that corresponds to their own interests. This does not occur with elected officials as they are democratically accountable for their actions. Additionally, party discipline can prevent individual members of the legislature from coming up with policy proposals that do not correspond to the interests of the legislative groups. One way to limit the risk of shirking by bureaucratic actors is through politicization.

The legislative proposal prepared by the executive or legislature is then subject to parliamentary approval. In this process, draft legislation might still undergo more or less fundamental changes. The extent of these changes strongly depends on whose consent is required for passing a law – in other words, the existence of veto points or veto players. Usually, a smaller number of actors possessing formal veto powers should speed up the decision-making process. Likewise, the ideological distance between veto players and – in the case of collective veto players – their internal cohesion are important for being able to predict the outcome of the policy-adoption process.

Web links

www.parliament.uk. Here information is supplied about aspects of decision-making in the British parliament.

www.polidoc.net. On this website election manifestos and other policy-relevant documents of political parties are presented and can be downloaded.

www.pippanorris.com. Professor Norris maintains a very instructive website on which she provides empirical data on the institutional characteristics of political systems.

www.internationalbudget.org. This website provides all kinds of information regarding budgets and the making of budgets.

www.bis.gov.uk/foresight. The Foresight Programme explores ways of using science and technology for British policy-making. The website offers numerous in-depth studies over a wide range of topics.

http://www-management.wharton.upenn.edu/henisz/polcon/contactinfo.html. Professor Henisz has developed a system for measuring political constraints. The resulting Political Constraint Index dataset can be downloaded from this website.

www.ipu.org. A website that gives insights into details about parliaments and elections all around the world. We recommend the PARLINE database, containing information on the structure and working methods of the parliamentary chambers in 188 countries.

Further reading

Aberbach, J.D., R.A. Putnam and B.A. Rockman (1981) *Bureaucrats and Politicians in Western Democracies*. Cambridge, MA: Harvard University Press. A classic read about the relationship between elected and appointed policy-making actors.

Caramani, D. (ed.) (2011) *Comparative Politics*. Oxford: Oxford University Press. This edited volume provides a concise yet compelling introduction to the main areas of comparative politics.

Jagannathan, R. and M. Camasso (forthcoming) *When to Protect? Decision-Making in Public Child Welfare*. Oxford: Oxford University Press. A compelling analysis of policy-making in a highly sensitive area.

König, T., G. Tsebelis and M. Debus (eds) (2010) *Reform Processes and Policy Change: Veto Players and Decision-making in Modern Democracies*. New York: Springer. A volume that offers a variety of advancements on the study of veto players.

Room, G. (2012) *Complexity, Institutions and Public Policy: Agile Decision-making in a Turbulent World*. Cheltenham: Edward Elgar. This theoretical book offers a different perspective on policy-making by systematically taking into account the implications of complex decision-making.

Schneider, A. and H. Ingram (1997) *Policy Design for Democracy.* Lawrence: University Press of Kansas. The major strength of this book is its presentation of numerous policy theories.

Chapter 7

Implementation

Reader's guide

In Chapter 2 we argued that a public policy is intended to solve a certain social problem that has reached the institutional agenda. As a rule, the problem that initiated the policy-making process can only be solved effectively if the adopted policy is properly put into practice. If a given policy is introduced but insufficiently implemented, it is possible that the ultimate result will be less desirable than the previous state. Despite the importance of this aspect, for a long time there has been the (implicit) assumption that once a policy is adopted, it will be implemented and then produce the desired results. This expectation rests upon a number of conditions, which may not be found in all political systems. Rather, implementation research has demonstrated that it is anything but a straightforward task to put public policies into practice. Most importantly, the specific interests of actors are likely to affect the outcomes. In this chapter, the central focus is on what has been called 'post-decisional' politics. We will approach the implementation of public policy from different analytical angles, including a clarification as to which actors implement public policy and a presentation of the major theoretical perspectives on implementation activities (which can combine 'top-down' and 'bottom-up' approaches). We then propose categories for assessing the degree to which a policy can be implemented effectively and identify factors that might hamper such implementation. The latter also include considerations about the design of public policies, thus underscoring the interlinkage between decision-making and implementation.

Policy implementation is the stage in the policy-making process where a policy is put into effect by the responsible bureaucracies. So implementation is the stage in the policy cycle where there is a connection between policy-makers and policy addressees, mediated by the implementers. In more technical terms, implementation involves the transformation of a policy output into a policy outcome. The attainment of the intended policy outcome is a necessary condition for bringing about the desired policy impact. However, it should be kept in mind that only the policy outcome can be directly affected by the implementers but not the policy impact since the latter might also by affected by additional factors. Therefore, all arguments made in this chapter solely concern the process of how policy outputs are turned into policy outcomes, leaving completely aside considerations about policy impacts.

What happens to a policy or political programme after its official passing by the government or the legislature? How do the formal transposition and the practical application of legal acts take shape? Which problems and deviations from the initial objectives can be observed? At first glance, it could be assumed that questions like these are relatively trivial. Why do problems in the execution of an apparently well-devised measure that was accepted by the cabinet and/or parliament subsequently emerge? In practice, numerous problems with implementation routinely occur. In this chapter we will show that the study of implementation is multi-faceted and demanding in both empirical and theoretical terms.

Analysing policy implementation always involves a judgement about the intended policy outcomes and about those actually achieved. Therefore, most approaches to implementation evaluate whether there is a difference between expected and achieved outcomes. Related to this is the often implicit assumption that there are 'implementation problems', that is, a policy cannot be put in place as intended by policy-makers due to the implementers' failure to overcome obstacles. Hogwood and Gunn (1984: 197) refer to such situations as 'non-implementation'; and they introduce a second type of implementation problems, i.e. 'unsuccessful implementation', which is seen to occur when a public policy fails to produce the intended outcome despite being fully implemented. While we only refer to implementation problems in the sense of non-implementation in this chapter, Hogwood and Gunn's second category suggests that the study of policy implementation is closely related to evaluation research. Indeed, Pressman and Wildavsky (1973) regarded policy implementation as the 'missing link' between policy-making and evaluation.

Who is involved in policy implementation?

In most polities, policy implementation is primarily carried out by different levels of bureaucracy. At the central level, there are the various national ministries (education, defence, trade, etc.), which form the core of the executive branch. Also at the central level, there are autonomous agencies located outside of the ministries that are charged with implementing public policy. These are set up with specialized expertise for dealing with complex or new policy areas. Therefore, in 1970, the United States government founded the Environmental Protection Agency, which is responsible for the implementation of environmental policy. Many countries, such as Ireland or the United Kingdom, followed the example of the United States and created such agencies.

This international trend of delegating implementation – and often also policy formulation – competencies to autonomous agencies is based on the assumption that these will improve overall implementation performance and efficiency (Bouckaert and Peters 2004). This is also related to the idea of separating politics from administration and insulating certain decisions from political considerations, which is expected to minimize deviations from the original intentions of policy-makers and prevent delays (see Pollitt and Talbot 2004; Pollitt *et al.* 2004). Regulatory agencies are a subgroup of such autonomous agencies and one of their main tasks is to implement public policy in market-related areas, such as electricity, telecommunications or water supply. These bodies carry out regulation using their own delegated power, resources and responsibilities (see Gilardi 2008).

While centrally located ministries and autonomous agencies play an important role in policy implementation, national policy is also implemented by public entities at the local level. Employment and to a certain extent also social policy is usually carried out by local employment agencies. In Germany, for example, employment agencies do not only support job seekers to find an employer, they are also responsible for processing applications for many kinds of social benefits, including child benefits, business start-up and part-time working allowances, unemployment benefits and insolvency payments, providing vocational and further training, and the integrating of older and disabled people into the labour market. In a similar vein, the 20 District Health Boards in New Zealand are responsible for implementing national health policy by providing or funding the provision of health care services.

There are also public policies that are implemented by multiple organizations, which might even be located at different levels of government. In such a situation, implementation involves collaborative efforts and brings inter-organizational relations to the fore. Recent empirical studies have pointed out that a considerable share of legislation requires multi-organizational structures (see Hall and O'Toole 2000). In this context, the role of inter-organizational networks has been emphasized as they can provide an effective means of coordination. Such networks are relatively stable structures through which individuals and organizations act in situations in which they are dependent on the contributions of others (Hanf and O'Toole 1992). Drug policy is an area that typically requires the collaborative efforts of different ministries and agencies to implement it properly due to its intersectoral character, which can involve the ministry of health and local health offices as well as other ministries and/or agencies working in the fields of education, finance, economy, trade, foreign affairs and criminal justice.

Depending on the specific policy to be implemented, bureaucracies can have more or less decisional discretion. For example, in the case of unemployment benefits specific conditions are defined for eligibility, the levels of benefits and the duration of their payment. Therefore, most bureaucratic decisions on the implementation of such benefits involve the application of the conditions specified in the legislation to the facts of the case at hand. Bureaucracies might, however, have greater leeway in the interpreting of policy outputs if these are characterized by vague policy contents or goals. An example of such a difficult to define policy goal is the achievement of sustainable development, which is a very broad concept that involves an ecological, a social and an economic dimension. In such cases, the bureaucracy can certainly shape public policy by providing an operational definition of vague policy objectives. As we will show later in this chapter, policy outputs characterized by vagueness, inconsistency and complexity have higher chances of being implemented inconsistently.

All in all, policy implementation is far from being a trivial activity. It involves multiple actors located in different public entities that may or may not have the same preferences concerning the way in which a given policy should be implemented. Thus, when looking at how implementation is carried out, it is not surprising that most studies concentrate on deviations from legislation. However, as we will outline in the next section, such deviations are not always perceived as problematic.

Key points

❏ Policy implementation is primarily carried out by bureaucratic actors.

❏ These can be ministries or autonomous agencies located at the central or the local level.

❏ There has been an international trend to transfer implementation competences to autonomous agencies, triggered by the idea that they can carry these tasks out in more efficient ways.

Analytical perspectives in implementation research

At the most basic level, implementation is about putting new public policy into practice. While at first glance this definition is straightforward, the empirical analysis is complex as it encompasses various actions by public and private actors that are directed at the achievement of certain goals specified in terms of their policy outputs (Van Meter and Van Horn 1975: 447). To illustrate this point, let us assume that a government has adopted a policy that requires food products to be labelled in a transparent and easy-to-understand manner in order to increase consumer trust (i.e. the policy objective). The food industry (i.e. the target group) may not comply with the requirements unless its products are to be scrutinized by the responsible administrative agency (e.g. the food standards agency). Thus, to achieve the intended policy outcome, compliance with the relevant policy has to be monitored. However, the policy could, in principle, also demand that a specific website is established on which consumers can complain about food products that are insufficiently labelled. Again, the target group of the policy would be the food industry and the policy outcome a modification of product labelling. This time, however, the activity of the implementers would involve the establishment and maintenance of the requested website. Many more examples could be given here, but what matters is that there is not only one way of implementing policy outputs and often implementation requires multiple actions, which further complicates analysis.

The diversity of activities is reflected in the theoretical perspectives adopted to describe and explain policy implementation. The traditional approach is characterized by a top-down perspective, which concentrates on policy outputs and investigates the extent to which the intended objectives have been achieved over time and why. In the late 1970s and early 1980s, the bottom-up perspective emerged. This perspective analyses the multitude of actors who interact at the operational level of a particular policy issue. Bottom-up models usually stress the strong interlinkages between the stages of policy formulation, implementation and reformulation (Sabatier 1986: 22). More recently, hybrid models of implementation have been advanced, which seek to overcome the divide between the other two approaches by incorporating elements of top-down, bottom-up and other theoretical models (Pülzl and Treib 2007: 90). In this section, we present the main characteristics of these three approaches.

Top-down models of policy implementation

In their path-breaking study on policy implementation, Pressman and Wildavsky (1973) demonstrated that great deviations and shifts in policy goals can occur during the implementation phase. The subtitle of their book concisely summarizes the central finding of the analysis: 'How Great Expectations in Washington Are Dashed in Oakland; or, Why It's Amazing that Federal Programs Work at all'. According to the authors, deviations in policy goals are likely if action depends upon a number of actors who are required to cooperate. Hence, the longer the implementation chain and the greater the number of actors involved in the process, the more difficult implementation becomes.

The approach of Pressman and Wildavsky corresponds to rational choice theories as they conceive of implementation as purposive action by different groups of actors with different preferences. Since the success of implementation depends on the cooperation of actors, there is a relatively high chance that problems will occur, which implies a mismatch between intended policy objectives and the actual outcomes. Put this way, implementation can be analysed by means of game theory, as outlined in Chapter 4. So implementation can be modelled as a 'one-shot' or a repeated game (see also Bardach 1977). The reasoning about the importance of the number of actors involved in the implementation process, i.e. the length of the implementation chain, resembles the argument underlying the theories of veto points and veto players presented in Chapter 6. In both cases, that is during decision-making and implementation, a greater number of actors can lead to conflict over policy goals as well as delays and deviations from what policy-makers originally intended.

The central finding of Pressman and Wildavsky that shifts in policy objectives can be frequently observed during the implementation stage is closely associated with the top-down approach (see Smith 1973; Van Meter and Van Horn 1975; Hood 1976; Sabatier and Mazmanian 1980; Mazmanian and Sabatier 1983; Hogwood and Gunn 1984; Sabatier 1986). Most importantly, this perspective makes a clear distinction between the stages of policy formulation and implementation (Hill 2009: 196). It is only on this basis that an actual comparison between policy requirements and their degree of actual implementation is possible. The degree of goal attainment serves as an indicator of implementation success; and effective implementation corresponds to a match between policy objectives and outcomes. If the objective of national legislation is, for instance, to set a certain standard for industrial emissions into the air, effective implementation is achieved as soon as the prescribed emission levels are met by the industry. Likewise, an effective implementation of bans on smoking in public buildings requires that appropriate steps are taken by the authorities in these buildings to make sure that nobody smokes inside. This can be achieved by no-smoking signs, the removal of ashtrays, monitoring and the announcement of sanctions.

In this context, Van Meter and Van Horn (1975) put forward a model in which they combine the characteristics of the policy to be implemented, institutional characteristics of the implementation agencies and how these are interrelated with other relevant organizations, contextual factors (including the economic, social and political environment) and the response of the implementers to all these factors. Based on this model, the authors hypothesize that implementation will be most successful when the policy output only requires marginal changes as compared to the status quo and when goal consensus among the public and private actors involved is high.

The logic of the top-down perspective is also well illustrated by the four-step model suggested by Sabatier and Mazmanian (1980). The model first addresses the extent to which the actions of implementing officials and target groups were consistent with the objectives and procedures outlined in a public policy. Next, they focus on the extent to which the objectives were attained over time. Thirdly, they evaluate the principal factors affecting policy outcomes. Finally, they suggest analysing whether and how the policy was reformulated on the basis of experience. Even though the main characteristics of policy evaluation will only be introduced in Chapter 8, it is apparent that the analytical perspective advanced by Sabatier and Mazmanian is 'evaluative' (see Laws and Hajer 2008: 411), especially when looking at the fourth step which points out a feedback process (Hill and Hupe 2009: 49). This observation holds true more generally for the various top-down models, as they all compare actual with expected policy outcomes in order to assess the degree to which they are congruent.

While the top-down perspective has produced many interesting insights into implementation processes, it has also been met with three sets of criticisms (Matland 1995: 147–8). First, this perspective takes policy outputs as the starting point of analysis and disregards actions taken earlier in the process, especially during policy drafting. Second, top-down models tend to see implementation as a purely administrative process that ignores political aspects. However, as already discussed in Chapter 4, bureaucratic actors may not be 'Weberian' in nature and always make independent decisions based on technical criteria, but might also pursue their own interests in accordance with the argument put forward by Niskanen (1971) and other theorists of public choice (for an overview, see Mueller 2003). Third, top-down models have been criticized for not taking into account local actors and the particular conditions for policy implementation at the 'street level'. These points of criticism paved the way for bottom-up models of policy implementation.

Bottom-up models of policy implementation

Bottom-up models regard effective implementation in a process-oriented way that abandons the divide between policy formulation and implementation (see Berman 1978; Lipsky 1980; Hjern and Porter 1981; Hjern 1982; Hjern and Hull 1982). Policy objectives and instruments are no longer defined as benchmarks to be reached; instead it is expected that they may undergo modifications during the process of implementation. Implementers have flexibility and autonomy to adjust policy in the light of particular local requirements and changes in the perception or constellation of policy problems, as well as new scientific evidence on the causal relationships between means and ends. Hence, effective implementation is not measured by the attainment of a certain centrally defined objective, but judged by the extent to which the perceived outcomes correspond with the preferences of the actors involved. The crucial question for evaluating implementation success is the extent to which a certain policy allowed for processes of learning, capacity-building and support-building in order to address problems associated with it in a decentralized way, consistent with the interests of the actors involved (see Wilson 1989; Schneider and Ingram 1997).

It is important to note that policy implementation occurs at two levels. Firstly, there is the macro-implementation level comprising central actors that devise a policy output. Secondly, local actors at the micro-implementation level react to macrolevel policies and develop their own programmes and implement them. According to Berman (1978), implementation problems stem from the fact that the macro-implementation level cannot influence microlevel implementers, leading to a variation in how the same national policy is implemented at the local level (Matland 1995: 148). This corresponds to the logic of the principal–agent problem which we outlined in Chapter 6: the agent (here, the local implementers) can be inclined to deviate from the principal (here, the centrally located actors). We will return to this point later in this chapter as agency problems represent an important source of imperfect implementation.

In this regard, Lipsky (1980) argues that the likelihood of local implementers or street-level bureaucrats deviating from centrally defined policy objectives stems from pressures imposed on them and how they cope with them. They develop methods of providing a service in a relatively routine way. These local implementers are oppressed by the bureaucracy within which they work and yet they possess discretionary freedom and autonomy. Against this background, street-level bureaucrats make choices about the use of scarce resources under pressure. So, increasing the monitoring of local implementers would not reduce the odds of imperfect implementation but increase the tendency to provide routine services and variations at the local level, as routines might vary from one local unit to another (see Hill and Hupe 2009: 52–3). Therefore, Hjern and Porter (1981), Hjern (1982) and Hjern and Hull (1982) suggest that bottom-up studies of implementation will be particularly insightful if they focus on microlevel implementers and their goals and preferences as well as the constraints they face.

This conception challenges the simplifying assumptions of the top-down perspective and tries to take into account the complexity of the implementation processes. Thus, it is emphasized that the formulation of clear-cut objectives often contrasts with the interests of politicians who have a preference for vague and ambiguous objectives in order to facilitate a positive evaluation later and to make detection of potential failures more difficult. In addition, the bottom-up perspective accounts for the fact that implementation processes are rarely characterized by a clear delineation of competencies between the political and administrative actors involved at different institutional levels. Hence, implementation is based less on hierarchically defined and controlled requirements, and instead can be understood as a bargaining between a great number of public and private actors as well as administrative agencies participating in the implementation process.

The precise mapping of the complexities of the implementation process inherent in the bottom-up approach also introduces problems when it comes to the measurement of success. As effective implementation is not measured on the basis of a comparison between initial objectives and actual achievements, but on the extent to which goals have been reached by taking into account the specific conditions 'on the ground', general and comparative assessments of effectiveness are difficult (Knill and Lenschow 2000). In addition, there are two further frequently expressed criticisms of bottom-up models (Matland 1995: 149–50). First, there is the normative criticism that in democratic polities local implementers should be subject to central control. Second, bottom-up models tend to over-emphasize the level of local autonomy as often it is the policy itself that defines how it should be implemented.

Hybrid models of policy implementation

In view of the specific problems of both top-down and bottom-up models, there have been increasing efforts to combine the two perspectives and enrich them with additional theoretical approaches (see Mayntz 1979; Windhoff-Héritier 1980; Elmore 1985; Sabatier 1986; Matland 1995; Winter 2003; O'Toole 2003). As a rule, hybrid models seek to integrate the 'macroworld' of the policy-makers with the 'microworld' of the implementers (McLaughlin, 1987: 177). One possibility is to integrate both approaches into one model (see Goggin *et al.* 1990; Winter 2003). Other authors (see Sabatier 1986; Matland 1995) identify additional conditions of scope that in a given constellation render a distinctive approach more or less analytically promising or suitable. These conditions include, the ambiguity of political objectives, the level of political conflict surrounding a policy decision, the complexity of policy networks, and government capacity (see Linder and Peters 1989; Knill and Lenschow 2000; Pülzl and Treib 2007).

Particularly insightful is the hybrid model of policy implementation advanced by Matland (1995), which analyses the ambiguity and conflict levels of policies to determine whether a top-down or a bottom-up approach is more appropriate for explaining a particular implementation process. Policy ambiguity refers to a lack of clarity of goals and/or means of achieving them. Policy conflict is the difference between the most preferred outcome of an implementation agency and the output that the agency has to implement. The conception of these two dimensions as being high or low gives way to four ideal-typical implementation processes: administrative, political, experimental and symbolic.

Administrative implementation involves low policy ambiguity and low policy conflict. Policy outcomes are determined by resources, and the process is compared to a machine, which is the central policy-making authority. All in all, administrative implementation fits with the top-down model.

Political implementation involves low policy ambiguity and high policy conflict. In such constellations, actors have clearly defined goals, though there is dissent when they are incompatible or a conflict occurs over the means of achieving them. Therefore, policy outcomes are determined by power or bargaining, which clearly indicates the top-down logic underlying this implementation process.

The remaining two implementation processes build on the bottom-up approach. Experimental implementation refers to a situation of high policy ambiguity and low policy conflict. Following this model, policy outcomes depend on the resources and actors present in the micro-implementation level, which are likely to vary from context to context. As this implementation process emphasizes the relevance of contextual conditions and the role of chance, it parallels the garbage can model (Cohen *et al.* 1972) and the multiple streams approach (Kingdon 2003). From this it follows that policy outcomes are hard to predict.

Symbolic implementation involves a situation in which there is high policy ambiguity and high policy conflict. The central principle is that coalitions of actors at the local level exist who control the available resources. However, the power of the various actor coalitions is again determined by contextual conditions. The preferences of actors' groups are likely to be based on their professional training. Among groups trained in different ways, there will be disagreement over proposals for policy implementation, leading to long battles and significant delays in attaining outcomes.

Key points

❏ There are three types of implementation models: top-down, bottom-up and hybrid.

❏ Top-down models primarily emphasize the ability of policy-makers to produce specific policy outcomes; most are characterized by an 'evaluative' strategy for analysis.

❏ Bottom-up models stress the characteristics of the actors implementing policy outputs; (local) implementers make ongoing choices themselves about the appropriate courses of action in specific contexts.

❏ Hybrid models integrate elements of both the above models and other theoretical models.

Implementation success: criteria and determinants

In this section we first outline how implementation effectiveness can be empirically assessed. The criteria we suggest are intended to provide a better understanding of the different activities related to policy implementation. We then provide some explanations for possible variations in the effectiveness of implementation.

Criteria of implementation success

The assessment of implementation is not only affected by the analytical perspective adopted, but also by the criteria that are applied (to measure 'successful' or 'perfect'). Based on the logic of top-down models, we suggest distinguishing between formal transposition and practical application (see Knill and Lenschow 1998; Weale *et al.* 2000; Winter 2003; Knill 2006; Hartlapp and Falkner 2009; Robichau and Lynn 2009). While there are some valid points of criticism concerning the top-down logic that we outlined above, it is clearly more suitable for providing a measurement of implementation.

Formal transposition focuses on the entirety of the specific provisions of a given public policy and their incorporation into the existing legal and administrative system. In so doing, bureaucrats have to ensure that this is done in a complete manner and within the time frame specified by the legal act by which a policy is adopted. Put differently, this stage is about the steps necessary to make a policy 'implementable' so that it can actually be put into practice. In some polities, policy-makers adopt detailed and specific laws, whereas in others they adopt general and vague laws that leave the bureaucrats with considerable discretion to fill in the policy details (Huber and Shipan 2002).

Although formal transposition is mostly unproblematic, it can sometimes still be a demanding task. This holds particularly true for federal states when the implementation of a new federal policy requires that the constituent units make adjustments to their respective policy arrangements (see Haider-Markel 1998; Huque and Watton 2010). Formal transposition can also be difficult when it is related to international agreements, such as the UN Convention on Climate Change, or supranational law. Formal transposition is particularly challenging in the context of the EU. In Chapter 3 we explained that the EU represents one of the few organizations that enacts supranational policies which must be transposed by its member states. Though we will discuss the EU's role in policy-making beyond national borders in detail in Chapter 10, here we want to point out that there is a sizable literature acknowledging that the transposition of EU policies by member states is marked by persistent deficits (see Knill and Lenschow 1998; Weale *et al.* 2000; Knill 2001, 2006; Falkner *et al.* 2005; Steunenberg and Toshkov 2009; Thomson 2009).

Practical application corresponds to the actual putting into practice of a policy. Depending on the content of a policy, practical application comprises different activities. It can refer to the provision of services defined by legislation, such as social benefits which are given to those entitled to them. Likewise, the actual provision of education, health care, infrastructure or equal opportunities for job applicants are the result of the practical application of corresponding public policies. However, this dimension is not the only aspect of practical application.

In most cases, the implementation of a policy entails that the policy addressees have to modify their behaviour in ways that it is fully in line with the obligations stemming from a public policy. An ideal outcome of practical application would be one in which organizations and individuals that are targeted by legislation voluntarily demonstrate the behaviour that conforms to the legislation in question, that is, that they comply with it. However, as non-compliance might occur, actions are required to enforce the policy.

There exists a wide range of non-coercive measures to achieve compliance. Governments can, for instance, make appeals to policy addressees to comply by underlining the respective policy's benefits. Likewise, implementers can provide information about a policy. More generally, it is the perception of the legitimacy of the policy by those it is addressed to that is crucial for compliance. Thus, as a rule, compliance is likely to be higher when non-compliance is widely perceived as socially unacceptable. In most cases, however, and especially when command-

and-control policies are employed, practical application involves monitoring and enforcement activities.

Monitoring is about surveillance, increased transparency and information gathering as to how well the target group actually complies with the requirements of a given public policy. This can be achieved in many different ways, for example by requesting compliance reports or carrying out announced or unannounced on-site inspections. Widespread monitoring activities are, for instance, speed controls on motorways or controls on drivers' blood alcohol concentration. If such activities reveal non-compliance, the next step is enforcement to ensure that the non-compliance stops and remedial action is taken. Enforcement powers available to implementers include prohibition notices, suspension of operational licences, injunctions and the carrying out of remedial works. For example, a driver exceeding road speed limits or being found to be driving while drunk may be punished by means of a fine or the temporary or even permanent loss of his or her driver's licence (see Table 7.1).

For effectively assessing implementation success, either of these two dimensions can be employed. As concerns the analytical insights, focusing on formal transposition is particularly promising for policies that are intersectoral and require collaborative efforts by many different organizations, and might yield interesting insights in federal states. As concerns practical application, the study of this dimension certainly gives a better understanding of the more substantive aspects of public policy that go beyond what is written in the law book, though it is more complex to assess due to the various types of activities related to it. Therefore, empirical studies will most likely generate major insights if

Table 7.1   *Criteria for measuring implementation success*

	Focus	Criteria
Formal transposition	Legal and administrative provisions for the transposition of requirements into the existing legal and administrative system	• Time frame • Completeness • Correct integration into the regulatory context
Practical application	Organizational and administrative structures and procedures	• Provision of policy-related services • Provision of non-coercive incentives for compliance • Monitoring and enforcement

they focus on specific aspects of practical application, that is, either on how well implementers provide a certain service or by which means they seek to induce the target population to change their behaviour.

Determinants of implementation success

We now turn to the most important factors that explain variation in implementation effectiveness, beginning with those factors that refer to the characteristics of policy outputs and then moving to institutional factors and the strategies for increasing their social acceptance.

Choice of policy instruments

An important theoretical debate centres on the question of whether the choice of policy instruments makes a difference regarding effective implementation (Mayntz 1979; Bressers and Klok 1988; Linder and Peters 1989; Howlett 1991; Knill and Lenschow 2000; May 2003). To illustrate this argument, we present the model of instrument preferences advanced by Howlett *et al.* (2009: 173–5). The assumption underlying the model is that certain policy instruments are better equipped than others to bring about the intended policy outcomes as they are easier to implement.

According to Howlett *et al.*, the appropriateness of the choice of policy instruments depends on two dimensions: the complexity of the policy environment, also known as the 'policy subsystem', and the capacity of the state to effect changes in the light of institutional constraints. Governments with a high capacity for facing complex policy environments are able to use directive instruments, including measures such as a government reorganization in order to create or modify policy subsystems. The next constellation refers to high-capacity governments faced with simple policy environments; these can achieve effective implementation by using authoritative instruments, involving the creation of specialized independent regulatory commissions or advisory committees, which help to cultivate ideas that favour compliance with public policy. In contrast, governments possessing a low capacity to cope with complex policy environments can rely on subsidy instruments such as grants or specific funding schemes to induce policy addressees to comply with the provisions of a policy. However, when low-capacity governments are confronted with simple policy environments they can use information instruments, such as campaigns or information disclosure, to induce compliance (see Table 7.2).

The logical consequence of this model is that implementation problems stem from the 'wrong' policy instruments being chosen by policymakers who are restricted by the ability of governments and the characteristics of the policy environment. From this it follows that a government that fails to evaluate correctly its capacity or the characteristics

Table 7.2   *Instrument choices in the light of capacity and subsystem characteristics*

		Complexity policy environment	
		High	**Low**
Capacity of the state	**High**	Directive instruments	Authoritative instruments
	Low	Subsidy instruments	Informative instruments

Source: Adapted from Howlett *et al.* (2009: 175).

of the policy subsystem is likely to experience problems in achieving compliance.

Precision and clarity of policy design

The second policy-related explanation for implementation problems concerns deficient policy formulation. Such problems of policy design can first of all be the result of vague and ambiguous policy objectives and requirements. For example, in 2004 the US State of Montana enacted a law to legalize medical marijuana, which is, however, defined so vaguely that it cannot be enforced (Hausen 2010).

Often, it is only on the basis of such imprecise formulations that the adoption of a policy is possible at all. High degrees of distributional conflict and politicization favour a negotiation context that is dominated by bargaining rather than problem solving, that is, the involved actors are primarily concerned with potential losses and gains than with analysing more thoroughly the extent to which there actually exists a sound causal relationship between policy objectives and the suggested policy instruments. As a result, distributional conflicts might lead to the formulation of ill-designed policies that are characterized by inaccurate assumptions about the causal relationship between policy problems and politically adopted remedies. This relationship between politics and the implementation process has already been acknowledged by Bardach (1977), who contended that conflicts that are not sufficiently resolved during the formulation stage bear a high risk of popping up again during the implementation process, where they possess far-reaching deficits (see also Winter 2003; Knill 2006).

The likelihood of deficient policy designs is not only affected by the degree of distributional conflicts characterizing a certain policy area. It also varies with the number of actors that are involved in the decision-making process. As was illustrated in Chapter 6, the greater the number of actors with veto potential and the more complex the overall decision-making structure, the higher is the probability for compromises based on open formulations and inconsistencies in policy design. An example is provided by the persistent deficits in implementing gender mainstreaming policies. In the Netherlands – a country typically ruled by multiparty coalition governments – vague formulations about the assignment of formal responsibility for gender mainstreaming at the local level have seriously hampered policy implementation. The formulation that gender equality should be integrated 'everywhere' entailed that many gender equality offices were closed because gender equality was regarded as 'the responsibility of everyone' (Verloo 2001: 8).

Control structures

Principal–agent theories constitute an important starting point for the explanation of implementation deficits. In these theories, it is assumed that implementation problems result from the differences between policy objectives and their actual implementation through the responsible administrative agencies. This difference is seen as an unavoidable consequence emerging from the configuration of modern political-administrative systems that are characterized by the delegation of competencies to subordinate administrative authorities. This delegation is of particular relevance with regard to the distinction between the tasks of policy formulation (usually taking place within central ministries) and the implementation of these policies (often delegated to agencies at the subnational or local level) (Howlett *et al.* 2009: 160–3).

Delegation entails the problem of bureaucratic drift, a problem that is inherent to the configuration of political-administrative systems, which is further aggravated by two factors. On the one hand, high organizational complexity might increase the number of agents and government levels that are involved in the implementation process and hence increase the potential for bureaucratic drift. Schnapp (2000) shows that bureaucratic drift is likely in countries with coalition governments that have a high number of coalition parties, namely Finland, Switzerland, Belgium and Japan. By contrast, it seems less likely in Spain, Canada, New Zealand, Greece and the United Kingdom since their governments are normally composed of one party only. The occurrence of bureaucratic drifts during implementation in governments consisting of several parties is hypothesized to be more likely since one of the coalition partners that could not realize its preferences during policy formulation might be willing to accept policy change if it knows it can attempt to modify policy outcomes during the implementation phase (Hammond and Knott 1996). On the other hand, a high degree of scientific or technological complexity of the underlying policy problem will increase the chances of different interpretations of policy objectives by principals and agents. The more specialized knowledge is needed to implement a public policy, the more likely is the implementer to possess an information advantage vis-à-vis policymakers, which facilitates deviations from the original policy guidelines.

There are two ways in which politicians can control the bureaucracy and the way it implements public policy. The first form is formal oversight, in which the parliament directly monitors agency behaviour to gain the information it needs to correct undesirable behaviour (see Aberbach 1990). This principally takes place by means of committee hearings and investigations (see Meier 2000). In the United States and United Kingdom, for instance, members of Congress or Parliament are frequently involved in 'casework', which concerns the handling of problems that occurred to citizens during the stage of policy implementation. Such cases typically involve delays in the provision of different kinds of social benefits or an unsatisfactory provision of certain services and/or infrastructure. Congressmen and Members of Parliament devote their resources to this casework since, in this way, they can demonstrate their responsiveness to the needs and problems of their electorate, which is expected to increase their chances for re-election (Anderson 2010: 219).

The second form is statutory control, in which the executive or the legislature designs the agency's structure and processes to favour some policies over others. While oversight occurs after the bureaucratic actors have implemented a policy, statutory controls are established before they act (Bawn 1997: 102). There are two forms of statutory controls: those designed around 'fire alarms' and those around 'stacked decks'. 'Fire alarms' are defined as a system in which the parliament establishes rules and informal practices that enable individual citizens and interest groups to examine administrative decisions and to 'raise the alarm' should they disagree strongly with specific decisions (McCubbins and Schwartz 1984: 427). Alternatively, legislation that delegates policy decisions to an agency may specify in great detail how the agency decisions are to be made. McCubbins *et al.* (1987) argued that these issues of agency structure and process can be designed strategically by legislators to 'stack the deck' in favour of groups that the legislators want to help. Additionally, courts can play an important role in ensuring that administrative agencies do not exploit their implementation powers.

So far, we have only concentrated on ways of controlling administrative agencies. However, Newton and van Deth (2010: 124–5) point out additional possibilities for reducing the risk of a bureaucratic drift. Firstly, politicians can appoint bureaucrats on the grounds of political considerations such as their ideological proximity to the party or parties to which the government and/or the parliamentary majority belong. Secondly, the potential of bureaucratic drift could be reduced by training bureaucrats in a manner that develops a professional ethos of public service. Thirdly, financial controls could be used as one form of oversight. Fourthly, an increasing share of open government might help to reduce delegation problems. The authors suggest the employment of 'sunshine laws', that is, a type of law that requires administrative agen-

---

Box 7.1 Delivery units for improving implementation

Imperfect policy implementation is widespread and therefore governments around the world are continuously looking for instruments to improve the process. Several governments (e.g. Australia, India, Indonesia, Malaysia and South Africa) have recently established delivery units at the centre of government to drive implementation improvements. The first such organization charged with optimizing implementation, and arguably the model for the more recent delivery units, is the United Kingdom prime minister's Delivery Unit, which was established by Tony Blair in 2001 and existed until October 2010. This unit monitored and reported on progress in relation to the prime minister's top delivery and reform priorities in the areas of climate change, education, health, fighting of crime, social exclusion and transport policy. Now that this Delivery Unit has been abolished, it will be interesting to see whether those countries that mimicked the United Kingdom in creating similar organizations will also follow its example and end them too in the near future.

---

cies to do their work in public through open meetings. Finally, maladministration might be reduced through the presence of ombudsmen.

It should be noted that most of the points mentioned above include assumptions about the behaviour of bureaucrats that correspond more to Niskanen than to Weber. Following Weber, bureaucrats should be guided by their professional ethos and thus behave in ways that serve their political masters. In contrast, the view purported by Niskanen stresses the self-interests of bureaucrats and their objective of maximizing them. However, the second suggestion by Newton and van Deth essentially approximates to the Weberian ideal of a bureaucrat.

Institutional Design

Except for very rare cases where policies to some extent are 'self-implementing', i.e. the declaration of policy requires no further actions to bring about the desired policy outcomes, the implementation of policies generally requires institutional structures and arrangements (O'Toole 2003: 234). In other words, policies generally have institutional implications, i.e. requirements for the establishment of appropriate structures and procedures for their proper implementation. A distinction can be made between policies that can be implemented by single organizations or authorities (Torenvlied 1996), and measures whose proper implementation entails horizontal and vertical coordination across several administrative units and levels (Hjern and Porter 1981). It is obvious that in the latter case much greater challenges to effective implementation exist than in the case of an integrated implementation structure: 'between or among organizations, the differing routines and specialized languages, not to mention distinct ways of seeing the world, mean that interorganizational implementation poses particularly daunting challenges' (O'Toole 2003: 235).

These challenges are based on the fact that the implementation of a policy in this way requires major changes in existing institutional structures. This aspect is of empirical importance with regard to implementation in federal polities. For example, Canada possesses one of the most decentralized frameworks for environmental policy implementation in the world. The provinces have supremacy over most environmental matters and are relatively free to set their own standards and carry out implementation activities (Huque and Watton 2010: 77–8). As a consequence of the well-developed competences of the provinces and the difficulties in achieving institutional cooperation across the different levels of government, the federal government has faced problems in the nationwide implementation of environmental policy. Therefore, this policy implementation is mainly carried out by the provinces, with federal policy only defining 'soft' environmental measures that can be implemented without coordination efforts.

The central argument here is that it is less the choice of the instrument per se that affects the implementation success of policies than the extent of necessary institutional modifications that arise from public policy (see Knill and Lenschow 1998; Knill 2001). This institutional perspective rests on two central assumptions: first, effective implementation is generally a question of effective institutional adaptation; second, the extent of institutional change is limited by existing institutional arrangements.

Although policies are generally directed at the specification of policy contents and instruments rather than institutional arrangements, there is often a tight linkage between policy content and the corresponding requirements of institutional implementation. Therefore, decisions on instruments to a certain extent always entail decisions on the corresponding institutional arrangements for their proper application. Consequently, implementation problems can be conceived of as problems of institutional change (Knill and Lenschow 1998).

The role of institutions has long been acknowledged in the literature on implementation. However, institutions were initially analysed mainly from the perspective of adequate institutional design. Analysts coming from the top-down perspective developed optimal structural and organizational arrangements that would permit effective implementation of a certain policy (see Pressmann and Wildavsky 1973). This reasoning relies on the implicit assumption that existing institutions would easily adapt to the suggested 'model' structure. Problems of institutional change were ignored. The bottom-up perspective assumes a similar malleability of existing institutional factors. Here, analysts are interested in the impact of varying institutional designs on the skills, resources and capacities of relevant actors. They are interested in the perfect design that serves to equip the implementing authorities with sufficient financial, legal and personal resources.

Without denying the importance of adequate institutional design, such a perspective remains incomplete as long as it ignores the problems associated with the process of adjusting the existing institutional arrangements to the defined 'ideal' arrangements. This latter aspect in particular, and to a lesser extent the gaps in the knowledge about appropriate institutional design, makes the implementation of public policies problematic.

This leads us to the second basic assumption of the institutionalist perspective: effective institutional adaptation to external requirements can only be expected within certain limits. It is one of the few generally accepted findings in the otherwise diverse research literature that institutional change, regardless of whether it is required explicitly or implicitly, rarely takes place in a smooth and unproblematic way. Existing institutions 'matter' and they do so mainly by constraining the options for future change and adaptations (see pp. 78–82).

An emphasis on institutional stability and continuity is, however, not synonymous with an entirely static understanding of institutional development. Rather institutions often find themselves in a permanent process of adaptation to their environment. However, the scope of these adaptations is restricted by the structuring effects of existing institutional arrangements. Institutional change is hence often limited to aspects that do not question the 'identity' of an institution (March and Olsen 1989; Thelen and Steinmo 1992).

This abstract argument is of limited explanatory value so long as we do not have any criteria to judge which particular institutional requirements stemming from public policy are likely to exceed the adaptation capacity of existing institutions and when they are not. To cope with this problem, Knill and Lenschow (1998) suggest a distinction between three levels of adaptation pressure, each of them linked to different expectations with regard to implementation effectiveness. This distinction is based on the understanding that institutionally grown structures and routines prevent easy modification of institutional arrangements (March and Olsen 1989; DiMaggio and Powell 1991). Hence, institutional adaptation appears to be more likely in cases where new policies imply incremental rather than fundamental departures from existing arrangements.

The first scenario refers to constellations where there is low pressure for institutional adaptation. In this case, the institutional implications of new policies are completely in line with existing arrangements, i.e. none or only marginal changes are demanded. Implementation is therefore expected to be relatively unproblematic, as adjustment requirements are very limited or completely absent. In the second scenario of high adaptation pressure, new requirements exceed the adjustment capacities of

existing institutions. Ineffective implementation is the probable consequence. Such constellations can be expected, for instance, when new
requirements contradict the strongly entrenched institutional elements of
policy arrangements. In this regard, Krasner (1988) differentiates between
two dimensions of institutional anchorage: 'institutional depth', which
refers to the extent to which institutional arrangements are embedded in
normative orientations and dominant belief systems; and 'institutional
breadth', which refers to the extent to which institutional arrangements
are interlinked with their environment.

   The third scenario of moderate adaptation pressure refers to constellations in which new policies require substantive adjustments of existing
institutions, though without challenging well-entrenched core patterns
within the political, legal and administrative system. While in such cases
there is a higher probability of an effective implementation of policies, it
cannot be taken for granted. In contrast with the two other scenarios, an
institutional perspective is insufficient to develop hypotheses on
expected implementation performance (in terms of institutional adjustments to new requirements). To answer this question we have to complement our analysis with a second explanatory step which considers the
particular interest constellation and institutional opportunity structures.
To what extent is there sufficient public support for adjusting to new
requirements? To what extent have actors who support regulatory change
sufficient powers and resources to realize their interests? As Figure 7.1
shows, institutional adaptation and hence effective implementation can
only be expected if they are facilitated by favourable contexts (Knill and
Lenschow 1998; Knill and Lehmkuhl 2002a).

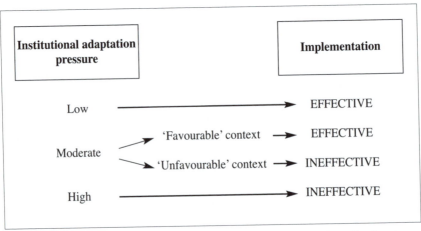

Figure 7.1   *Institutional adaptation pressure and implementation effectiveness*

Source: Knill and Lehmkuhl (2002a).

Box 7.2   Implementation of Mexican environmental policy

Mexico has emulated various environmental protection standards of the United States. This transfer of policies was primarily motivated by the country's wish to become a member of the North American Free Trade Agreement (NAFTA). To avoid criticism from the US public concerning environmental issues, the Mexican government displayed notable efforts to bring its legislation in line with that of its northern neighbour. Despite legal reforms, environmental degradation is still occurring in Mexico due to insufficient policy implementation. Of course, there are many reasons why the authorities face such implementation problems. One of the main reasons is that the transfer of US environmental protection standards turned out to be the wrong choice as they are technically too demanding for the country. This point is best illustrated by Mexican wastewater standards, which were originally sector-specific as is the case in the United States. However, since it became clear that the Mexican authorities lack the necessary institutional infrastructure for monitoring such a sophisticated regulatory approach, wastewater standards have been modified in a manner to make them 'implementable' (Knill *et al.* 2008a). This entailed the abolition of the ambitious initial standards and the establishment of a new regulatory system that does not differentiate between industry sectors. The modification of the regulatory approach reduced the extent of non-compliance, but the overall state of compliance is still far from perfect.

Administrative capacities

While the factors discussed so far are particularly focused on the willingness of actors to achieve effective implementation, the focus on administrative capacities entails a different perspective that is concerned with the ability rather than willingness to comply with given policy requirements. In other words: varying implementation effectiveness can also be explained by different capacities, which affect the opportunities available for effective formal and practical implementation. As already mentioned, implementation is generally carried out by a designated government agency that has responsibility for the new policy measure. Theoretically the responsible agency should be equipped with the necessary resources to ensure that the policy is carried out as intended, though in reality this does not always occur. For successful implementation, the entity concerned must possess sufficient resources to be able to translate the policy objectives into an operational framework. Particular emphasis is placed on human capacity (administrative and technical expertise) as well as financial, technical and organizational resources (see Gerston 2004: 103). The less developed these capacities, the more important becomes the allocation of existing resources in the light of political priorities.

Box 7.3   Alcohol control in Russia

Consumption of alcoholic beverages has been one of the most significant public health problems in Russia for many decades. For a long time, the government tried to conceal the severity of these problems and the mortality related to alcohol consumption. Prior attempts to control its consumption have been unsuccessful, in part due to the government's reliance on alcohol revenue and its inability to implement creative and manageable solutions. In this context, Levintova (2007) examines the implementation of the 2005 federal alcohol control law in the Russian Federation. She finds that poor organizational capacities prior to implementation have been a major impediment to its realization. Specifically, as of 1 January 2006, excise stamps for imported products were to be affixed on alcoholic beverages. However, in mid-January the Russian government issued a six-month extension in response to a serious shortage of excise stamps. Even though this extension allowed for the printing of additional stamps, most alcohol quickly disappeared from store shelves, with many consumers turning to illicit sources. Consequently, in autumn 2006 almost 200 Russians died and thousands were hospitalized due to alcohol induced poisoning, reportedly from drinking alcohol tainted with industrial spirits. More generally, models of alcohol control often advocated by 'Western' policy consultants ignore the preponderance of home-made alcohol. Under such circumstances, taxing alcohol will most likely have little impact – and may even be counter-productive.

Social acceptance

As already outlined above, the main purpose of policy implementation is to modify the behaviour of policy addressees. While there are many policy-specific and institutional factors that might hamper this goal, it is ultimately the social acceptance of public policy that matters for successful implementation. There are certainly some policy measures that are welcomed by policy addressees, such as increases in social benefit levels. By the same token, there is legislation that is less well received either because it imposes costs on the target group or because its implications are not well understood. In such cases, implementers might approach interest groups to seek their support actively for the policy measure in question (Anderson 2010: 227). Interest groups can communicate the exact content of the law to their members and convince them of the advantages it entails.

However, the involvement of interest groups in policy implementation is an ambivalent strategy. On the one hand, there have been cases in which policies failed because of a lack of interest group support. In 2011, the German government introduced E10 gasoline (which is produced with up to 10 per cent ethanol content) as one of several measures for replacing fossil fuels with renewable energy. German consumers have refused to purchase this product with the result that gas stations are sitting on ample reserves of it while the non-ethanol gasoline is in short supply. Among the various arguments advanced for explaining the broad rejection of E10 gasoline, one is that the government failed to ensure the support of the German Automobile Club, which is very influential in forming its members' preferences on traffic-related policy. On the other hand, interest groups can be inclined to demand 'corrections' to public policy at the implementation stage in exchange for their support.

Even though there is this ambivalence about interest group participation in policy implementation, there are situations where decision-makers have no choice but to include them. Particularly controversial policy issues that seem unlikely to be accepted by the public are likely to require broad support by interest groups and other private actors such as social movements (see Haider-Markel 2001).

Key points

❑ When measuring implementation effectiveness, it is useful to distinguish between formal transposition and practical application.

❑ Formal transposition is about taking the necessary steps with regard to the accommodation of a policy into the legal and administrative system to make it 'implementable'.

❑ Practical application refers to what is usually conceived of as policy implementation. It involves the provision of services on the one hand and monitoring and enforcement activities on the other.

❑ There are six principal factors affecting implementation effectiveness: choice of policy instruments, policy design, control structure, institutional design, administrative capacity and social acceptance.

Conclusions

Once the government has taken a decision on a public policy, the stipulations of that policy must be put into action to bring about the behavioural changes intended by the policy-makers. Therefore, unless the stipulations of a given policy are actually implemented, the problem originally initiating the policy process will persist. At first glance, implementation appears as an automatic continuation of the policy-making process. Yet there often exists a substantial gap between the passage of new legislation and its application, which is addressed by implementation research. The bureaucracy is delegated a significant degree of power during the implementation stage of the policy process because of its discretion in interpreting the actual intent, method and scope of a policy decision. During implementation, administrative agencies by no means always follow unrestrictedly political guidelines and, even if they do so, in some cases results deviate remarkably from political expectations. The role of bureaucracy during implementation reveals a contradictory picture of great interest. On the one hand, bureaucracies are essential for making policies work; but, on the other hand, senior bureaucrats are often more experienced and better trained than their political masters, which paves the way for bureaucratic drift.

Previous considerations have made clear that both the formal transposition and practical application of a policy in general are based on complex processes. These can be analysed from different perspectives (top-down versus bottom-up) and by shedding light on various factors that are expected to affect implementation effectiveness. The implementation stage of the policy process is by definition an operational phase where policy is actually translated into action with the desire to solve some public problem. We have identified six key challenges which we believe can routinely impede the effective implementation of public policy. In this context, the question of whether and under what conditions the implementation of policies can be characterized as effective or ineffective cannot be answered in terms of a single cause, but needs to take into account different aspects.

Web links

www.inece.org. This is the website of the International Network for Environmental Compliance and Enforcement. It is a valuable source of information about the implementation of environmental policy.

www.eif.oeaw.ac.at/compliance. This database provides an overview of qualitative academic research on the application and transposition of EU law in the member states.

www.eif.oeaw.ac.at/implementation. This website complements the previous one by providing an overview of quantitative academic research on the application and transposition of EU law in the member states.

www.healthpolicyinitiative.com/policyimplementation. This is a useful tool for training people in how to interview policy-makers about influences on health policy implementation.

www.apsc.gov.au/publications09/devolvedgovernment.htm. Here a link is given to an electronic book that gives an overview of challenges regarding policy implementation through the federal government in Australia.

Further reading

Bardach, E. (1977) *The Implementation Game: What Happens After a Bill Becomes a Law*. Boston: MIT Press. A classic book about the complex process of policy implementation.

Dyer, C. (2001) *Operation Blackboard: Policy Implementation in Indian Elementary Education*. Oxford: Symposium Books. This book examines the failure to establish a minimum norm of essential facilities for primary schools in India.

Falkner, G., O. Treib, M. Hartlapp and S. Leiber (2005) *Complying with Europe: EU Harmonisation and Soft Law in the Member States*. Cambridge: Cambridge University Press. This book provides one of the few accounts of the implementation of EU policies beyond formal transposition.

Hill, M. and P. Hupe (2009) *Implementing Public Policy: An Introduction to the Study of Operational Governance*. Thousand Oaks, CA: Sage. This book is a very comprehensive treatise on all aspects related to policy implementation.

Lipsky, M. (1980) *Street-level Bureaucracy*. New York: Russell Sage Foundation. This is another classic book that we recommend for further reading.

Pressman, J. and A. Wildavsky (1973) *Implementation*. Berkeley, CA: University of California Press. An influential book with respect to policy implementation that is helpful in understanding how implementation actually works.

Chapter 8

Evaluation

Reader's guide

Policy-making does not end with the passage and implementation of legislation. Several questions emerge afterwards. Has the policy attained its objectives? What are its unintended effects? Is the failure to meet the policy goals related to the design of the public policy or its implementation? Policy evaluation tackles these and related questions about expected and unexpected policy outcomes and impacts. By definition, evaluation studies make judgements about the quality of public policies, which implies that negative findings can, in principle, reinitiate the policy-making process with the objective of improving existing policy arrangements. While this definition might give the impression that evaluation studies are only carried out by experts who possess the required knowledge and techniques for making such judgements, many actors are in fact involved in the process. The large number of potential stakeholders at this policy stage results from the fact that there is a 'political' component to policy evaluation, meaning that statements about the success and failure of a given public policy are likely to be used for generating positive or negative images of those in power. Therefore, to understand fully policy-making the evaluation stage cannot be left out. To illustrate the central topics, we will first give an overview of the different types and methods of policy evaluation, before moving on to the role that theories play in this process. This is followed by a discussion of the political characteristics of policy evaluation and the role of 'evidence' in policy-making.

Policy evaluation is about comparing the intended and actual effects of public policies and can refer to insights regarding policy outcomes and/or impacts. Generally speaking, two types of evaluation can be distinguished: formative and summative (Scriven 1967). Formative evaluation has the purpose of improving a certain policy measure – also known as 'a programme' – by providing advice to implementing actors and other stakeholders. This evaluation type is useful for fostering internal development and improvement. Summative evaluation takes place at the end of policy implementation and assesses whether the policy has attained the intended objectives. It represents an external assessment intended for policy-makers who are involved in overseeing the programme and who may utilize the findings to make decisions about its continuation. The literature also distinguishes between outcome evaluation and impact evaluation. These concepts have nothing to do with policy outcomes or impacts. Impact evaluation concerns the establishing of a causal link between the policy and its effects, which can be either policy outcomes or impacts. Outcome evaluation, by contrast, is simply the assessing of the effects of a policy but without firmly linking them to its output.

Put this way, it becomes clear that policy evaluation is essentially about generating information, which can then be used for many different purposes, such as improving public policy, supporting the views of proponents or critics, or responding to political pressure. It is possible or even desirable that a new policy cycle will begin if the overall verdict is that the evaluated public policy does not meet its objectives. While evaluation is a useful and even necessary device of policy-making in modern states, it is seldom a straightforward task. Some of the factors that can complicate evaluation activities include:

- the identification of policy goals
- the appropriate definition and measurement of performance indicators
- the isolation of a policy's effects from other factors
- the political context

The first three challenges can be resolved by a carefully developed research design, which concerns making decisions regarding the structure and strategy of investigation, which provides the framework for the generation and analysis of data (Burnham *et al.* 2008: 39; see also King *et al.* 1994). In contrast, the fourth issue, about the political context in which evaluation takes place, cannot be fully controlled. Although evaluation research attempts to assess a policy in the most objective manner, these activities occur in a political environment, meaning that policy-makers might be interested in emphasizing those findings that help to portray them in a positive light.

Besides the potential threat of instrumentalization, there are also practical constraints stemming from the political context. As such, policymakers often want immediate information on policy effects, though many public policies have long-term effects that will not be known in the short term, forcing researchers to project effects rather than actually measuring them. Accordingly, 'all public policy evaluations ... are projects in both *political* science and political *science*' (King *et al.* 2007: 480). In this chapter, we provide an introduction that highlights the scientific and political characteristics of policy evaluation.

Types and methods of evaluation

As already hinted above, policy evaluation can be conducted in many ways and for different purposes. So we will now outline the main types of evaluation and provide some background knowledge regarding the methodologies that can be used to assess the effects of public policies.

Types of evaluation

Actors involved in evaluation are diverse, ranging from researchers, consulting firms, think tanks and NGOs to courts, political bodies (such as parliamentary commissions) and the executive. The diversity of actors that might participate in or conduct policy evaluation reflects the different types of evaluation.

Administrative evaluation
Administrative evaluation is usually carried out within government bodies and examines the delivery of government services. It is performed by specialist agencies; financial, legal and political overseers; or private consultants. The main objective of administrative evaluation is to ensure that public policies attain their goals at the least possible cost and least burden on the policy addressees (Howlett *et al.* 2009: 185). Administrative evaluation not only emphasizes the effectiveness of public policy but also its efficiency, that is, whether the best possible effect is achieved by the lowest possible use of resources. It also involves scrutiny of individuals and corporations in terms of their compliance with legislation (Hessing *et al.* 2005: 249). This makes it clear that there is a direct connection between policy implementation and evaluation.

There exist many different techniques for administrative evaluation, including: process, effort, efficiency and effectiveness evaluation (Howlett *et al.* 2009: 186). Process evaluation is about exploring possibilities for making operating procedures more efficient. Effort evaluation assesses the amount of effort governments put into attaining their policy objectives (e.g. in terms of budgets or personnel resources). Efficiency evaluation is about a public policy's costs and the ways of accomplishing the same goals at lower costs. Effectiveness evaluation compares the intended goals of a policy or programme with the ones actually achieved. These four forms have recently been complemented by performance indicators and benchmarks that are designed to allow public-sector efforts to be compared. In a comparative study, Pollitt (2006) showed that British administrations could push such performance indicators faster and further than in other European countries, due to the characteristics of their political system and their more individualistic and risk-accepting administrative culture.

While administrative evaluation is predominantly concerned with the *ex post* assessment of the delivery of government services, there also exist *ex ante* techniques, known as policy appraisal, that seek to inform decision-makers by predicting the effects of policy proposals (see Turnpenny *et al.* 2008, 2009). The most widely used form of policy appraisal is regulatory impact analysis, which includes various methods to assess ex ante the impact of proposed regulatory policies on target populations. The aim of this administrative procedure is to increase the empirical basis of political decisions and to make the regulatory process more transparent and to increase accountability (Radaelli 2004: 723). Thus, regulatory impact analysis is directly related to the stage of problem definition with the objective of enhancing the quality of regulation, that is, of achieving 'better regulation'. The OECD and its 1997 guidelines on regulatory impact assessment played a central role in the international diffusion of this evaluation technique (Radaelli 2009: 31–2) and today it is in place in most of its member countries (Sager and Rissi 2011: 151).

Judicial evaluation

Judicial evaluation is clearly different from administrative evaluation as it is principally concerned with legal issues relating to the way in which policies are developed and implemented. Depending on the political system, judicial evaluation is either initiated by the judiciary or when requested by individuals or organizations presenting a legal complaint against any given policy measure. In the most extreme case, a judicial evaluation can declare a policy (or rather the legal act on which it is based) as unconstitutional and ask the legislature to develop modifications to it (see pp. 114–15). Thus, judicial evaluation represents one of the few means by which private actors can challenge the activities of public actors. Moreover, public actors can utilize judicial evaluation as a means for achieving compliance with public policy (Hessing 2005: 197).

In the United States, especially, the courts also evaluate whether a programme adopted by the government is in compliance with the intent of the law in question. Thus, in some polities 'judicial evaluations may move from the determination of the scope of government authority to the determination of whether such authority was used appropriately in a given situation' (Adolino and Blake 2011: 26). In this context, Howlett *et al.* (2009: 189) point out that in parliamentary systems, judicial evaluation focuses on whether or not courts, tribunals or government agencies have acted within their powers, indicating that the evaluation is mostly confined to procedural issues. In political systems with a constitutionally entrenched division of powers, such as the United States, judicial evaluation concentrates more directly on legislative and executive actions per se.

Political evaluation
Howlett *et al.* (2009: 189–91) identify political evaluation as a third category, in addition to administrative and judicial evaluation. This is based on a rather unsystematic and technically not very sophisticated way of gathering and interpreting information about public policies. Thus, strictly speaking, political evaluation is not an evaluation activity in the classical sense but rather a tool for framing public policy in a positive or negative way (see Fischer 1995, 2003). The purpose of this kind of political evaluation is strongly related to aspects of party competition. Political parties who had supported the adoption of a certain public policy have a strong interest in declaring it a success, while opposing parties will strive to draw a negative picture. However, political evaluation is not confined to political parties. Many other actors participating in policy-making, such as think tanks or interest groups, can use it for their purposes. This way, there is a certain risk that evaluations are used as political instruments rather than for measuring policy effects. We will return to this aspect of policy evaluation and discuss it in more detail later in this chapter.

Scientific evaluation
Policy evaluation can also constitute a social scientific activity which aims to provide neutral answers to the question of whether a given public policy is effective or not. This entails that scientific evaluation is conducted by social scientists in accordance with certain minimum research standards (see King *et al.* 1994). As a consequence, it can only be carried out by experts who are trained in a specific way and are familiar with the required research techniques. While it is, in principle, possible to base policy decisions on scientific evaluation, this is often hampered by practical considerations (see Rossi *et al.* 2004: 23–6).

A systematic scientific evaluation requires resources that are often not available to policy-makers. Most importantly, it requires time and, especially in situations where the findings are to be used for the formulation of public policy, is difficult to provide. Time can also be an issue for summative evaluation, since the time frame of policy-makers is limited by election periods and the fact that they want their policy successes to be backed by evidence before elections. However, in order to make valid statements about policy outcomes and/or impacts, an observation period of a certain length is needed. Unless this is granted, scientific evaluation cannot produce an accurate assessment of policy effects.

More generally, scientific evaluation is part of evaluation research, which represents a distinct discipline in social science. This body of research aims to discuss methodological issues related to the assessment of policy success, the establishment of causality, and techniques of analysis. There has been a lively debate in evaluation research concerning how to integrate theoretical considerations and improve theory construction. Although such considerations about the practice of policy evaluation also form part of the scientific debate, it is clear that evaluation research is only loosely related to the political process that produces public policies, which distinguishes it from the previous three evaluation types. However, we want to stress that there have been instances in which scientific evaluation research has informed subsequent policy-making. The negative income tax experiments that were conducted in the 1960s and 1970s in the United States, for instance, informed later welfare policies by projecting how elastic labour supply would be for varying amounts of welfare guarantees.

Evaluation methods

Evaluation studies can concentrate on the effectiveness of a policy and assess whether it ameliorates a given social problem. Evaluation studies can also assess the efficiency of a policy: that is, whether the minimal resources have been used. This difference between effectiveness and efficiency is reflected in different types of evaluations: (quasi-)experimental, qualitative, economic and performance. Economic evaluations and performance measurements are mostly employed for administrative evaluation and address efficiency concerns, although the latter can also be useful for evaluating effectiveness. (Quasi-)experimental and qualitative methods are predominantly utilized for the purpose of scientific evaluation and are mainly interested in the effectiveness of a policy.

Experimental models
Experimental models are strongly connected with social science methods as they prioritize the accuracy and objectivity of the information generated. Social experiments essentially assess the effectiveness of a policy by testing whether it has led to changes in the outcomes and/or impacts that

it was designed to bring about. Social experiments tackle this basic question by providing potentially unbiased estimates of the policy's effects. That is, they attempt to produce an estimate of effects that is entirely attributable to the policy itself, rather than other factors. In other words, experimental evaluation studies are concerned with exploring causality, that is, an association between a cause and an effect (see Brady 2010).

The simplest of all experimental designs is the two-group post-test randomized experiment. One group is affected by a given policy (experimental group) and the other group (comparison group) is not. The members of the two groups are assigned randomly. The two groups are then measured after the experimental group was affected. Randomization provides measures which, if the experiment is properly designed and its control requirements adhered to, provide strong evidence of policy outcomes and/or impacts, independent of confounding factors.

Although experimental designs are often regarded as the scientifically most rigorous standard, several factors can impede their application, e.g. considerations about ethical issues, costs or practicability. As a result, quasi-experimental designs are more frequently used in evaluation research than experimental ones. They correspond to an experiment in which one has little or no control over the allocation of a specific programme. Hence, the key difference is that a quasi-experimental design lacks random assignment: the logic of comparison is based on non-equivalent groups that potentially differ from each other in many ways other than the presence of the programme whose effect is being evaluated (Cook and Campbell 1979: 6).

The most frequently applied quasi-experimental strategy is the non-equivalent comparison group design. The designation 'non-equivalent' means that the comparison group can be selected in any number of ways, with the exception that access to the policy cannot be determined through random allocation. Data is gathered for the characteristics of the groups before they are affected by a given policy (pre-test data) and after (post-test data). Pre- and post-test data are collected for the comparison and experimental groups at the same time. If the experimental group turns out to display altered characteristics in the post-test data which are absent in the comparison group, it would be reasonable to conclude that the policy being evaluated did indeed have an effect (Rubin and Babbie 2009: 164–5; see Figure 8.1).

Experimental and quasi-experimental evaluation studies often gather empirical information by surveying a large number of respondents. They tend to employ quantitative methods for analysing the data. Quantitative research refers to the systematic empirical investigation of quantitative properties and their relationships (for an overview, see Oakshott 2009). The process of measurement is central to quantitative research because it provides the fundamental connection between empirical observation and

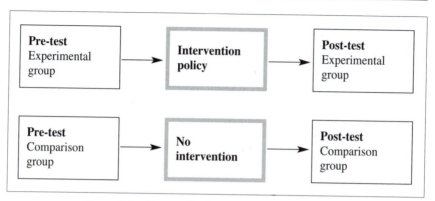

Figure 8.1 *Non-equivalent comparison group design*

theory. However, designing a quantitative study may be more demanding than the executing of it. Once data are collected, it may be difficult to correct for problems of poor model specification and low data quality (Sprinz 1999). Therefore, sources of uncertainty and selection bias should be minimized during the early stages of analysis. From this it follows that the preparation of experimental and quasi-experimental evaluation studies requires a certain time frame.

To assess the scientific value of (quasi-)experimental approaches, there are four criteria. The first one is internal validity, which concerns whether the research design allows for attributing observed changes to the public policy being evaluated, i.e. the cause, and not to other possible causes. The second criterion is construct validity, which can be regarded as a 'labelling' issue. If an experiment seeks to assess, let us say, fertility decisions, is this really what it measures? The third criterion, external validity, is about generalizing the evaluation findings across populations of persons, settings and time. The guiding question is whether the same results might be received if, for example, the experimental and control groups had different characteristics or were composed in different ways. The fourth is conclusion validity, which refers to the degree to which conclusions reached about causal relationships in the data are reasonable (see Shadish *et al.* 2001).

Qualitative evaluation
Evaluators can also employ qualitative methods for assessing the effects of a public policy. These are best at taking a peek at 'why' or 'how' some policy might have produced the outcomes it has. Qualitative evaluations emphasize the importance of observation, the need to retain the complexity of the evaluation context, and the value of subjective human interpretation in the evaluation process. Qualitative approaches, such as semi-structured or unstructured interviews and focus group discussions,

> ## Box 8.1   Welfare reform and fertility decisions
>
> In 1992, the US State of New Jersey adopted a policy known as the Family Cap that denies additional cash benefits to any child born ten or more months after a woman receives welfare benefits while still on the welfare rolls. This entails a benefit loss of $102 a month for the second-born child and $64 a month for any subsequent births. Jagannathan *et al.* (2010) evaluated the impact of these monetary penalties on the fertility decisions of poor women. They used data from a classical experimental design with 8,393 female welfare recipients in New Jersey, randomly assigned to experimental and control groups, based on the last four digits of the welfare payee's social security number. This resulted in an experimental group which consisted of 5,501 individuals and a control group of 2,892. While women receiving welfare benefits were found to be less likely to give birth to additional children, the monetary penalties were only decisive for a very small percentage of these cases, especially accounting for the fertility behaviour of short-term African American recipients. The authors concluded that social rather than economic factors arising from the new policy were responsible for the changes in fertility behaviour. Since the initiation of Family Cap, women in New Jersey on welfare rolls have been constantly under pressure to 'do the right thing', which is most likely the reason for a decrease in birth probability.

are more open-ended than quantitative methods and are most valuable for collecting and analysing data that do not readily reduce to numbers. They are particularly useful for exploratory research as they tend to build from these experiences upwards, seeking patterns but keeping an open stance towards the new or unexpected. To establish a causal link between policy outputs and outcomes and/or impact, they should be combined with (quasi-)experimental methods.

The qualitative approach starts with data gathering which is based on many different techniques, such as: narratives; direct and indirect (unobtrusive) observations; interactions between stakeholders and the evaluator; documentary evidence; and other sources of information. The approach then constructs an understanding of the programme. In this context, qualitative evaluations pursue a holistic approach in as much as they take into account different points of view on the policy measure in question and its effects on all the stakeholders. Thus, an evaluation is not just realized from the implementing actor's perspective, but also takes into account the affected population's viewpoints (McDavid and Hawthorn 2006: 176).

The data is subsequently analysed through in-depth studies, which may rely on counterfactual arguments for contrasting the actual outcomes with the expected ones. To be sure, analysing qualitative data can be a challenging task. For example, qualitative evaluators pay attention to actual words people have used during the interviews, which can result in considerable complexity and make it difficult to summarize and present findings. At the same time, however, they provide an ideal tool for learning about the performance of a policy when data collection capacities are limited.

Economic evaluation

Economic evaluations involve the identification, measurement, valuation and then comparison of the costs (inputs) and benefits (outcomes/impacts) of two or more alternative policies. The costs and consequences of alternative interventions or scenarios are compared to find the best use of scarce resources, thus focusing on the efficiency of a policy. It is predominantly used for administrative evaluations. They differ according to their scope and intent. They can have a very narrow focus, in which evaluators are only concerned about the resource consequences for the implementing agency (for instance, in the case of child benefits, for the ministry for family affairs or its equivalent). In these evaluations, a new intervention which shifts costs to another agency may be preferred. Alternatively, economic evaluations can examine wider social costs. In these evaluations, a new intervention that shifts relative costs but does not reduce total costs may not be desirable.

A country that has adopted economic evaluation as a formal tool for guiding the design of health policies is South Korea. In 2001, it used economic evaluations for decisions on pricing and the extent of health insurance coverage of new medical technologies, encompassing pharmaceuticals, equipment and diagnostic technology, that were necessary within the context of amending the act on national health insurance (Yang *et al.* 2008: 183). The number of Asian countries preparing for the adoption of economic evaluation for making health policy is rising: China, Taiwan and Thailand have already elaborated their own guidelines in this policy area (Yothasamut *et al.* 2009).

The three main types of economic evaluation are cost–benefit analysis, cost–effectiveness analysis and cost–utility analysis. They all address efficiency issues with regard to social interventions. Cost–benefit analysis involves weighing the total expected costs against the total expected benefits of one or more actions in order to choose the best option. To this end, benefits and costs are often expressed in money terms and are adjusted for time value, so that all flows of benefits and costs over time are expressed on a common basis in terms of their present value (see Shapiro 2011). Cost–effectiveness analysis compares the relative costs and outcomes of two or more policies. It is distinct from cost–benefit analysis, which assigns a monetary value to the measure of effect. It is often used in the field of health services, where it may be inappropriate to monetize health effects. Typically it is expressed

---

Box 8.2   Nursing intervention in Sweden

Traffic injuries can cause physical, psychological and economic impairment, and affected individuals may also experience shortcomings in their post-accident care and treatment. Against this background, Franzén *et al.* (2009) analysed the cost-effectiveness of nursing interventions via telephone follow-up by examining costs and quality-adjusted life years (i.e. a year of life adjusted for its quality or its value. A year in perfect health is considered equal to 1, whereas the value of a year in ill health would be discounted). Car occupants, cyclists and pedestrians aged between 18 and 70 years and attending the Emergency Department of Umeå University Hospital in Sweden after being injured on the road were randomly assigned to an experimental or comparison group. The experimental group received routine care supplemented by nursing care via telephone follow-up over half a year, while the comparison group received routine care only. The analysis revealed that nursing intervention by telephone follow-up provided a cost-effective method giving improved quality-adjusted life years at a very low cost. This held particularly true where injuries were rather minor.

---

in terms of a ratio where the denominator is a gain in health from a measure (e.g. years of life) and the numerator is the cost associated with the health gain. Similarly, cost–utility analysis involves looking at whether an action should be undertaken. Due to the strong overlap between the concepts of cost–effectiveness and cost–utility analysis, the latter is usually referred to as a specific case relating to health care and life expectancy.

Performance measurement
In contrast with the previous evaluation types, performance measurement can either take into account effectiveness or efficiency considerations. Performance measurement differs from the previous forms of evaluation with respect to the use of the information gathered, since implementing actors and programme managers are expected to be accountable for achieving the intended goals. Moreover, the analytical focus is mostly at the managerial level. Performance measurement is about the use of organizational resources relative to a predefined goal, characterized by an ongoing monitoring and reporting of policy accomplishments (see Pollitt 2006). This definition clearly indicates that reporting is a central activity to performance measurement. It is typically conducted by programme or agency management. In this sense, it and programme evaluation are complementary in gathering information to reduce the uncertainty around a policy measure. The fundamental purpose behind the measurement is – akin to policy evaluation – to improve interventions: 'performance is not only a concept, but also an agenda' (van Dooren *et al.* 2010: 4).

Originally, performance measurement emerged in the United States at the level of local government, where it was possible to assess inputs and outputs of local government services. In the United Kingdom, it was an essential component of the general reform of the civil service in the 1980s under the Thatcher government. Government publications of that time made explicit the hypothesized links between increased managerial efficiency, a forecast decline in public spending and economic growth (Pollitt 1986: 159).

However, this idea of improving the effectiveness of public services through the use of private sector principles is not confined to Conservative governments. During the New Labour period in the United Kingdom (1997–2010) there was a clear drive towards increasing transparency in the performance of public services through the introduction of targets in all areas of the public sector (Radnor and McGuire 2004: 245). One of many examples of this was the Modernising Social Services reform, which advanced a particular form of performance measurement in the area of social care. It should, however, be noted that the new Conservative–Liberal Democrat coalition has removed a number of these targets since assuming office.

More generally, in the last three decades, performance measurement has emerged as a major trend among many OECD countries (Kouzmin *et al.* 1999). The growing popularity of this type of measurement can be substantively attributed to the reform process known as 'new public management' (McDavid and Hawthorn 2006: 300). Again, this indicates that performance measurement has become a mainstream tool of administrative evaluation.

Summing up: the main elements of an evaluation
There is no fundamental incompatibility between the evaluation types outlined above; each of them addresses a valuable dimension and thus complements our understanding of a given policy's effects. In recent years attention has increasingly turned to how one might integrate results from evaluations that use different strategies, carried out from different perspectives, and using different methods. Regardless of which strategy a researcher adopts, there are some elements that are inherent to each evaluation. Loosely following Rossi *et al.* (2004) and McDavid and Hawthorn (2006), eight steps can be regarded as essential for carrying out an evaluation.

The first step requires the identification of the clients of the evaluation (e.g. policy-makers, scientific community, beneficiaries of the policy measure). Second, clear-cut evaluation questions or criteria have to be formulated. The third step is about the assessment of the resources available to carry out the evaluation project (time, personnel, organizational infrastructure, etc.), which is followed by the need for a detailed analysis of the intended effects of the policy measure as the fourth step. The fifth step is about the selection of the most appropriate evaluation strategy (e.g. a (quasi-)experimental versus a qualitative design). The next two steps are about the development of measures and gathering of data and the carrying out of the data analysis.

As concerns data analysis other methods than those discussed above can be employed, including techniques for describing the distributional characteristics of the data (see Burnham *et al.* 2008: ch. 5). Such descriptive techniques include bar charts, line graphs and tables reporting the frequency of observations for the individual categories, thus allowing for a comparative assessment of the data. For example, one could prepare a table that shows the consumption of alcoholic beverage before and after the adoption of an increased alcohol tax, broken down by age groups and/or gender. In this way, the expected effect (i.e. lower consumption) can be investigated as to whether or not it is observable in the entire target population or only parts of it. The eighth and final step is about the publication of the results and presentation of recommendations for improving the existing policy measure.

Key points

❏ We can distinguish between administrative, judicial, political and scientific evaluation.

❏ Of these four types, political evaluation is the least systematic.

❏ In terms of evaluation methods, we can differentiate between (quasi-)experimental models, qualitative evaluation, economic evaluation and performance measurement. These methods are not competing but complementary. The first two are mostly utilized for scientific evaluation, whereas the latter two represent tools of administrative evaluation.

❏ There exist certain criteria that all evaluation activities must meet. Thus, despite the different evaluation methods, eight general steps can be identified for conducting policy evaluation.

Theory in policy evaluation

Traditionally, policy evaluation has been dominated by method-driven approaches, which seek to uncover the empirical relationship between a public policy and its outcomes and/or impacts by means of using a 'rigorous' research methodology. While data collection and empirical analysis are still central to evaluation activities, theory-based approaches have become a mainstream practice in scientific evaluation and to a certain extent also in administrative evaluation – it should, however, be noted that theories are not relevant for judicial or political evaluation.

Most fundamentally, the theory-driven approach to evaluation 'examines conditions of program implementation *and* mechanisms that mediate between processes and outcomes as a *means* to understand when and how programs work' (Weiss 1997: 41). This definition clearly suggests that theory-driven evaluation is concerned with uncovering causal relationships and not with limiting itself to empirical ones. The reason for addressing causality in the context of policy evaluation is the intent to draw conclusions about how public policies work and to make recommendations for policy improvement (Chen and Rossi 1989, 1992; Chen 1990, 2005; Rogers *et al.* 2000). This requires an explicit theory of how the public policy under study causes the intended or observed effects (Rogers *et al.* 2000: 5–6).

What does 'theory' mean in the context of policy evaluation? The term is used in many different ways within different theory-based approaches in the literature (Blamey and Mackenzie 2007: 442). However, there exist two main types of theories that play a role in policy evaluation: programme theory and social science theory. For the sake of completeness, we want to highlight that Donaldson and Lipsey (2006) mention evaluation theory as a third type. Evaluation theory is mostly concerned with evaluation practice and the corresponding literature mainly sheds light on what evaluation attempts to do and what seem to be effective approaches based on the information provided by past evaluations. In our understanding, it is inaccurate to refer to this perspective as a 'theory' as it is mainly a discussion among professionals about effective evaluation practice. As a consequence, we will limit our presentation to programme theory and social science theory.

Programme theory

Programme theory is more modest than fully fledged social science theories. It mostly concerns assumptions that guide the way a certain public policy or specific programme is implemented and expected to bring about change in social conditions (Donaldson and Lipsey 2006: 64). These assumptions can be developed before a programme is implemented or after it has been running for some time (Astbury and Leeuw 2010: 364–5). Programme theory is composed of three interrelated components: impact theory, service utilization plans and organizational plans.

Organizational and service utilization plans together constitute the 'process theory', alternatively known as the 'logic model'. To explain these components in detail, we follow the description provided by Rossi *et al.* (2004: 139–68).

Impact theory refers to the assumptions about the change process triggered by the public policy in question and the resolution of social problems. It describes a cause-and-effect sequence and is therefore typically represented as a graph that specifies relationships among policy actions, outcomes, impacts and other factors. Other ways of illustrating the hypothesized relationships are tables or narratives. It should be noted that public policy often works indirectly by changing some critical aspect of the situation, which should then lead to the achievement of the actual policy goal.

At the centre of attention are the transactions between the public policy and the target population. A simple impact theory would be that more people decide to get vaccinated against influenza because they are exposed to information regarding the virus. A more complex impact theory involves a longer causal chain between the incentives provided by a programme and the intended policy goal. To illustrate this, we rely on mentorship programmes, which some governments support actively. The idea of these programmes is to bring young people together with individuals working in enterprises, for example, and who offer guidance and encouragement. Through mentorship young people may gain confidence in their abilities, prepare more intensively for a career and apply for higher education, which, in turn, increases the overall number of students who enrol in higher education. In the long term, this leads to an increase in the share of highly qualified individuals, which should yield a positive impact on the economy. An evaluation that lacks the specification of an adequate impact theory can be useful for determining whether a certain policy outcome or impact was produced; but it will face difficulties in explaining *why* it was produced or not. Evaluation with a poorly specified impact theory is known as a 'black box' evaluation (Chen and Rossi 1989, 1992; Chen 1990, 2005; Weiss 1995, 1997).

To attain the changes in social conditions posited by impact theory, the requisite services must be provided to the target population. To this end, a service utilization plan is required, which is constituted by the public policy's assumptions and expectations about how to reach the target population. In addition, it involves considerations about the provision and sequence of service contacts and the ways of concluding the relationship when services are no longer supplied. Similar to impact theory, the service utilization plan also describes policy–target transactions, though it adopts a different perspective by focusing on the target population and its environment. With regard to the information campaign about influenza vaccination, the service utilization plan could be that a sufficient number of informative posters are put up and that information is also provided by other media in order to take into account the fact that different types of information devices reach different subgroups of the target population.

The third component relates to the organizational plan, which refers to the necessary resources, personnel, infrastructure, administration and general organization. This plan is articulated from the perspective of policy management. It is about the functions the public policy is expected to fulfil and the resources required for that. A central role is played by those activities that constitute the public policy's role in the target–policy transactions that are expected to resolve social problems. In addition, the organizational plan must include functions that represent preconditions for the service supply. Organizational plans usually include a number of assumptions and propositions. For example, if at least one informative poster about influenza vaccination is put up at each bus stop, then the intended service delivery, i.e. provision of vaccination, will be requested by the target population. This reasoning is then complemented by propositions about the required resources.

Where does the information about the three components of programme theory come from? Impact theory is ideally informed by appropriate social science theory, whereas process theory (i.e. service utilization and organizational plans) usually comes almost entirely from the programme and its context (Donaldson and Lipsey 2006: 64; see also Chen 1990, 2005; Astbury and Leeuw 2010). Since programme theory is based on practical information, it can, in principle, also be utilized for administrative evaluation. In such cases, however, the scientific component related to impact theory tends to be based on implicit theories held by those managing the programme. Therefore, programme theory can often only unfold its potential in the context of scientific evaluation.

Social science theory

While programme theory seeks to uncover causality by focusing on the characteristics of a certain public policy or programme, social science theory allows for the inclusion of factors external to the subject being evaluated. The broadening of factors taken into consideration while performing evaluation activities can be considered to be helpful for assessing the likelihood of accomplishing the intended policy goals. From this it follows that social science theories facilitate the evaluation of conditional effects of policy outputs, i.e. they make predictions as to which conditions and which policy outcomes and/or impacts are most (un)likely.

Social science theories are not particularly concerned with policy evaluation, but they are still suitable for this purpose as they posit generalizable causal statements. However, their use for evaluation requires a sufficient knowledge of them and therefore they are predominantly adopted for the purpose of scientific evaluations. Most theories we have become acquainted with in this book can, in principle, be employed for policy evaluation. For example, theories of learning (see p. 254) can be easily adapted in order to explain why a certain public policy can be expected to be successful or not. Similarly, rational choice theory might serve as a basis for policy evaluation (see pp. 82–92). Jagannathan *et al.* (2010), for instance, emphasize the importance of the target group's financial considerations – or put in more technical terms, their cost–benefit calculation – for predicting the effectiveness of welfare reform.

More generally, the theories related to policy implementation which we discussed in Chapter 7 are particularly promising as a basis for explaining the extent to which observed policy outcomes and impacts correspond with intended effects. Policy evaluation might be designed in such way as explicitly to take into account the acceptance of a certain public policy. It can draw attention to the critical role played by interest groups to ensure effective implementation and goal attainment.

According to Astbury and Leeuw (2010: 375) most efforts of theory-driven evaluation today seem to pay scant attention to causal mecha-

Key points

❏ Policy evaluation can be either method-driven or theory-driven; the latter approach offers the advantage that the 'black box' between policy outputs and policy outcomes and/or impacts can be opened.

❏ Theory plays a particularly important role for scientific and, to a certain extent, also for administrative evaluation. Theoretical considerations are irrelevant for judicial and political evaluation.

❏ There are two central types of theories relevant for policy evaluation: programme theory and social science theories.

❏ Programme theory is based on assumptions about the working of a programme and is composed of impact theory, service utilization plans and organizational plans.

❏ Social science theories can be employed to provide a more complete explanation of observed policy outcomes and/or impacts. They can also be utilized to inform an impact theory.

nisms, even though it is central to this perspective. Social science theories provide an important tool for moving ahead and systematically taking into consideration the context in which policy outputs are made and implemented (see Connell *et al.* 1995; Weiss 1995, 1997; Pawson and Tilley 1997; Connell and Kubisch 1998). In addition, the integration of social science theories might be useful for evaluation measurement and decisions concerning the most appropriate design for an evaluation study (Donaldson and Lipsey 2006: 65).

The political dimension of policy evaluation

The results of policy evaluation can be utilized to achieve certain political goals. Moreover, the decision to start a new policy process with the objective of replacing an existing public policy with a new one is based on political considerations. In this section, we address these two political dimensions of policy evaluation.

Policy evaluation versus political evaluation

There exist two fundamentally different points of view on evaluation activities. On the one hand, scientific realists argue for the possibility of an objective description. They advocate a separation of facts and values with the aim of producing politically neutral knowledge. This perspective is based on the assumption that there exists a set of clear-cut policy goals and that there is agreement on the indicators on the basis of which the evaluation is to be carried out (see Pawson and Tilley 1997). On the other hand, social constructivists – also sometimes labelled as post-positivists – claim that evaluation research is entirely subjective. They stress that evaluation does not study public policy as such, but its interpretation, which entails that the evaluation process itself is based on values and therefore is socially constructed (see Fischer 1995). However, both sides seem to agree that evaluation cannot be practised without being somehow influenced by political judgement (Taylor and Balloch 2005: 1–2).

A helpful perspective for understanding the important difference between policy evaluation and political evaluation is provided by McConnell (2010: 45–54). Even though in his book he concentrates on the concept of 'policy success', the reasoning can still be applied to what is of interest here, namely the extent to which evaluation can be political. According to the author, policy success can be assessed on the basis of four dimensions.

First, a policy is successful when the implementing actors achieve the objectives laid down in a legal act. This dimension overlaps with implementation studies (see Chapter 7). A more demanding approach is represented by the second dimension that concentrates on the question of whether a policy output produces the intended outcomes and/or impacts. A third dimension is the benefit it brings to the target group. The fourth dimension is about meeting the criteria of the respective policy domain. Different policy areas are characterized by different values being widely held by their relevant policy community, such as precaution in environmental policy. Thus, a policy may be deemed successful when it concurs with these specific standards. From this discussion of policy success we can derive what *policy* evaluation should ideally be about, that is, an assessment of these four dimensions.

Political success is clearly different from policy success (McConnell 2010: 49–54). The first dimension of political success refers to increasing electoral prospects. As explained in Chapter 4, the central objective of elected officials is to stay in power. To attain this, the governing party will try to employ evaluation to demonstrate that the public policies it made whilst in office are successful. The second dimension refers to the process of policy-making. A policy measure can be successful in this regard if it: involves a narrow definition of the policy problem that triggered the policy process; gives the appearance of dealing with the problem; and helps to counter critics or gain support from the most relevant actors. A policy corresponding to these criteria can help to keep more difficult-to-solve policy problems off the decision agenda and ease the business of governing. The third dimension is about values and direction of government. A policy measure might be politically successful in helping to forge new approaches to policy-making. Political evaluation would provide the information necessary to achieve success with regard to these three dimensions.

The understanding of the political success of a public policy makes political evaluation different from objectively assessing expected and unexpected policy effects. In short, it is about the purposeful use of information to stay in power. Bovens *et al.* (2008: 320) argue that even the decision to make an evaluation could be politically motivated; for example, by 'the replacement of key officials, elections that produce government turn-overs, incidents or figures that receive publicity and trigger political calls for an investigation, and so on'. This concurs with the argument advanced by Rossi *et al.* (2004: 37) that actors initiating evaluation might have hidden agendas: 'occasionally, an evaluation is commissioned to provide a rationale for a decision that has already been made behind the scenes to terminate a program, fire an administrator, and the like'. Alternatively, evaluation can become political to the extent that policy-makers ignore recommendations to discontinue programmes on the basis of a negative evaluation (see Quinn and Magill 1994).

The politics of policy evaluation has also been discussed in terms of the diffusion of regulatory impact assessment. According to Turnpenny *et al.* (2009: 645), the US-based literature posits that elected politicians want regulatory impact assessment performed so as to receive information on whether the ministerial departments and agencies are disadvantaging important political constituencies. Thus, the adoption of policy appraisal is perceived as a means of politically controlling the bureaucracy. More generally, the institutional context of polities has been found to be decisive for the actual use of this tool (Radaelli 2004). Sager and Rissi (2011), for instance, demonstrate that the specific institutional characteristics of the Swiss polity have prevented the success of regulatory impact assessment. As at the Swiss federal level, various direct democratic instruments (e.g. referendums) are used. When drafting legislation it is more important to include the opinions of most actors than the results of policy appraisal. Thus, the full potential of *ex ante* evaluations cannot be exploited.

Another way in which policy evaluation can become political is by telling evaluators what they should find. This aspect specifically relates to the increasing dominance of evaluation research as 'contractual research' (Wollmann 2007: 399). This form of evaluation entails an agreement between the evaluator and the client. The client agrees to fund the evaluation, defines the subject matter and the leading research questions, and approves the evaluation method. The evaluator, in turn, agrees to complete the evaluation within a specified time period and budget. By receiving funding from an external source, i.e. the client, the evaluator loses independence regarding the subject matter, the research questions and methods. While this is already undesirable in terms of academic research, contractual evaluation might also bear the risk that the evaluator is asked to deliver a type of *ex ante* defined results. It is important that policy evaluators are aware of their social responsibility.

Evidence-based policy-making

In the traditional policy cycle introduced in Chapter 1, evaluation follows policy implementation. Based on the assessment of what works out and what does not, policy-makers might improve public policy by initiating a new policy process. However, the decision to utilize the findings of evaluation is a political one. Classical policy analysis as it emerged in the 1960s strongly built on the evaluative rationality applied to public problems, that is, to improve policy outcomes and impacts by applying analytic methodologies to policy assessment. Evidence-based policy-making represents a recent effort to reform policy processes by prioritizing decision-making criteria that are evidence-based and to stimulate processes of policy-oriented learning (Howlett 2009b: 154). The idea underlying evidence-based policy-making is that governments can learn from experience and avoid repeating the errors of the past. In other words, it is an approach that is designed to help politicians make 'well-informed' decisions about policies by putting the best available evidence at the heart of policy formulation and implementation.

To understand better what evidence-based policy-making is about, we have to return to Chapter 6, in which we discussed how policy proposals are drafted. In an ideal world, these proposals would represent the most effective or, indeed, most efficient way of resolving a social problem, howsoever defined. In reality, however, many factors influence the design of public policy. These include experts, ideas, international organizations and interest groups. In a complementary vein, the partisan ideology of elected and appointed politicians and their private interests can be decisive for the design of a policy. This suggests that a policy proposal is not necessarily drafted in a way to ensure that the solution to the social problem is attained. It is this possible flaw in designing public policy that the concept of evidence-based policy-making seeks to remedy.

In the United Kingdom, for instance, under the New Labour government (1997–2010) the profile of evidence-based policy was raised (Wells 2007; Boaz *et al*. 2008). Numerous publications acknowledge this drive. In 2000, for instance, a report by the Performance and Innovation Unit called for policy analysis to be placed at the heart of policy-making (Wilson 2008: 159). Another publication showing the growing importance of evaluation is the 2003 'Magenta Book: Guidance Notes for Policy Evaluation and Analysis'.

At the international level, the use of evaluation – as one principal component of evidence-based policy – varies strongly across countries. Canada, Germany, Sweden and the United States are broadly considered as 'pioneers' in the use of evaluation. A bit later, in the 1970s and 1980s, countries such as Denmark, France, the Netherlands, Norway, Switzerland and the United Kingdom also institutionalized evaluation. Yet a sizeable group of countries only adopted such an evaluation culture during the 1990s, including Finland, Ireland, Italy and Spain (Viñas 2009: 459). Other European countries such as Belgium still have a notably less developed evaluation culture (Varone *et al*. 2005).

Exactly what constitutes the 'evidence' in evidence-based policy-making remains contentious in the literature. It is, however, clear that evaluation is only one instrument for informing policy decisions. More generally, Head (2008) suggests that three types of evidence are especially relevant in modern states: scientific knowledge, policy management knowledge and political knowledge. Scientific knowledge – to which we can also attribute evaluation if based on a scientific methodology – is the product of the systematic analysis of current and past conditions and trends, and the analysis of the causal interrelationships that explain them. Policy management knowledge is the 'practical wisdom' of professionals and the organizational knowledge associated with managing programme implementation. The political form of knowledge resides primarily in politicians, political parties, organized groups and the media. Political knowledge is related to a wide range of activities, including considering and adjusting strategies or tactics, undertaking agenda-setting, determining priorities, and building coalitions of support. Head's central argument is that evidence-based policy cannot exclusively rely on scientific knowledge but must be complemented by the other two forms in order to be feasible and effective in policy formulation.

While evidence-based policy-making appears to be a sensible approach in theory, there are several practical limitations. Governments are under constant pressure to solve problems and characteristically do not have the time to study things as much as they want. Consequently, they are often required to make a policy decision based on an 'informed guess' instead of waiting for a more complete answer. The second limitation is that many policy initiatives rest on assumptions about the future that are not testable. Policy-makers have to make predictions about future impacts against the credibility of the sources of the information and their own common sense.

The capacity of governments actually to practice evidence-based policy-making is also crucial (Howlett 2009b). Cohen and Levinthal (1990) introduced the term 'absorptive capacity' for the ability of a firm to innovate. As described by them (1990: 133), absorptive capacity has two constituent components: the capacity to adopt ideas from the outside world (i.e. adoption capacity) and the capacity to create new inventions (i.e. invention capacity).

Adolino and Blake (2011: 27) adapted the logic of this model to governmental learning on the basis of evaluation. According to these authors, governments are most likely to learn from the past when they have expertise and good information acquired through communication with so-called policy networks (see pp. 200–5). If the exchange between government and policy networks is intense, learning will take place in government and society. By the same token, in the case of a high-capacity government with minimal links to policy networks, learning based on evaluation findings will be restricted to the government itself. In constellations where governments have little expertise or insufficient information, learning will take place at much lower levels, even if the government in question interacts intensely with policy networks.

Evidence-based policy-making is a rationalist concept that stresses the possibility of objective information. An important criticism of it has been the constructivist or interpretative position which argues that even scientific knowledge is socially constructed. From this perspective, scientific evidence cannot inform the design of public policy without being affected by beliefs and principles as well as particular theoretical frames and interpretations of the world (see Sanderson 2002: 6). Another line of criticism is advanced by Marston and Watts (2003: 158), who argue that there is a risk that evidence-based policy can be misused by political elites to increase their strategic control over the definition of the nature of policy problems, which could turn into a threat to open and democratic policy-making. Finally, it is important to note that there are different 'levels' of evidence that might inform policy-making (Camasso 2003).

In health policy, for instance, Brownson *et al.* (1999: 90) state that there are at least two levels of evidence: one focusing on the importance of a particular health condition and its link with some preventable risk factor; and another one that concentrates on the relative effectiveness of specific interventions to address a particular health condition. Depending on which level of evidence is taken into consideration, different or even contradictory policy recommendations can be derived. This further underlines the fact that basing policy decisions on evidence does not eliminate the need for choosing from a variety of policy options.

In reality, evidence-based policy-making is only practised in a few policy areas. One area in which evidence is systematically taken into consideration when making policy is the health sector, but even there Shimkhada *et al.* (2008) found that this does not happen very extensively. One of the factors impeding the more systematic use of evidence in policy-making refers to the structural barriers to communication between researchers and decision-makers. Even in the United Kingdom

---

Key points

❑ It is important to distinguish between policy evaluation and political evaluation. The first is about comparing the expected and observed effects of a public policy; the second is about utilizing formally or informally derived information about public policy for political purposes.

❑ There are many different ways in which an evaluation can be political. What they all have in common is the objective of helping elected officials to stay in power or to induce a change in the partisan composition of government.

❑ Evidence-based policy-making is about using experience or new information to avoid a repetition of the errors of the past or to find better resolutions to policy problems by means of policy-oriented learning. It is a political decision as to whether or not base policy formulation on evidence.

❑ The 'evidence' to be used when formulating public policy does not only refer to findings of evaluation studies, but also includes other types of information. However, there are many different definitions in the literature.

where the political will to establish evidence-based policy-making was considerable, the policy areas in which this approach was advanced were limited (Boaz *et al*. 2008: 242).

Conclusions

Evaluation is about assessing the expected and unexpected outcomes and impacts of public policy. There are multiple strategies for designing an evaluation study. Most importantly, the evaluator should be clear about whether the principal interest is on assessing the effectiveness or efficiency of a policy measure. Once this decision has been taken, he or she can choose from various evaluation methods. Another important question relates to the purpose of the evaluation. The findings will depend on the way evaluation is realized since an exclusively objective assessment of policy effects is hardly possible. From this it follows that the findings of evaluation studies – regardless of how well they are designed – should always be seen in the social context in which they were undertaken.

We have further learned in this chapter that evaluation is an integrative part of evidence-based policy-making and thus important for providing feedback to policy-makers. The recent popularity of this approach can be seen to reflect the growing uncertainties surrounding policy-making and the increasing complexity of policy decisions; scientific evidence appears to offer a way of controlling this uncertainty and reducing complexity. Depending on the results of the evaluation process, a new policy cycle can be initiated with the aim of terminating or modifying the newly established policy. Thus, evaluation presents an important tool for policy-making because it might bring an issue back to the political agenda and motivate policy actors to improve the policy design. However, whether lessons for future policy decisions are actually drawn from evaluation findings is a political decision.

Web links

www.itcproject.org. On this website, the International Tobacco Control Policy Evaluation Project publishes a wide range of evaluation papers with respect to policy measures designed to combat smoking.

www.policy-evaluation.org. This is an online database of web resources related to social policy evaluation.

www.socialpsychology.org. This page contains links to numerous web-based experiments, such as on judgements and attitudes. Although it is not directly about experimental policy evaluation, it is still helpful for understanding the logic of social experiments.

www.socialresearchmethods.net. On this website there are many resources and links to other websites that deal with applied social research methods.

www.spear.govt.nz. The purpose of this site is to provide a platform for the New Zealand social policy research and evaluation sector. It contains several interesting research reports and gives a good overview of the practical side of public policy evaluation.

www.eval.org. This is the website of the American Evaluation Society.

www.evaluationcanada.ca. This is the website of the Canadian Evaluation Society.

www.aes.asn.au. This is the website of the Australasian Evaluation Society.

www.evaluation.org.uk. This is the website of the UK Evaluation Society.

Further reading

Bardach, E. (2008) *A Practical Guide for Policy Analysis: The Eightfold Path to More Effective Problem Solving*. Washington, DC: CQ Press. This book provides a helpful complement to this chapter as it systematically links the first stage of the policy cycle with the final one.

McConnell, A. (2010) *Understanding Policy Success: Rethinking Public Policy*. Basingstoke: Palgrave Macmillan. This book provides a holistic understanding of policy evaluation by framing it in the context of policy success.

Nagel, S.S. (ed.) (2001) *Handbook of Public Policy Evaluation*. Thousand Oaks, CA: Sage. This is a comprehensive collection of essays on policy evaluation with some instructive theoretical sections.

Rossi, P.H., M.W. Lipsey and H.E. Freeman (2004) *Evaluation: A Systematic Approach*. Thousand Oaks, CA: Sage. A useful resource that provides insights into a wide range of evaluation-related topics.

Shadish, W.R., T.D. Cook and D.T. Campbell (2001) *Experimental and Quasi-Experimental Designs for Generalized Causal Inference*. Belmont, CA: Wadsworth. A valuable book on research design for advanced readers.

Vedung, E. (2000) *Public Policy and Program Evaluation*. New Brunswick, NJ: Transaction Publishers. An introduction that manages to connect evaluation with other policy-analytical topics.

Chapter 9

Governance: A Synoptic Perspective on Policy-Making

Reader's guide

The governance concept focuses on patterns of political steering, that is, the institutionalized relationship between public and private actors, in order to resolve social problems. It concerns both hierarchical and non-hierarchical modes of political steering, and it is particularly the recognition of the non-hierarchical forms that distinguishes governance from government, i.e. the traditional mode of hierarchical intervention, which we have implicitly employed as the point of reference in previous chapters. The second innovative feature of the governance concept relates to the fact that it allows for a more holistic view of policy-making that cuts across policy stages. This is attained by placing the forms of cooperation between public and private actors centre stage. In this way, the governance perspective can be employed to scrutinize processes of problem definition and agenda-setting as well as decision-making, implementation and, to a certain extent, even evaluation. The chapter begins with an introduction of the central concepts and modes of governance. We also address the question of whether there has been a shift from hierarchical to non-hierarchical forms of political steering over time. We then present a typology of governance types, to provide a better understanding of how public and private actors might cooperate in the policy-making process and to what extent their relationship is characterized by a dominant position of the state. Finally, we discuss and apply the different criteria for evaluating the extent to which governance might be characterized as 'good' or 'bad'.

The term 'governance' has made an impressive career from the early 1990s onwards. It has developed into the catchword for an ever-growing number of studies in the social sciences. At the same time, it is used as a 'magic formula' – often in terms of 'good governance' – in political speeches and documents, both at the domestic and international level. However, as is often the case with new concepts, there is no consensus regarding its meaning and specific applicability (Kooiman *et al.* 2008: 2). The definition of the term varies considerably across different sub-fields and research strands of the social sciences (see Pierre and Peters 2000: 7; Kohler-Koch and Rittberger 2006). This lack of a common meaning can be traced to the fact that the concept is used not only in an analytical way, but also in a normative sense (Doornbos 2001).

This basic assessment, however, does not mean that governance and related research are not of relevance for the study of public policy. On the contrary, it implies a new perspective on public policy that cuts across the distinction of policy stages made in the previous chapters. In placing patterns and forms of coordination between public and private actors at centre stage, a governance focus implies that processes of problem definition, agenda-setting, decision-making, implementation and, to a certain extent, evaluation are interpreted through a different analytical lens. The governance perspective sheds light on specific policy regimes understood as institutional forms and instruments shaping processes of collective action. The focus is hence on general patterns of policy-making in a given policy sector and country, and potential changes in these patterns over time.

Central concepts and modes of governance

When taking a closer look at the rich literature on governance, we are confronted with different, partially overlapping definitions and concepts. To get a clearer understanding of the relevance of the governance concept, we need to differentiate and classify these approaches. On this basis, we can turn to a more detailed discussion of different modes of governance from a policy-analytical perspective.

Governance concepts

Despite its prominence in public policy analysis, there is no generally accepted definition of the term 'governance' (Kooiman *et al.* 2008: 2). On the basis of various classification attempts (Mayntz 2010: 37–8; see also Rhodes 1996, 1997: 46–60; Benz and Dose 2010), two general conceptions of governance can be distinguished.

The first – rather broad – definition conceives of governance as political steering and hence purposeful attempts at coordinating individual action in order to achieve certain policy goals. Thus, governance refers to the collective settlement of social affairs in a polity, including a broad range of different modes, such as hierarchical intervention and non-hierarchical steering, based on cooperation between public and private actors or patterns of private self-governance.

In contrast to this conception of governance as classification of different modes of political steering, the term is also widely used to describe a distinctive mode of steering, namely non-hierarchical approaches (Peters and Pierre 1998). Rhodes (1996: 660), for instance, refers to governance as self-organizing, inter-organizational networks. These networks encompass not only public, but also private actors. Cooperation is based on the need to exchange resources and negotiation over shared policy objectives and solutions.

Especially in the literature on global governance (Czempiel and Rosenau 1992), this more narrow definition of governance is particularly emphasized. In this debate, governance is restricted to non-hierarchical modes of political steering, i.e. it is explicitly delineated from 'government' as the traditional mode of hierarchical intervention. This distinction is based on the understanding that beyond the nation-state attempts at collective coordination necessarily have to be based on non-hierarchical modes as the option of hierarchical intervention is restricted to the nation-state (Zürn 2004). We will revisit this argument in Chapter 10.

It is in the context of this latter distinction between governance and government that an emphasis on the governance concept, in the sense of 'good governance', has emerged. This development has been particularly driven by international organizations like the World Bank, who have stressed the positive effects of non-hierarchical patterns of political steering that emerge from broad societal participation in policy-making, especially in the field of development policy (Knill 2004; see Table 9.1).

Table 9.1 *Overview of governance concepts*

Definition of governance	Description
Governance as classification of modes of political steering.	Deliberate collective coordination of individual action; including both hierarchical and non-hierarchical modes.
Governance as distinctive mode of political steering.	Non-hierarchical modes of political steering.

Modes of governance

Basically, we find a distinction between three governance modes in the literature, namely hierarchy, markets and networks (Knill and Lenschow 2003, 2005; Knill and Tosun 2009; Lütz 2010). Before outlining these different modes, it is important to stress that they are all mutually present in modern states. Hence, it would be inaccurate to equate them with institutionalist approaches that assign countries to certain categories with regard to their policy arrangements (see Esping-Andersen 1990; Castles 1998). Rather, the different modes can vary in the same country regarding their dominance in the individual policy areas. Moreover, the dominance of a mode can change, as we will show in the next section.

Governance by hierarchy stresses the role of formal rules and procedures that are binding for both public and private actors. Most importantly, however, the state has a monopoly on the use of force to bring private actors into compliance with public policy. From this it follows that the state has a sanctioning power that exceeds that of private actors to a great extent, indicating that the relationship between public and private actors is asymmetrical. Compared to other types of coordination such as markets or networks, the state plays a key role in policy-making within this mode. It hierarchically intervenes to produce and supply common goods (e.g. infrastructure, education or clean air) and defines the legal framework without which no economic activities could be realized.

By supplying common goods the state generates fair conditions for all market participants and a reliable framework for economic activities, which represents the main advantage of hierarchical governance. In contrast, the disadvantage of this mode of governance is a decoupling of the state from the policy needs of private actors and an insufficient knowledge of the 'actual' problems they are confronted with. This has important implications for our previous discussion of problem definition and agenda-setting in Chapter 5. In constellations that are characterized by hierarchical governance it is possible that the problems that receive attention from policy-makers might deviate from what citizens regard as problems, leading to public policy that may not be accepted or is difficult to implement.

Governance by markets represents the opposing model to hierarchical governance as it is based on the idea that goods and services are allocated efficiently without intervention by the state. Markets provide individual and corporate actors with an ideal setting for exchanging resources based on price. This argument is founded on the assumption that the prices of goods and services contain all the information relevant for their exchange and, therefore, that exchange relationships can emerge between all kinds of market participants. Based on the price, market participants can judge whether it is advantageous to agree to a transaction or not.

Another central assumption of market governance is that actors are rational, i.e. that they seek to maximize their own well-being, so that they are likely to produce negative externalities that cause harm to third persons and hence lower society's overall welfare level (see pp. 83–4). Usually, the most effective way of internalizing negative externalities is provided by state intervention, which is also needed to define the basic rules required to make sure that markets function at all. Thus, the logical consequence of trying to remedy the disadvantages of market governance would be to strengthen governance further by increasing the established hierarchy. At the same time, the hierarchical definition and enforcement of the rules of the game (including such elementary things as property rights) constitute basic requirements for the emergence and functioning of markets.

The third mode of coordinating the relationship between public and private actors is network governance. The literature on this challenges the conventional wisdom that the market is the only efficient system of a non-hierarchical coordination of societal actors. An important discussion unfolded as to whether networks are only a combination of elements of market and hierarchy or whether they would be better understood as a specific form of governance in their own right (Powell 1990; Provan and Kenis 2008: 232; Raab and Kenis 2009: 205).

Policy networks are defined as stable sets of interdependent public and private actors who interact informally to achieve distinctive but interdependent goals (Laumann and Knoke 1987; Schneider 1992, 2006). The members of a policy network are linked to one another through the exchange of policy-relevant information, expertise and additional resources (Rhodes and Marsh 1992: 10). The basic idea is that policy networks provide the governing resources to intervene in policy areas, which are not available within the state apparatus (Kenis and Schneider 1991: 41). Policy networks can participate in the preparation of decisions taken by the executive or the legislature, i.e. policy drafting, and help to implement them. Governments will, in principle, work most closely with those groups offering the most valuable resources (see Daugbjerg 1998).

Patterns of cooperation in policy networks may take many different forms, including not only forms of horizontal coordination between public and private actors, but also patterns of societal self-governance, for instance so-called private interest governments (Streeck and Schmitter 1985). With such private interest governments, opposing interests are not represented by independent organizations, but are internalized within regulatory regimes that subject the activities of private agents to a self-imposed discipline. Minimum quality standards imposed collectively on an industry by producers, a situation common to agricultural

---

Box 9.1   Drug policy implementation through local networks

The concept of network governance has received notable attention with regard to the implementation of public policies. In this context, policy networks are expected to yield a positive impact on the implementation process as they facilitate non-hierarchical coordination and provision of additional resources. They can play an important role in increasing the acceptance of public policies through communication. The study by Percival (2009) sheds light on the impact of local policy networks on the implementation of drug policy reform in the US state of California. The main idea of the reform is that non-violent drug offenders are placed in mandatory treatment programmes instead of being sent to prison. The analysis reveals that the implementation of the drug policy reform varies considerable across the individual counties and that this variation can be attributed to the characteristics of the local policy networks. These networks are composed of public health and justice agencies as well as public and private drug treatment facilities. Decisive for the effectiveness of policy implementation are the monetary resources available to local policy networks, the extent to which members agree with the interpretation of policy goals, the overall expertise and collaborative capacity.

---

industries, are often achieved by self-regulation. Another area in which self-regulation is applied refers to situations in which the industry limits or controls its activities. For example, in many countries the alcohol industry regulates itself when it comes to advertising its products.

All these different patterns of non-hierarchical governance in policy networks are based on negotiations between the involved actors. Decisions are not imposed in a top-down manner but are negotiated. It is this importance of negotiations for the development and implementation of public policy that characterizes this mode of governance and hence constitutes its distinctive feature relative to 'classical' approaches to policy-making (Kooiman *et al.* 2008: 2). Against this background we can understand why many scholars restrict the term governance in order to bring out this distinctive feature – implying that we are confronted with two different meanings of the term, as the discussion above has already highlighted.

Network governance emphasizes mutual trust and complementarity of resources that are expected to result in reciprocal actions. The fact that networks are both relatively loosely coordinated and stable brings about the exchange of resources that cannot be reflected in prices, i.e. in intangible goods. These resources can be tacit knowledge or competences that only emergence when the resources of different actors are shared. If conflicts between network participants arise these are resolved by discussion and negotiations rather forcing the affected actors to leave the network.

The disadvantage of network governance is the emergence of a distinction between 'insiders' (those actors actually incorporated into and consulted in decision-making and implementation) and 'outsiders' (those interests to which access is denied). Those who are members of the network benefit from having insider status, though this comes at the price of systematically excluding other actors (Lütz 2010: 139). This has important implications for fundamental principles of democratic politics that stress the importance of inclusion for policy-making. In extreme cases, network governance might become 'undemocratic' and produce policy outputs that, for society as a whole, are less desirable than those attained by hierarchical or market governance.

Changes in governance modes: from hierarchies to markets to networks?

An important topic within the governance debate centres on the question as to whether there has been a shift in governance modes from hierarchy towards non-hierarchical approaches to political steering. So far, however, there is a lack of empirical studies that would allow a systematic answering of this question. Against this background, it is hard to judge whether the political and, to some extent, scientific emphasis on new modes of governance is 'rhetoric or reality' (Holzinger *et al.* 2006). It should also be emphasized that changes in modes or the scientific discovery of new modes of governance might to a lesser extent be driven by actual empirical changes, and more by analytical innovations, meaning that the same empirical phenomenon is being seen through different lenses. So it is very difficult to disentangle empirical and analytical developments in the governance debate.

Notwithstanding these limitations, some general developments can be identified. A first pattern refers to attempts at increasing and improving hierarchical governance capacities during the 1960s and 1970s. For a long time, governance corresponded to government, that is the hierarchical steering of society by state interventions. With the emergence of unexpected societal conflicts and economic problems in the 1960s and 1970s, the interventionist state came under attack. The main argument advanced by political scientists and politicians was that the interventionist state based on hierarchical governance is ill-equipped to resolve the newly emerging social and economic problems of modern states. These developments strongly challenged the trust placed in the ability of governments to steer and plan societally – an aspect that became increasingly apparent with the detection of far-reaching deficits in implementation. Consequently, top-down policy-making based on command-and-control instruments and coercive techniques of policy implementation were perceived as old-fashioned and ineffective for increasing public welfare.

As a first consequence, the wish to reduce the hierarchical components in policy led to a new relationship between political and administrative actors. While hierarchical governance assigns bureaucracy the sole function of implementing public policy, criticism of the interventionist state favoured the evolution of a new approach that regarded political and administrative actors as interrelated in one system, i.e. the political-administrative system (Jann and Wegrich 2010: 178). The reforms were summarized under the heading of the 'active state', since reformist efforts departed from the old bureaucratic styles of merely administrating the public sector and found a more proactive style of encompassing policy planning and engineering social reforms (Reichard 2003: 347; see also Seibel 2001).

This pattern of extended hierarchical governance was increasingly challenged by implementation and evaluation research that had revealed far-reaching deficits with regard to the effectiveness of this technocratic approach (Taylor and Balloch 2005: 4). At the same time, the takeover of neoliberal parties in many Western democracies – in particular the United Kingdom and the United States – implied that the encompassing involvement of government was increasingly questioned. This coincided with activities of market liberalization and privatization of state monopolies at the international and EU level. These developments favoured extensive reforms, entailing that the state should delegate those tasks that it could not fulfil in a satisfactory manner to private actors, including industry and societal organizations.

Thus, since the 1980s, we observe a second pattern of changes in governance modes that is characterized by political attempts to reduce hierarchical governance and instead to rely on market coordination. This implied that governments no longer provided public goods and services themselves, but reduced their role to establishing regulatory frameworks for the provision of these goods and services by private actors. The 'interventionist state' has been increasingly replaced by the 'regulatory state' (Majone 1994).

The regulatory state thesis postulates that the provision of common goods has basically been left to the market, with the role of the state being confined to defining the rules and incentive structures of private actors in such a way that socially desirable outcomes are achieved. This is well illustrated by the global wave of privatization in areas such as the postal service, telecommunications, railways and many other common goods previously provided and managed by the state. Often, privatization went hand in hand with the creation of regulatory agencies (see p. 150). This 'rolling back' of the state, as a result of deregulation, privatization and administrative reforms, has partly changed the functional role of interventionist policies: it no longer provides the common goods, but rather enables them to be provided.

At the administrative level, the growing influence of market mechanisms led to the rise of new public management which governments since the 1980s have used to modernize the public sector. In a nutshell, new public management assigns to elected officials only the role of defining long-term policy goals; and apart from that they are expected to delegate competences to operative agencies and institutions. Further, new public management regards the public–private dichotomy as obsolete. Consequently, the idea of competition can also be applied to the delivery of public services, which is theorized as making the entire process more efficient. Introducing competition also provides benchmarks and other bases for comparison which is at odds with the classical understanding of public administration. This is also underlined by a preference for output control (e.g. definition of policy or programme targets) over input control (e.g. the selection of personnel) (see Peters and Pierre 1998: 227–31; see also Hood 1991; Pollitt and Bouckaert 2000; Norman 2003).

It is questionable though if and to what extent these developments entail fundamental or gradual shifts in governance modes. On the one hand, it is well-acknowledged that privatization, deregulation and the shift to new public management were not similarly pronounced across countries. Germany, for instance, has been much less affected than the United Kingdom (Pollitt and Bouckaert 2000; Knill 2001). On the other hand, it should not be overlooked that – regardless of the country in question – the public provision of common goods and the dominance of interventionist governance has hardly been completely reversed. The emphasis on markets basically entailed a shift rather than a reduction in hierarchical intervention. Hierarchical provision has been replaced by hierarchical market regulation.

A third pattern in the discussion about changes in modes of governance refers to the emphasis of policy networks that can be observed from, especially, the 1990s onwards. This discussion developed rather independently of the emphasis on market mechanisms, though it was primarily driven by the acknowledgement of increasing needs for cooperation between public and private actors. The emergence and growth of policy networks as a new form of governance is interpreted as the result of two developments. On the one hand, policy networks emerge from a loss of internal sovereignty of the state arising from growing organizational complexity and societal differentiation and fragmentation. As a consequence, governments can no longer effectively intervene in societal processes, but need to rely on cooperation with societal actors. On the other hand, the growing integration of nation states into international institutions and globally integrated markets leads to a loss of external sovereignty. National governments need to coordinate their activities with a broad range a public and private actors operating at the domestic and international level.

As a consequence, it is argued that over time a shift away from hierarchical intervention towards more cooperative forms of interaction between public and private actors has occurred (Héritier 2002: 3; Grande 2009: 78). The growth and emergence of these patterns is generally referred to as 'modern governance' (Kooiman 1993) or 'governance in the modern state' (Mayntz 2010).

It should, however, be noted that modes of governance coexist and that different policy challenges might require different modes of governance. This point is well made by the encompassing volume on governance success, edited by Bovens *et al.* (2001a). In the introduction, the editors underscore the point that a government coping with industrial decline must apply a different governance mode than a government that, for example, wants to achieve success in the reform of health care, the liberalization of financial markets or the containment the AIDS epidemic.

More generally, notwithstanding the fact that public and private contributions are equally relevant in more cooperative forms of governance, it is important to emphasize that the overall responsibility for providing common goods still lies with the state. The state plays a central and active role and disposes of powers and resources which are not available to societal actors. In particular, governments may provide important incentives (the state may offer financial support, or delegate power, or it may refrain from direct and potentially less effective state intervention) in order to stimulate and increase the integration and organization of societal interests (Streeck 1994: 18; Knill and Lehmkuhl 1998).

Key points

❑ The term 'governance' has many different meanings in the literature; here we conceive of it as the purposeful collective coordination of individual action to achieve policy goals.

❑ The literature has identified three main governance modes, namely hierarchy, markets and networks. These modes of governance are present in each polity, but their dominance might vary across policy areas and change over time.

❑ The extent to which hierarchy has been replaced by markets and policy networks as dominant governance modes is difficult to assess empirically. This can be traced to the fact that market governance needs not mean a reduction in hierarchical governance.

❑ With regard to policy networks it is questionable whether the perception of change is triggered by the adoption of networks as a new scientific paradigm or by real-world developments.

Finally, it is questionable if and to what extent policy networks are really a new development or only indicate that political steering is analysed through a distinctive analytical perspective that explicitly takes account of the fact that public and private actors cooperate in the formulation and implementation of public policies. The emphasis of governance without government and the role of policy networks might stem form analytical as well as real-world changes. In other words, policy networks might be a new scientific paradigm as much as they might be a new empirical development.

Four ideal types of governance

We have seen above that the distinction between different modes of governance might to some extent be problematic. This holds true in particular for the distinction between markets and hierarchies. The reliance on market governance need not mean a reduction of hierarchical governance, but may even depend to some extent on hierarchical intervention. The reliance on market governance might lead to a shift in patterns of hierarchical governance, that is, from the state as the provider to the state as the regulator of public goods. At the same time, policy networks are often used as a catch-all category emphasizing that public and private actors cooperate in the policy-making process. This, however, would be to overlook the fact that this cooperation might take rather different forms, with public and private actors playing rather different roles. So far we have only limited insights into the causes that lead to changes in the reliance on different governance modes across countries and policy sectors.

In an attempt to address these problems, Knill and Lenschow (2003) identify four ideal types of governance (see also Knill and Lehmkuhl 2002a, 2002b; Knill 2004, 2008). This typology is based on two analytical distinctions. On the one hand, the focus is on the degree of cooperation between public and private actors in the policy-making process; on the other hand, a basic distinction is made between hierarchical and non-hierarchical modes. This distinction is assessed through the degree of legal obligation that characterizes collective policy solutions.

Depending on the specific configuration of these two dimensions, four basic governance types can be distinguished:

- interventionist governance
- regulated self-governance
- cooperative governance
- private self-governance

Table 9.2   *Four ideal types of governance*

		Cooperation of public and private actors	
		High	**Low**
Degree of legal obligation	**High**	Regulated self governance	Interventionist governance (government)
	Low	Cooperative governance	Private self governance

Source: Knill and Lehmkuhl (2002b: 49).

The first pattern of interventionist governance corresponds to hierarchy or government and covers not only the hierarchical provision of public goods but also the reliance on market mechanisms through the hierarchical definition of regulatory frameworks governing market interactions. The three remaining ideal types cover different forms of governance in policy networks. While in reality one might often observe a more variegated picture than is offered by ideal types, they still have the virtue of providing a standard against which real-world systems can be compared and potential differences explained (see Table 9.2).

Interventionist governance

Interventionist governance refers to constellations which reflect the classical scenario of policy-making, namely the limited governance capacity of private actors in view of the underlying incentive structure, which can only be compensated for by external power, i.e. it requires the hierarchical intervention of the state. Although this scenario does not exclude the involvement of private actors, the overall responsibility for the provision of public goods lies with the state. In general, this pattern is characterized by a hierarchical relationship between public and private actors, with the state intervening 'from above' into society through highly detailed and legally binding requirements, i.e. on the basis of clearly defined rules and regulations which have to be complied with by the public and private actors concerned ('command and control').

Regulated self-governance

Regulated self-governance refers to constellations in which hierarchical intervention through legally binding rules is accompanied by more cooperative relationships between public and private actors during the formulation and implementation of public policies. Regulated self-governance implies that the participation of society takes place on the basis of clearly formalized and institutionalized procedures, although the state still plays a dominant role in the final decision on policy contents and regulatory arrangements. In this context, the relationship between public and private actors might be arranged in various ways: private actors might participate in policy-making and implementation; competencies might be delegated to private organizations; or regulatory frameworks for private self-governance might be cooperatively developed. Often, regulated self-governance can only be achieved under the 'shadow of hierarchy' (Mayntz and Scharpf 1995), the state being capable of relying on traditional forms of intervention should there be governance failures (Peters 1998).

Cooperative governance

The remaining governance patterns – cooperative governance and private self-governance – crucially differ from the previous patterns with respect to two factors: the voluntary character of policy-making and the fact that private actors rather than the state play a dominant role in policy formulation and implementation. In the case of cooperative governance, the definition and application of instruments does not occur on the basis of legally binding requirements, but through negotiations and voluntary agreements between public and private actors. Decisions are not taken unilaterally by public actors and then forced on society. Rather policies are the result of bargaining processes, in which both public and private actors participate on an equal standing. While regulated self-governance still means that governments hierarchically define the rules of the game for private governance, cooperative governance means that public and private actors cooperate in the development of such rules.

Instead of hierarchical intervention through legally binding instruments, the focus is on cooperation between state and society. On the one hand, it is the objective of these arrangements to allow for the negotiation of cooperative arrangements by including a broad range of public and private actors. On the other hand, a second feature of this pattern of 'joint policy-making' is the objective of replacing hierarchical intervention by voluntary agreements between public and private actors, such as industry associations.

Private self-governance

While in cooperative governance, the definition and implementation of public policies is based on close cooperation between state and society, these tasks are completely in the hands of private actors in private self-governance. Similar to cooperative governance, governance here is based on voluntary rather than legally binding instruments. An example is the declaration of the car industry in many countries to reduce car exhaust emissions to a certain level within a given period of time.

In this scenario, the provision of public goods basically depends on the governance capacity of private actors. Nevertheless, in such constellations states might still play a role in providing complementary governance contributions, hence 'refining' and guiding societal self-governance. For instance, public actors can increase the legitimacy of private governance by officially acknowledging the outcomes of private governance (Ronit and Schneider 1999; Lehmkuhl 2000) or by mediating and moderating between conflicting interests, stimulating communication and coordination between different actors (Willke 1995). Finally, as shown in recent studies on the role of international standardization in the information technology and communications sector, the activities of private actors might restrict the role of public actors (Knill and Lehmkuhl 1998; Knill 2001).

In conclusion, the above considerations indicate that governance patterns might vary strongly across countries and policy sectors, depending on the level of legal obligation present in political steering activities as well as the degree of cooperation between public and private actors in policy-making. Governance by public or private actors should not be seen as exclusive alternatives, but as mutually reinforcing.

Which model for which season? The relevance of institutional and political capacities

It would be wrong to assume that there is a free choice between the different governance models identified above, regardless of the particular context in which a certain political problem has to be addressed. Governance models cannot be understood in the light of mere ideological orientations or political preferences of the governing party, but against the backdrop of specific institutional and political structures which might vary across countries and policy sectors and so determine the governance capacity of public and private actors, i.e. their formal and factual ability to shape the formulation and implementation of public policies. By affecting the cost–benefit calculations of the actors involved and by defining a certain distribution of powers and resources between them, the existing institutional structures have an important impact on the capacity for governance by public or private actors.

The basic factor affecting the governance capacity of national governments is the structural potential for policy adjustments that aim at coping with new problems. For instance, economic and technological challenges may imply that common goods can no longer be provided if the existing policy arrangements are relied upon. Rather, fundamental policy adjustments at the national level might be necessary. Hence, the governance capacity of national governments can be expected to increase with the structural potential for such adjustments. The reform capacity also may vary from country to country and from policy to policy.

The potential for policy-making depends on the particular institutional arrangements characterizing a country's legal, administrative and political system (Knill 1999). It decreases with the number of formal and factual institutional veto points that affect the opportunities for national governments to initiate and push through institutional reforms against political and societal resistance (see pp. 135–6). Although the level of reform capacity does not make it possible to predict the timing or the concrete content and direction of policy reforms, it does indicate the structural potential of national governments to maintain their governance capacity by adjusting policy arrangements in the light of the challenges emerging from economic internationalization. These considerations suggest that the more governments need to rely on broad political support when developing their policies, the more do governance models – which incorporate private actors into the formulation and implementation of public policies (regulated self-governance, cooperative governance or even private self-governance) – constitute appropriate alternatives. However, as for public actors, the governance capacity of private actors cannot simply be taken for granted. Rather the participation of private actors in governance itself is crucially dependent on certain institutional preconditions. The most important factor refers to their organizational structures, namely that the level of private governance capacity will increase with both the strength and the degree of the organization of private actors.

Organizational strength defines the extent to which organizations are able to influence, monitor and sanction the behaviour of their members, i.e. the extent to which the organizations have sufficient autonomy to make decisions on behalf of their members and are capable of ensuring their compliance with these decisions. The level of organizational strength is generally expected to increase with certain organizational properties such as centralization and the degree of organization within a specific domain (Streeck and Schmitter 1981).

The degree of organization refers to the extent to which private actors are organized or willing to contribute to the provision of common goods by private organizations. As shown in Chapters 3 and 4, the size of the group and the extent to which organizations might offer 'selective incentives' for cooperation might play an important role in this context. The degree of organization may have important repercussions on the resources of the actors involved, including financial, personnel and technological capacities as well as scientific expertise. Examples of effective private governance reveal that – particularly with respect to complex technological problems – private actors must, surely, have more appropriate resources for developing corresponding solutions than do bureaucracies (Knill and Lehmkuhl 1998; Cutler 1999; Donahue and Zeckhauser 2011).

The successful incorporation of private actors into policy-making therefore cannot be assumed to constitute a feasible governance mode without prior consideration of the organizational structures in which these actors operate. Private self-governance or cooperative governance will not work, if the involved associations have no representative monopoly or are not able to ensure the rule-following behaviour of their members when it comes to the implementation of policy decisions. In other words, private governance is of little help, if societal structures are weakly developed.

In summary, determining the extent to which public and private actors will contribute to the solution of policy problems requires a detailed analysis of the particular context that characterizes the strategic constellation underlying the provision of a certain common good. The question then is: what patterns of interaction should be developed, given the variations in the governance capacities of private and public actors? For instance, where institutional constellations enjoy high governmental, but weak societal, governance capacities, then interventionist governance or regulated self-governance are still the most appropriate ways to address

Key points

- ❑ The combination of the degree of hierarchy and the extent of cooperation between public and private actors produces four ideal types of governance: interventionist governance, regulated self-governance, cooperative governance and private self-governance.

- ❑ Interventionist governance refers to the classical understanding of policy-making through government, which grants the state a dominant role vis-à-vis private actors.

- ❑ The state is still dominant in situations of regulated self-governance, but private actors participate in policy-making in a formalized and institutionalized manner.

- ❑ Cooperative governance involves voluntary agreements between public and private actors.

- ❑ With private self-governance the provision of public goods completely depends on the governance capacity of private actors; the state only provides guidance in this processes.

- ❑ The appropriateness of these governance types for policy-making depends on the institutional and political context.

political problems. In the case of the opposite scenario (weak government, strong society), private self-governance or cooperative governance are the more viable alternatives.

The institutional strength of state and society thus constitutes an important aspect that affects the patterns of governance in a certain country or policy sector. As institutional configurations might vary across both sectors and countries, it is highly unlikely that ideological changes or common challenges emerging from globalization will yield an overall convergence in governance patterns.

When is governance good?

While the institutional and political context affects the appropriateness of governance patterns in the light of different problem constellations, they are not the only aspects that inform the choice of governance arrangements. In addition, the decision whether a certain mode of regulation reflects 'good governance' or not requires clarity about the normative benchmarks of such an evaluation (Baldwin *et al.* 2011: 76). When considering the current political and scientific discussion on 'good governance', it becomes obvious that these criteria are debatable. The main conflict deals with the question of whether the input or the output legitimacy of public policy should serve as the primary evaluation criterion (Scharpf 1999).

With respect to output factors, particular attention is paid to two aspects: (1) the extent to which a political system has the capacity of taking political decisions in a certain area; and (2) the extent to which these decisions are actually implemented and complied with. With respect to input legitimacy, the focus is primarily on the democratic quality of the governance process (for a detailed discussion, see Knill 2004; Knill and Lenschow 2005).

Decision-making capacity

A necessary, albeit not sufficient, condition for effective governance is the capability of governments to take a policy decision. As already mentioned in the previous section, this capacity cannot be taken for granted, but varies across different political systems, depending on the specific institutional rules characterizing the decision-making process.

However, the capacity of governments to take political decisions is not only affected by the institutional configuration in which they operate, but also by the underlying mode of governance. In other words, there exists a close linkage between this capacity and the respective levels of discretion and obligation implied by different modes of governance. As a general rule, one can expect the decision-making capacity of political systems to increase the more that powers and discretion are delegated to lower institutional levels (decentralization) and to private actors. The more the precise specification of policies is left to other actors or institutional levels, the less difficult it is to adopt these policies at the central level. The more policy discretion is delegated to potential veto players or policy opponents, the less will they mobilize against the policy in question.

Consequently, the ability to reach decisions can be expected to be lowest when governance follows the pattern of hierarchical intervention, with prescribed requirements that are detailed and legally binding and which affect the interests of many public and private actors who might resist the adoption of corresponding decisions. By contrast, a consensus between conflicting interests and the adoption of a certain policy will be less cumbersome and time-consuming when the degree of detailed governmental intervention into society 'from above' is lower. For instance, if the actors addressed by a certain decision have no obligation to comply with it, there is a relatively low probability of political resistance.

Implementation effectiveness

Good governance not only depends on legislative decisions, but also on the extent to which these decisions are actually implemented and complied with. Generally, implementing agencies or private actors have to take the necessary steps to fulfil the objectives spelled out in legislation or underlying agreements in both formal and practical terms. To what extent do the governance modes differ with respect to these aspects?

A specific advantage of hierarchical intervention lies in the fact that precise and obligatory rules have a higher potential for effective implementation, as the force of law can be used to impose fixed standards or objectives (Baldwin *et al.* 2011: 35). In the absence of legally binding requirements, by contrast, this 'push factor' is lacking and compliance rests solely on the 'goodwill' of the implementers. Hence, from this perspective, hierarchical intervention and regulated self-governance achieve a higher ranking than private self-governance and cooperative governance.

However, hierarchical 'push' is not the only factor affecting the implementation of policies. Of similar importance are 'pull factors', i.e. aspects which influence the willingness of implementing bodies and policy addressees to comply with regulatory rules. It has been argued that governance patterns that are responsive to the motivations and interests of implementers and the target actors contribute to implementing the regulation in question effectively. Analysing the different modes of governance from this perspective, we find that such patterns are particularly relevant with respect to regulated self-governance and co-governance. At first sight, private self-governance seems to rely positively on pull factors, as the incentive to escape top-down policies causes private regulators to formulate and comply with their own rules. This incentive, though, depends on the presence of a coercive threat. If it is perceived as weak, industry may respond to the opposite incentive to cheat. Private actors might implement rules in a rather light-handed way as the threat of enforcement or later top-down intervention, in case of self-governance failure, is low (Baldwin *et al.* 2011: 58).

These considerations suggest that implementation effectiveness will be highest in cases of regulated self-governance. Here, effective compliance is not only driven by hierarchical 'push', but also by societal 'pull'. For all other governance modes, at least one factor is missing. Most problematic in this respect is the pattern of private self-governance, at least in those constellations in which governmental threats of hierarchical intervention in the case of weak compliance are not feasible or credible.

Democratic legitimacy

With regard to democratic legitimacy, the focus is generally on questions of due process and accountability of governance patterns. 'Due process' relates to the decision-making and the implementation phase and claims public support on the basis of equal and wide participatory rights granted to those affected by policy decisions.

The issue of participatory rights refers to the scope of participation in the formulation of regulatory policy by those affected or involved in the implementation. At first glance, it seems to be quite obvious that private self-governance, co-governance as well as regulated self-governance constitute better alternatives than hierarchical intervention with regard to this criterion. These approaches all allow for the incorporation and participation of private actors in the formulation and implementation of public policies.

A closer look, however, reveals that this initial evaluation overlooks the problem of unequal access opportunities. On the one hand, and as already emphasized by Olson (1965), not every societal interest group is equally powerful. Hence, the opportunities to exert political influence might vary, with economic interests being typically represented much more strongly than 'public' interests, such as environmental or consumer protection. Participation therefore need not automatically coincide with equality of representation.

In addition, participatory patterns of policy-making usually imply a distinction between 'insiders' and 'outsiders'. This problem is particularly severe, for instance, in arrangements of regulated self-governance. While certain societal actors are granted a representational monopoly, other interests are excluded. This problem is even more pronounced in private self-governance. In this case, there is a high possibility that regulation will only take into account the interests of the actors directly affected (e.g. the industry in a certain sector), while the input of the general public (consumers, residents, etc.) remains very limited.

From these considerations it follows that, in terms of equal participation and access, neither regulated self-governance nor co-governance nor private self-governance necessarily constitute better alternatives to hierarchical intervention. If and to what extent this is the case is crucially dependent on the specific rules regulating the access of interested actors to policy-making.

With respect to the second dimension of due process – substantive equality – decentralization and legal discretion (as inherent in private self-governance and co-governance) may turn out to be a problem. Discretion opens up room for the unequal treatment of the target groups, inconsistencies within or between policies and distortions of the market due to different local policy patterns. The insistence on substantive equality is not uncontroversial, however, as it may go hand in hand with a great insensitivity to the circumstances experienced by those affected by policy decisions. Uniform rules do not take account of different administrative structures, established technologies or the salience of problems at subnational levels. Hence, we need to distinguish between policy content that requires uniform application due to the presence of certain problem types and policy content that can be achieved flexibly.

In other words, while decentralization is likely to impact positively on the level of access and participation, discretion does not contribute to substantive equality. The relative importance of this latter criterion varies with the policy intent. Second, the choice of steering mechanisms also affects due process. The hierarchical model contributes to substantive equality, while treating the openness of procedures and involvement of stakeholders as secondary; the more cooperative models emphasize the openness of the process more than equal outcomes.

Policy-makers may claim democratic legitimacy, even in cases where the public has not been involved in the rule-making process if they have, nevertheless, the opportunity of exercising public control over the policy authority (accountability). Both parliamentary and direct public control are enhanced by decentralizing policy tasks to regional or local public authorities or private actors through the use of discretionary instruments. The fact that in practice this may result in some confusion as to the placing of responsibility does not negate their potential to bring about a higher level of control, especially in a multilevel system. On the other hand, self-governance is clearly most problematic in terms of public control. Besides the remote sanctioning powers of public authorities, self-governance systems risk being captured by groups who are not representative of the general public – or even those affected by the policy – and becoming isolated from public oversight.

Key points

❏ Whether governance is 'good' or not can be evaluated on the basis of three dimensions: a political system's decision-making capacity; the implementation of its decisions; and its democratic legitimacy.

❏ Decision-making capacity might be expected to be low in the case of hierarchical intervention, but to increase with more cooperative forms of governance.

❏ Effective policy implementation is a function of hierarchical 'push' and societal 'pull'. Based on this reasoning, effective implementation is most likely in the case of regulated self-governance.

❏ Democratic legitimacy centres on the participation in and accountability of policy-making. With regard to the first, all governance types are problematic to some extent. The same holds true for accountability, although self-governance systems appear particularly problematic.

Conclusions

The governance concept provides a new perspective on policy-making as it moves beyond the policy cycle and patterns of how public and private interact. Governance is at the same time a complex concept that is applied differently in the literature. It is not only used to classify different modes of political steering (including hierarchy, markets and networks), but also as a notion representing a particular mode of steering, namely non-hierarchical patterns, which yields a distinction between government (hierarchy) and governance.

We have seen that precise statements on the extent to which there is a shift away from hierarchical modes of governance towards market competition or policy networks is difficult to assess. This can be traced to the fact that the reliance on market mechanisms need not automatically entail a reduction in hierarchical governance. At the same time, the increasing reference made to network governance might be not only a result of empirical shifts, but also be triggered by changes in the analytical perspective on the policy process. So it is difficult to judge whether non-hierarchical forms of political steering are on the rise.

Based on the degree of cooperation between public and private actors and the degree of legal obligation characterizing policy outputs we have further developed the discussion of different governance modes and identified different ideal types of governance. On this basis, we further discussed potential factors that account for varying governance patterns across countries and sectors. We have also showed that the classification of governance as 'good' or 'bad' strongly depends on the normative benchmark that is applied. In this regard, we differentiated between decision-making capacity, implementation effectiveness and democratic legitimacy.

The governance perspective is suitable for investigating the initial policy stages that consist of problem definition and agenda-setting as it might indicate whether the perspectives of all participants in the policy process have the same chances of being acknowledged during policy-making. Additionally, utilizing the governance concept also provides a clearer understanding of policy formulation and adoption. As we have illustrated, the general scope of participation and the extent to which policy-making is characterized by the creation of 'insiders' and 'outsiders' has far-reaching consequences for policy outputs. In this context, a central finding we made in Chapter 7 was that a poorly designed policy that lacks broad public acceptance is likely to fall short of its goals. It is also likely that the findings of evaluation studies are one source for changing forms of governance.

While the governance debate often more or less implicitly focuses on more cooperative forms, it is important to stress that hierarchical interventions continue to be widely used in modern states and that this is actually quite positive. No governance model works equally well for all constellations. Rather appropriate governance arrangements have to be designed carefully by taking into account the specific institutional and problem structures at hand. Even less hierarchical types of governance, in many instances, still indicate the need of a strong involvement of the state, either via classical patterns of hierarchical intervention or through institutionalized forms of cooperation between government and private actors. Modes of private self-governance hardly constitute a viable alternative to state intervention.

The evaluation of different governance modes shows that what is seen as good governance strongly varies with the respective evaluation criterion that is applied. Regardless of the criterion, it becomes apparent also at this stage that a simple demise of the state would mean 'throwing out the baby with the bath water'. Rather, effective and legitimate governance is crucially dependent upon the involvement of the state.

Web links

http://info.worldbank.org/governance/wgi/index.asp. The Worldwide Governance Indicators project reports indicators for 213 economies over the period 1996–2010 for six dimensions of governance.

www.eu-newgov.org. The website of the Integrated Project on New Modes of Governance provides publications on governance in Europe.

http://www.oecd.org/findDocument/0,3770,en_2649_33735_1_1_1_1_1,00.html. This is a link to the OECD Directorate for Public Governance and Territorial Development. It offers numerous publications and documents, especially on the topic of 'good governance'.

http://www.wcfia.harvard.edu/research_activities/harvard_mit_private_governance/overview. The Harvard–MIT Private Governance Working Group is a forum for scholars to discuss research on private governance, and it hosts some interesting publications and might be consulted for learning about relevant conferences and other events.

http://www.glogov.org/. The Global Governance Project is a joint research programme of 13 European research institutions. The project's website is a good resource of recent publications on governance.

http://www.brookings.edu/governance/Issues-in-Governance-Studies.aspx. At this website issues of the periodic series of papers in Issues in Governance Studies, published by the reputable US Brookings Institute, can be downloaded.

Further reading

Bovaird, T. and E. Löffler (eds) (2009) *Public Management and Governance*. London: Routledge. A volume that illustrates the increasing role the governance concept plays in public management.

Eliadis, P., M. Hill and M. Howlett (eds) (2005) *Designing Government: From Instruments to Governance*. Montreal/Kingston: McGill-Queens University Press. The strength of this book is that it systematically illuminates the relationship between policy instruments and governance, constituting an innovative approach to the study of governance.

Hale, T. and D. Held (eds) (2011) *The Handbook of Transnational Governance: Institutions and Innovations*. New York: Wiley. A comprehensive volume addressing some essential topics in transnational governance.

Kjær, A.M. (2004) *Governance*. Oxford: Polity. This book is a good complement to the first section of this chapter on the different concepts of governance.

Levi-Faur, D. (ed.) (2012) *The Oxford Handbook of Governance*. Oxford: Oxford University Press. This volume covers the main research topics in the study of governance.

Pollitt, C. and C. Talbot (eds) (2004) *Unbundled Government: A Critical Analysis of the Global Trend to Agencies, Quangos and Contractualisation*. London: Routledge. A coherent collection of articles on the consequences of cooperative forms of governance and the delegation of tasks to private actors.

Chapter 10

Public Policies beyond the Nation State

Reader's guide

The development of public policies is not restricted to the nation state. Rather governments have always cooperated at the international level in order to address common problems that cannot be effectively addressed by individual countries. In fact, it was the existence of transboundary effects and externalities that stimulated the creation of international regimes such as the Basel Convention governing the international movement of hazardous waste or the United States–Canada Great Lakes water quality regime. As a result, there is an increasing number of public policies that reach beyond the nation state. While interdependencies are certainly one of the most important drivers of this process, social, political, economic and technological changes equally contribute to it. In light of these developments, it is our central objective in this chapter to identify analytical factors that influence the formulation and implementation of public policies beyond the nation state, that is, international public policies. We will first offer a general assessment of the rationales for international cooperation and provide an overview of the actors and institutions involved in policy-making beyond the nation state. This step involves combining public policy analysis with the disciplines of international relations and comparative political economy. We will then address interest constellations and mechanisms affecting the dynamics of policy formulation at the international level. Finally, we turn to the peculiarities and challenges that characterize the implementation of these policies. In this way, we take up once again two important stages of the policy-making process, namely decision-making and implementation.

Since the 1990s, there has been a growing shift in scholarly attention from the national to the international and global level of policy-making. Students of public policy, international relations and comparative political economy have become more and more interested in the factors affecting the formulation and implementation of public policies beyond the nation state as well as potential interactions between policy-making at the international and the domestic level. In response to the real-world developments of increasing international cooperation and growing economic and technological interdependencies between states, as well as the considerable progress in the process of European integration, scholars of public policy and international relations have begun to focus on theories and patterns of global governance (Czempiel and Rosenau 1992; Young 1994; Stone 2008; see also Chapter 9).

The shift in scholarly attention has not only been characterized by a partial convergence in terms of the analytical concepts and the subjects of analysis of the different fields of political science, i.e. public policy, international relations and comparative political economy – it has also been characterized by the rise of a new catchword, 'globalization', which has been seen as the crucial driving force behind the development of public policies beyond the state. The problem with this term is, however, that it still lacks a comprehensive and generally accepted definition.

On the one hand, 'globalization' can be seen as an intensified version of interdependence between states driven by economic liberalization, which has rendered nation states increasingly sensitive and vulnerable to each other. This vulnerability, in turn, constitutes an important driving force for international cooperation, i.e. the establishment of international organizations and regimes to manage and regulate these interdependencies (Cooper 1968). On the other hand, 'globalization' can be characterized as a phenomenon that is qualitatively different from mere interdependence, and as even being caused by the latter. According to this understanding, instead of being linked to nation states, 'globalization' refers to increasing cross-border transactions by private actors.

As this book is concerned with *public* policies, our focus is on nation states rather than private actors. Hence we will start from the problem of interdependence between states and consider 'globalization' in terms of the phenomenon of increasing interdependence (seee Braun and Gilardi 2006). The starting point of this chapter therefore concerns the conditions and patterns of international cooperation. Public policies beyond the nation state refer to the formulation and implementation of policies via international organizations and regimes. This does not lead to a neglect of the role of private actors in this process: they are integrated into the analysis insofar as they participate in the making of public policies. Purely private policies, such as codes of conduct or private arbitration, are not taken into account as they are beyond the scope of this book (see Chapter 1).

This analytical choice is further justified by the fact that after the 'big wave' of globalization research and debates on 'governance without government', it is generally acknowledged that the nation state still matters a lot in the development of policies beyond it, more than was assumed in the early stages of the global governance debate. Paraphrasing the study by Evans *et al.* (1985) and Weiss (1998), it seems fair to say that the 'state is back in' in the globalization debate, at least to a much greater extent than some scholars had assumed during the 1990s (Héritier 2002; Holzinger *et al.* 2008a, 2008b; Tömmel and Verdun 2009). In light of these developments, we will identify analytical factors that are central to influencing the formulation and implementation of international public policies.

Public policies beyond the nation state: general assessment

There is a consensus in the literature that political, social, economic and technological changes generally discussed under the term 'globalization' – here understood as the intensification of interdependencies between states – have significantly affected the conditions for national policy-making. In particular, the increasing integration of national markets and the emergence of transnational information and communication networks challenge the autonomy and effectiveness of national governments in defining and providing public goods by developing appropriate policy responses (Cerny 1995; Kobrin 1997; Knill and Lehmkuhl 2002a, 2002b; Holzinger 2008).

On the one hand, economic and technological interdependencies have created a range of problems that exceed the scope of national sovereignty and can therefore no longer be sufficiently resolved by the unilateral action of national governments. Examples include the regulation of electronic commerce and the protection of intellectual property rights over digital information. On the other hand, the emergence of globally integrated markets poses new challenges for the regulation of domestic problems. More specifically, it has been claimed that globalization puts pressure on national governments to redesign national regulations for avoiding excessive regulatory burdens imposed on domestic industries.

In view of this constellation, national governments frequently try to cooperate and to establish international regimes and organizations in order to maintain their capacity to address social and political problems that extend beyond the parameters of national sovereignty. International regimes are generally defined as 'implicit or explicit principles, norms, rules and decision-making procedures around which actors' expectations converge in a given area of international relations' (Krasner 1983: 2; see also Hasenclever *et al.* 1997). International organizations, by contrast, refer to stable forms of cooperation founded on the grounds of an international agreement (Simmons and Martin 2002; Higgott 2008). Indeed, the number, relevance and regulative activities of international regimes and organizations have grown steadily over the past few decades (see Breitmeier *et al.* 2006; Reinalda 2009). National policy-makers delegate tasks and competences to organizations that are in a better position than national governments to develop policy responses to problems exceeding the scope of national boundaries.

As a result, the development of international public policies is characterized by the involvement of a huge and still growing range of different international – both governmental and non-governmental – organizations whose relevance might vary from sector to sector and issue to issue. To get a basic understanding of these developments, we first have to learn more about the reasons driving general trends towards policy-making beyond the nation state. We will then provide an overview of institutions and areas of international public policy.

Public policy beyond the nation state: underlying rationales

Why do national governments engage in the delegation of powers to international regimes and organizations? Which factors account for the rise in international organizations and regimes and their growing differentiation and institutionalization? To explain this development, two aspects must be taken into account, namely, constellations in which the scope of the underlying problem exceeds the scope of territorially bounded regulatory structures, and restrictions on national policy options as a result of economic interdependencies between states.

Incongruence between transnational problem structures and regulatory structures
In many instances, the development of public policies beyond the nation state is driven by the existence of transnational problems that cannot be effectively addressed by the unilateral action of individual countries. Typical examples of transnational problems can be found, for instance, in the environmental field. Problems, such as climate change and global warming, have implications at a global scale and require far-reaching international cooperation (including more or less all states) for the development of solutions that still have not yet been adopted. In addition, many transboundary problems exist that can be addressed by the cooperation of smaller groups of countries, such as water pollution of transboundary rivers where downstream countries might suffer from polluting

activities in upstream countries. An example is the Great Lakes Water Quality Agreement of 1978 concluded by the governments of Canada and the United States. Problems of transnational scope, however, are not restricted to the transboundary effects of environmental pollution, but can also be observed in many other areas, such as global diseases, migration, the regulation of international financial markets (Sinclair 1999) or the international harmonization of telecommunication, broadcasting or internet standards (Schmidt and Werle 1998; Akdeniz 2008).

As transnational problems might vary in scope, the range of countries whose cooperation is needed in order to develop policy responses might also differ. While many problems (like climate change, financial market regulation or telecommunications standardization) have a worldwide range, other problems can be addressed by setting up regional regimes and organizations (like the EU) or multilateral cooperation between a few countries (e.g. the Mediterranean Commission on Sustainable Development).

In addition, it is important to emphasize that not every problem triggered by globalization is necessarily of global scope and hence not every problem created by globalization exceeds the regulatory scope of national governments. It might well be that a problem created by economic and technological interdependence can still be sufficiently resolved within the territorial boundaries of one nation state, while such solutions are no longer feasible for other problems.

Under certain conditions, even problems of global scope might be effectively resolved within national boundaries. Such constellations are possible when the extent to which a good is provided is determined by the largest individual contribution – that is, by the 'best shot' (Hirshleifer 1983; Holzinger 2002). Despite the fact that the scope of the problem exceeds a single jurisdiction and thus impedes authoritative rule-making, other actors might accept the contribution of a single actor. An example of this scenario is the provision of a global system for the administration of internet addresses and domain names. One state (the United States) has resolved the problem for all other states by developing an appropriate system (Knill and Lehmkuhl 2002b).

However, this is only one of the basic options concerning the ways in which individual contributions and the provision of a public good can be linked. In many cases the level of provision is based on the sum of individual contributions, e.g. the activities of individual states addressing the problem of global warming. It is conceivable that the provision of the good is determined by the smallest individual contributions, that is the 'weakest link' (Holzinger 2002). For instance, the control of illegal and harmful content on the internet is de facto determined by the country with the lowest regulatory standards, given that providers of such material can move their services across national borders. It is becoming apparent that in both of these cases, activities of individual states are no longer sufficient for coping with problems of global scope. Hence, there is a need for transnational solutions.

Economic interdependencies

The need to develop public policies beyond the nation state emerges not only from the existence of problems that exceed the scope of territorially bounded regulatory structures, but also from restrictions on governmental options to address domestic problems. These restrictions result from global market integration intensifying economic interdependencies between states.

With the increasing abolition of national trade barriers, there is the potential that the international mobility of goods, workers and capital puts pressure on nation states to redesign domestic market regulations to avoid excessive regulatory burdens (Goodman and Pauly 1993; Keohane and Nye 2000). As a consequence, national governments compete over the optimal design of domestic regulations in order to attract foreign capital and to improve the competitive position of their economy. On the one hand, the presence of mobile capital can induce governments to attract capital from elsewhere by lowering regulatory requirements (e.g. social or environmental standards), and, on the other, the threat to remove domestic capital can exert pressure on governments to lower the level of environmental and labour regulation (Drezner 2001: 57–9).

While much research effort has been dedicated to the almost classical question of the extent to which regulatory competition induces races to the regulatory top or bottom between countries (Vogel 1995; Scharpf 1997b; Holzinger 2002; Holzinger and Knill 2008; Tosun 2012), much less emphasis has been placed on the fact that countries might anticipate and reduce potential competition effects and their induced restriction on the national set of feasible strategies by international cooperation. In other words, countries that are strongly integrated economically may seek to avoid problems of collective action by harmonizing regulatory standards. Hence, they may pre-empt potential effects of regulatory competition in order to maintain their 'steering potential' (see Knill and Lehmkuhl 2002a, 2002b; Knill *et al.* 2008b).

A case where these effects are certainly most pronounced is the EU. Although economic integration has always been a core objective of European integration, the establishment of the Single Market has been accompanied by enduring efforts to harmonize social, environmental and consumer protection regulation. European integration in these areas at least partially emerged as a result of intersectoral spillovers that demanded responses in policy areas that did not originally belong to the Community's field of activity. To put it more generally, developments in international cooperation do not always occur independently from one

Box 10.1   EU polity

The EU operates through a system of supranational institutions and intergovern-
mentally made decisions negotiated by the member states. Important institutions
include the Council of the EU, the European Council, the European Parliament,
the European Commission and the European Court of Justice (for an overview,
see Hix and Høyland 2011). The Council of the EU is the legislative body. It
meets regularly in ten different formations depending on the policy topic on the
agenda, e.g. agriculture and fisheries, competitiveness or environment. Every
meeting of the Council is attended by one minister from each member state. The
European Council consists of the heads of state or government of the member
states, together with its appointed president, and the president of the
Commission. This body has no legislative functions, but defines the general
political directions and priorities of the EU. The European Parliament – together
with the Council – is responsible for policy-making and the EU budgetary
process. The European Parliament exercises democratic supervision over the
European Commission. It has the power to dismiss it by adopting a motion of
censure by two-thirds of its members. The Parliament is the only EU organ that is
directly legitimized by elections, which are held every five years. Members of
the Parliament are organized into seven Europe-wide political groups and do not
form national blocks. The Commission is composed of one Commissioner from
each member state appointed for a five-year term by agreement between the
member states, who are subject to approval by the Parliament. It has two important roles. On the one hand, it enjoys considerable powers in agenda-setting and
drafting EU policies, given its exclusive right of formally initiating policy proposals. On the other hand, the Commission acts as the 'guardian of the treaties'
and has to ensure that the legislation adopted by the Council and the European
Parliament are being implemented in the member states. The judiciary branch of
the EU is the European Court of Justice. It is composed of one judge from each
member state.

another, but rather push and pull each other (Lindberg and Scheingold
1970; Burley and Mattli 1993).

Overview: organizational forms and areas of international public policy

The making of public policies beyond the nation state is characterized by
the involvement of a huge amount of different organizational forms and
touches on a broad range of different policy sectors. At a general level,
these organizational forms can be distinguished along two criteria: (1)
whether they are governmental or non-governmental; and (2) whether
they are of international or national scope.

The role and influence of national governments is of crucial importance
for understanding the emergence of policies beyond the nation state.

Cooperation between national governments constitutes the precondition of any international public policy. Often, but not always, this cooperation entails the establishment of international organizations. Similar to national politics, the making of public policies beyond the nation state, in many instances, is characterized by the involvement and participation of various NGOs. With regard to these, a general distinction is made between non-profit organizations representing public interests, such as environmental protection, development aid or human rights, and organizations representing private sector interests, such as business associations or individual companies. Again, these organizations can be both national and international in scope, including international NGOs such as Amnesty International, the International Red Cross, Médecins Sans Frontières or the International Union for the Conservation of Nature, along with international interest groups, multinational corporations and national organizations who seek to influence the policy position of their governments in international negotiations. Moreover – and again comparable to national politics – the making of international public policies can entail the widespread participation of scientific experts and advisory boards operating at the national and international level (Puchala and Hopkins 1983: 78; Haas 1992).

As it is impossible to offer an exhaustive list of organizations and sectors of international public policy, in this section we take a different point of departure by suggesting some basic analytical criteria that help to structure this highly complex field. In so doing, our focus is on three dimensions, namely the form, the geographical scope and the sector of international cooperation. As the focus of this book is on *public* policies and hence on decisions and activities adopted by governments, our discussion concentrates on specific features of intergovernmental cooperation. Without denying the potential influence of non-governmental actors and institutions, we consider this analytical choice to be a more appropriate starting point for offering a basic overview of developments in public policy beyond the nation state.

Forms of international cooperation

As already emphasized, any public policy beyond the nation state requires some form of international cooperation. Three basic patterns can be distinguished: international organizations, international regimes and coalitions or groupings. The most prominent form of international cooperation is the establishment of international organizations. These are established by a treaty that has to be ratified by the member states' governments to provide the organization with its own legal personality. The establishment of an international organization entails the delegation of specific competences by member states and the establishment of administrative structures and resources to fulfil these tasks (Snidal and Abbott 2000; Simmons and Martin 2002; Higgott 2008).

Apart from these general characteristics, however, as we have already pointed out in Chapter 3, international organizations strongly differ in their functions, competences and organizational features (Pevehouse and Warnke 2005; Bauer and Knill 2007; Volgy *et al.* 2009). While some primarily serve as a neutral forum for debate others are characterized by the far-reaching delegation of national policy competencies, with the EU being the most developed example. While some organizations, like the EU, the OECD or the UN, cover a broad range of different sectors, others are restricted to single issues. These differences are reflected in varying administrative structures and resources. They range from very small treaty secretariats, such as the Ozone Secretariat with a staff of only 18 employees (see Bauer 2009) to large and complex bureaucracies, such as the UN Secretariat with a staff of over 12,000 just at its headquarters. In 2007 the *Yearbook of International Organizations* counted 964 intergovernmental organizations and 1,202 sub-organizations (emanations of their parent organization) (Union of International Associations 2008: 3).

International cooperation, however, need not exclusively be based on the establishment of an international organization but might be restricted to setting up treaty-based regimes. Many international treaties have not been set up as international organizations with their own legal personalities and administrative structures and instead rely on national administrations or ad hoc commissions. Some forms of international cooperation such as the G8 or G27 lack even a treaty basis, implying that – in a legal sense – they exist only as simple groupings or coalitions of states (Pevehouse and Warnke 2005).

Geographical scope

In addition to differences in the precise form and scope of responsibilities (single issue versus multi-issue) as well as the establishment of an administrative body, international cooperation might vary in its geographical scope. Four basic patterns can be empirically observed.

First, international cooperation can be of global scope, implying that membership is generally open to all nations. Examples include the UN and its specialized agencies, the Universal Postal Union, Interpol, the WTO and the IMF. Second, cooperation can be restricted to countries belonging to certain regions of the world. This category includes the EU, the Council of Europe, NATO, the African Union, the Organization of American States, the Association of Southeast Asian Nations (ASEAN), the Arab League, and the Organization for Security and Co-operation in Europe (OSCE). Third, international cooperation might be based on cultural criteria, including member countries that are characterized by similar linguistic, ethnic, religious or historical traditions. An illustrative example is the Nordic Council, which was formed in 1952 and has 87 elected members from Denmark, Finland, Iceland, Norway and Sweden as well as from the three autonomous territories of the Faroe Islands, Greenland and Åland. Fourth, cooperation can be based on functional considerations, such as the Convention for the Protection of the Marine Environment of the North-East Atlantic of 1972, of which the following countries are members: Belgium, Denmark, Finland, France, Germany, Iceland, Ireland, Luxembourg, the Netherlands, Norway, Portugal, Spain, Sweden, Switzerland and the United Kingdom.

Policy sectors
International cooperation can be found in a broad range of different policy sectors. Some international organizations like the UN, cover a policy spectrum that is more or less comparable to the scope covered by national governments (see pp. 51–3). In addition to these encompassing organizations, we find single-issue organizations in many different policy sectors. Basically, international cooperation is particularly pronounced in the following areas: security, human rights, social affairs (humanitarian aid, health care, education), environmental protection, economic regulation and technical standardization. These areas are characterized by the need to pool resources for effectively solving existing problems or a reduction in economic costs by means of harmonization. The second point predominantly holds true for international cooperation on economic regulation and technical standardization.

So far, we have concentrated on general patterns regarding the rationales as well as the forms, geographical scope and sectors of international cooperation. While these merely descriptive accounts offer a first overview of policy developments beyond the nation state, they still leave open the important questions of why countries with heterogeneous interests actually agree on common solutions and if and to what extent international agreements are actually complied with. These issues will be investigated in the following sections.

Key points

❑ The development of public policies beyond the nation state is driven by problems of transnational scope and growing economic interdependence between states.

❑ Types of international cooperation vary in their organizational forms, their geographical scope and the policy sectors they cover.

Policy formulation: typical interest constellations and interaction

The huge variety in forms and patterns of international cooperation implies that processes of policy formulation differ widely. This holds true in particular with regard to the relevant rules used for decision-making and the extent to which member states have delegated autonomous powers to international organizations. In the case of the EU, the European Commission constitutes a very powerful player at the stage of policy formulation, given the Commission's formal and exclusive right to initiate policy proposals as well as its attempts to build up informal and close working relationships with national civil servants, policy experts and interest associations (Egeberg 2006; Trondal 2010). As a result, processes of policy formulation in the EU are not easily comparable to those of other international organizations, where such autonomous powers are less developed.

In light of this constellation, the focus of this section is on the more general discussion of factors that render international cooperation more or less likely. When can we expect international cooperation to be successful? When are the involved countries able to achieve common policy solutions? When, by contrast, does the heterogeneity of member state interests yield a less favourable scenario for international cooperation?

To be sure, one could certainly argue that the joint development of policies at the international level is generally a highly difficult exercise. This can be related to two aspects that characterize policy-making beyond the nation state: the potentially high heterogeneity of national interest positions, and the very demanding quorums (in some cases, unanimity) for adopting joint solutions. International cooperation entails challenges for decision-making that are typical of multilevel systems, with policy adoption at the international level requiring the consent of most or all actors at national level (Scharpf 1988; Moravcsik 1993; Benz 2003).

In certain cases, these problems of joint decision-making can to some extent be reduced by the creation of so-called package deals. The latter require various decisions to be linked with one another during negotiations; concessions by individual countries in one area are thus compensated by the concessions of other states in other areas. Another possibility which can sway countries to give up their resistance is (monetary) compensation for the costs which arise for them during the implementation of planned measures (see Scharpf 1997b). The means of doing so are limited, though, as most international organizations do not have any specific financial resources from which such compensatory payments can be made. In other words, the opportunities to overcome decision-making problems in international negotiations seem rather restricted.

This general statement, however, is in surprising contrast with the very far-reaching developments in international cooperation that can be observed empirically. Obviously, there are ways to overcome success-fully the above-mentioned difficulties; and three aspects are of particular significance. First, national interest constellations may be defined to a great extent by the underlying problem type. This implies that the chances for successful international cooperation may vary from case to case. Second, there is evidence that international cooperation may be facilitated by the active efforts of individual states at the international level to influence the content and form of regulations according to their interests. These interests are particularly associated with minimizing the potential costs of administrative and institutional adaptation and at the same time securing the competitiveness of national industries. Third, it must not be underestimated that the interest constellations during inter-national negotiations can change as a result of learning processes and the diffusion of ways of perceiving and solving problems between the involved states. These processes, which are promoted by institutionalized forms of interaction between the involved actors, have significant ramifi-cations for the specific form and content of international policies.

The problem type

In the literature it is generally argued that the peculiarities of an under-lying policy problem have a significant impact on the politics involved in providing it. Basically, three distinct constellations are identified: coordi-nation, agreement and defection. For their part, each of these is charac-terized by a specific problem in resolving conflicts of interest. Depending on underlying interest constellations, international coopera-tion between the involved countries might be more or less difficult to achieve (Knill and Lehmkuhl 2002a, 2002b).

Coordination problems refer to constellations in which the involved countries have a strong common interest in the development of joint solutions and in which there is agreement between the countries upon the specific policy solution. Hence, international cooperation presumes com-munication between the involved countries. In the absence of strong interest conflicts between the involved negotiation partners, agreements may be achieved rather swiftly. For each individual country, international cooperation constitutes rational behaviour.

As soon as international cooperation aims at redistribution, however, it becomes more difficult to achieve an international agreement between states or collective action between private actors. Generally, such agree-ment problems are characterized by a common interest in the develop-ment of a common solution and by a pronounced disagreement about the kind of solution to be selected. In many instances, such constellations

Box 10.2   The Universal Postal Union

An example of the international coordination of national postal policies is through the Universal Postal Union (UPU). International postal communications were originally governed by bilateral agreements which answered the particular needs of each country. This system, involving as it did a great variety of rates calculated in different currencies and according to different units of weight and different scales, made it complicated to operate the service and hampered its development. The invention of steam navigation and the railway brought about a change in the postal system. Countries began to realize that, if international communications were to keep pace with the means of transport, formalities would have to be standardized and reduced. To simplify the complexity of this system, several countries (in particular the United States and Germany) called for an international solution, which led to the establishment of the UPU in 1874. The UPU is one of the oldest international organizations within the UN system and currently has 191 member states.

Its general purpose lies in the coordination of the activities of national postal authorities. Among the principles governing its operation, as set forth in the Universal Postal Convention and the General Regulations, two of the most important were the formation of a single territory by all signatory nations for the purposes of postal communication and uniformity of postal rates and units of weight. An important achievement of the treaty was that it ceased to be necessary, as it often had been previously, to affix the stamps of any country through which one's letter or package would pass in transit: the stamps of member nations would be accepted for the entire international route. The major purpose of the UPU is to ensure the technical and administrative compatibility and collaboration of national postal systems. While international cooperation at the level of the UPU might not be free of conflicts between member states, coordination rather than distribution is at the heart of its activities. At the same time, all countries share a common interest in cooperation (Brown 2001: 135).

can be observed when it comes to the international harmonization of standards, for example with regard to digital broadcasting. To ensure the compatibility and interconnectivity of their products, producers are generally interested in common standards. For reasons of economic competitiveness, however, they might prefer different options; e.g. they may try to promote their own product as the 'solution' to which other companies would have to adjust (Schmidt and Werle 1998).

A typical example that illustrates international agreement problems refers to the harmonization of environmental product standards in integrated markets. Product standards specify the quality and technical characteristics of a certain product, such as emission standards for passenger cars or the lead content of fuels. They have to be distinguished from process standards that typically define restrictions on the use of specific

---

Box 10.3   Indian ban on Chinese toys

China is a major manufacturer and exporter of toys. On many occasions, countries or regions with high consumer protection standards such as Australia, Canada, the United States and the EU have temporarily banned Chinese toys from their markets as some of them were found to pose health and safety risks. In 2009, India also imposed such a ban. This was lifted six months later, but the Indian trade ministry explained that Chinese toys, in order to be imported, would need to obtain certificates showing they conformed to standards prescribed by safety bodies such as the International Organization for Standardization or the American Society for Testing and Materials. In response to international calls, the authorities in China are now showing an increased interest in taking corrective action.

---

inputs or specify requirements, technologies or processes for industries. An example is the specification of emission standards for combustion plants (see Knill *et al.* 2008a; Knill and Tosun 2009; Tosun and Knill 2011).

In the case of product standards, we can expect all states to have a shared interest in common standards. Different national product standards and authorization procedures would pose restraints on industries in all countries and be at odds with the purpose of integrated markets. We are thus faced with a situation in which all states have an interest in harmonization and thus a common interest in international regulation (Holzinger 2002: 69).

The conflict of interest mainly relates to the level of regulation: poorer countries tend to prefer lower standards than rich countries. In developed countries, citizens may attach a high priority to issues like environmental quality. Accordingly, these countries may be willing to bear the costs of a more ambitious environmental policy. In developing member states, these issues are assumed to be of only secondary priority, since the population is less willing to bear the costs brought about by strict regulations (Scharpf 1997b; Holzinger 2002; Knill *et al.* 2008a).

In the literature, it is argued that those states that are interested in higher standards enjoy a more favourable negotiation position. This can be attributed to the fact that under certain conditions, high-regulating countries have the opportunity to introduce trade restrictions for products that do not adhere to their national levels. This is the case if the member states are entitled to enforce market segmentation, for health or environmental reasons for example, under the rules of the EU and WTO (Holzinger and Knill 2005, 2008).

The constellation of national interests facilitates the international harmonization of product standards at a high level of regulation. As a conse-

---

Box 10.4   The California effect

David Vogel (1995) has demonstrated that for product standards the erection of exceptional trade barriers can not only contribute to preventing a race to the bottom, but under certain conditions can also contribute to the tightening of regulations in individual states. This applies in particular when producers in states with low product standards are highly dependent on exports to states with stricter regulations. In order to avoid being confronted with different standards, those industries will press for a harmonization of regulations, which results in the elevation of standards in less strictly regulated markets. Vogel describes this effect using the example of California, whose stricter emissions regulations for automobiles triggered an increase in the standards of other US states (see Knill and Liefferink 2007: ch. 5).

---

quence, the establishment of integrated markets such as the European Single Market rarely result in the often-feared races to the bottom when it comes to the regulation of product standards. Rather, the above-mentioned constellation might bring about races to the top in which the dynamics of market integration cause the member states collectively to elevate their national standards (Vogel 1995; Scharpf 1997b; Holzinger and Knill 2005, 2008).

While, in principle, bargaining between actors can still resolve agreement problems, the prospects for international cooperation are gloomier for defection problems. The basic difference between problems of coordination or agreement and problems of defection is that, notwithstanding their common interest in the provision of a certain public good (e.g. reduction of transboundary air pollution) and corresponding cooperation agreements, when there are defection problems the involved countries prefer to free-ride, taking advantage of the contributions of the others. Among states, the risk of defection might either hamper the emergence of an international agreement or cause serious compliance problems.

This scenario is typical for the international harmonization of regulations that define common standards for industrial processes. In contrast to product standards countries have no common interest in international harmonization. For poor countries, in light of the lower level of economic development, harmonization at a high level would severely threaten existing industrial sectors. Harmonization at a low level would not be an attractive option either, because national industries would thus be exposed to increased competition from highly productive companies from the rich countries, who could offer their products at much cheaper prices. Rich countries, by contrast, would prefer international harmonization at their high regulatory level. If they cannot achieve this objective, harmonization at a lower level would be the second-best solution from an economic standpoint, in order to improve their competitive position vis-à-vis their competitors from the poorer member states. However, in light of the high priority attached to social and environmental protection in many rich countries, politically asserting the second solution is not viable. Thus national governments prefer the continuation of different national standards over international regulations at a low level (Scharpf 1996: 119–20; Holzinger and Knill 2005, 2008).

Compared to product standards, we should expect a less dynamic development with regard to the international harmonization of process regulations. First, for process standards there is no common harmonization interest across countries. Second, potential dynamics emerging from market segmentation are absent. No country can restrict the import of products which were produced under conditions which do not correspond with their own regulations on air quality control or water protection. Hence, if the regulation of production processes implies an increase in the costs of production, potentially hampering the international competitiveness of an industry, regulatory competition will exert downward pressures on economic regulations (Holzinger 2002). It is expected that governments will lower taxes, social or environmental standards in the face of lobbying or threats to exit made by the respective industry.

However, this sceptical view is frequently challenged by empirical findings. For example, the EU has passed very strict process standards in important areas such as air and water pollution control, chemical control and waste policy, which were not always at the level of the most ambitious member state, though in fact did go far beyond the standards of the least regulated states (Sbragia 2000; Knill and Liefferink 2007; Holzinger *et al.* 2008a, 2008b). It appears that member states often accept measures whose implementation is associated with significant economic and institutional costs (Héritier *et al.* 1996; Jordan 1999; Knill *et al.* 2008a). In other words, there is a considerable gap between theoretically forecasted cases of failure to achieve harmonization and empirical observations of successful international cooperation in many instances.

As a consequence, the distinction of different problem types and related interest constellations cannot provide a complete account of international cooperation. Nevertheless, this theoretical model contains important hypotheses which can serve as a point of departure for analysis and can be modified and further developed according to empirical findings. There are two patterns that characterize the formation of public policies beyond the nation state: the role of leader countries when it comes to transferring their regulatory patterns to the international level, and institutionalized forms of learning and policy diffusion (see Braun and Gilardi 2006). We will examine these factors more closely in the following sections.

The innovative potential of leader countries

Regardless of the specific problem type and constellation of national interests, the dynamics of international cooperation may be affected by the pioneering activities of leader countries. The latter are typically characterized by very advanced patterns of domestic regulation in a certain policy field, such as environmental or social policy. Compared to the developments in other countries and at the international level they are first movers. They adopt innovative regulations, even though these policies might entail competitive disadvantages for their industries and that they cannot presume that others might follow. In light of this constellation they seek to incorporate their national regulations into the international legislative process to the greatest possible extent. The activities of leader countries may thus constitute an important driving force of international cooperation, even in the case of interest constellations that at first glance hardly seem to provide a sufficient basis for the adoption of joint solutions.

Such patterns have been observed, in particular, for harmonization activities at the level of the EU. The fact that we observe European harmonization towards the most rather than the least stringent of existing member state regulations has been explained by the dynamics resulting from the activities of pioneer countries in influencing EU policies (Héritier *et al.* 1996; Jänicke and Weidner 1997; Liefferink and Andersen 1998; Jänicke and Jacob 2004).

These dynamics emerge from the interest of national governments in minimizing the institutional costs of adjusting domestic regulatory arrangements to EU policy requirements. In particular, highly regulating countries with a comprehensive and consistently developed regulatory framework might face considerable problems with adjustment, if European policies reflect regulatory approaches and instruments that depart from domestic arrangements.

As a result, these countries have a strong incentive to promote their own approaches at the European level. The most promising way to do this is to rely on the strategy of the 'first move'; i.e. to try to shape European policy developments at the stages of problem definition and agenda-setting rather than later in the process. This requires that member states have to win the support of the EU Commission, which has the formal monopoly over initiating policies at the EU level. The Commission, in turn, is generally interested in strengthening and extending supranational policy competencies. As a consequence, only those domestic initiatives that fit with these objectives have the chance of succeeding. This specific interaction of national and supranational interests favours the development of innovative and ambitious policies at the EU level, hence driving EU harmonization towards stricter regulation.

What impact do these dynamics have on policy-making and the level of regulation at the international level? Firstly, we should bear in mind that this mechanism to a considerable extent accounts for the broad spectrum of instruments and patterns of regulation, which reflect different regulatory traditions at the national level, as it is not always the same countries that assert themselves in situations marked by regulatory competition. Secondly, the influence of leader countries can help to prevent the often feared race to the bottom in social or environmental policy.

Against this background, there is considerable potential for an ongoing expansion of more stringent regulations at the international, and particularly the EU, level. This general trend of course does not rule out the possibility of negotiations breaking down in individual cases or international regulatory approaches partially lagging behind those of individual member states. Nevertheless, the role of leader countries might enhance the scope and level of international regulatory cooperation in the long term.

Deliberation and diffusion

Up to now we have presumed that the interests of nation states are consistent and defined clearly during international negotiation processes. An agreement can only be expected when the preferences of national governments are compatible or distributional conflicts can be avoided by concessions, package deals or compensation payments. In other words, a relatively static constellation of national interests is assumed, which defines the options for the design of policy measures at the international level.

However, Joerges and Neyer (1997) have demonstrated that this form of intergovernmental bargaining is by no means the only mode of interaction characterizing international negotiations. Other instances can be observed in which the patterns of interaction are influenced to a lesser extent by actors defending and asserting national policy positions than by a collective problem-solving orientation. In such cases, national representatives develop a common understanding of problems and solutions, such that national ideas and interests are not regarded as static.

Such processes are facilitated by a specific form of interaction which is described by Joerges and Neyer as deliberation. With deliberations, the main focus is placed on discussion and reasoning on the basis of scientific and technical insights rather than on strategic bargaining to assert national interests. This 'deliberative problem solving' facilitates learning processes between negotiating partners (see Stone 2008; Howlett and Joshi-Koop 2011). Transnational networks of experts or epistemic communities emerge (Haas 1992) in which converging ideas, assumptions and convictions develop by means of the collective professional orientation and socialization of the participating actors. This in turn provides the basis for a convergence of positions of national interest (see Chapter 11).

However, the development of this kind of problem-solving orientation cannot be taken for granted for all negotiations at the international level. We can identify three factors which can facilitate deliberative problem-solving. First, the chances for deliberative problem solving increase with the uncertainty surrounding the policy's possible distributive effects. In such constellations, national interests and problem definitions are less structured in advance and can be modified more easily. Second, institutionalized interactions between national representatives over a longer period enhance the diffusion of scientific and technical expertise between the member states of an international organization. Third, and related to the last aspect, the stimulation of such processes of transnational policy learning presupposes the existence of institutional arrangements which allow for the regular and continuous exchange of arguments and ideas between national experts and representatives. The development of these structural arrangements varies across international organizations and is most developed in the EU.

Deliberative problem-solving processes not only lead to the convergence of national policy positions and so to agreement at the international level, but also to a facilitating of the international diffusion of innovative policy concepts, independently of the adoption of international measures. For example, analysts frequently observe the emulation and transfer of policies and regulatory instruments that have proven to be particularly successful in one country (see Simmons and Elkins 2004; Volden 2006; Gilardi *et al.* 2009). The trend towards internationally converging structures and regulatory patterns that are frequently obtained (Bennett 1991; Holzinger and Knill 2005; Knill 2005) can in turn contribute to a decrease in national conflicts of interests over decisions on international measures.

Kern *et al.* (2001), for instance, show that international organizations play an important role in accelerating and facilitating cross-national policy learning. They constitute important channels for multilateral communication and policy diffusion. Kern demonstrates that – compared to policy exchange resting on bilateral and horizontal communication between countries – policy models spread much broader and faster if these countries are members of the same international organization. These results are confirmed by a macro-quantitative analysis on environmental policy convergence by Holzinger *et al.* (2008a, 2008b). Analysing policy developments in 24 Western countries between 1970 and 2000 for a broad range of different policy measures and standards, they find not only an impressive degree of cross-national convergence, but also that this development has to a considerable extent been driven by processes of communication in international organizations.

Log jam or progress? Conflict in international policy-making

The analysis up to now has shown that international policy-making is marked by different constellations of national interests and patterns of consensus building. Depending on the analytical perspective, we arrive at different assessments of the possibilities for successful cooperation. Nevertheless, we can conclude with a number of general observations.

As a rule, there are more favourable conditions for extensive international harmonization in product regulation than in process regulation. This can be traced back to two factors: on the one hand, the harmonization of product standards facilitates market integration and thus is associated with advantages for all involved countries; on the other hand, those states that advocate a high level of regulation are in a better negotiation position, because they have the legal means to enforce high standards single handedly, if need be. Both of these preconditions exist in the area of process regulation.

However, we should not infer from this that all attempts to harmonize process regulation will fail or result in suboptimally low regulatory standards. Depending on how countries anticipate they will be affected in economic and ecological terms by regulatory proposals, the constellation of national interests can have a different impact on the capacity for action at the international level. An important factor which tends to help overcome political impasses results from the first-mover activities of pioneer countries.

Finally, the interest constellation between countries cannot always be viewed as a static factor. Policy may be altered because of the deliberation and diffusion that may take place, under certain conditions, during institutionalized cooperation at the international level. Deliberation and diffusion in turn facilitate the convergence of national understandings of problems and solutions. By these means failures in negotiation can be avoided or overcome.

Key points

❏ The chances for successful international cooperation are strongly affected by the underlying problem type and the related constellation of national interests. A basic distinction can be made between problems of coordination, agreement and defection.

❏ The pioneering activities of leader countries that adopt innovative domestic policies can stimulate international cooperation.

❏ Processes of transnational policy learning driven by deliberation and diffusion can improve the basis for international cooperation.

Policy implementation

The fact that countries have adopted common policies at the international level, by no means guarantees that the very same countries are also willing and able to implement them. In Chapter 7, we saw that implementation problems – even in merely domestic settings – are fairly widespread. This is even more the case when it comes to the formal and practical transposition of international or supranational law. Compared to national policies the implementation of international policies is characterized by features that further reduce the likelihood of effective compliance. These features particularly aggravate implementation problems with regard to those factors which we mentioned in Chapter 7, namely deficient policy design, control deficits, and the preferences and strategies of the involved actors.

Deficient policy design

International policies are generally more vulnerable to design deficits than national policies. This can be traced to the more cumbersome and complex decision-making process involved, entailing the participation of many actors with often highly heterogeneous interests. In many negotiation constellations at the international level, options for resolving distributional conflicts between the involved countries by compensation payments or packages are rather limited. As a consequence, agreement on common policies can often only be achieved by compromise formulae that grant national governments sufficient leeway to adjust international policy requirements in the light of domestic conditions and interest constellations.

A first pattern that can be observed comprises policy designs that allow member states a high discretion with regard to the interpretation of policy requirements. This is with good reason, as it permits member states to accommodate their specific interests. At the same time, however, this freedom leads to cross-country differences in the application of international rules which were originally intended to be uniform.

An example of such regulations is formed by the series of EU directives (i.e. legislative acts that require member states to adopt measures in order to implement their provisions) on water quality, for instance for bathing water, where countries themselves are free to define the bodies of water to which the directives apply. This form of self-definition, combined with the unclear wording of the classification criteria, leaves it open to member states to decide whether they want to apply the directive or not, depending on their specific environmental policy goals. In the directive on the quality of bathing water, for example, 'bathing water' is defined as a body of water 'in which bathing is explicitly authorised by the competent authorities of each member state, or bathing is not prohibited and is traditionally practised by a large number of bathers'. This definition certainly leaves a lot of room for interpretation (Knill 2008: 73–88).

A second way of balancing conflicting national interests is by the use of vague and open legal terms that leave a lot of room for interpretation during national implementation. In international environmental regulation, for instance, we find two recurring and vague legal terms, where approval requirements are defined on the basis of the 'technological state of the art' and in line with 'economically reasonable' technical obligations. Very different judgements can be made when deciding if a measure is 'economically reasonable' or if the requirements linked to the current 'state of technology' are fulfilled.

Third, member states opposing a certain policy are often appeased by granting them specific exemptions. These can refer to both formal and substantive regulatory requirements. A common example of the former category is the possibility of exceeding compliance deadlines. International policies normally define a point in time as to when certain provisions (e.g. maximum permissible values) come into effect or as to when certain standards must be achieved. In some cases, however, member states are given the opportunity to deviate from this deadline if certain conditions are fulfilled. For instance, the EU bathing water directive allows member states to deviate from the generic implementation deadline by ten years in exceptional cases. In order to do so, the states must present adequate reasons for non-compliance as well as water management plans.

Exemptions referring to the latter category of substantive aspects typically refer to the scope and level of regulatory requirements and might vary from case to case, dependent on the specific regulatory issue. These specific exemptions sometimes grant individual countries extensive means to deviate from international requirements, usually resulting in the watering down of the initial common goal. The EU directive on large combustion plants, for example, contains various special agreements accommodating the interests of individual member states. Thus, new plants with a capacity of more than 400 megawatts are allowed to exceed twice-over the stipulated emission limit for sulphur dioxide, as long as they are in operation for less than 2,200 hours per year. This provision was included following pressure from France, where so-called 'peak-load plants' are used to cover peaks in demand which cannot be accommodated at short notice by nuclear power (see Knill and Liefferink 2007: ch. 10).

These various exceptions, extensions and vague legal terms entail that individual countries often have considerable room for manoeuvre in implementing international policies, despite often seemingly 'uniform' policy design. This, in turn, results in a differentiation of international policy effects at the national level. In most cases, such differentiation leads to a diluting of original policy objectives. Hence, regulations allowing for deviations from initial policies can be characterized as design deficits. They are a considerable part of the story behind implementation deficits in international policy.

Control deficits

In Chapter 7 we saw that many implementation problems are linked to control deficits; i.e. constellations in which political principals are not able to control the agents that implement policy. For several reasons, implementation of international policy is particularly vulnerable to agency drift, which typically entails more or less far-reaching deviations from the formal and practical requirements of any policy.

First, given its nature as a multilevel process, the implementation of international policies usually involves more institutional levels and actors than is usually the case for national political systems. As each of these actors (international bureaucrats, national politicians, administrative agencies, street-level bureaucrats, transnational and national interest groups) might pursue different objectives, there is a high likelihood of deviation from initial policy goals (Pressman and Wildavsky 1973; Winter 2003).

Second, in monitoring the implementation of international law, international bureaucracies possess very limited resources for enforcing the cooperation of the public and private actors participating in the implementation process. On the one hand, responsibility for the execution of international policies generally lies with the member states. This means that international bodies have no competence to intervene directly in the implementation process at the domestic level. The defining characteristic of international law is the lack of a centralized enforcement mechanism. When international law is enforced, this is done by states themselves (Brewster 2009). Even in the EU, where the Commission is responsible for ensuring and monitoring the implementation of EU law in the member states, its powers are fairly restricted. Although the Commission can initiate infringement proceedings with the European Court of Justice against member states that do not comply with EU law, it has very limited opportunities to intervene directly in national implementation processes. As a consequence, even for the EU – where control powers are comparatively well-developed – many studies emphasize the presence of far-reaching implementation deficits (see Tallberg 2002).

On the other hand, a major obstacle to controlling effectively the implementation of international law is linked to problems with data and monitoring. International organizations are strongly dependent on information provided by the member states. Implementation deficits can hence only be discovered if they are reported as such by member states or if failures are reported to the international body concerned by national interest groups or citizens. Though, in this way, potential deficits in formal transposition can still be detected rather easily, the detection of implementation deficits is much more difficult when it comes to the practical application of international law.

In view of their limited competences and resources, international bodies are unable to monitor and control the implementation of international policies as they are practised in member states. Instead, they have to rely on information provided by national authorities or complainants. This entails problems for comparing implementation performance across countries. The more developed are administrative monitoring capacities and structures of interest organization in a country, the more likely is it that potential implementation problems will be detected and reported. This leads to a paradoxical constellation where countries with higher implementation capacities face a higher risk of being accused of failing to implement than countries in which such capacities are less developed.

In summary, the implementation of international policy can generally be expected to suffer from far-reaching control deficits. The latter can be traced not only to the huge number of institutional levels and actors that are involved in the implementation process, but also to the lack of comprehensive data on implementation effectiveness and the underdeveloped ability of international bodies to sanction both formal and practical non-compliance.

Preferences and strategies of the involved actors

The high dependence on the willingness and capacity of national governments to implement effectively international law underlines the crucial relevance of the interests of national actors in accounting for varying degrees of implementation. The central role of national actors and, in particular, national governments in ensuring compliance is underscored by the fact that international law has no direct effect at the member state level; i.e. in order to become effective international law has to be transposed into national law by national legislation. In a similar vein, the fact that international law is not superior to national law entails that national transposition legislation can be annulled by new national law at any time. It is important to emphasize, however, that these characteristics do not apply to the relationship between EU law and national law. According to decisions by the European Court of Justice, EU legislation is not only superior to national law (and hence cannot easily be reversed by national legal acts), but also becomes effective at the national level even without transposition legislation being already in place (Brewster 2009; Nollkaemper 2009).

This leads us to the general question as to when we might expect national governments to transpose and apply effectively international policies. Several factors should favour effective implementation. First, it may be argued that international law and organizations are endogenous to the collective preferences of states, as are their membership criteria and decision-making rules. Hence, high rates of compliance can be due to the fact that international agreements may not depart much from what states would have done in their absence (Bueno de Mesquita 2009: ch. 11). Second, there is evidence that states are generally concerned about their international reputation. A state that violates international law develops a bad reputation, which leads other states to exclude the violator from future cooperative opportunities. Anticipating a potential loss of future gains, states have an incentive to implement effectively international policies, even if the latter are not in their immediate interests (Brewster 2009). Compliance with international law, according to this view, can be instrumental in building leaders' reputations and increasing their chances of political survival (Bueno de Mesquita 2009: 353).

However, these arguments can be challenged on various grounds. First, as emphasized by Martin and Simmons (1998: 743), once established, institutional arrangements will constrain and shape domestic policy choices, even as they are constantly challenged and reformed by member states. International institutions are therefore not only subject to the decisions of states, but at the same time impact on subsequent governmental activities. Even if we assume that, at the time of adoption, a certain international policy was fully in line with the interests of national governments, subsequent developments at the domestic level might put this initial congruence into question.

Such developments can be linked to changing policy salience at the national level or to changes in government. It may not be taken for granted that the government in office when a certain international policy was negotiated and the government that is in office when it comes to the implementation of these policies have similar interests with regard to the regulation of the issue at stake. In addition, swift changes in international rules are often prevented by the fact that international decision-making processes usually require high quorums (Pierson 1996). In these situations of so-called joint decision traps, a few countries or even only one state that is in favour of the status quo can block reform attempts by other countries (Scharpf 1988).

Second, the reputation argument raised above needs modification. The extent to which reputation concerns will lead to compliance will depend on how national governments weigh the potential costs of being excluded from future cooperative agreements and the degree to which they are tempted to renege on international agreements to play to the domestic audience and therefore to increase their chances of re-election.

Box 10.5   Implementation of international agreements in federal systems

Numerous empirical analyses have demonstrated that the implementation of the provisions of international agreements is likely to depend on domestic actor and institution constellations. Against this backdrop, Paquin (2010) asks whether the existence of federal political systems affect implementation, by examining Belgium and Canada. The Belgian system is characterized by substate actors who have the role of co-decision, in which pronounced intergovernmental mechanisms are in place. In Canada, by contrast, the decision-making process is more centralized and intergovernmental mechanisms are poorly institutionalized. The analysis reveals that the Belgian system displays higher implementation effectiveness, largely because its substate actors have an important role at every step of the conclusion of an international treaty.

In conclusion, there is a considerable potential that countries – even if they initially agree with international regulations and laws – deviate from international policy objectives during the implementation stage. The major reasons for such deficits are linked to inadequate policy designs and control deficits as well as the preferences and strategies of the domestic actors involved in the implementation process, in particular national governments. Although these problems are to a certain extent also present when it comes to the implementation of merely national policies, they can be considered as rather fundamental with regard to compliance with international ones.

Key points

- ❑ The implementation of international policy often suffers from deficient policy design (such as vague legal terms, extensions and exceptions).

- ❑ Control deficits constitute a crucial problem for the implementation of international policy, given that international organizations generally lack enforcement powers.

- ❑ The specific multilevel constellation characterizing the implementation of international law facilitates domestic deviations from original policy objectives in the light of changing interests and the strategic behaviour of national governments.

Conclusions

We have seen that the development of public policies beyond the nation state can be driven by varying rationales, including economic interdependencies between countries as well as the emergence of problems of transnational scope that cannot be effectively addressed by unilateral responses. As a result of these factors, states cooperate internationally in many different organizational forms and policy sectors, although the development of international policy competencies varies from sector to sector and issue to issue.

Given the fact that international policy formulation typically requires the accommodation of many, often highly heterogeneous, interests, joint agreement among the involved countries cannot be taken for granted. The fact that we can nevertheless sometimes observe far-reaching international cooperation can be explained by three factors – the underlying problem type, the facilitating role of pioneer countries, and cross-national policy-learning and diffusion. Finally, we have seen that – compared to national policies – the implementation of international laws is much more vulnerable to non-compliance and deviation from initial policy objectives. This can be traced, in particular, to deficiencies in policy design and control deficits as well as the interests of domestic actors in charge of implementation.

Weblinks

www.rff.org/News/ClimateAdaptation/Pages/international_timeline.aspx. This website provides information about the implementation of internationally defined strategies for combating climate change.

www.idpc.net/. Here information is provided by a global network of NGOs and professional networks to develop policy solutions to the transboundary problem of drug use and trafficking.

www.ilo.org/ilolex/english/index.htm. This is the database of international labour standards, another issue that has increasingly become addressed at the international level.

www.ilo.org/dyn/natlex/natlex_browse.home?p_lang=en. This is a complementary database on national labour standards that provides a useful repository of information about labour legislation.

Further reading

DeSombre, E.R. (2006) *Flagging Standards: Globalization and Environmental, Safety, and Labor Regulations at Sea*. Cambridge, MA: MIT Press. An analytically compelling account of shipping as one of the most globalized industries.

Hoekman, B.M. and M.M. Kostecki (2010) *The Political Economy of the World Trading System*. Oxford: Oxford University Press. An informative introduction to international trade and the nature and functioning of the WTO.

Keck, M.E. and K. Sikkink (1998) *Activists beyond Borders: Advocacy Networks in International Politics*. Ithaca: Cornell University Press. An important book about how international civil society can affect policy-making.

Skogstad, G. (ed.) (2011) *Policy Paradigms, Transnationalism, and Domestic Politics*. Toronto: University of Toronto Press. A stimulating collection of case studies on how transnational activities shape policy paradigms in areas ranging from same-sex unions to the regulation of genetically modified organisms.

Vogel, D. (1995) *Trading Up: Consumer and Environmental Regulation in the Global Economy*. Cambridge, MA: Harvard University Press. A book that quickly familiarizes the reader with the policy-shaping powers of international economic integration.

Vogel, D. and R.A. Kagan (eds) (2004) *Dynamics of Regulatory Change: How Globalization Affects National Regulatory Policies*. Berkeley, CA: University of California Press. A collection of research highlighting the impact of globalization in various policy fields.

Chapter 11

Policy Change and Policy Convergence

Reader's guide

We now turn to one of the most central topics in the study of public policy, namely the occurrence and determinants of policy change. The analysis of policy change is again an issue that cuts across the different stages of the policy cycle and therefore allows us to combine different theoretical perspectives and analytical concepts. Changes in public policies can be studied by relying on the agenda-setting process and by referring to implementation problems and the (negative) findings of evaluation studies. In addition, the theories discussed in the context of decision-making may be equally helpful in scrutinizing events of policy change. The institutional characteristics of polities again prove to be important for facilitating or impeding policy change. Yet it is, in particular, the broad nature of the topic that renders the systematic analysis of policy change a challenging task in terms of assessment and explanation of change – an issue we will address in the first part of this chapter. In a second step we will turn to cross-national policy convergence and the analysis of the aggregate consequences of policy adjustments in individual countries. The central question addressed by research on policy convergence concerns the extent to which national policies become more similar over time. We discuss basic types and dimensions of the convergence concept and differentiate it from related concepts, including policy transfer, policy diffusion and isomorphism. Based on this discussion, a third step focuses on the causes and conditions that trigger cross-national policy convergence.

Policy change is of central importance to the study of public policy. Under which conditions can we expect adjustments or transformations of existing policies? Why do some policies remain in place, despite their limited functionality, while others are changed? Do policies follow a sequential path of development? Why do policies generally change incrementally but sometimes radically? These are only some of the central questions that have guided research on policy change over recent decades.

Notwithstanding the considerable progress made in sustained research activities related to these issues, we are still left with open questions and challenges. On the one hand, we face a broad variety of theoretical frameworks that assess policy change from different analytical perspectives and that pursue different research interests. On the other hand, the measurement of policy change is not comparable across different studies. This can be traced to the fact that policies contain many elements and dimensions that may be subject to change, implying that there is no consensus as to the object of change. Researchers are often interested in the occurrence or non-occurrence of change, while neglecting the question of the direction of change (policy expansion versus policy reduction).

In recent years, the study of policy change has gained additional impetus from research activities that concentrate on the cross-national aggregate effects of change. The central question here is on the causes and conditions that lead to cross-national policy convergence. To what extent do policy changes at the domestic level result in increasing or decreasing policy homogeneity across countries? Answers to these questions not only depend on the way convergence is conceptualized and measured, but also on the specific factors that affect national policy developments in individual cases.

Policy change: theories, measurement and general patterns

The study of policy change may be considered a core area of public policy (Capano 2009; Howlett and Cashore 2009; Knill *et al.* 2010; Tosun 2012), with the major interest being on the description and explanation of changes in dominant policy patterns in different fields. In the literature, we find many ways by which policy change is measured. So far, no dominant and generally accepted approach has emerged. As a consequence, the theoretical and empirical findings of varying studies are not commensurable, as the dependent variable is conceptualized and measured very differently. This conceptual diversity is reflected in a broad variety of basic theoretical approaches to the study of policy change.

In this section we will provide an overview of the key approaches to the study of policy change. This will also include a critical assessment of the state of the art and suggestions for possible solutions. We will proceed in three steps. After a discussion of central theoretical frameworks that account for policy change and policy stability, we turn to key issues associated with the measurement and operationalization of policy change, before presenting expectations about the overall direction of policy change, i.e. the relationship between policy expansion and policy reduction.

Theories of policy change

In Chapter 4, we discussed a broad range of basic theoretical approaches that could serve as a starting point for analysing public policy, broadly distinguishing between structure-based, institution-based and interest-based frameworks. Frameworks used to explain policy change and policy stability can also be classified along these lines and hence be linked to the broader concepts mentioned in Chapter 4. However, theories of policy change differ not only in the extent to which they emphasize the role of structure, institutions and actors as explanatory factors, but also in the extent to which they link these factors into more complex theoretical frameworks.

More specifically, theories of policy change can be classified in the light of their underlying causal logic. On the one hand, we find approaches that are based on a 'linear-additive' view of causality, in which a clear separation between dependent and independent variables is assumed (Capano 2009: 16). Such approaches typically address the question of *why* policy change occurred or not. Independent variables generally refer to macrofactors, such as socio-economic conditions, the strength of societal interest groups, changes in government, party political positions, and international influences (Schmidt 1998). On the other hand, there are approaches characterized by the 'logic of combinative causality', in which possible combinations of causal conditions capable of generating a specific result are sought (Ragin 2006). The theories in this tradition are primarily concerned with the question as to how different variables can be associated with each other according to Boolean logic rather than in a simple positive or negative fashion (Capano 2009: 16).

In the following, we will focus our discussion on the combined causality models, as these account for a broad variety of potential components of policy change (John 2003). This is well-documented by the fact that we have already referred to some of these theories in our analysis of agenda-setting patterns in Chapter 5. In restricting our focus to these models, we do not neglect the relevance of linear-additive approaches, which have not only been comprehensively addressed in Chapter 4, but will also be of relevance for explaining policy convergence below.

Although combinative causality frameworks used to explain policy change are characterized by an inclusive approach that integrates structures, institutions and actors, they generally place particular emphasis on certain explanatory elements. So, for example, the advocacy coalition framework and other theories of policy learning have a strong focus on actors and their changing preferences and beliefs. The punctuated equilibrium framework, the path-dependency framework and veto player theory, by contrast, are primarily concerned with institutional factors; while the multiple stream approach emphasizes chance and contingency, with structures, institutions and actors being considered of equal explanatory relevance.

Policy change as change in preferences and beliefs: advocacy coalitions and policy learning

The advocacy coalition framework developed by Sabatier (1988, 1998), Sabatier and Jenkins-Smith (1993, 1999) and recently modified by Sabatier and Weible (2007) is one of the most comprehensive approaches to policy change. It employs the structure of beliefs in the governing coalitions of so-called policy subsystems – semi-autonomous networks of policy participants that focus on a particular policy issue, usually within a geographical boundary – to predict changes in shared beliefs that lead to changes in policy. The framework posits a three-tiered hierarchical belief system, including deep-core beliefs, which are ontological and normative, basic political values, which constitute the 'glue' that ties coalitions together, and policy- or instrumental-level positions. In this sense, an advocacy coalition consists of actors from a variety of market, state and civil society institutions at all levels, which share the abovementioned basic beliefs (i.e. on policy goals and other perceptions) and seek to manipulate the characteristics of institutions in order to achieve these goals.

Against this background, policy change or its absence is affected by three factors. First, policy change may stem from the interaction of competing advocacy coalitions within a policy subsystem. The emerging conflicts are then mediated by 'policy brokers', that is, actors who are more concerned with system stability than achieving policy goals. Second, changes exogenous to the policy subsystem (such as external shocks, pressure caused by a problem, or changing socio-economic conditions) can lead to policy-oriented learning. Third, the encompassing institutional parameters, such as constitutional rules, constrain the actions of the advocacy coalitions, which should preserve the policy status quo.

Box 11.1   Changes in Swiss drug policy

Swiss drug policy has been substantially modified over the last three decades. Originally rather prohibitionist, during the early 1980s public and social services were created to help protect injecting drug users against HIV and AIDS. Needle exchange programmes were set up and users were offered and encouraged to be vaccinated against hepatitis. According to Kübler (2001) this harm reduction approach can be understood by applying the advocacy coalition framework. The policy change can be substantially explained as a competition between coalitions who advocate different belief systems regarding problems and policy. The AIDS epidemic is considered a crucial external factor that helps the harm reduction coalition to overthrow the hegemonic abstinence coalition.

Belief systems and interests are the main factors of the support of advocacy coalition for a given policy. Nevertheless, the chances of an advocacy coalition succeeding depends on a plethora of additional factors. These include resources such as money or expertise but also external factors such as the nature of the problem or public opinion. Of these external factors, some are relatively stable over time and therefore predictable, whereas others are subject to greater change (Howlett *et al.* 2009: 83).

The importance of learning as a trigger of policy change is not restricted to the advocacy coalition framework. Indeed, numerous explanations of policy change are based on notions of learning, including the concepts of 'political learning' (Heclo 1974), 'government learning' (Etheredge 1981), 'social learning' (Hall 1993) and 'lesson-drawing' (Rose 1991) (for an overview, see Bennett and Howlett 1992: 275). Advancement on the lesson-drawing approach includes the more recently developed concepts of 'rational learning' and 'Bayesian learning' (see Meseguer Yebra 2009). Both conceive of governments as rational actors looking for appropriate policy solutions that work well abroad (see Gilardi *et al.* 2009; Gilardi 2010). In the case of Bayesian learning, governments additionally update their beliefs on the consequences of policies with all the available information about policy designs and choose the one that is expected to yield the best results.

In the literature, particular attention has been paid to Hall's (1993) theoretical argument about social learning, which conceptualizes policy-making as a process that usually involves three central variables: the first is the overarching goal that guides a policy in a particular field; the second is the policy instrument used to attain those goals; and the third is the precise setting of this instrument. These three elements jointly form a 'policy paradigm'. According to Hall's reasoning, policy change is most likely for the policy setting (i.e. 'first-order change') but becomes more difficult when it comes to policy instruments (i.e. 'second-order change') and even more so with goals (i.e. 'third-order change'). Changes in policy settings are considered to be relatively unproblematic since they can be achieved by using existing instruments and with reference to existing goals. In a similar way, instrumental changes are considered to be more likely than goal changes, as the latter imply a departure from dominant and institutionally strongly entrenched ideas of how to perceive and resolve specific political problems.

Learning also represents an important factor in the policy subsystem adjustment model put forward by Howlett and Ramesh (2002). The authors' model builds on the critique that the advocacy coalition framework treats endogenous factors – i.e. the advocacy coalitions themselves and exogenous factors such as macroeconomic shocks – individually. As a result of this analytical distinction, there is little to prevent the conflating of exogenous and endogenous processes for explaining the nature of policy change. The authors argue that exogenous factors can induce subsystem adjustments by producing new policy regimes, i.e. by affecting endogenous factors. The four resulting types of adjustments include 'policy learning', 'venue change', 'systemic perturbations' and 'subsystem spillovers'.

With the first two types actors located within the existing subsystem use exogenous factors, such as new information, to pursue desired policy goals. In these cases, policy change is initiated by exogenous factors but subsequently shaped in large part by the goals and strategies of actors internal to the subsystem. Systemic perturbations can generally be seen as exogenous events that draw new attention to a policy sector, such as the occurrence of a financial crisis. Crises bring new actors or new ideas and policy goals to the forefront of policy-making and can produce dynamic policy change. Much like a systemic perturbation, a subsystem spillover is generated by exogenous factors, which promote the merging or integration of previously separate subsystems into a single policy domain.

Linking policy change and institutional change: punctuated equilibriums, path-dependency and veto points
The punctuated equilibrium framework advanced by Baumgartner and Jones (2002, 2009) seeks to explain why political processes are usually characterized by stability and incrementalism, but occasionally produce fundamental shifts from the past. As we have already seen in Chapter 5, where we discussed the model with a specific perspective on agenda-setting, this framework conceives of the given institutional setting as crucial in influencing policy dynamics and the degree of change. According to this framework, institutions are strictly conservative. Thus, policy change can only happen if exogenous challenges and

transformations help the advocates of change to create new images for policy issues. By the same token, endogenous factors in a policy sub-system are of less relevance for policy change (see Howlett and Cashore 2009).

Closely linked to historical institutional accounts of policy-making (Thelen and Steinmo 1992) are models that interpret policy change as a path-dependent development. Such models conceive of policy change as sequential development, with previous decisions having a decisive impact on subsequent ones. The sequential development can be driven by two logics. On the one hand, self-reinforcing sequences can account for the long-term reproduction of existing policy patterns as a result of increasing returns, which once a policy is adopted delivers increasing benefits to the actors concerned. Hence, over time it becomes increasingly difficult to transform existing arrangements or select previously available options, even though the existing approach has been widely recognized as suboptimal (Pierson 2000; Hacker 2004; Howlett and Rayner 2006). On the other hand, reactive sequences conceive of policy development as involving temporally ordered and causally connected events. Each event within the sequence is in part a reaction to previous events. With reactive sequences, the final event is typically the dependent variable under investigation, and the overall chain of events can be seen as a path leading up to this outcome (Mahoney 2000: 509).

Depending on the underlying sequential logic, we might arrive at different expectations about policy change and policy stability. According to the self-reinforcing sequence, the expected pattern is policy stability, with change being restricted to incremental adjustments of existing arrangements. Path-breaking changes can only be expected in constellations of institutional destabilization through some kind of exogenous shock (Howlett and Cashore 2009: 35). If policy development is analysed as a reactive sequence, by contrast, it is likely that path-dependency will coincide with major changes.

Path-dependency models are at the same time highly contingent and deterministic (Thelen 1999; Knill and Lenschow 2001; Mahoney 2006). Contingency plays an important role in explaining initial policy decisions, since the framework assumes that chance, minor events and marginal factors can trigger off a new path. At the same time, the deterministic bias becomes apparent in the conception of policy development as a sequential process (Capano 2009: 25).

The importance of institutional factors is also highlighted by theoretical work on veto points (Immergut 1990; Immergut and Anderson 2007) and veto players (Tsebelis 2002), which have developed into central analytical concepts for explaining policy stability. Both perspectives emphasize ways in which political institutions can obstruct policy change. In doing so, the veto point theory highlights the relevance of the legislative process which is conceived as a chain of political decisions taken in a series of policy arenas. However, veto player theory goes a step further by taking the policy preferences of the players into account.

Policy change by chance: the multiple stream approach
The multiple stream approach put forward by Kingdon (2003) under-scores the possibility of policy change through agenda-setting. According to this perspective, policy change depends on three factors. The first is the need for a changing perception or definition of a given policy problem. Policy-makers have to be persuaded to pay more attention to one problem than all the others. The second factor refers to the development of appropriate solutions. Because competing proposals can be attached to the same problem, getting a proposal on the 'short list' typically takes time and the willingness to pursue it by using many tactics. Proposals are likely to be more successful if they are seen as technically feasible, compatible with policy-makers' values, reasonable in cost, and appealing to the public. The third factor is that the politics process refers to political factors that influence the chances of successfully coupling problems and solutions, such as changes in elected officials, political climate or mood (e.g. conservative, tax averse), and the voices of advocacy or opposition groups.

Similar to the 'garbage can' model (Cohen *et al.* 1972), Kingdon's conception of agenda-setting emphasizes the relevance of chance, and therefore qualifies for the view that policy-making is an (entirely) rational process. The major strength of the model lies in its basic simplicity (its emphasis on independent streams, change and contingency), which provides a counter-intuitive tool with which to interpret empirical reality. At the same time, the model remains highly open with regard to the specification of relevant explanatory factors and causal mechanisms (Capano 2009: 21). This holds true especially for statements on the potential interactions between the three streams and their mutual adaptation.

In summary, we have seen that there are many frameworks that allow for the analysis of policy change from different analytical perspectives (for an overview, see Capano 2009; Howlett *et al.* 2009; Tosun 2012). These approaches differ not only in the relevance they attach to different explanatory factors, but also by their different basic expectations about policy development. While institution-based accounts place stronger emphasis on policy stability, with radical change being triggered by alterations in the institutional setting, theories of policy learning are generally better able to assess different degrees or orders of policy change.

Measurement of policy change

A thorough explanation of policy change presupposes – as a necessary condition – the development of a sound concept of measurement for the phenomenon under study. However, while students of public policies are increasingly concerned with the analysis of policy change, conceptual choices and problems related to the assessment of change are rarely made explicit. As Capano (2009: 14) correctly observes, 'the definition of what is change represents a strategic issue for the researcher. It really makes a substantial difference if policy change is defined in terms of the transformation of the definition of the issues in question, or as the structure and content of the policy agenda, or in terms of the content of the policy programme, or as the outcome of implementation of policy'.

However, specifying the object of change is only one, if important, challenge to be overcome. There are several additional problems deserving analytical attention. Firstly, policy change is a dynamic concept and thus attention must be paid to the time frame within which processes of change are observed. Secondly, the evaluation of the degree of policy change (e.g. radical versus incremental) is affected by different levels of abstraction. Thirdly, policy change is a multifaceted concept with respect to the direction as well as the dimensions of change. Finally, the likelihood of policy expansion relative to policy reduction must be specified. From this it follows that the researcher must outline how he or she conceives of the occurrence, direction and intensity of policy change. In this section we take up these challenges and provide some guidance for more accurately analysing policy change.

Temporal issues regarding policy change

When addressing the phenomenon of policy change, we need to observe at least two points in time in order to assess that a policy has changed its characteristics. Therefore, studies of policy change must be based on data which – depending on the specific research focus – cover periods of years or even decades (Howlett and Cashore 2009: 35). To receive the most convincing empirical evidence of policy change, the number of observations should be as large as possible. Ideally, this would imply observations for each year over a sufficiently long period of time. As such, the selection of the time axis represents one of the most challenging tasks in the study of policy change as the conclusions to be drawn from the analysis are highly contingent on the observation period. The main problem arises from 'censoring', i.e. the incomplete recording of information at the beginning or end of the event that is of interest.

Figure 11.1 illustrates four frequent forms of censoring. We randomly defined an observation period starting in 1990 and ending in 2010. The two crosses (X_1 and X_2) symbolize an episode of policy change, taking

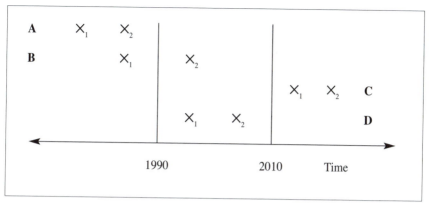

Figure 11.1   *Types of censoring*

Source: Based on Blossfeld *et al*. (2007: 40).

place during an infinite period of time. Yet, the only available empirical information refers to the observation window, which is marked by two vertical lines. Observations A to D are used to differentiate between episodes of change and the accuracy of their empirical assessment.

Observation A is completely censored on the left, implying that both moments of policy change occurred before the beginning of the observation. Hence, we would merely observe the prevalence of the status quo and therefore underestimate the likelihood of any policy change. Observation B is partially censored on the left so that we merely observe one moment of change instead to two. Accordingly, we might overestimate the scope of the change since we are missing information about the previous level of change. Observation C is completely censored on the right, implying that the start and end time of the episode of change is located after the end of the observation. Again, we would wrongly conclude that no change has occurred. What we in fact want is a time frame which enables us to observe the entire episode of change in order to arrive at correct conclusions with regard to the occurrence of change, as shown by observation D.

To reduce the risk of censoring, it is essential to select the observation period in accordance with the empirical characteristics of the object of analysis or – even better – in line with theoretical considerations. For example, if we are interested in changes to public policy arrangements in Canada due to the entering into office of a cabinet composed of the Canadian Conservative Party, we would need to start the observation with the 2006 elections that brought them into power. If we started to measure policy change any later than 2006, it would be possible to underestimate the extent to which public policies have changed due to the new partisan composition of the government. Accordingly, the identification of the relevant time axis is a crucial step for examining policy change and should receive enhanced attention within the development of the research design.

Policy change at different levels of abstraction
When is change fundamental and when is it incremental? Sabatier and colleagues, for instance, approach the issue by focusing on changes in the beliefs of the coalitions of the actors concerned. On this basis, they distinguish between two degrees of change, namely changes in core beliefs and changes in secondary aspects, with the former being much more difficult to achieve than the latter (Sabatier and Jenkins-Smith 1993, 1999; Sabatier and Weible 2007). Another widely used distinction, which we have already mentioned at various times, is made by Hall (1993) who differentiates between three levels of policy change, as already mentioned: (1) policy paradigms (the overarching goal that guides a policy in a particular field); (2) policy instruments (the means used to achieve these goals); and (3) the precise setting or calibration of those instruments. Also Baumgartner and Jones (2002, 2009) distinguish between different magnitudes of policy change, namely exceptional large-scale changes (punctuations) and – as they assume is the general rule – incremental or minor adjustments.

However, the assessment of whether changes affect the policy core or only secondary aspects strongly depends on the evaluation benchmark and the detailed analysis and interpretation of the underlying case by the individual researcher. Respective judgements can only be made by taking account of the specific policy issue. The same problem applies to the identification of policy paradigms and the distinction between incremental and fundamental change that Baumgartner and Jones make. In other words, the evaluation of the degree of policy change crucially depends on the measuring rod against which change is assessed. It makes a big difference in terms of theorizing as to whether we explain the change of a certain policy (e.g. with regard to the atmospheric emissions of large combustion plants) 'on the spot' (i.e. by focusing on the reasons that caused the change at a certain point of time in a given country) or whether we adopt a more abstract perspective on one and the same change, interpreting it in the light of long-term changes or changes taking place in many other countries (Knill and Lenschow 2001; Capano 2009).

Policy density and policy intensity: directions and dimensions of policy change
Change is defined as any departure from the status quo. What is often overlooked is that policy change involves two directions, namely expansion and reduction (Knill *et al.* 2009, 2010). Policy expansion implies

that a new policy is introduced or an existing one is intensified. By the same token, policy reduction means that a policy or parts of it have been abolished without substitution. This still leaves us with limited guidance for actually assessing the characteristics of policy change. To remedy this situation, we suggest a differential measurement of policy change based on two basic dimensions: policy density and policy intensity. By doing this, we distinguish different types of change that refer to varying policy dimensions. So, we pay attention to the presence of a policy, the instruments a policy utilizes and the setting of those policy instruments. Our framework represents a refinement and extension of these categories.

This way, we deliberately restrict our focus to changes in policy outputs, hence we exclude other potential objects of policy change (such as problem definition or agenda-setting). This is not to say that the latter are not worth studying. Rather, we use this specific focus in order to highlight how problems of measuring the direction and intensity of policy change can be addressed.

The dimension of *policy density* describes the extent to which a certain policy area is covered by governmental activities. It tells us something about the legislative penetration and internal differentiation of a policy field or subfield. Hence, it measures the extensiveness or breadth of governmental intervention. Any increase in it indicates policy expansion; any decrease can be interpreted as policy reduction.

Changes in policy density can be assessed by two indicators: the number of policy targets and the number of policy instruments that are applied in a given policy field or subfield. The number of policy targets offers a more general measurement of the breadth of policy activity, i.e. the higher the number of policy targets the broader the policy involvement of a country in a given sector.

This point can be illustrated by the example of clean air policy – a subfield of environmental policy. To reduce air pollution, governments might rely on a variety of different measures. On the one hand, they can regulate the amount of pollutant emissions into the air: policies would refer to the different substances that are targeted, i.e. there might be a policy on the reduction of emissions of carbon dioxide. On the other hand, governments can adopt policies that define minimum requirements for air quality. Again, we can conceive of different measures that prescribe such standards for different pollutants. These types of legislative activities are only examples that indicate the universe of potential policy options within clean air policy. Any increase in the number of policy items in a given policy field or subfield indicates an increasing breadth of policy involvement and hence a higher density of regulation, i.e. policy expansion – regardless of the strictness of the policy requirements. Any decrease, by contrast, means a lower level of state involvement and hence a reduction of policies.

The second indicator for assessing policy density is defined by the number of policy instruments that are applied. This measures policy density on a less general level than the number of policies. This can be traced to the fact that a change in the number of instruments need not coincide with a change in the number of policies, as a policy can be characterized by different instruments. Knowing that a certain policy has been adopted tells us nothing about the specific means by which the intended effects of the policy could be achieved. To reduce the amount of carbon dioxide emissions into the air, for instance, governments can rely on a broad array and combination of instruments, including command-and-control approaches (i.e. the definition of legally binding emission standards), economic incentives (such as environmental taxes or emission trading systems) or industrial self-regulation and voluntary agreements. Even if the number of policies in a given field remains constant over time, the number of policy instruments can increase or decrease, implying respective changes in policy density.

Given this approach, it is important to emphasize that not every change in the composition of policies or instruments has to coincide with reduction or expansion. Any substitution of policies or instruments that will not affect the number of the respective measures cannot be interpreted as policy change in these terms. For instance, if a command-and-control instrument is replaced by a market-based approach, we would not interpret this as policy change but rather as a substitution and preservation of the status quo in terms of policy density.

Policy intensity, by contrast, refers to the level of policy intervention. On the one hand, it is defined by the settings of the applied policy instruments, i.e. the levels of policy requirements. The characterization of changes in instrument settings depends on the nature of the item in question. For tax rates, for instance, a lowering of the setting implies policy reduction; whereas for environmental pollution standards, the lowering of the maximum permissible limits would be interpreted as policy expansion, since it increases the overall level of environmental protection.

On the other hand, policy intensity varies with the scope of policy intervention. The scope of the latter increases with the number of cases, constellations or targets that are covered by a certain policy. If, for instance, a government altered the conditions for welfare benefits in such a way that not only national citizens, but also foreigners living in the country might apply, this would mean an increase in policy scope and policy expansion. In a similar vein, the scope of regulation of carbon dioxide emissions from power plants would increase if the benchmark (for instance, the generated power per year) for plants falling under the regulation was lowered, implying that more companies are covered by the respective legislation.

Table 11.1   *Dimensions and indicators of policy change*

Dimension	Subdimensions	Indicators
Policy density	Policy target density	(Cumulative) difference in the number of policy targets which were introduced or abolished.
	Instrument density	(Cumulative) difference in the number of instruments which were introduced or abolished
Policy intensity	Intensity level	Development of policy strictness/policy generosity over time (difference in number and/or degree of measures with increasing and decreasing effects)
	Intensity scope	Development of scope of a policy over time (difference in number and/or degree of measures with increasing and decreasing effects)

Source: Based on Knill *et al.* (2010: 417).

Based on the above considerations, we can construct an aggregate measure of changes in policy density by calculating the cumulated difference between policies introduced and abolished and adding this information to the cumulated difference between instruments introduced and abolished. Likewise, a combined assessment of the cumulated difference between increases and decreases in policy levels and scope allows us to come up with an aggregate measure of changes in policy intensity. Note, however, that a summative combination of these two dimensions cannot be achieved since they address different aspects of policies. Table 11.1 summarizes our conceptual approach by outlining the dimensions, subdimensions and indicators of policy change.

General patterns of policy change: policy expansion versus policy reduction

Various theoretical considerations suggest that the emergence of policy reduction and policy expansion are not equally likely. Rather we should expect that – independent of the country, policy area, change indicator and time period in question – instances of expansion should occur more frequently than those of reduction. The central argument behind this is that – for various reasons – the adoption of new as well as stricter or more generous policies generally meets less political resistance than terminating or cutting back regulations or public services. As stated already by Bardach (1976: 129), 'the American political system, like most others, rewards novelty and innovation'.

A first factor that might reduce the likelihood of reduction refers to sunk costs: efforts spent setting up legal and organizational structures for implementing a certain programme. Increasing returns on path-dependency might lead to constellations where suboptimal policies are continued rather than replaced (North 1990). Second, anti-termination or anti-dismantling coalitions consisting of actors who benefit from the status quo might mobilize strong political resistance (Bardach 1976; deLeon 1997; Bauer 2006). The formation of such coalitions is favoured by so-called ratchet effects that emerge from individuals adjusting, out of habit, more easily to increasing than sinking benefits (Duesenberry 1949).

A basic expectation then is that we should observe a continuous growth of policy density and policy intensity over time, regardless of the policy field and country under investigation. If the number of instances of expansion is regularly higher than the number of instances of reduction, there should be a clear tendency for continuous policy expansion over time.

This general expectation is analogous with the law of growing state activities that had been formulated by the economist Adolph Wagner in 1893. As outlined in Chapter 4, Wagner proposed that the share of income composed of public expenditure will increase over time in both absolute and relative terms. As nations progressively industrialize, the share of the public sector in the national economy grows continually. The increase in state expenditure is needed because of three main reasons, namely socio-political factors (the expansion of the state's social functions over time), economic factors (an increase of state involvement in the sciences, technology and various investment projects as a result of scientific and technological progress) and historical factors (increases in servicing debts) (see Schmidt 1998: 161).

However, a major problem with Wagner's argument (and the subsequent scientific debate) has to be seen in terms of the fact that the data on public expenditure are taken as the central indicator for measuring the growth of state activities. In this way, the regulatory and legislative activity of governments is only taken into account insofar as these activities result in public spending. In addition, expenditure data are often difficult to obtain, with the consequence that analysts rely on input data (i.e. the budget) as a proxy. Against the backdrop of these difficulties, the analysis of policy output patterns constitutes a promising starting point that complements Wagner's argument and at the same time avoids certain problems with regard to empirical testing and data validity.

Key points

❑ Theories of policy change can be divided into three basic approaches: (1) models that analyse policy change in terms of the changing preferences and beliefs of the actors involved; (2) models analytically linking institutional change and policy change; and (3) contingency models emphasizing the role of chance.

❑ The measurement of policy change is a complex task and is confronted with several challenges, including (1) selection problems regarding the time period under investigation; (2) the lack of generally accepted benchmarks for assessing the degree of change; and (3) the lack of concepts and indicators for measuring the direction of change.

❑ We suggest policy density and policy intensity as concepts for assessing policy change. Policy density describes the extent to which a certain policy area is covered by governmental activities. Policy intensity refers to the level of policy intervention.

❑ The general expectation on the aggregate direction of change is that policy expansion should be more likely than policy reduction.

Cross-national policy convergence: concept, measurement and dimensions

So far, we have analysed key issues concerning policy change from a purely country-specific perspective. We have presented different concepts and theoretical approaches that seek to describe and explain the occurrence, degree and direction of policy change in a given country at a certain point in time. The focus on individual countries, however, does not allow for systematically comparing the dynamics of policy change across countries. What are the consequences of national change in comparison to developments in other countries? Do national policy changes entail growing policy similarity across countries and hence policy convergence? Or can we observe an opposite pattern of policy divergence, with national policies moving further apart over time?

With regard to these questions there is a long-standing scholarly debate as to whether national public policies become more similar over time. On the one hand, several studies emphasize a clear trend towards policy convergence, implying the development of similar or even identical policies across countries (for an overview, see Bennett 1991; Drezner 2001; Heichel *et al.* 2005). For example, there are hints that national environmental policy arrangements have become increasingly similar over time (Holzinger *et al.* 2008a, 2008b). On the other hand, there are many studies – typically in the tradition of the new institutionalism (see Hall and Taylor 1996) – that modify or even challenge the general expectation of cross-national policy convergence. Emphasizing important differences in national institutions and opportunity structures for domestic actors, these studies expect diverging or at least parallel, rather than converging, policy developments across countries. For instance, cross-national policy convergence is of a notably limited magnitude in the case of welfare state arrangements (Esping-Andersen 1990; Starke *et al.* 2008).

In the discussion on policy convergence, reference is often made to closely related concepts like policy diffusion, policy transfer and institutional isomorphism. So we first have to differentiate convergence from these concepts, before focusing on different types of policy convergence that are distinguished in the literature. In a third step, we need to show that, in addition to these different types, different dimensions of convergence can be identified, which refer to the degree, direction and scope of convergence (see Knill 2005; Holzinger and Knill 2005; Holzinger *et al.* 2007; Holzinger *et al.* 2008a, 2008b).

Related, but different: the concepts of policy convergence, policy transfer, policy diffusion and institutional isomorphism

Policy convergence is generally defined as increasing policy similarity over time (Kerr 1983: 3). Notwithstanding this broadly accepted understanding, policy convergence is often equated with partially overlapping concepts, such as isomorphism, policy transfer or policy diffusion. While policy convergence is related to results, *policy transfer* is concerned with processes and describes a development that might, but need not, lead to cross-national policy convergence. Policy transfer is not restricted to merely imitating the policies of other countries, but can include profound changes in the content of the exchanged policies (Rose 1991; Dolowitz and Marsh 1996, 2000; Radaelli 2000). Accordingly, Dolowitz and Marsh (2000: 5) define policy transfer as 'processes by which knowledge about policies, administrative arrangements, institutions and ideas in one political system (past or present) is used in the development of policies, administrative arrangements, institutions and ideas in another political system'.

Similar to transfer, *policy diffusion* refers to processes (rather than effects) that might result in increasing policy similarities across countries, hence leading to policy convergence (Elkins and Simmons 2005: 36). Diffusion is generally defined as the socially mediated spread of policies across and within political systems, including communication and influencing processes which operate both on and within the populations of those who adopt the policies (Rogers 2003: ch. 2). Diffusion studies typically start out from the description of adoption patterns for certain policy innovations over time. In a subsequent step, they analyse the factors that account for the empirically observed spreading process.

Policy diffusion and policy transfer share a number of similarities, such as their focus on process, which can make it difficult analytically to distinguish them from one another (see Karakhanyan *et al.* 2011). Yet, they are conceptually distinct inasmuch as they have differing empirical foci and dependent variables. Diffusion studies typically start out from a rather general perspective. While analyses of policy transfer investigate the underlying causes and contents of singular processes of bilateral or multilateral policy exchange, the dependent variable in diffusion research refers to general patterns characterizing the spread of innovations within or across political systems. The diffusion literature focuses more on the spatial, structural and socio-economic reasons for particular adoption patterns than on the reasons for individual adoptions as such (Bennett 1991: 221; Jordana and Levi-Faur 2005; Garrett *et al.* 2008; Gilardi 2008). Diffusion studies often reveal a rather robust adoption pattern, with the cumulative adoption of a policy innovation over time following an S-shaped curve (Gray 1973). Relatively few countries adopt an innovation during the early stages. Over time, the rate of adoption increases, until the process gets closer to saturation and then slows down again.

From these considerations it also follows that policy transfer and policy diffusion differ from policy convergence in important ways. First, differences exist with respect to their underlying analytical focus. While diffusion and transfer are concerned with process patterns, convergence studies place a particular emphasis on effects. Transfer and diffusion thus reflect processes which under certain circumstances might result in policy convergence. This does not imply, however, that the empirical observation of converging policies must necessarily be the result of transfer or diffusion (Drezner 2001). It is conceivable that policy convergence is the result of similar but relatively isolated domestic events. Second, the concepts differ in their dependent variable. Convergence studies typically seek to explain changes in policy similarity over time. By contrast, transfer studies investigate the content and process of policy transfer as the dependent variable, while the focus of diffusion research is on the explanation of adoption patterns over time (Levi-Faur 2002; Elkins and Simmons 2005; Jordana and Levi-Faur 2005; Gilardi 2008).

The particular focus underlying the analysis of policy convergence places it in close proximity to the concept of *isomorphism* which has been developed in organizational sociology (see Chapter 4). The central question underlying studies on isomorphism refers to the reasons which

Table 11.2   *Policy convergence and related concepts*

	Policy convergence	Isomorphism	Policy transfer	Policy diffusion
Analytical focus	Effects	Effects	Process	Process
Empirical focus	Policy characteristics	Organizational structures	Policy characteristics	Policy characteristics
Dependent variable	Similarity change	Similarity change	Transfer content; transfer process	Adoption pattern

Source: Knill (2005: 768).

lead organizations to become more similar over time. For example, Bellé (2010) demonstrates that the adoption of performance-related pay in Italian municipalities can be explained by isomorphism. There is thus a broad overlap between studies on policy convergence and isomorphism, with the major difference between the two concepts constituting their empirical focus. The literature on isomorphism concentrates on the increasing similarity of organizational and institutional *structures and cultures*. Studies on policy convergence, transfer or diffusion, by contrast, focus on changes in national *policy characteristics* (see Table 11.2).

Following the above considerations, policy convergence can be defined 'as any increase in the similarity between one or more characteristics of a certain policy (e.g. policy objectives, policy instruments, policy settings) across a given set of political jurisdictions (supranational institutions, states, regions, local authorities) over a given period of time. Policy convergence thus describes the end result of a process of policy change over time towards some common point, regardless of the causal processes' (Knill 2005: 768).

Types and measurement of policy convergence

In the literature, four basic convergence types are distinguished which are associated with different concepts of measurement, namely sigma (σ), beta (β), gamma (γ) and delta (δ) convergence (see Sala-i-Martin 1996; Heichel *et al.* 2005). The most common type is σ-convergence. Following this approach, convergence occurs if there is a decrease in variation of policies among the countries under consideration over time. Measures are usually based on the total variation, standard deviation, measures of association and algebraic distances.

The study of β-convergence focuses on mobility. This form occurs when laggard countries catch up with leader countries, implying, for instance, that the former strengthen their regulatory standards more quickly and fundamentally than the latter (Sala-i-Martin 1996). An example of this measurement is provided by Holzer and Schneider (2002), who analyse the asylum policy arrangements of policy laggards (i.e. countries with hardly any legislation in place) and policy frontrunners (i.e. countries with elaborate legislation). Here, β-convergence occurs when the degree and speed of tightening asylum regulations in formerly liberal countries is higher than in formerly restrictive ones. To give another example, β-convergence would occur when countries with lenient environmental protection standards tightened their regulations faster than those applying strict regulations right from the beginning. In the literature, this mode of policy convergence has also been discussed under the heading of 'catching up'.

β-convergence only allows for the identification of processes of catching-up, but gives no information on the extent to which catching-up is accompanied by processes of overtaking between countries. In response to this problem, the concept of γ-convergence is applied (Boyle and McCarthy 1999). For the analysis of γ-convergence, country-rankings for different points in time are compared to assess the pattern, and not just the speed, of mobility of countries. If countries in the first ranks fall behind or countries in the last ranks catch up over time, convergence occurs. Policy change is analysed by simple measures of association. A low degree of similarity between rankings indicates high mobility of countries over time. The concept of γ-convergence adds an additional perspective to the study of policy convergence as it may occur where other approaches do not detect changes. Country rankings may change without a significant decrease in cross-country variation (Holzinger *et al.* 2011).

In contrast to the measurement of homogeneity and mobility changes, the final convergence type concentrates on changes in the distance between policy outputs and an exemplary policy model, e.g. a model promoted by an international organization or a front-runner country. Based on the algebraic notation of 'distance' (δ), this concept is referred to as δ-convergence (Heichel *et al.* 2005). With its reference to an exemplary policy model or benchmark, δ-convergence adds aspects of the direction of convergence to the analysis (Heichel *et al.* 2008: 83; see Table 11.3).

Convergence dimensions

Even if we restrict our focus to the conception of convergence as the growing similarity of policies over time, i.e. σ-convergence, this still leaves a broad range of options as how to assess empirically and evaluate

Table 11.3 *Four forms of policy convergence*

Convergence type	Concept	Measurement
σ-convergence	Decrease in the variation of national policies	Changes in total variation or standard deviation
β-convergence	Mobility of policies	Group-wise comparison of changes in total variation or standard deviation
γ-convergence	Changes in country performance rankings	Association measures
δ-convergence	Changes in the distance between policy outputs and an exemplary policy model	Algebraic distances

increasing or decreasing policy similarity (Heichel *et al.* 2005; Holzinger and Knill 2005: 778–9). Basically, three dimensions can be distinguished: the degree, direction and scope of convergence. With regard to degree, the focus is on the extent to which we can actually observe an increase in policy similarity across countries over time. In other words, the degree of convergence is higher, the more the variation across countries has decreased over time.

The direction of convergence, by contrast, indicates the extent to which convergence coincides with an upward or downward shift of the mean policy position from time t_1 to t_2. Convergence at the top or bottom presupposes therefore both a decrease in variation and a shift of the mean (Botcheva and Martin 2001: 4). The direction of convergence is usually related to the extent of state intervention or to the strictness of regulation. Lax standards or laissez-faire policies are identified with the 'bottom', strict standards or interventionist policies with the 'top' (Drezner 2001: 59–64). However, the direction of convergence can only be measured whenever the policies under consideration can be viewed as 'scalar', or can be measured, which can be associated with a normative judgement on the extent of an intervention. Typical examples are the levels of environmental and consumer protection or the level of welfare benefits. However, it is not always easy to identify what the top and the bottom are in a policy, because this may vary in the light of different value judgements. For example, in media regulation there are two competing goals: restricting harmful content on the one hand and promoting freedom of information on the other hand (Holzinger and Knill 2005: 779).

Table 11.4 *Dimensions of policy convergence*

Convergence dimension	Research question	Measurement
Convergence degree	How much convergence can be observed?	Changes in total variation or standard deviation (for σ-convergence)
Convergence direction	Where does convergence occur (top or bottom)?	δ-convergence
Convergence scope	Which countries and policies are affected?	Relationship of affected countries/policies in comparison to the whole sample

The scope of convergence describes the range of countries that are potentially affected by a certain convergence factor. For example, if we talk about compliance with international law we would not expect any convergence effects on countries which are not members of the international institutions in which harmonization efforts take place. The scope of convergence increases with the number of countries and policies that are actually affected by a certain factor, with the reference point being the total number of countries and policies under investigation (see Table 11.4).

Key points

❑ Policy convergence is defined as an increase in the similarity between one or more characteristics of a certain policy across a given set of political jurisdictions over a given period of time.

❑ There are three concepts that are closely related to policy convergence: policy transfer, policy diffusion and isomorphism.

❑ The literature distinguishes between four basic convergence types which are associated with different concepts of measurement: sigma (σ), beta (β), gamma (γ) and delta (δ). These convergence types entail distinctive analytical perspectives on the same empirical phenomenon and hence might also yield different evaluations of convergence or divergence.

❑ In addition to different types, convergence can also be assessed along different analytical dimensions, namely degree, direction and scope.

Causes and conditions of cross-national policy convergence

The literature on convergence and its related concepts offers a broad range of causal factors in order to explain changes in the similarity of policies across countries. At a very general level, these factors can be grouped into two categories: (1) causal mechanisms triggering convergent policy changes across countries and (2) facilitating factors which influence the effectiveness of these mechanisms (Knill 2005).

Causal mechanisms

With respect to causal mechanisms, five central factors can be found in the highly diverse literature (see Bennett 1991; DiMaggio and Powell 1991, Dolowitz and Marsh 2000; Drezner 2001; Hoberg 2001; Knill 2005; Holzinger and Knill 2005, 2008; Braun and Gilardi 2006; Holzinger *et al.* 2011). First, cross-national policy convergence might simply be the result of similar, but *independent problem-solving* of different countries when responding to parallel pressure from problems (e.g. ageing of societies, environmental pollution or economic decline); that is, policy convergence is caused by countries reacting to similar policy problems. Just as individuals open their umbrellas simultaneously during a rainstorm, governments may decide to change their policies in the presence of tax evasion, environmental pressures such as air pollution, or an ageing population. As Bennett notes, the analyst of policy convergence 'must avoid the pitfall of inferring from transnational similarity of public policy that a transnational explanation must be at work' (1991: 231).

Second, emphasis is placed on convergence effects emerging from *compliance with international law*. As shown in Chapter 10, there are several reasons that favour the setting up of international organizations and regimes, including economic interdependencies and problems of transnational scope that cannot be effectively addressed by unilateral action. International cooperation typically involves the adoption of common rules by signatory countries, i.e. the member states are legally obliged to comply with international law. While the specific design of international rules is of course determined in negotiations between member countries (rather than hierarchically defined by international organizations), these rules, once adopted, constitute an important source of domestic policy convergence.

The degree to which compliance with international law triggers cross-national convergence varies with the legal specification of international law. Specificity is particularly high if international law requires the harmonization of national standards. Convergence effects are less pronounced, by contrast, if legal rules are defined in a less rigid way, leaving member states broad leeway for selecting appropriate instruments to comply with international policy objectives.

Third, several studies emphasize convergence effects stemming from the *imposition of policies*. This refers to constellations where countries or international organizations force other countries to adopt certain policies by exploiting asymmetries in political or economic power. While legal requirements are the crucial mechanism linking international policy-making and national policy change, the domestic effects of imposition are based on asymmetries of political power rather than legal obligation.

A typical scenario of imposition is the conditionality enforced by international organizations. First, conditionality can be based on the exchange of policies for loans. For instance, it is argued that the spread of neoliberal monetary and trade policies to developing countries was driven by such forms of conditionality. Governments pressed by international financial institutions switched to liberal trade regimes (see Dolowitz and Marsh 1996: 347). In a similar vein, the IMF required fundamental policy reforms in Greece as a precondition for granting monetary support in the aftermath of the global financial crisis of 2008. A second form of conditionality is the exchange of policy adjustments for membership in international institutions. It has been argued that the EU accession of Central and Eastern European countries has been governed by this principle (Schimmelfennig and Sedelmeier 2004; Knill and Tosun 2009). Those Central and Eastern European countries that wished to join the EU had to comply with the *acquis communautaire*, i.e. the entirety of European law, and with the so-called Copenhagen criteria, which require that a state has the institutions to preserve democratic governance and human rights and has a functioning market economy in place. As a result, in the pre-accession period agenda-setting and policy drafting were directly affected by the EU in these counties (Tosun 2012).

Sometimes, it might be difficult to draw a clear analytical borderline between international negotiations characterized by symmetric relations of power and those characterized by asymmetric ones. In negotiations at the international or European level, it will almost always be the case that some states are more influential than others. It is hence not always easy to decide whether the power constellations imply a voluntary or an imposed agreement from the perspective of individual countries (Holzinger and Knill 2008: 41).

Fourth, *regulatory competition* emerging from the increasing economic integration of European and global markets has been identified as an important factor that drives the mutual adjustment of policies across countries. Besides legal obligations and political power, internationalization can trigger national policy change via the route of market forces. In general, theories of regulatory competition predict that countries adjust policy instruments and regulatory standards in order to cope with com-

Box 11.2   Environmental policy convergence in Europe

The question of if and to what extent different international factors trigger convergence in environmental policy has been systematically addressed by the ENVIPOLCON project (see Knill 2005; Holzinger *et al.* 2008a, 2008b, 2011; Holzinger and Knill 2008). The empirical findings of this project strongly suggest that environmental policy converged in Europe in the period 1970–2000. On the one hand, environmental policies have on the whole grown more alike (σ-convergence), though at the same time they have moved in an 'upward' direction, thus becoming stricter. Hence, a 'race to the bottom' due to regulatory competition – i.e. a lowering of environmental standards by countries as a consequence of engaging in competitive markets, as often referred to in the literature – does not appear to have taken place.

This astonishing rate of cross-national policy convergence can be explained as the result of the effects of two international influences. First, the research findings provide evidence that compliance with international law constituted an important driving force for policy convergence. Second, communication within transnational networks also turns out to have been a major driving force. In contrast, competition effects play a negligible explanatory role. Regulatory competition has not led to environmental races to the bottom.

The project findings also show that environmental leader countries are able to pull along the laggards. This applies, first, to environmental standard setting through international law. The establishment of legally binding agreements at the international level typically implies that low-regulating countries adjust their standards to the level of the environmental leader countries. In other words, the leaders are generally able to set the pace in international environmental harmonization. In addition, this effect is also relevant in the absence of legally binding agreements. Communication and information exchange alone can induce laggard countries to raise their standards as they seek to avoid being blamed as 'pollution havens'.

petitive pressures emerging from international economic integration. The more exposed a country is to competitive pressures following high economic integration (emerging from its dependence on the trading of goods, capital and services with other countries), the more likely it is that its policies will converge with those of other states with international exposure. In other words, the degree of convergence depends on the level of competitive pressures to which countries are exposed.

Finally, cross-national policy convergence can simply be caused by transnational communication. Under this heading, there are several mechanisms which all rest on communication and information exchange among countries (see Holzinger and Knill 2005, 2008). They include lesson-drawing (where countries deliberately seek to learn from successful problem-solving activities in other countries), joint problem-solving activities within transnational elite networks or epistemic communities, the promotion of policy models by international organizations with the objective of accelerating and facilitating cross-national policy transfer and the emulation of policy models.

The basic assumption here is that information exchange and common problem-solving activities at the international level favour cross-national policy learning and so alter the beliefs and expectations of domestic actors (Holzinger and Knill 2005: 782). One could certainly argue that communication is also of relevance with regard to the other mechanisms of imposition, international harmonization or regulatory competition. In these cases, however, communication and information exchange are basically a background condition for the operation of the mechanisms rather than the central factor that actually triggers convergence.

The extent to which communication in transnational networks has repercussions on national policies is affected by various factors. First, the frequency of interaction at the international level is of importance. The more regularly that national actors meet, the higher are the chances for policy learning. International organizations and regimes display considerable variance in this regard. The same holds true for the second factor: organizational differentiation and the institutionalization of information exchange. The higher the number of forums and bodies in which national policy-makers and experts can meet, the higher the learning potential (Heichel *et al.* 2008: 91; see also Table 11.5).

Table 11.5   *Causes of cross-national policy convergence*

Factor	Mechanism	Effect
Independent problem-solving	Parallel problem pressure	Independent similar response
Compliance with international law	Legal obligation	Direct 'prescription' of policy change
Policy imposition	Political power	Direct 'prescription' of policy change
Regulatory competition	Economic pressure	Indirect change via redistribution of power between actors
Transnational communication	Learning	Indirect change via alteration of actor beliefs

Source: Holzinger *et al.* (2008a: ch.3).

Facilitating factors

What are the potential facilitating factors that affect the degree of cross-national policy convergence? The first group of factors refers to characteristics or, more precisely, the similarity of the countries under investigation. It is argued that converging policy developments are more likely for countries that are characterized by high *institutional similarity*. Policies are transferred and properly implemented only insofar as they fit with existing institutional arrangements (see Knill and Lenschow 1998; Knill 2001). In other words, the adoption of similar policies across countries varies with the compatibility between transnational concepts and domestic policy legacies. The degree of expected convergence will decrease with the cost of adopting the policy concept in question (Knill 2001). The same scenario applies to constellations in which adoption of the new policy entails high economic costs or is likely to face strong political opposition (e.g. in the case of strong redistributive effects among coalitions of national actors). *Cultural similarity* also plays an important role in facilitating cross-national policy transfer. In their search for relevant policy models, decision-makers are expected to look to the experiences of those countries with which they share an especially close set of cultural ties (Strang and Meyer 1993). Finally, *similarity in socio-economic structures and development* has been identified as a factor that facilitates the transfer of policies across countries (see, for instance on environmental policy, Jänicke 1988).

The second group of facilitating factors that can be analytically distinguished is composed of the characteristics of the underlying policies. In this context, the *type of policy* has been identified as a factor that influences the likelihood of convergence. The expectation is that policies involving high distributional conflicts between coalitions of domestic actors will diffuse and so converge to a lesser extent than policies with comparatively small redistributional consequences. A second argument about the impact of policy characteristics on convergence concentrates on different *policy dimensions*. As mentioned above, Hall (1993), for instance, distinguishes between policy paradigms, policy instruments and settings, arguing that change (and consequently convergence) is most difficult in relation to goals, given their deep embeddedness in the dominant beliefs of domestic actors. Instruments and, even more, settings, by contrast, can be adjusted without necessarily demanding ideational change; hence convergence on the latter dimensions is more likely than on paradigms. This view, however, is not uncontested in the convergence literature (see Lenschow *et al.* 2005; Radaelli 2005).

Key points

❏ There are five major causes of national policy change: parallel problem pressure, compliance with international law, policy imposition, regulatory competition and transnational communication.

❏ The effects of these factors on cross-national policy convergence are conditioned by several factors, including the institutional, cultural and socio-economic similarity between countries as well as the type and dimension of the underlying policy.

Conclusions

In this chapter we have focused on two central and related topics within the study of public policy, namely policy change and policy convergence. We have addressed the phenomenon of policy change and have seen that there exists a broad range of different theoretical frameworks that are used to account for policy change and policy stability. These approaches analyse and interpret change from different analytical perspectives and hence should be viewed as complementary rather than contradictory. With regard to the assessment of policy change, we have made clear that the researcher must pay attention to several issues in order to attain a correct assessment of the characteristics of change. Most importantly, the findings are contingent on the observation period. In addition, the evaluation of the degree of change is affected by the analytical level of abstraction. We also emphasized the need to disaggregate the concept of policy change into policy density and stringency in order to provide an accurate empirical account. Finally, we have explained why there is a differing expectation with regard to the likelihood of the occurrence of policy expansion and reduction. For a number of reasons, policy reduction – and in the most extreme case policy termination – is less likely as compared to policy expansion. From this it follows that the general expectation regarding policy change is one of policy expansion.

In addressing the question of the potential aggregate effects of national policy developments, we focused on the extent to which national policy change can lead to cross-national policy convergence. To answer this, we first discussed the concept of policy convergence and how it relates to similar, partially overlapping concepts like diffusion, transfer and isomorphism. Second we introduced the four major types of policy convergence, namely sigma (σ), beta (β), gamma (γ) and delta (δ) convergence. Third, we provided insights into different convergence dimensions (degree, direction and scope). We argued that these three dimensions are helpful for further characterizing processes of policy convergence.

Finally, we turned to factors affecting the degree of cross-national policy convergence, distinguishing between causal mechanisms (parallel problem pressure, international harmonization, policy imposition, regulatory competition and transnational communication) and facilitating factors (institutional, cultural and socio-economic similarity between countries, as well as policy type and policy dimension).

Web links

www.polver.uni-konstanz.de/knill/forschung-projekte/environmental-policy-con-vergence-in-europe-envipolcon/. This website presents the data on environmental policy convergence employed by Holzinger *et al*. (2008a, 2008b).

www.polver.uni-konstanz.de/knill/forschung-projekte/confronting-social-and-environmental-sustainability-with-economic-pressure-balancing-trade-offs-by-policy-dismantling-consensus/. This website introduces the CONSENSUS project, which provides data on social and environmental policy change in 24 OECD countries between 1976 and 2005.

http://ec.europa.eu/education/higher-education/doc1290_en.htm. Information is available here about the Bologna Process and its diffusion.

www.oecdobserver.org. This website is a good resource for learning more about policy innovations triggered by the OECD.

www.zew.de/en/publikationen/taxation/eta.php. This website provides a tool for comparing corporate tax levels in the individual member states of the EU.

www.ub.edu/spanishpolicyagendas. This major research project sheds light on policy developments in Spain and addresses the question of whether Spanish policies have converged towards European ones.

Further reading

Dobbins, M. (2011) *Higher Education Policies in Central and Eastern Europe: Convergence towards a Common Model?* Basingstoke: Palgrave Macmillan. An in-depth analysis of Central and Eastern European countries and their responses to the Bologna Process.

Garrett, G., F. Dobbin and B. Simmons (eds) (2008) *The Global Diffusion of Markets and Democracy*. Cambridge: Cambridge University Press. A book that brings together cutting-edge research on policy diffusion.

Gilardi, F. (2008) *Delegation in the Regulatory State: Independent Regulatory Agencies in Western Europe*. Cheltenham: Edward Elgar. This book provides insights well beyond the processes of policy diffusion.

Holzinger, K., C. Knill and B. Arts (eds) (2008a) *Environmental Policy Convergence in Europe? The Impact of International Institutions and Trade*. Cambridge: Cambridge University Press. The studies brought together in this edited volume all represent important contributions to the study of policy convergence.

Mahon, R. and S. McBride (eds) (2008) *The OECD and Transnational Governance*. Vancouver: University of British Columbia Press. An instructive book about the OECD's role as 'policy ideas generator' in a plethora of economic and social policy domains.

Roy, R.K. and A.T. Denzau (2003) *Fiscal Policy Convergence from Reagan to Blair: The Left Veers Right*. London: Routledge. This book scrutinizes the process of adopting common fiscal policies.

Chapter 12

Conclusions: Future Challenges for Public Policy Analysis

In this chapter we will briefly summarize the main characteristics of policy-making on the basis of the explanations given in the course of this book. Then we will point to open questions that aptly characterize the state of the art in public policy analysis. As we will show, there are still various avenues along which the state of research can be improved. We summarize these points and put forward a research agenda to stimulate future inquiry.

What have we learned?

Policy-making is a complex process. Often, the factor which has stimulated the promulgation of a public policy in one political system does not necessarily lead to the same outcome in another political system. Therefore, the analysis of policy-making usually focuses on single stages of the complete policy-making process. We have learned that the possibility of influencing the agenda – along with defining the nature of a social problem – is an important source of power as legislative institutions grant an advantage to those who address a problem and propose a solution to it first: those known as 'first movers'. Due to this characteristic, several groups of actors compete with one another in order to be able to set the agenda in accordance with their preferences: politicians, the bureaucracy, the mass media, interest groups, international organizations and epistemic communities. As agenda-setting efforts often overlap, it is difficult to say which particular group of actors dominates this process.

With respect to policy formulation, in most polities the executive and the ministerial bureaucracy emerge as important actors, whereas with policy adoption executive–legislative relations come to the fore. We have demonstrated that power fragmentation can drastically influence policy adoption, which then can only be achieved by means of negotiation and the search for compromise. If the political system displays a concentration of power, policy adoption is less challenging. We have also demonstrated that, despite the need to receive approval by many actors (e.g. the majority of parliament to give its consent to a policy proposal), political systems still manage to produce effective solutions to social problems.

Once the government has taken a decision on a public policy, the stipulations of that public policy must be put into action to bring about the desired change intended by policy-makers. Therefore, unless the stipulations of a given public policy are actually carried out, the problem will persist. At first glance, the stage of policy implementation appears to be an automatic continuation of the decision-making process. Yet there is often a substantial gap between the passage of new legislation and its application, which is addressed by implementation research. We have drawn attention to six key challenges which we believe can routinely impede the effective implementation of public policy: the choice of policy instruments, policy design, control structure, institutional design, administrative capacity and social acceptance. The question of whether and under what conditions the implementation of policies can be characterized as effective or ineffective cannot be answered by a single cause, but needs to take into account a complex configuration of different aspects. Considerations regarding policy implementation are also an important aspect of the rich body of literature on governance, which we discussed at length in Chapter 9. However, the governance concept does not only allow for shedding light on the implementation of public policies but also on how they come about. Further to this, the governance perspective can be used to address questions about whether or not a certain public policy has attained its predefined objectives, thus allowing an analysis of aspects that typically lie in the realm of the next stage of the policy cycle, namely policy evaluation.

Generally speaking, in the evaluation stage, the floor is opened to different types of 'experts' and their appraisal of whether a policy performs well or poorly. Essentially, policy evaluation is a systematic process for assessing the design, implementation outcomes and impacts of public policies. To this end, evaluation studies use a wide range of social science research methods, including various qualitative and quantitative techniques. These methods can be used to evaluate public policies in a way that supplies information to policy-makers and administrative actors or uses it for scientific debate. Once the results of a policy evaluation are available, policy-makers can decide whether the measure in question is effective or not. In the latter case, the consequence could be policy change. However, we have also stressed that besides policy evaluation there also exists political evaluation. This is not an evaluation activity in the classical sense but rather a tool for framing public policy in a positive or negative way. In this regard, actors who had designed or supported the adoption of a certain public policy have a strong interest in declaring it a success, while those actors that could not realize their policy preferences will usually strive to draw a negative picture. It is therefore important to delineate clearly policy evaluation from political evaluation.

We have seen that the concept of policy change has received increasing scientific attention. This research perspective concerns the adoption of a new policy or the amendment or repeal of an existing one. There exists a broad range of different theoretical frameworks to account for policy change and policy stability. These approaches analyse and interpret change from different analytical perspectives and are thus complementary rather than contradictory. We explained that there are three topics deserving particular attention when studying policy change. Firstly, policy change is a dynamic concept and thus enhanced attention must be paid to the time frame within which the processes of change are observed. Secondly, assessments of the degree of change might be affected by the level of analytical abstraction from which change is evaluated. Thirdly, policy change is a multifaceted concept with respect to the direction as well the dimensions of change.

We have highlighted that there are various national causes of policy change, such as learning processes. Likewise, public policies are increasingly affected by various international factors. There is a consensus in the literature that political, social, economic and technological changes generally discussed under the buzzword of globalization have significantly affected the conditions for national policy-making. In particular, the increasing integration of national markets and the emergence of transnational information and communication networks challenge the autonomy and effectiveness of national governments in defining and providing public goods by developing appropriate public policies.

On the one hand, economic and technological interdependencies have created a range of problems that exceed the scope of national sovereignty and can therefore no longer be sufficiently resolved by the unilateral action of national governments. On the other hand, the emergence of globally integrated markets poses new challenges for the regulation of domestic problems. In view of this, national governments cooperate to establish international regimes and organizations in order to maintain their capacity to address social and political problems that extend beyond the parameters of national sovereignty. As a result, the development of international public policies is characterized by the involvement of a huge and still growing range of different international – both governmental and non-governmental – institutions whose relevance might vary from sector to sector and issue to issue. Against this backdrop, we posed the question of whether public policies across countries are becoming more similar. There is indeed empirical evidence supporting the occurrence of convergence in various policy areas such as environmental protection.

In Chapter 3 we argued that public policies are primarily determined by the institutional configurations and the preferences of actors participating in the policy-making process. The institutions establish formal rules and determine which actors participate in policy-making and what role they play. To understand better how the various interactions between institutions and actors affect public policy decisions, we can use theories that are an indispensable tool for analysis. As explained in Chapter 4, the variety of policy-analytical theories can be roughly divided into structure-based models, institution-based models and interest-based models. All of these theories advance our understanding of how public policies come about by shedding light on different aspects. They represent an important further development of the initial attempts to explain public policies which were characterized by the use of typologies and taxonomies. Altogether, we can state that public policy analysis has experienced a steady expansion of sophisticated theories and empirical research and provides many insights into how public policies affect out daily lives.

How can we move ahead?

The insights summarized above indicate that public policy analysis has developed into a seminal research perspective of political science. Despite notable advances in empirical and theoretical terms, there are still several challenges within the state of the art. The points to which we turn now are not intended as criticism but rather as an invitation to question some of the approaches broadly employed in this area of study. Thus, the study of policy-making cannot only advance by illuminating new empirical phenomena at the national or international level, but also by approaching well-established key concepts from a fresh perspective. This involves revisiting the use of typologies and taxonomies, the development of more integrated theoretical models, the combination of different research methodologies as well as the systematic linking of policy outputs, policy outcomes and policy impacts. In addition, research on the selection of policy or governance instruments bears a potential for further advancing the state of research.

Improving the development of typologies and taxonomies

As we have seen in Chapter 2, typologies and taxonomies have been central to public policy analysis. Essentially, both are classifications, i.e. they are based on a process of grouping entities by similarity. The main difference is that typologies conceptually separate a given set of items multi-dimensionally, whereas taxonomies classify them on the basis of empirically observable and measurable characteristics (Smith 2002: 381). The fundamental idea is that they illustrate the causal relationship between two or more theoretical constructs in a parsimonious way. For example, the relationship between regime types (distinguished between parliamentary, presidential and semi-presidential systems) and the frequency of pension policy change (categorized, for instance, as low, moderate and high frequency change).

Yet, typologies and taxonomies must satisfy two conditions in order to have analytical leverage. Firstly, the classes formed must be exhaustive, meaning that for N policies to be classified there must be an appropriate category for each. Secondly, there must be only one class within which any one policy can be classified (Bailey 1994: 3). In other words, for a typology to be valid, it must be both exhaustive and mutually exclusive. Recalling Lowi's (1964) typology (pp. 16–19), there are four categories to which policies can be assigned: regulatory, distributive, redistributive and constitutive. For this typology to be valid, every policy type present in a country must be assigned to exactly one of these four categories. If there is a policy that cannot be assigned to any category, the typology loses its analytical power. The same occurs if a policy can be assigned to multiple categories.

While the definition and creation of typologies and taxonomies may look straightforward, many of the classifications used in public policy analysis do not meet the standards defined above, i.e. they are not exhaustive and/or not exclusive (Collier *et al.* 2010: 157). A typology that fulfils these criteria is Wilson's matrix of types of politics, which distinguishes between concentrated and diffuse costs and benefits of regulation, giving way to a 2 × 2 matrix (pp. 19–21).

Examples of classifications that fail (fully) to meet these criteria are the above-mentioned Lowi typology and Peters's (2010) classification of the relationship between interest groups and bureaucratic actors (see p. 128). Peters differentiates between legitimate, clientela, parantela and illegitimate relationships. The main problem here is that clientela and parantela relationships can equally be assigned to the first category as they also refer to an interaction between bureaucrats and interest groups that is 'legitimate'. What is analytically more interesting with clientela and parantela relationships is that access is granted to very few interest groups. Yet, the granting of selective access is also the case with (neo-)corporatist systems of interest mediation, i.e. a form that Peters assigns to the category of legitimate relationships, which are characterized by the privileged position of organized labour and employers vis-à-vis other interest groups. Another problem with this classification is that the final category, i.e. illegitimate relationships, remains isolated from the other forms, even though what basically characterizes it is that some interest groups are systematically excluded from policy-making. Therefore, an analytically more compelling classification would simply distinguish between restricted and unrestricted access of interest groups to policy-makers.

This does not mean that we generally disapprove of this instrument. In fact, both typologies and taxonomies are important tools for grouping and analysing empirical information. Rather, we want to underscore the fact that more attention should be paid to conceptual and methodological issues when developing or using classifications. Collier *et al.* (2010), for instance, outline how typologies that do not meet the criteria of exhaustiveness and mutual exclusiveness can be reorganized to bring them into conformity with these criteria. As a result, we believe that a critical discussion and reorganization of existing – and often very influential and analytically interesting – typologies represents a promising avenue for future research.

Linking different analytical perspectives

We have seen throughout this book that the study of public policies is characterized by a variety of different analytical approaches and theoretical perspectives. While this certainly constitutes a common pattern of research activity in most other disciplines and areas, analytical variety per se can hardly be considered a sufficient condition for advancing our understanding of policy-making. To be sure, we do not want to be advocates of analytical streamlining. On the contrary, the application of different perspectives and theories is an enormous stimulus for innovation. However, in order really to advance our knowledge with regard to the study of public policies, it is crucial to make the application of different analytical lenses more explicit and to look for ways effectively to link different perspectives.

On the one hand, diversity becomes apparent by the fact that – albeit being basically related to the same empirical subject – theories and analytical approaches often focus on the different elements involved in making one and the same policy. This becomes most pronounced in the distinction of different policy stages. Agenda-setting theories, for instance, strongly differ from accounts of decision-making or policy implementation. We are hence confronted with a broad range of different theories that explain the development, adoption and application of a policy. This is – as such – plausible and appropriate. However, so far, few theoretical attempts have been made to investigate potential linkages between these different theories.

What difference, for instance, does it make for decision-making, if agenda-setting follows a certain pattern, let us say, the inside-access model rather than the outside-initiative model (see Cobb *et al.* 1976)? Under which conditions does problem definition matter for decision-making? To what extent does decision-making affect implementation performance? Up to now, we only have very broad and anecdotal statements concerning potential interactions, but lack a systematic understanding. This is definitely not to argue for a search for a grand theory of public policy, though there is a need to improve our understanding of potential interfaces between what have so far been highly isolated and theoretical endeavours. In fact, this might be seen as the flipside of the policy cycle as a heuristic. As we have stressed at various points, in our view the policy cycle framework is analytically helpful as it helps to disaggregate policy-making in order to make it explainable. Yet, perhaps it is now time to reconsider this approach and suggest process-related explanations for policy choices and their implementation.

On the other hand, theoretical variety emerges from the fact that the same empirical phenomenon is analysed from different levels of abstraction. A case in point is the empirical analysis of policy change as presented in Chapter 11. This can make a big difference in terms of whether we explain the change of a certain policy (e.g. in relation to air emissions of large combustion plants) 'on the spot' (i.e. by focusing on the reasons that caused the change at a certain point of time in a given country) or whether we adopt a more abstract perspective on one and the same change, interpreting it in the light of long-term changes or changes taking place in many other countries. Often, these differences in analytical lenses are not made sufficiently explicit, leading to irrelevant or even false theoretical debates as empirical developments are measured in different ways. For instance, by taking a micro-perspective 'on the spot', policy changes that might seem incremental could be interpreted as fundamental by taking a more long-term view. It is not the faulty collection or interpretation of empirical data, but the application of different analytical perspectives, that results in contrasting assessments of change.

While this may not sound too serious, it may have far-reaching implications with respect to underlying theoretical considerations as well as the conclusions to be drawn from the analysis. More specifically, it is often overlooked that scholars view and measure change using different levels of analysis. For example, the privatization of state-owned utilities might appear dramatic from an individual or organizational perspective; it might even constitute a sectoral revolution. But at the same time the mode of the reform may remain in line with the legal and administrative traditions of the country in question and, on this basis, be judged as incremental or less significant (see Knill and Lenschow 2001).

False theoretical debates and contradictions are hence often simply the result of the fact that different analytical and/or empirical lenses and – linked to this – evaluations of the same empirical phenomenon are not clearly spelled out. For instance, we are often confronted with ongoing debates with respect to the explanatory power of interest-based versus institution-based approaches (see Chapter 4). In this regard, it is overlooked that these approaches can operate at different levels of analysis ('on the spot' in the case of the former, versus 'bird's eye' in case of the latter) and hence arrive at different explanations and interpretations that are – in fact – compatible with, rather than contradicting, each other.

For instance, historical institutionalists typically prefer to analyse sectoral developments against the background of the general macro-institutional context. Immergut (1992), for example, analyses developments in health politics in the light of varying political structures that confront reformers with different institutional veto points. Dobbin (1994) explains cross-national variation in 19th-century railways policy by the impact of varying conceptions of the state and the market in different countries. This is not to say that approaches that stress the importance of institutions as independent explanatory factors automatically focus on state structures. There are many sociological studies that are explicitly concerned with organizational life (March and Olsen 1984, 1989, 2008). But these studies also evaluate developments at lower levels in the light of the more abstract, in this case organizational, perspective.

By contrast, interest-based approaches, which conceive of institutions merely as an intervening variable structuring strategic interaction, tend to assess institutional changes 'on the spot', i.e. the levels of empirical observation and analytical evaluation are identical. The analyst follows the affected actors through the institutional jungle, viewing change through his or her eyes. Changes in the structure of regulatory agencies, for instance, are not evaluated in the light of a macro-institutional context (such as the relationship between state and market), but by reference to the distribution of power between different actors situated in the regulatory environment (Knill 2001: 23–5).

Taking account of the fact that institution-based and interest-based approaches analyse the same empirical development from different levels, reduces the risk of engaging in muddled debates. Watching out for different levels of analysis helps us to understand that different approaches explain different aspects of the same empirical phenomena, and hence might arrive at varying evaluations and assessments of change. The acknowledgement of different levels of analysis not only helps to avoid muddled debates, but opens up an interesting space for the complementary linkage of institution- and interest-based approaches (see Knill and Lenschow 2001: 197). While institution-based approaches are well-equipped to account for broader patterns of policy change, they must be complemented by interest-based approaches in order to understand fully concrete policy choices. The crucial question is therefore not to decide which approach is theoretically superior, but to link them in a synergetic way.

In general, students of public policy should make more explicit the distinctive analytical perspectives they apply, as different perspectives might not only entail different research questions, but also different interpretations of the same empirical phenomena as well as different theoretical choices. At the same time, more clarity on analytical scope provides the basis for the linking of complementary perspectives and the establishing of analytical interfaces between them. Both aspects constitute a major challenge for policy analysis, but will at the same time offer exciting opportunities to advance strongly our understanding.

Linking qualitative and quantitative research

The study of public policies is characterized by a bifurcation between qualitative analyses investigating policy-making (with in-depth case studies for a small number of cases) and macro-quantitative studies focusing on policy patterns over longer time periods and analysing a large number of countries. While the application of different research designs is certainly highly important, very few attempts have been made to combine effectively qualitative and quantitative research. Instead, two distinctive research traditions have emerged which concentrate not only on different research questions, but also on different theoretical approaches.

The macro-quantitative tradition of policy analysis typically concentrates on the comparative analysis and explanation of governmental activities in different countries (Schmidt 1996; Zohlnhöfer 2006). The basic research focus is on the explanation of cross-country differences in the policy area under investigation. The theoretical framework is usually based on a rather fixed set of explanatory variables, including socio-economic factors, the role of interest groups, the influence of political parties, institutional factors, veto players, international influences, policy legacies and path dependencies. The relative explanatory power of these factors is typically tested on the basis of multivariate regression models that allow for the inclusion of a larger number of independent variables. Mostly, the country sample is restricted to the OECD countries. The main dependent variables of interest are based on expenditure data in different policy fields (such as government spending in social, health or education policy), state revenues (e.g. taxes, privatization revenues), or macro-economic indicators (e.g. growth rates or inflation) (see, e.g., Busemeyer 2007; Gilardi *et al.* 2009; Gilardi 2010; for a discussion, see Kittel 2006). Qualitative policy studies, by contrast, are less homogeneous in terms of their underlying research design, dominant research questions, theoretical approaches and choice of indicators. In addition to single case studies, we find small-*n* designs that compare one or more policy sectors for a few countries, sometimes entailing comparisons over time. Case selection is driven by analytical concerns (with the primary objective of maximizing variation in the dependent and independent variables) and not restricted to particular world regions. The research focus is not exclusively on the analysis of policy change or the explanation of policy differences, but often includes one or more stages of the policy cycle, such as agenda-setting, decision-making, implementation or evaluation. Given the more diverse set of research questions it addresses, the theoretical toolbox applied in qualitative policy analysis is less standardized than in the quantitative research tradition, though it generally covers the different theories outlined in Chapter 4 and hence also the standard variables used in macro-quantitative studies. The big difference between large-*n* and small-*n* designs is less related to overall approaches than to the distinctive variables that are selected in the context of different theoretical frameworks. While quantitative studies can only test such variables for which respective data are available, or at least available in such a way that they are suitable for statistical analysis, this restriction does not apply for qualitative studies, which often include the generation of data as well as its analysis.

This holds true, for instance, with regard to the assessment of interest positions and strategies of the involved actors which – in many instances – require a detailed analysis on the basis of interviews and relevant documents. In a similar vein, the way institutional factors might structure individual ideas and beliefs (as is assumed in sociological institutionalism) is hardly suitable for quantitative analysis. The latter is usually restricted to the role of institutional veto points as potential hurdles for policy change. A similar pattern also holds for the dependent variable. Qualitative analyses display a great diversity in this regard and focus on a broad variety of different policy elements, such as policy ideas, policy instruments and policy settings. They typically concentrate on policy outputs that are often highly difficult to assess for large-*n* studies.

It is hence quite obvious and also hardly new that qualitative and quantitative research endeavours have their own distinctive mutual strengths and weaknesses. While the latter face important restrictions with regard to data availability and so the testability of certain explanatory factors, they offer the possibility for generating general statements on cross-national policy patterns and their underlying causes. Qualitative accounts, by contrast, do not allow for generalization and systematic testing in view of their limited focus, but face fewer restrictions with regard to data availability and the selection of indicators.

Both research strands of policy analysis could benefit from integrated research designs in which both approaches are effectively combined (Gilardi 2008; Fearon and Laitin 2010). This is further enhanced by the fact that they focus on different, yet complementary, indicators and elements of public policies, namely policy outcomes and impacts on the one hand and policy outputs on the other. Qualitative analyses could also be used in order to check for 'spurious correlation' in quantitative studies, i.e. a relationship between variables that have no direct causal connection, and to provide guidance concerning the fine-tuning of the theoretical argument by advancing causal mechanisms (Ragin 1987; Yin 1994; Lieberman 2005: 444). For instance, case studies can be selected on the basis of the results of a quantitative study which has revealed some disconfirming cases, i.e. cases that are apparently incorrectly predicted by our theoretical model. Often researchers tend to exclude such outliers from their regression models despite the fact that they can have important implications for the slope of the regression model and the explained variance (Ebbinghaus 2005: 140).

Tosun (2012), for instance, uses such an integrated research design to explain the regulation of genetically modified maize in Central and Eastern Europe and Latin America. The findings of the complementary case study show that the inaccurate explanatory power of the statistical analysis primarily stems from problems in gathering appropriate data for the key variables as well as shortcomings in the theoretical model. The second point mainly refers to the policy positions of the left-wing Latin American parties that do not oppose genetically modified crops for environmental reasons, as assumed by the theoretical model, but because of their anti-globalization and anti-American ideologies. Without the qualitative analysis, the role of the Latin American political parties' ideology for explaining whether or not the commercial cultivation of genetically modified crops is allowed would not have been understood.

There are hence good reasons to combine systematically both research traditions. The systematic linkage of quantitative and qualitative research designs constitutes a major challenge for future policy studies and bears high potential to improve our theoretical understanding of public policies.

Towards more encompassing assessments of policy change

Notwithstanding the ever increasing amount of both quantitative and qualitative studies the analysis of policy change still suffers from important weaknesses. First, in many instances, policy change is assessed by looking at a few policy issues within a given policy field, such as industrial or car exhaust emissions in the case of clean air policy. By adopting such a selective focus, however, we only get an incomplete and potentially unrepresentative picture of what is going on with regard to the whole policy field in question. This particularly holds true if the analytical criteria for the issue selection are not made explicit. These problems are especially pronounced in quantitative studies which often rely on a small number of indicators for assessing policy change.

Second, in some policy areas change is often measured on the basis of impact data rather than the measurement of legislative outputs. The latter are primarily examined in case studies. Quantitative research, by contrast, especially for reasons of data availability, in most instances relies on policy impacts. For example, with regard to environmental policy, the most frequently used indicators are levels of environmental quality or aggregate data on pollutant emissions and degradation levels of certain environmental media, e.g. deforestation rates. Likewise, assessments of energy policy are often based on changes in consumption patterns or energy production. Another example is provided by health policy, where policy change is often measured by changes in expenditure levels, health care resources (e.g. density of physicians) and activities (vaccination rates) as well as health status (e.g. life expectancy) and risk factors (tobacco consumption). More generally, expenditure levels (which can either represent policy outcomes or impacts) are widely used as proxies for policy change, which may or may not have direct relationships with changes in policy outputs.

Such proxies are easily accessible through international organizations like the OECD or the World Bank, but they are also analytically quite distant proxies of governmental decisions. The use of impact data, however, entails potential validity problems because intervening variables cannot sufficiently be controlled for. Even though there should be, in principle, a connection between the actual decisions taken by governments (i.e. policy outputs) and their real effects (i.e. policy impacts), this relation might be influenced by a multitude of additional variables. As a result, it is very demanding to extract the net effect of governmental decision on changes in, for example, environmental quality. From this, policy impacts must be seen as indirect indicators of political decisions and therefore as being ill-suited for examining whether certain factors create political pressures that weaken or tighten certain policies.

This point can be well illustrated by some examples taken from the research literature. Lower levels of carbon dioxide emissions may depend on plant modernization, energy efficient conservation investments, output shifts from more- to less-energy-intensive final goods, and fuel switching from coal and oil to natural gas and renewable energies (Aubourg *et al.* 2008). None of these factors can be directly related to political decisions made by the government. Instead, they reflect alterations in the behaviour of the regulated community that may or may not be the result of new legislation. Similar reservations are also expressed by Green-Pedersen (2004, 2007) regarding the use of expenditure data for changes in welfare state policies, even though in this case these data mostly represent policy outcomes and are therefore more closely related to policy outputs. In addition to the difficulties in controlling intervening factors, a major problem with expenditures on, for example, unemployment benefits is that they can rise due to increased numbers of the unemployed rather than to any changes in legislation. Another point mentioned by Green-Pedersen is the problem related to 'time lags': especially in the case of welfare state retrenchment, public policies are designed to have gradual rather than immediate effects. Thus, newly adopted legislation entailing retrenchment may not yet be visible in expenditures.

In summary, the assessment of policy change suffers from problems of eclectic and potentially insufficiently valid measurements. In Chapter 11, we outlined potential ways that these deficits can be overcome. In general, our suggestion is to measure policy change on the basis of outputs rather than outcomes or impacts. This way, validity problems can be overcome. Although the collection of data on policy outputs constitutes a particular challenge for large-*n* projects, researchers should be prepared to undertake this effort instead of merely relying on easily accessible impact data.

More broadly, this suggestion may entail a 'cultural' change in policy research and political science in general. Especially in recent years there seems to be an imbalance in the evaluation of research activities. High emphasis is placed on causal inference, and in particular on statistical analysis, sometimes regardless of the quality of the data at hand and the soundness of the indicators selected for operationalization. The mere collection and description of empirical data, by contrast, is seen as a less worthwhile endeavour, notwithstanding its fundamental importance for any serious analysis. In short, much more research effort, resources and journal space should be dedicated to the collection and presentation of empirical data. It is only on the basis of sound and encompassing data that new knowledge can be generated. While this statement applies to many other scientific disciplines, it is particularly pronounced for the analysis of policy change.

Systematic comparison of output, outcome and impact data

Better and more encompassing data on policy outputs would also offer new opportunities for systematically analysing the extent to which changes in policy outputs actually result in changes in policy impacts. This comparison would offer new opportunities and input for the study of policy implementation. So far, implementation studies have been primarily based on small-*n* designs. This can be traced to the fact that the analysis of the extent to which policy addressees and implementing authorities actually complied with the policy in question requires in-depth analysis of the behaviour of these actors, their underlying beliefs and perceptions. Given these requirements, our knowledge of implementation processes is still deficient and based mainly on the accumulation of case study evidence.

The systematic comparison of data on policy outputs, outcomes and impacts can be seen as an opportunity to reduce systematically this research gap. Assuming that implementation constitutes a crucial link between outputs and impacts, implementation effectiveness can be measured and compared for a large number of countries. For instance, if increases in the strictness of environmental standards coincide with improvements in environmental quality, this points to effective implementation, while the opposite scenario indicates implementation problems, at least when sufficiently controlling for the effects of other variables, such as economic growth or industrial production levels. Different levels of implementation effectiveness can then be explained by focusing on the various factors outlined in Chapter 7. Based on this general pattern and assessment, additional case studies would then help to illuminate further our understanding of causal mechanisms. At the same time, quantitative findings could serve as a starting point for systematically integrating the findings of already existing case studies on policy implementation.

Strengthening the focus on policy instruments and governance modes

In Chapters 2 and 9 we explained that policy-makers can choose between different policy instruments and institutional forms of governance to induce changes in the behaviour of the target population. Despite the hints given in the literature that the selection of policy instruments and governance modes may depend on truly 'political' considerations (see Schneider and Ingram 1990; Lascoumes and Le Galès 2007; Kassim and Le Galès 2010), only a few empirical studies have systematically addressed this important aspect of policy-making. There are two perspectives that appear particularly promising for future research.

The first one concerns the question as to whether policy-makers in different countries also have different preferences for certain policy instruments or institutional forms of governance, such as hierarchy, markets or networks. For example, can we observe that some countries are more likely to rely on authoritative tools (e.g. command-and-control regulation) for reducing the number of traffic accidents than to employ tools that are based on the use and distribution of information? Is there a group of countries that generally prefers incentive tools over authority tools for reducing environmental degradation? These are only some examples of research questions that wait to be evaluated in detail. Remarkably, such a research perspective could be easily accommodated within the scholarship on policy styles presented in Chapter 2 and might even help to revive it by offering a more feasible analytical lens than the original concept.

The second analytical perspective refers to the role of political parties. Throughout this book we have seen that in most polities political parties play a key role in policy-making. However, our knowledge about how exactly political parties define public policy is still limited. In Chapter 6 we learned that ideology matters since political parties are likely to limit public policies to those alternatives that correspond to their most fundamental beliefs. What we do not know is whether or not ideology also affects the policy or governance instruments that political parties propose. For example, it would be plausible to hypothesize that Liberal parties – which tend to support civil liberties and advocate a minimum of state intervention – are less likely to propose public policies that employ authoritative tools than, for example, Conservative parties. It would be equally reasonable to argue that this holds true only for certain policy areas such as the regulation of the internet or data protection. Furthermore, one could argue that all political parties, regardless of their ideologies, must accept all kinds of policy or governance tools since they refer to different functions of the state. On the basis of the existing literature we cannot make any general statements about whether or not political parties have preferences for specific policy instruments or governance modes. Yet for a more complete understanding of policy-making, it would be desirable to improve our knowledge.

References

Aberbach, J. (1990) *Keeping a Watchful Eye: The Politics of Congressional Oversight* (Washington, DC: The Brookings Institution).

Aberbach, J.D., R.D. Putnam, and B.A. Rockman (1981) *Bureaucrats and Politicians in Western Europe* (Harvard: Harvard University Press).

Aberbach, J.D., H.-U. Derlien, R. Mayntz and B.A. Rockman (1990) 'American and German Federal Executives: Technocratic and Political Attitudes', *International Social Science Journal*, 123(9): 13–17.

Adolino, J. and C. Blake (2011) *Comparing Public Policies: Issues and Choices in Six Industrialized Countries* (Washington, DC: CQ Press).

Akdeniz, Y. (2008) *Internet Child Pornography and the Law – National and International Responses* (Aldershot: Ashgate).

Aldrich, J.H. (2008) 'Political Parties In and Out of Legislatures', in R.A.W. Rhodes, S.A. Binder and B.A. Rockman (eds), *The Oxford Handbook of Political Institutions* (Oxford: Oxford University Press).

Anderson, J. (2010) *Public Policymaking: An Introduction* (Belmont, CA: Wadsworth Publishing).

Armingeon, K. (2002) 'The Effects of Negotiation Democracy: A Comparative Analysis', *European Journal of Political Research*, 41(1): 81–105.

Astbury, B. and F.L. Leeuw (2010) 'Unpacking Black Boxes: Mechanisms and Theory Building in Evaluation', *American Journal of Evaluation* 31(3): 363–81.

Aubourg, R.W., D.H. Good and K. Krutilla (2008) 'Debt, Democratization, and Development in Latin America: How Policy Can Affect Global Warming', *Journal of Policy Analysis and Management*, 27(1): 7–19.

Austen-Smith, D. and J.R. Wright (1992) 'Competitive Lobbying for a Legislator's Vote', *Social Choice and Welfare*, 9(1): 229–57.

Axelrod, R. (1984) *The Evolution of Cooperation* (New York: Basic Books).

Axelrod, R. and W.D. Hamilton (1981) 'The Evolution of Cooperation', *Science*, 211(4489): 1390–6.

Bacchi, C.L. (2009) *Analysing Policy: What's the Problem Represented to be?* (Frenchs Forest: Pearson Education).

Bachrach, P. and M.S. Baratz (1962) 'Two Faces of Power', *American Political Science Review*, 56(4): 947–52.

Bailey, K.D. (1994) *Typologies and Taxonomies – an Introduction to Classification Techniques* (Thousand Oaks: Sage).

Baldwin, R., M. Cave and M. Lodge (2011) *Understanding Regulation: Theory, Strategy, and Practice* (Oxford: Oxford University Press).

Bardach, E. (1976) 'Policy Termination as a Political Process', *Policy Sciences*, 7(2): 123–31.

Bardach, E. (1977) *The Implementation Game: What Happens After a Bill Becomes a Law* (Boston: Massachusetts Institute of Technology Press).

Bardach, E. (2008) *A Practical Guide for Policy Analysis: The Eightfold Path to More Effective Problem Solving* (Washington, DC: CQ Press).

Basinger, S. and M. Hallerberg (2004) 'Competing for Capital: The Effects of Veto Players, Partisanship, and Competing Countries' Domestic Politics on Tax Reform', *American Political Science Review*, 98(2): 261–76.

Battaglini, M. and O. Giraud (2003) 'Policy Styles and the Swiss Executive Federalism: Comparing Diverging Styles of Cantonal Implementation of the Federal Law on Unemployment', *Swiss Political Science Review*, 9(1): 285–308.

Bauer, M.W. (2006) 'Politikbeendigung als policyanalytisches Konzept', *Politische Vierteljahresschrift*, 47(2): 147–68.

Bauer, M.W. and C. Knill (2007) *Management Reforms in International Organizations* (Baden-Baden: Nomos).

Bauer, S. (2009) 'Does Bureaucracy Really Matter? The Authority of Intergovernmental Treaty Secretariats in Global Environmental Politics', *Global Environmental Politics*, 6(1): 23–49.

Baumgartner, F.R. and B.L. Leech (2001) 'Issue Niches and Policy Bandwagons: Patterns of Interest Group Involvement in National Politics', *Journal of Politics*, 63(4), 1191–213.

Baumgartner, F.R. and B.D. Jones (2002) *Policy Dynamics* (Chicago: University of Chicago Press).

Baumgartner, F.R. and B.D. Jones (2009) *Agendas and Instability in American Politics* (Chicago: University of Chicago Press).

Baumgartner, F.R., S. De Boef and A. Boydstun (2008) *The Decline of the Death Penalty and the Discovery of Innocence* (New York: Cambridge University Press).

Baumgartner, F.R., C. Breunig, C. Green-Pedersen, B.D. Jones, P.B. Mortensen, M. Neytemans and S. Walgrave (2009a) 'Punctuated Equilibrium in Comparative Perspective', *American Journal of Political Science*, 53(3): 602–19.

Baumgartner, F.R., J.M. Berry, M. Hojnacki, D.C. Kimball and B.L. Leech (2009b) *Lobbying and Policy Change: Who Wins, Who Loses, and Why?* (Chicago: University of Chicago Press).

Bawn, K. (1997) 'Choosing Strategies to Control the Bureaucracy: Statutory Constraints, Oversight, and the Committee System', *Journal of Law, Economics, and Organization*, 13(1): 101–26.

Béland, D. and R.H. Cox (2011) 'Introduction: Ideas and Politics', in D. Béland and R.H. Cox (eds), *Ideas and Politics in Social Science Research* (Oxford: Oxford University Press).

Béland, D. and A. Lecours, (2007) 'Federalism, Nationalism and Social Policy Decentralisation in Canada and Belgium', *Regional and Federal Studies*, 17(4): 405–19.

Béland, D. and A. Lecours (2008) *Nationalism and Social Policy: The Politics of Territorial Solidarity* (Oxford: Oxford University Press).

Bellé, N. (2010) 'Così Fan Tutte? Adoption and Rejection of Performance-Related Pay in Italian Municipalities: A Cross-Sector Test of Isomorphism', *Review of Public Personnel Administration*, 30(2): 166–88.

Bemelmans-Videc, M.-L., R.C. Rist and E. Vedung (eds) (2003) *Carrots, Sticks and Sermons. Policy Instruments and Their Evaluation* (New Brunswick/London: Transaction Publishers).

Bendor, J., Taylor, S. and R. van Gaalen (1985) 'Bureaucratic Expertise versus Legislative Authority: A Model of Deception and Monitoring in Budgeting', *American Political Science Review*, 79(4): 1041–60.

Bennett, C.J. (1991) 'What is Policy Convergence and what Causes It?', *British Journal of Political Science*, 21(2): 215–33.

Bennett, C.J. and M. Howlett (1992) 'The Lessons of Learning: Reconciling Theories of Policy Learning and Policy Change', *Policy Sciences*, 25(3): 275–94.

Benz, A. (2003) 'Compounded Representation in EU Multilevel Governance', in B. Kohler-Koch (ed.), *Linking EU and National Governance* (Oxford: Oxford University Press).

Benz, A. and N. Dose (2010) 'Von der Governance-Analyse zur Policytheorie', in: A. Benz and N. Dose (eds), *Governance: Regieren in komplexen Regelsystemen – Eine Enführung* (Wiesbaden: VS).

Berman, P. (1978) 'The Study of Macro- and Micro- Implementation', *Public Policy*, 26(2): 157–84.

Bernauer, T. and L. Caduff (2004) 'In Whose Interest? Pressure Group Politics, Economic Competition and Environmental Regulation', *Journal of Public Policy*, 24(1): 99–126.

Bernhagen, P. (2008) *The Political Power of Business. Structure and Information in Public Policy-Making* (Abingdon: Routledge).

Berry, W.D. (1990) 'The Confusing Case of Budgetary Incrementalism: Too many Meanings for a Single Concept', *Journal of Politics*, 52(1): 167–96.

Beyme, K. von (1985) *Political Parties in Western Democracies* (Aldershot: Gower).

Birchfeld, V. and M.M.L. Crepaz (1998) 'The Impact of Constitutional Structures and Collective and Competitive Veto Points on Income Inequality in Industrialized Democracies', *European Journal of Political Research*, 34(2): 175–200.

Birkland, T.A. (2006) *Lessons of Disaster: Policy Change after Catastrophic Events* (Washington, DC: Georgetown University Press).

Birkland, T.A. (2010) *An Introduction to the Policy Process: Theories, Concepts, and Models of Public Policy* (Armonk, NY: M.E. Sharpe).

Birmingham, K. (1998) 'Public Pressure Alters French Vaccination Policy', *Nature Medicine*, 4(11): 1217.

Black, R.C. and R.J. Owens (2009) 'Agenda Setting in the Supreme Court: The Collision of Policy and Jurisprudence', *Journal of Politics*, 71(3): 1062–75.

Blamey, A. and M. Mackenzie (2007) 'Theories of change and realistic evaluation: Peas in a pod or apples and oranges?', *Evaluation* 13(4): 439–55.

Blondel, J. (1990) 'Types of Party Systems', in P. Mair (ed.) *The West European Party System* (Oxford: Oxford University Press).

Blossfeld, H., K. Golsch and G. Rohwer (2007) *Techniques of Event History Modeling using Stata. New approaches to Causal Analysis* (Mahwah: Erlbaum).

Boaz, A., Grayson, L., Levitt, R. and W. Solesbury (2008) 'Does Evidence-Based Policy Work? Learning from the UK Experience', *Evidence and Policy*, 4(2): 233–53.

Börzel, T.A. and T. Risse (2010) 'Governance Without a State: Can It Work?', *Regulation and Governance*, 4(2): 113–34.

Botcheva, L. and L. Martin (2001) 'Institutional Effects on State Behavior: Convergence and Divergence', *International Studies Quarterly*, 45(1): 1–26.

Botterill, L. (2009) 'The Role of Agrarian Sentiment in Australian Rural Policy' in F. Merlan and D. Raftery (eds), *Tracking Rural Change: Community, Policy and Technology in Australia, New Zealand and Europe* (Canberra: ANU Press).

Bouckaert, G. and B.G. Peters (2004) 'What is Available and what is Missing in the Study of Quangos?', in C. Pollitt and C. Talbot (eds), *Unbundled Government* (London: Routledge).

Bouwen, P. (2004) 'Exchanging Access Goods for Access: A Comparative Study of Business Lobbying in the European Union Institutions', *European Journal of Political Research*, 43(3): 337–69.

Bovaird, T. and E. Löffler (eds) (2009) *Public Management and Governance* (London: Routledge).

Bovens, M., Hart, P.'t and B.G. Peters (eds) (2001a) *Success and Failure in Public Governance. A Comparative Analysis* (Cheltenham: Edward Elgar).

Bovens, M., Hart, P.'t and B.G. Peters (2001b) 'Analysing Governance Success and Failure in Six European States', in M. Bovens, P.H. Hart and B.G. Peters (eds), *Success and Failure in Public Governance. A Comparative Analysis* (Cheltenham: Edward Elgar).

Bovens, M., Hart, P.'t and S. Kuipers (2008) 'The Politics of Policy Evaluation', in M. Moran, M. Rein and R.E. Goodin (eds), *The Oxford Handbook of Public Policy* (Oxford: Oxford University Press).

Boyle, G.E. and T.G. McCarthy (1999) 'Simple Measures of Convergence in per capita GDP: A Note on Some Further International Evidence', *Applied Economics Letters*, 6(6): 343–7.

Brady, H.E. (2010) 'Causation and Explanation in Social Science', in J.M. Box-Steffensmeier, H.E. Brady and D. Collier (eds), *The Oxford Handbook of Political Methodology* (Oxford: Oxford University Press).

Braun, D. and F. Gilardi (2006) 'Taking "Galton's Problem" Seriously Towards a Theory of Policy Diffusion', *Journal of Theoretical Politics*, 18(3): 298–322.

Bräuninger, T. and M. Debus (2009) 'Legislative Agenda-Setting in Parliamentary Democracies', *European Journal of Political Research*, 48(6): 804–39.

Braithwaite, V., T. Makkai and Y. Pittlekow (1996) 'Inglehart's Materialism-Postmaterialism Concept: Clarifying the Dimensionality Debate through Rokeach's Model of Social Values', *Journal of Applied Social Psychology*, 26(17): 1536–55.

Braybrooke, D. and C. Lindblom (1963) *The Strategy of Decision* (New York: Free Press).

Breitmeier, H., O.R. Young and M. Zürn (2006) *Analyzing International Environmental Regimes: From Case Study to Database* (Cambridge: MIT Press).

Bressers, H. and P.-J. Klok (1988) 'Fundamentals for a Theory of Policy Instruments', *International Journal of Social Economics*, 15(3–4): 22–41.

Breunig, C., C. Koski and P.B. Mortensen (2010) 'Stability and Punctuations in Public Spending: A Comparative Study of Budget Functions', *Journal of Public Administration Research and Theory*, 20(3): 703–22.

Brewster, R. (2009) 'The Limits of Reputation on Compliance', *International Theory*, 1(2): 323–33.

Brown, C. (2001) *Understanding International Relations* (Basingstoke: Palgrave Macmillan).

Brownson, R.C., J.G. Gurney and G.H. Land (1999) 'Evidence-Based Decision Making in Public Health', *Journal of Public Health Management and Practice* 5(5): 86–97.

Budds, J. and G. McGranahan (2003) 'Are the Debates on Water Privatization Missing the Point? Experiences from Africa, Asia and Latin America', *Environment and Urbanization*, 15(2): 87–113.

Budge, I. and M. Laver (1986) 'Office Seeking and Policy Pursuit in Coalition Theory', *Legislative Studies Quarterly*, 11(4): 485–506.

Budge, I., I. Crewe, C. McKay and Prof K. Newton (2001) *The New British Politics* (London: Longman).

Bueno de Mesquita, B. (2009) *The Predictioneer's Game* (New York: Random House).

Burley, A.M. and W. Mattli (1993) 'Europe Before the Court: A Political Theory of Legal Integration', *International Organization*, 47(1): 4176.

Burnham, P., K.G. Lutz, W. Grant and Z. Layton-Henry (2008) *Research Methods in Politics* (Basingstoke: Palgrave Macmillan).

Busemeyer, M.R. (2007) 'Determinants of Public Education Spending in 21 OECD Countries, 1980–2001', *Journal of European Public Policy*, 14(4): 582–610.

Byng R., I. Norman and S. Redfern (2005) 'Using Realistic Evaluation to Evaluate a Practice-Level Intervention to Improve Primary Healthcare for Patients with Long-Term Mental Illness', *Evaluation*, 11(1): 69–93.

Cairney, P. (2009) 'The "British Policy Style" and Mental Health: Beyond the Headlines', *Journal of Social Policy*, 38(4): 1–18.

Cairney, P. (2011) 'The New British Policy Style: From a British to a Scottish Political Tradition?', *Political Studies Review* 9(2): 208–20.

Camasso, M. (2003) 'Treatment evidence in a non-experimenting practice environment: Some recommendations for increasing supply and demand', in A.R. Roberts and K.R. Yeager (eds), *Evidence-Based Practice Manual: Research and Outcome Measures in Health and Human Services* (Oxford: Oxford University Press.)

Cameron, D. and R. Simeon (2002) 'Intergovernmental Relations in Canada: The Emergence of Collaborative Federalism', *Publius*, 32(2): 49–71.

Campbell, C. and G.K. Wilson (1995) *The End of Whitehall: Death of a Paradigm?* (Oxford: Blackwell).

Campbell, J.L. (1998) 'Institutional Analysis and the Role of Ideas in Political Economy', *Theory and Society*, 27(3): 377–409.

Capano, G. (2009) 'Understanding Policy Change as an Epistemological and Theoretical Problem', *Journal of Comparative Policy Analysis: Research and Practice*, 11(1): 7–31.

Capoccia, G. and R.D. Kelemen (2007) 'The Study of Critical Junctures: Theory, Narrative, and Counterfactuals in Historical Institutionalism', *World Politics*, 59(3): 341–69.

Caramani, D. (2011) 'Party Systems', in D. Caramani (ed.), *Comparative Politics* (Oxford: Oxford University Press).

Carey, J. M. (2008) 'Legislative Organization', in R.A.W. Rhodes, S.A. Binder and B.A. Rockman (eds), *The Oxford Handbook of Political Institutions* (Oxford: Oxford University Press).

Castles, F. (1998) *Comparative Public Policy. Patterns of Post-War Transformation* (Cheltenham: Edward Elgar).

Cerny, P.G. (1995) 'Globalization and the Changing Logic of Collective Action', *International Organization*, 49(4): 595–625.

Champion, D. and S. Chapman (2005) 'Framing Pub Smoking Bans: An Analysis of Australian Print News Media Coverage, March 1996–March 2003', *Journal of Epidemiology and Community Health*, 59(8): 679–84.

Chang, H.F. (2003) 'Risk Regulation, Endogenous Public Concerns, and the Hormones Dispute: Nothing to Fear But Fear Itself?', *Southern California Law Review*, 77(4): 743–76.

Chappell, L. (2001) 'Federalism and Social Policy: The Case of Domestic Violence', *Australian Journal of Public Administration*, 60(1): 59–69.

Chen, H.T. (1990) *Theory-Driven Evaluations* (Thousand Oaks: Sage).

Chen, H.T. (2005). *Practical Program Evaluation: Assessing and Improving Planning, Implementation, and Effectiveness* (Thousand Oaks: Sage).

Chen, H.T. and P. Rossi (1989) 'Issues in the Theory-Driven Perspective', *Evaluation and Program Planning*, (12)4: 299–306.

Chen, H.T. and P. Rossi (1992) *Using Theory to Improve Policy and Program Evaluations* (Westport: Greenwood Press).

Cobb, R.W. and J.F. Coughlin (1998) 'Are Elderly Drivers a Road Hazard? Problem Definition and Political Impact', *Journal of Aging Studies*, 12(4): 411–27.

Cobb, R.W. and C.D. Elder (1983) *Participation in American Politics: The Dynamics of Agenda-Building* (Baltimore: Johns Hopkins Press).

Cobb, R.W., J.-K. Ross and M.-K. Ross (1976) 'Agenda Building as a Comparative Political Process', *American Political Science Review*, 70(1): 126–38.

Coen, D. (2007) 'Empirical and Theoretical Studies in EU Lobbying', *Journal of European Public Policy*, 14(3): 333–45.

Coen, D. and J.J. Richardson (eds) (2009) *Lobbying the European Union: Institutions, Actors, and Issues* (Oxford: Oxford University Press).

Cohen, B.C. (1963) *The Press and Foreign Policy* (Princeton: Princeton University Press).

Cohen, M. and D.A. Levinthal (1990) 'Absorptive Capacity: A New Perspective on Learning and Innovation', *Administrative Science Quarterly*, 35(1): 128–52.

Cohen, M., March, J. and J. Olsen (1972) 'A Garbage Can Model of Organizational Choice', Administrative Science Quarterly, 17(1): 1–25.

Cohler, A.M., B.C. Miller and H.S. Stone (eds) (1989) *Montesquieu: The Spirit of the Laws* (Cambridge: Cambridge University Press).

Colebatch, H.K. (ed.) (2006) *Beyond the Policy Cycle: The Policy Process in Australia* (Crows Nest: Allen & Unwin).

Collier, D., J. Laporte and J. Seawright (2010) 'Typologies: Forming Concepts and Creating Categorial Variables', in J.M. Box-Steffensmeier, H.E. Brady and D. Collier (eds), *The Oxford Handbook of Political Methodology* (Oxford: Oxford University Press).

Colomer, J. M. (ed.) (2008) *Comparative European Politics* (London: Routledge).

Connell, J.P. and A.C. Kubisch (1998) 'Applying a Theory of Change Approach to the Evaluation of Comprehensive Community Initiatives: Progress, Prospects and Problems', in K. Fulbright-Anderson, A.C. Kubisch and J.P. Connell (eds), *New Approaches to Evaluating Community Initiatives. Volume 2: Theory, measurement and analysis* (Washington, DC: Aspen Institute).

Connell, J., A. Kubisch, L. Schorr and C. Weiss (eds) (1995) *New Approaches to Evaluating Community Initiatives: Concepts, Methods and Contexts* (Washington, DC: Aspen Institute).

Cook, T. and D. Campbell (1979) *Quasi-Experimentation: Design and Analysis Issues for Field Settings* (Boston: Houghton Mifflin).

Cooper, R.N. (1968) 'The Economics of Interdependence', *The International Executive*, 10(4): 3–5.

Cox, G.W. and M.D. McCubbins, (1986) 'Electoral Politics as a Redistributive Game', *Journal of Politics*, 48(2): 370–89.

Cox, R.H. (2004) 'The Path Dependence of an Idea: Why Scandinavian Welfare States Remain Distinct', *Social Policy and Administration* 38(2): 204–19.

Cram, L. and J.J. Richardson (eds) (2004) *Policy Styles in the European Union* (London: Routledge).

Crenson, M.A. (1971) *The Un-Politics of Air Pollution: A Study of Non-Decisionmaking in the Cities* (Baltimore: Johns Hopkins Press).

Crepaz, M.M.L. (2002) 'Global, Constitutional, and Partisan Determinants of Redistribution in 15 OECD Countries', *Comparative Politics*, 34(2): 169–88.

Cutler, A.C. (1999) 'Private Authority in International Trade Relations: The Case of Maritime Transport', in A.C. Cutler, V. Haufler and T. Porter, (eds), *Private Authority and International Affairs* (Albany: State of New York University Press).

Cutler, A.C., Haufler, V. and T. Porter (1999) 'The Contours and Significance of Private Authority in International Affairs', in A.C. Cutler, V. Haufler and T. Porter (eds), *Private Authority and International Affairs* (Albany: State University of New York Press).

Cyert, R.M. and J.G. March (1963) *A Behavioral Theory of the Firm* (Englewood Cliffs, NJ: Prentice Hall).

Czempiel, E.-O. and J.N. Rosenau (eds) (1992) *Governance Without Government: Order and Change in World Politics* (Cambridge: Cambridge University Press).

Dahl, R. (1957) 'Decision-Making in a Democracy: The Supreme Court as a National Policy-Maker', *Journal of Public Law*, 6: 279–95.

Dahl, R. (1958) 'A Critique of the Ruling Elite Model', *American Political Science Review*, 52(2): 463–69.

Dahl, R. (1961) *Who Governs? Democracy and Power in an American City* (Yale: Yale University Press).

Dahl, R. and C.E. Lindblom (1953) *Politics, Economics, and Welfare* (New York: Harper).

Daugbjerg, C. (1998) 'Linking Policy Networks and Environmental Policies: Nitrate Policy Making in Denmark and Sweden 1970–1995', *Public Administration* 76(2): 275–94.

Daugbjerg, C. and J. Studsgaard (2005) 'Issue Redefinition, Venue Change and Radical Agricultural Policy Reforms in Scandinavia and New Zealand', *Scandinavian Political Studies*, 28(2): 103–24.

Daynard, R.A., Hash, L.E. and A. Robbins (2002) 'Food Litigation: Lessons from the Tobacco Wars', *Journal of the American Medical Association*, 288(17): 2179.

DeLeon, P. (1997) 'Afterward: The Once and Future State of Policy Termination', *International Journal of Public Administration*, 20(12): 2195–212.

Depauw, S. and S. Martin (2009) 'Legislative Party Discipline and Cohesion in Comparative Perspective', in D. Giannetti and K. Benoit (eds), *Intra-Party Politics and Coalition Governments in Parliamentary Democracies* (London: Routledge).

Derlien, H.-U. (1995) 'Public Administration in Germany: Political and Societal Relations', in J. Pierre (ed.), *Bureaucracy in the Modern State. An Introduction to Comparative Public Administration* (Aldershot: Edward Elgar).

Dery, D. (1984) *Problem Definition in Policy Analysis* (Lawrence: University Press of Kansas).

Dery, D. (2000) 'Agenda Setting and Problem Definition', *Policy Studies*, 21(1): 37–47.

DeSombre, E.R. (2006) *Flagging Standards: Globalization and Environmental, Safety, and Labor Regulations at Sea* (Cambridge, MA: MIT Press).

DiMaggio, P. and W.W. Powell (1991) 'The Iron Cage Revisited: Institutional Isomorphism and Collective Rationality in Organizational Fields', in W.W. Powell and P. DiMaggio (eds), *The New Institutionalism in Organizational Analysis* (Chicago: University of Chicago Press).

Diwakar, R. (2007) 'Duverger's Law and the Size of the Indian Party System', *Party Politics*, 13(5): 539–62.

Dobbin, F. (1994) *Forging Industrial Policy: The United States, Britain, and France in the Railway Age* (Cambridge: Cambridge University Press).

Dobbins, M. (2011) *Higher Education Policies in Central and Eastern Europe: Convergence towards a Common Model?* (Basingstoke: Palgrave Macmillan).

Dobbins, M. and C. Knill (2009) 'Higher Education Policies in Central and Eastern Europe: Convergence toward a Common Model?', *Governance*, 22(3): 397–430.

Dolowitz, D.P. and D. Marsh (1996) 'Who Learns What from Whom: A Review of the Policy Transfer Literature', *Policy Studies*, 44(2): 343–57.

Dolowitz, D.P. and D. Marsh (2000) 'Learning from abroad: The Role of Policy Transfer in Contemporary Policy Making', *Governance*, 13(1): 5–24.

Donahue, J. and R.J. Zeckhauser (2011) *Collaborative Governance: Private Roles for Public Goals* (Princeton: Princeton University Press).

Donaldson, S.I. and M.W. Lipsey (2006) 'Roles for theory in contemporary evaluation practice: Developing practical knowledge', in I. Shaw, J.C. Greene and M.M. Mark (eds), *The Handbook of Evaluation: Policies, Programs, and Practices* (London: Sage).

Dooren, W. van, Bouckaert, G. and J. Halligan (2010) *Performance Management in the Public Sector* (London: Routledge).

Doornbos, M. (2001) 'Good Governance: The Rise and Decline of a Policy Metaphor?' *Development Studies*, 37(6): 93–108.

Dorey, P. (2005) *Policy Making in Britain: An Introduction* (London: Sage).

Döring, H. (1995) *Parliaments and Majority Rule in Western Europe* (Frankfurt am Main: Campus).

Downs, A. (1957) *An Economic Theory of Democracy* (New York: Harper and Row).

Downs, A. (1967) *Inside Bureaucracy* (Boston: Little, Brown).

Downs, A. (1972) 'Up and Down with Ecology: The "Issue Attention Cycle"', *The Public Interest*, 28: 38–50.

Drezner, D.W. (2001) 'Globalization and Policy Convergence', *International Studies Review*, 3(1): 53–78.

Duesenberry, J.S. (1949) *Income, Saving and the Theory of Consumer Behavior* (Cambridge: Harvard University Press).

Dunleavy, P. (1991) *Democracy, Bureaucracy & Public Choice: Economic Explanations in Political Science* (Hemel Hempstead: Harvester Wheatsheaf).

Duverger, M. (1954) *Political Parties: Their Organization and Activity in the Modern State* (New York: Wiley).

Dye, T.R. (2005) *Understanding Public Policy* (Englewood Cliffs, NJ: Prentice Hall).

Dye, T.R. and H. Zeigler (2006) *The Irony of Democracy: An Uncommon Introduction to American Politics* (Belmont: Thomson Higher Education).

Dyer, C. (2001) *Operation Blackboard: Policy Implementation in Indian Elementary Education* (Oxford: Symposium Books).

Dyson, K. (1980) *The State Tradition in Western Europe. A Study of an Idea and Institution* (Oxford: European Consortium for Political Research Press).

Eavey, C.L. and G.J. Miller (1984) 'Bureaucratic Agenda Control: Imposition or Bargaining?', *American Political Science Review*, 78(3): 719–33.

Ebbinghaus, B. (2005) 'When Less is More: Selection Problems in Large-N and Small-N Cross-National Comparisons', *International Sociology*, 20(2): 133–52.

Egeberg, M. (1995) 'Bureaucrats as Public Policy-Makers and their Self-Interest', *Journal of Theoretical Politics*, 7(2): 157–67.

Egeberg, M. (2006) 'Executive Politics as Usual: Role Behaviour and Conflict Dimensions in the College of European Commissioners', *Journal of European Public Policy*, 13(1): 1–15.

Eichbaum, C. and R. Shaw (2007) 'Ministerial Advisers, Politicization and the Retreat from Westminster: The Case of New Zealand', *Public Administration*, 85(3): 609–40.

Eichbaum, C. and R. Shaw (2008) 'Revisiting Politicization: Political Advisers and Public Servants in Westminster Systems', *Governance*, 21(3): 337–63.

Eisner, M.A., J. Worsham and E.J. Ringquist (2006) *Contemporary Regulatory Policy* (Boulder: Lynne Rienner Publishers).

Eliadis, P., M. Hill and M. Howlett (eds) (2005) *Designing Government: From Instruments to Governance* (Montreal: McGill-Queen's University Press).

Elkins, Z. and B. Simmons (2005) 'On Waves, Clusters, and Diffusion: a Conceptual Framework', *The Annals of the American Academy of Political and Social Science*, 598(1): 33–51.

Elmore, R. F. (1985) 'Forward and Backward Mapping', in K. Hanf and T. Toonen (eds), *Policy Implementation in Federal and Unitary Systems* (Dordrecht: Martinus Nijhoff).

Engel, C. (2010) 'The Behaviour of Corporate Actors: How Much Can We Learn from the Experimental Literature?', *Journal of Institutional Economics*, 6(4): 445–75.

Enjolras, B. and R.H. Waldal (2007) 'Policy-Making in Sport. The Norwegian Case', *International Review for the Sociology of Sport*, 42(2): 201–16.

Ennser, L. (2010) 'The homogeneity of West European party families: The radical right in comparative perspective', *Party Politics*, 17(1): 1–21.

Erne, R. (2011) 'Interest associations', in D. Caramani (ed.), *Comparative Politics* (Oxford: Oxford University Press).

Ertl, H. (2006) 'Educational Standards and the Changing Discourse on Education: The Reception and Consequences of the PISA Study in Germany', *Oxford Review of Education*, 32(5): 619–34.

Esping-Andersen, G. (1990) *The Three Worlds of Welfare Capitalism* (Cambridge: Polity Press).

Etheredge, L.S. (1981) 'Government Learning: An Overview', in S.L. Long (ed.), *The Handbook of Political Behavior* (New York: Pergamon).

Evans, P.B., Rueschemeyer, D. and T. Skocpol (eds) (1985) *Bringing the State Back* (Cambridge: Cambridge University Press).

Fairbrass, J. and A. Jordan (2001) 'European Union Environmental Policy and the UK Government: A Passive Observer or a Strategic Manager?', *Environmental Politics*, 10(2): 1–21.

Falkner, G., O. Treib, M. Hartlapp and S. Leiber (2005) *Complying with Europe? Theory and Practice of Minimum Harmonisation and Soft Law in the Multilevel System* (Cambridge: Cambridge University Press).

Fearon, J.D. and D.D. Laitin (2010) 'Integrating Qualitative and Quantitative Methods', in J.M. Box-Steffensmeier, H.E. Brady and D. Collier (eds), *The Oxford Handbook of Political Methodology* (Oxford: Oxford University).

Fedson, D.S. (2005) 'Preparing for Pandemic Vaccination: An International Policy Agenda for Vaccine Development', *Journal of Public Health Policy*, 26(1): 4–29.

Feick, J. and W. Jann (1989) 'Comparative Policy Research: Eclecticism or Systematic Integration?', *MPIfG Discussion Paper*, 89(2).

Ferejohn, J. (1974) *Pork Barrel Politics; Rivers and Harbors Legislation, 1947–1968* (Stanford: Stanford University Press).

Fink S. (2008) 'Politics as Usual or Bringing Religion Back In? The Influence of Parties, Institutions, Economic Interests, and Religion on Embryo Research Laws', *Comparative Political Studies*, 41(12):1631–56.

Fischer, F. (1993) 'Citizen Participation and the Democratization of Policy Expertise', *Policy Sciences*, 26(3): 165–87.

Fischer, F. (1995) *Evaluating Public Policy* (Belmont: Wadsworth).

Fischer, F. (2003) *Reframing Public Policy: Discursive Politics and Deliberative Practices* (Oxford: Oxford University Press).

Fischer, F. (2006) *Professional Expertise in Deliberative Politics: Knowledge, Policy, and Empowerment* (Oxford: Oxford University Press).

Fischer, F., G.J. Miller and M.S. Sidney (eds) (2007) *Handbook of Public Policy Analysis: Theory, Politics, and Methods* (Boca Raton, FL: CRC Press).

Franzén, C., U. Björnstig, C. Brulin and L. Lindholm (2009) 'A Cost-Utility Analysis of Nursing Intervention via Telephone Follow-Up for Injured Road Users', *BMC Health Services Research* 9(1): 98.

Freeman, G.P. (1985) 'National Styles and Policy Sectors: Explaining Structures Variation', *Journal of Public Policy*, 5(4): 467–90.

Frey, B. (1994) 'Direct Democracy: Politico-Economic Lessons from Swiss Experience', *American Economic Review*, 84(2): 338–42.

Gaines, B.J. and C. Crombez (2004) 'Another Look at Connections Across German Elections', *Journal of Theoretical Politics*, 16(3): 289–319.

Gallagher, M. (2011) 'Elections and Referendums', in D. Caramani (ed.), *Comparative Politics* (Oxford: Oxford University Press).

Gallagher, M. and P. Mitchell (2008) 'Introduction to Electoral Systems', in M. Gallagher and P. Mitchell (eds), *The Politics of Electoral Systems* (Oxford: Oxford University Press).

Gallagher, M., M. Laver and P. Mair (2005) *Representative Government in Modern Europe. Institutions, Parties, and Government* (New York: McGraw-Hill).

Gamble, A. (1988) *The Free Economy and the Strong State. The Politics of Thatcherism* (London: Macmillan).

Gamkhar, S. and J. Vickers (2010) 'Comparing Federations: Lessons from Comparing Canada and the United States', *Publius*, 40(3): 351–56.

Ganghof, S. (2011) 'Veto Player', in B. Badie, D. Berg-Schlosser and L. Morlino (eds), *International Encyclopedia of Political Science* (Los Angeles: Sage).

Ganghof, S. and T. Bräuninger (2006) 'Government Status and Legislative Behaviour. Partisan Veto Players in Australia, Denmark, Finland and Germany', *Party Politics*, 12(4): 521–39.

Garrett, G., F. Dobbin and B. Simmons (eds) (2008) *The Global Diffusion of Markets and Democracy* (Cambridge: Cambridge University Press).

Gerston, L.N. (2004) *Public Policy Making: Process and Principles* (Armonk: M.E. Sharpe).

Gibson, J.L. (2008) 'Judicial Institutions', in R.A.W. Rhodes, S.A. Binder and B.A. Rockman (eds), *The Oxford Handbook of Political Institutions* (Oxford: Oxford University Press).

Gilardi, F. (2008) *Delegation in the Regulatory State: Independent Regulatory Agencies in Western Europe* (Cheltenham: Edward Elgar).

Gilardi, F. (2010) 'Who Learns from What in Policy Diffusion Processes?' *American Journal of Political Science*, 54(3): 650–66.

Gilardi, F., K. Füglister and S. Luyet (2009) 'Learning From Others: The Diffusion of Hospital Financing Reforms in OECD Countries', *Comparative Political Studies*, 42(4): 549–73.

Goetz, K.H. (2008) 'Governance as a Path to Government', *West European Politics*, 31(1): 258–79.

Goggin, M.L., A. Bowman, J.P. Lester and L.J.J. O'Toole (1990) *Implementation Theory and Practice: Toward a Third Generation* (Glenview: Scott/Foresman/ Little, Brown).

Golden, M. and L. Picci (2008) 'Pork Barrel Politics in Postwar Italy, 1953–94', *American Journal of Political Science*, 52(2): 268–89.

Goodman, J. and L. Pauly (1993) 'The Obsolescence of Capital Controls? Economic Management in an Age of Global Markets', *World Politics*, 46(1): 50–82.

Grande, E. (2009) 'Perspektiven der Governance-Forschung: Grundzüge des Forschungsprogramms des Münchener Centrums für Governance-Forschung', in E. Grande and S. May (eds), *Perspektiven der Governance-Forschung. Schriften des Münchner Centrums für Governance-Forschung* (Baden-Baden: Nomos).

Grando, M.T. (2010) *Evidence, Proof, and Fact-Finding in WTO Dispute Settlement* (Oxford: Oxford University Press).

Gray, V. (1973) 'Innovation in the States: A Diffusion Study', *American Political Science Review*, 67(4), 1174–85.

Greenberg, G.D., J.A. Miller, L.B. Mohr and B.C. Vladeck (1977) 'Developing Public Policy Theory: Perspectives from Empirical Research', *American Political Science Review*, 71(4): 1532–43.

Green-Pedersen, C. (2001) 'Minority Governments and Party Politics: The Political and Institutional Background to the "Danish Miracle"', *Journal of Public Policy*, 21(1): 53–70.

Green-Pedersen, C. (2004) 'The Dependent Variable Problem within the Study of Welfare State Retrenchment: Defining the Problem and Looking for Solutions', *Journal of Comparative Policy Analysis* 6(1): 3–14.

Green-Pedersen, C. (2006) 'Long-Term Changes in Danish Party Politics. The Rise and Importance of Issue Competition', *Scandinavian Political Studies*, 29(3): 221–37.

Green-Pedersen, C. (2007) 'More than Data Questions and Methodological Issues: Theoretical Conceptualization and the Dependent Variable "Problem" in the Study of Welfare Reform', in J. Clasen and N.A. Siegel (eds), *Investigating Welfare State Change. The 'Dependent Variable Problem' in Comparative Analyses* (Cheltenham: Edward Elgar).

Green-Pedersen, C. and R. Stubager (2010) 'The Political Conditionality of Mass Media. When do Parties Follow Mass Media Attention?', *British Journal of Political Science*, 40(3): 663–77.

Grossman, G. and E. Helpman (2001) *Special Interest Politics* (Cambridge: MIT Press).

Guetzkow, J. (2010) 'Beyond Deservingness: Congressional Discourse on Poverty, 1964–1996', *Annals of the American Academy of Political and Social Science*, 629(1): 173–97.

Gustafsson, G. and J.J. Richardson (1979) 'Concepts of Rationality and the Policy Process', *European Journal of Political Research*, 7(4): 415–36.

Gustafsson, G. and J.J. Richardson (1980) 'Post-Industrial Changes in Policy Style', *Scandinavian Political Studies*, 3(1): 21–37.

Haas, P. (1992) 'Introduction: Epistemic Communities and International Policy Coordination', *International Organization*, 46(1): 1–35.

Hacker, J. (2004) 'Privatizing Risk without Privatizing the Welfare State: The Hidden Politics of Social Policy Retrenchment in the United States', *American Political Science Review*, 98(2): 243–60.

Haider-Markel, D.P. (1998) 'The Politics of Social Regulatory Policy: State and Federal Hate Crime Policy and Implementation Effort', *Political Research Quarterly*, 51(March): 69–88.

Haider-Markel, D.P. (1999) 'Creating Change – Holding the Line: Agenda Setting on Lesbian and Gay Issues at the National Level', in E.D.B. Riggle and B. Tadlock (eds), *Gays and Lesbians in the Democratic Process: Public Policy, Public Opinion, and Political Representation* (New York: Columbia University Press).

Haider-Markel, D.P. (2001) 'Implementing Controversial Policy: Results from a National Survey of Law Enforcement Department Activity on Hate Crime', *Justice Research and Policy*, 3(1): 29–61.

Hale, T. and D. Held (eds) (2011) *The Handbook of Transnational Governance: Institutions and Innovations* (New York: Wiley).

Hall, P.A. (ed.) (1986) *Governing the Economy: The Politics of State Intervention in Britain and France* (New York: Oxford University Press).

Hall, P.A. (1993) 'Policy Paradigms, Social Learning and the State', *Comparative Politics*, 25(3): 275–96.

Hall, P.A. and Taylor, R.C.R. (1996) 'Political Science and the Three New Institutionalisms', *Political Studies*, 44(5): 936–57.

Hall, R.L. and A.V. Deardorff (2006) 'Lobbying as Legislative Subsidy', *American Political Science Review*, 100(1): 69–84.

Hall, T.E. and L.J.J. O'Toole (2000) 'Structures for Policy Implementation: An Analysis of National Legislation, 1965–1966 and 1993–1994', *Administration & Society*, 31(6): 667–86.

Hall, W.D. (2003) 'The Australian Policy Debate about Human Embryonic Stem Cell Research', *Health Law Review*, 12(2): 27–33.

Hallerberg, M. (2010) 'Empirical Applications of Veto Player Analysis and Institutional Effectiveness', in T. König, G. Tsebelis and M. Debus (eds), *Reform Processes and Policy Change: Veto Players and Decision-Making in Modern Democracy* (New York: Springer).

Hammond, T.H. (1986) 'Agenda Control, Organizational Structure, and Bureaucratic Politics', *American Journal of Political Science*, 30(2): 379–420.

Hammond, T.H. (2003) 'Veto Points, Policy Preferences, and Bureaucratic Autonomy in Democratic Systems', in G.A. Krause and K. Meier (eds), *Politics, Policy, and Organizations* (Ann Arbor: University of Michigan Press).

Hammond, T. H. and J. Knott (1996) 'Who Controls the Bureaucracy?: Presidential Power, Congressional Dominance, Legal Constraints, and Bureaucratic Autonomy in a Model of Multi-Institutional Policy-Making', *Journal of Law, Economics, and Organization*, 12(1): 119–66.

Hammond, T.H., Bonneau, C.W. and R.S. Sheehan (2005) *Strategic Behavior and Policy Choice on the U.S. Supreme Court* (Stanford: Stanford University Press).

Hanf, K. and L.J.J. O'Toole (1992) 'Revisiting Old Friends: Networks, Implementation Structures and the Management of Inter-organizational Relations', *European Journal of Political Research*, 21(1–2): 163–80.

Hanhimaki, J.M. (2008) *The United Nations: A Very Short Introduction* (Oxford: Oxford University Press).

Hardin, G. (1968) 'The Tragedy of the Commons Science', *Science*, 162: 1243–48.

Hartlapp, M. and G. Falkner (2009) 'Problems of Operationalisation and Data in EU Compliance Research', *European Union Politics*, 10(2): 291–315.

Hasenclever, A., Mayer, P. and V. Rittberger (1997) *Theories of International Regimes* (Cambridge: Cambridge University Press).

Hausen, J. (2010) 'Medical Marijuana Laws too Vague, Law Enforcement, Lawyers Say', www.bozemandailychronicle.com/news/article_7e4b4f40–92bf-11dfbbb6-001cc4c03286.html.

Hayes, M.T. (2006) *Incrementalism and Public Policy* (Lanham: University Press of America).

Hayes, M.T. (2007) 'Policy Characteristics, Patterns of Politics, and the Minimum Wage: Toward a Typology of Redistributive Policies', *Policy Studies Journal*, 35(3): 465–80.

Hazama, Y. (1996) 'Constitutional Review and the Parliamentary Opposition in Turkey', *The Developing Economies*, 34(1): 316–38.

Head, B.W. (2008) 'Three Lenses of Evidence-Based Policy', *Australian Journal of Public Administration*, 67(1): 1–11.

Heckathorn, D.D. and S.M. Maser (1990) 'The Contractual Architecture of Public Policy: A Critical Reconstruction of Lowi's Typology', *Journal of Politics*, 52(4): 1101–23.

Heclo, H. (1974) *Modern Social Politics in Britain and Sweden: From Relief to Income Maintenance* (New Haven: Yale University Press).

Heclo, H. (1978) 'Issue Networks and the Executive Establishment', in A. King (ed.), *The New American Political System* (Washington, DC: American Enterprise Institute Press).

Heichel, S., J. Pape and T. Sommerer (2005) 'Is there Convergence in Convergence Research? An Overview of Empirical Studies on Policy Convergence', *Journal of European Public Policy*, 12(5): 817–40.

Heichel, S., Holzinger, K., Sommerer, T., Liefferink, D., Pape, J. and S. Veenman (2008) 'Research Design, Variables and Data', in K. Holzinger, C. Knill and B. Arts (eds), *Environmental Policy Convergence in Europe? The Impact of International Institutions and Trade* (Cambridge: Cambridge University Press).

Henrekson M. (1993) 'Wagner's Law: A Spurious Relationship?', *Public Finance*, 48(2): 406–15.

Héritier, A. (2002) 'Introduction', in A. Heritier (ed.), *Common Goods: Reinventing European and International Governance* (Lanham: Rowman & Littlefield).

Héritier, A. (2002) 'New Modes of Governance in Europe: Policy-Making without Legislating?', in A. Héritier (ed.), *Common Goods: Reinventing European and International Governance* (Lanham: Rowman & Littlefield).

Héritier, A., C. Knill and S. Mingers (1996) *Ringing the Changes in Europe: Regulatory Competition and the Transformation of the State* (Berlin: De Gruyter).

Hessing, M., M. Howlett and T. Summerville (2005) *Canadian Natural Resource and Environmental Policy: Political Economy and Public Policy* (Vancouver: UBC Press).

Hibbs, D. (1977) 'Political Parties and Macroeconomic Policies', *American Political Science Review*, 71(4): 467–87.

Higgott, R. (2008) 'International Political Institutions', in R.A.W. Rhodes, S.A. Binder and B.A. Rockman (eds), *The Oxford Handbook of Political Institutions* (Oxford: Oxford University Press).

Hill, M.J. (2009) *The Public Policy Process* (Harlow: Pearson).

Hill, M.J. and P. Hupe (2009) *Implementing Public Policy: An Introduction to the Study of Operational Governance* (Thousand Oaks: Sage).

Hirschman, A.O. and C.E. Lindblom (1962) 'Economic Development, Research and Development, Policy Making: Some Converging Views', *Behavioral Science* 7(2): 211–22.

Hirshleifer, J. (1983) 'From Weakest-Link to Best-Shot: The Voluntary Provision of Public Goods', *Public Choice*, 41(3): 371–86.

Hix, S. and B. Høyland (2011) *The Political System of the European Union* (Basingstoke: Palgrave Macmillan).

Hjern, B. (1982) 'Implementation Research: The Link Gone Missing', *Journal of Public Policy*, 2(3): 301–08.

Hjern, B. and C. Hull (1982) 'Implementation Research as Empirical Constitutionalism', *European Journal of Political Research*, 10(2): 105–16.

Hjern, B. and D.O. Porter (1981) 'Implementation Structures: A New Unit of Administrative Analysis', *Organization Studies*, 2(3): 211–27.

Hoberg, G. (2001) 'Globalization and Policy Convergence: Symposium Overview', *Journal of Comparative Policy Analysis: Research and Practice*, 3(2): 127–32.

Hodge, G.A. and C. Greve, (2007) 'Public–Private Partnerships: An International Performance Review', *Public Administration Review*, 67(3): 545–58.

Hoekman, B.M. and M.M. Kostecki (2010) *The Political Economy of the World Trading System* (Oxford: Oxford University Press).

Hogwood, B.W. and L.A. Gunn (1984) *Policy Analysis for the Real World* (Oxford: Oxford University Press).

Hogwood, B.W. and B.G. Peters (1983) *Policy Dynamics* (New York: St. Martin's Press).

Hollander, R. and H. Patapan (2007) 'Pragmatic Federalism: Australian Federalism from Hawke to Howard', *Australian Journal of Public Administration*, 66(3): 280–97.

Holzer, T. and G. Schneider (2002) *Asylpolitik auf Abwegen: Nationalstaatliche und europäische Reaktionen auf die Globalisierung der Flüchtlingsströme* (Opladen: Leske & Budrich).

Holzinger, K. (2002) 'The Provision of Transnational Common Goods: Regulatory Competition for Environmental Standards', in A. Héritier (ed.), *Common Goods: Reinventing European and International Governance* (Lanham: Rowman & Littlefield).

Holzinger, K. (2008) *Transnational Common Goods: Strategic Constellations, Collective Action Problems, and Multi-level Provision* (Basingstoke: Palgrave Macmillan).

Holzinger, K. and C. Knill (2005) 'Causes and Conditions of Cross-National Policy Convergence', *Journal of European Public Policy*, 12(5): 775–96.

Holzinger, K. and C. Knill (2008) 'Theoretical Framework: Causal Factors and Convergence Expectations', in K. Holzinger, C. Knill and B. Arts (eds), *Environmental Policy Convergence in Europe? The Impact of International Institutions and Trade* (Cambridge: Cambridge University Press).

Holzinger, K., C. Knill and A. Schäfer (2006) 'Rhetoric or Reality? "New Governance" in EU Environmental Policy', *European Law*, 12(3): 403–20.

Holzinger, K., H. Jörgens and C. Knill (eds) (2007) 'Transfer, Diffusion und Konvergenz von Politiken', *PVS Politische Vierteljahresschrift, Sonderheft 39* (Wiesbaden: VS).

Holzinger, K., C. Knill and B. Arts (eds) (2008a) *Environmental Policy Convergence in Europe? The Impact of International Institutions and Trade* (Cambridge: Cambridge University Press).

Holzinger, K., C. Knill and T. Sommerer (2008b) 'Environmental Policy Convergence? The Impact of International Harmonization, Transnational Communication and Regulatory Competition', *International Organization*, 62(4): 553–87.

Holzinger, K., C. Knill, and T. Sommerer (2011) 'Is There Convergence of National Environmental Policies? An Analysis of Policy Outputs in 24 OECD Countries', *Environmental Politics*, 20(1): 20–41.

Hönnige, C. (2009) 'The Electoral Connection: How the Pivotal Judge Affects Oppositional Success at European Constitutional Courts', *West European Politics*, 32(5): 963–84.

Hood, C. (1976) *The Limits of Administration* (London: John Wiley & Sons).

Hood, C. (1986) *The Tools of Government* (Chatham: Chatham House)

Hood, C. (1991) 'A Public Management for All Seasons', *Public Administration* 69(1): 3–19.

Hood. C. and H.Z. Margetts (2007) *The Tools of Government in the Digital Age* (Basingstoke: Palgrave Macmillan).

Hooghe, L., G. Marks and A.H. Schakel (eds) (2008) 'Regional Authority in 42 Democracies, 1950–2006: A Measure and Five Hypotheses', *Regional and Federal Studies*, 18(2–3): 111–302.

Howlett, M. (1991) 'Policy Instruments, Policy Styles and Policy Implementation: National Approaches to Theories of Instrument Choice', *Policy Studies Journal*, 19(2): 1–21.

Howlett, M. (2002) 'Understanding National Administrative Cultures and Their Impact upon Administrative Reform: A Neo-Institutional Model and Analysis', *Policy, Organisation & Society*, 21(1): 1–24.

Howlett, M. (2003) 'Administrative Styles and the Limits of Administrative Reform: A Neo- Institutional Analysis of Administrative Culture', *Canadian Public Administration*, 46(4): 471–94.

Howlett, M. (2009a) 'Government Communication as a Policy Tool: A Framework for Analysis', *The Canadian Political Science Review*, 3(2): 23–37.

Howlett, M. (2009b) 'Policy Analytical Capacity and Evidence-Based Policy-Making: Lessons from Canada', *Canadian Public Administration*, 52(2): 153–75.

Howlett, M. and B. Cashore (2009) 'The Dependent Variable Problem in the Study of Policy Change: Understanding Policy Change as a Methodological Problem', *Journal of Comparative Policy Analysis: Research and Practice*, 11(1): 33–46.

Howlett, M. and S. Joshi-Koop (2011) 'Transnational Learning, Policy Analytical Capacity, and Environmental Policy Convergence: Survey Results from Canada', *Global Environmental Change* 21(1): 85–92.

Howlett, M. and E. Lindquist (2004) 'Policy Analysis and Governance: Analytical and Policy Styles in Canada', *Journal of Comparative Policy Analysis*, 6(3): 225–49.

Howlett, M. and M. Ramesh (2002) 'The Policy Effects of Internationalization: A Subsystem Adjustment Analysis of Policy Change', *Journal of Comparative Policy Analysis*, 4(3): 31–50.

Howlett, M., M. Ramesh and A. Perl (2009) *Studying Public Policy: Policy Cycles and Policy Subsystems* (Oxford: Oxford University Press).

Howlett, M. and J. Rayner (2006) 'Understanding the Historical Turn in the Policy Sciences: A Critique of Stochastic, Narrative, Path Dependency and Process-Sequencing Models of Policy-Making over Time', *Policy Sciences*, 39(1): 1–18.

Huber, J.D. and C.R. Shipan (2002) *Deliberate Discretion: the Institutional Foundations of Bureaucratic Autonomy* (Cambridge: Cambridge University Press).

Hueglin, T.O. and A. Fenna (2006) *Comparative Federalism: A Systematic Inquiry* (Peterborough: Broadview Press).

Hug, S. and G. Tsebelis (2002) 'Veto Players and Referendums around the World', *Journal of Theoretical Politics*, 14(4): 465–516.

Huque, A.S. and N. Watton (2010) 'Federalism and the Implementation of Environmental Policy: Changing Trends in Canada and the United States', *Public Organization Review*, 10(1)71–88.

Immergut, E.M. (1990) 'Institutions, Veto Points, and Policy Results: A Comparative Analysis of Health Care', *Journal of Public Policy*, 10(4): 391–416.

Immergut, E.M. (1992) *Health Politics: Interests and Institutions in Western Europe* (Cambridge: Cambridge University Press).

Immergut, E.M. (2008) 'Institutional Constraints on Policy', in M. Moran, M. Rein and R.E. Goodin (eds), *The Oxford Handbook of Public Policy* (Oxford: Oxford University Press).

Immergut, E.M. and K.M. Anderson (2007) 'Editors' Introduction: The Dynamics of Pension Politics', in E.M. Immergut, K.M. Anderson and I. Schulze (eds), *The Handbook of West European Pension Politics* (Oxford: Oxford University Press).

Immergut, E.M. and K.M. Anderson (2008) 'Historical Institutionalism and West European Politics', *West European Politics*, 31(1–2): 345–69.

Inglehart, R. (1997) *Modernization and Postmodernization* (Princeton: Princeton University Press).

Ingram, P. and K. Clary (2000) 'The Choice-within-Constraints New Institutionalism and Implications for Sociology', *Annual Review of Sociology*, 26: 525–46.

Jackson, G. (2010) 'Actors and Institutions', in G. Morgan, J. Campbell, C. Crouch, O.K. Pedersen and R. Whitley (eds), *The Oxford Handbook of Comparative Institutional Analysis* (Oxford: Oxford University Press).

Jagannathan, R. and M. Camasso (forthcoming): *When to Protect? Decision-Making in Public Child Welfare* (Oxford University Press: Oxford).

Jagannathan, R., Camasso, M.J. and C. Harvey (2010) 'The Price Effects of Family Caps on Fertility Decisions of Poor Women', *Journal of Social Service Research*, 36(4): 346–61.

Jahn, D. (1998) 'Environmental Performance and Policy Regimes: Explaining Variations in 18 OECD Countries', *Policy Sciences*, 31(2): 107–31.

Jänicke, M. (1988) 'Structural Change and Environmental Impact: Empirical Evidence on Thirty-One Countries in East and West', *Environmental Monitoring and Assessment*, 12(2): 99–114.

Jänicke, M. and K. Jacob (2004) 'Ecological Modernisation and the Creation of Lead Markets', *Global Environmental Politics*, 4(1): 1–18.

Jänicke, M. and H. Weidner (1997) *National Environmental Policies: a Comparative Study of Capacity-Building* (Berlin: Springer).

Jann, W. and K. Wegrich (2007) 'Theories of the Policy Cycle', in F. Fischer, G. Miller and M. Sidney (eds), *Handbook of Public Policy Analysis: Theory, Politics, and Methods* (Boca Raton: CRC Press).

Jann, W. and K. Wegrich (2010) 'Governance und Verwaltungspolitik: Leitbilder und Reformkonzepte', in A. Benz and N. Dose (eds), *Governance: Regieren in komplexen Regelsystemen – Eine Enführung* (Wiesbaden: VS).

Jerit, J. (2006) 'Reform, Rescue, or Run Out of Money? Problem Definition in the Social Security Reform Debate', *Harvard International Journal of Press/Politics*, 11(1): 9–28.

Joerges, C. and J. Neyer (1997) 'Transforming Strategic Interaction into Deliberative Problem-Solving: European Comitology in the Foodstuffs Sector', *Journal of European Public Policy*, 4(4): 609–25.

John, P. (2003) 'Is there Life after Policy Streams, Advocacy Coalitions, and Punctuations: Using Evolutionary Theory to Explain Policy Change', *Policy Studies Journal*, 31(2): 481–98.

John, P. (2006) *Analysing Public Policy* (London: Continuum).

Jones, B.D. (2001) *Politics and the Architecture of Choice: Bounded Rationality and Governance* (Chicago: University of Chicago Press).

Jones, B.D. and F.R. Baumgartner (2005) *The Politics of Attention: How Government Prioritizes Problems* (Chicago: University of Chicago Press).

Jordan, A.G. (1999) 'The Implementation of EU Environmental Policy: a Policy Problem Without a Political Solution?', *Environment and Planning C: Government and Policy*, 17(1): 69–90.

Jordan, A.G. (1981) 'Iron Triangles, Woolly Corporatism or Elastic Nets? Images of the Policy Process', *Journal of Public Policy*, 1(1): 95–124.

Jordana, J. and D. Levi-Faur (2005) 'The Diffusion of Regulatory Capitalism in Latin America: Sectoral and National Channels in the Making of a New Order', *Annals of the American Academy of Political and Social Science*, 598(1): 102–24.

Josling, T. (2010) 'WTO Compliance and Domestic Farm Policy Change', in V.E. Ball, R. Fanfani and L. Gutierrez (eds), *The Economic Impact of Public Support to Agriculture: An International Perspective* (Berlin: Springer).

Kahneman, D. and A. Tversky (1982) 'Judgement Under Uncertainty: Heuristics and Biases', in D. Kahneman, P. Slovic and A. Tversky (eds), *Judgement Under Uncertainty: Heuristics and Biases* (Cambridge: Cambridge University Press).

Kahneman, D., P. Slovic and A. Tversky (eds) (1982) *Judgement Under Uncertainty: Heuristics and Biases* (Cambridge: Cambridge University Press).

Karakhanyan, S., van Veen, K. and T. Bergen (2011) 'Educational Policy Diffusion and Transfer: The Case of Armenia', *Higher Education Policy*, 24(1): 53–83.

Karembu, M., D. Otunge and D. Wafula (2010) *Developing a Biosafety Law: Lessons from the Kenyan Experience* (Nairobi: ISAAA AfriCenter).

Kassim, H. and P. Le Galès (2010) 'Exploring Governance in a Multi-Level Polity: A Policy Instruments Approach', *West European Politics*, 33(1): 1–21.

Kato, J. (1994) *The Problem of Bureaucratic Rationality: Tax Politics in Japan* (Princeton: Princeton University Press).

Katz, R.S. (2011) 'Political Parties', in D. Caramani (ed.), *Comparative Politics* (Oxford: Oxford University Press).

Keating, M. (2005) *The Government of Scotland: Public Policy Making after Devolution* (Edinburgh: Edinburgh University Press).

Keating, M. (2009) 'Putting European political science back together again', *European Political Science Review*, 1(2): 297–316.

Keating, M., Cairney, P. and E. Hepburn (2009) 'Territorial Policy Communities and Devolution in the United Kingdom', *Cambridge Journal of Regions, Economy and Society*, 2(1): 51–66.

Keck, M.E. and K. Sikkink (1998) *Activists beyond Borders: Advocacy Networks in International Politics* (Ithaca: Cornell University Press).

Kelemen, D.C. (2006) 'Suing for Europe: Adversarial Legalism and European Governance', *Comparative Political Studies*, 39(1): 101–27.

Kenis, P. and V. Schneider (1991) 'Policy Networks and Policy Analysis: Scrutinizing a New Analytical Toolbox', in B. Marin and R. Mayntz (eds), *Policy Networks. Empirical Evidence and Theoretical Considerations* (Frankfurt am Main: Campus).

Keohane, R. and J. Nye (2000) 'Globalisation: What's New? And What's Not? (And So What?)', *Foreign Policy*, 118: 104–12.

Kern, K., H. Jörgens and M. Jänicke (2001) 'The Diffusion of Environmental Policy Innovations: A Contribution to the Globalisation of Environmental Policy', *Discussion Paper* FS II 01–302, Berlin: WZB.

Kerr, C. (1983) *The Future of Industrial Societies: Convergence or Continuing Diversity?* (Cambridge: Cambridge University Press).

Kettl, D.F. (2008) 'Public Bureaucracies', in R.A.W. Rhodes, S.A. Binder and B.A. Rockman (eds), *The Oxford Handbook of Political Institutions* (Oxford: Oxford University Press).

Kim, D. (1990) 'The Transformation of Familism in Modern Korean Society: From Cooperation to Competition', *International Sociology*, 5(4): 409–25.

King, G., R. Keohane and S. Verba (1994) *Designing Social Inquiry: Scientific Inference in Qualitative Research* (Princeton: Princeton University Press).

King, G., E. Gakidou, N. Ravishankar, R.T. Moore, J. Lakin, M. Vargas, M. María Téllez-Rojo, J.E. Hernández Ávila, M. Hernández Ávila and H. Hernández Llamas (2007) 'A "Politically Robust" Experimental Design for Public Policy Evaluation, with Application to the Mexican Universal Health Insurance Program', *Journal of Policy Analysis and Management*, 26(3): 479–506.

Kingdon, J.W. (2003) *Agendas, Alternatives, and Public Policies* (New York: Longman).

Kinney, E. (2002) 'The Emerging Field of International Administrative Law: Its Content and Potential', *Administrative Law Review*, 54(1): 415–33.

Kitschelt, H. and S.I. Wilkinson (eds) (2007) *Patrons, Clients and Policies: Patterns of Democratic Accountability and Political Competition* (Cambridge: Cambridge University Press).

Kittel, B. (2006) 'A Crazy Methodology? On the Limits of Macroquantitative Social Science Research', *International Sociology*, 21(5): 647–77.

Kittel, B. and H. Obinger (2003) 'Political Parties, Institutions, and the Dynamics of Social Expenditure in Times of Austerity', *Journal of European Public Policy*, 10(1): 20–45.

Kjær, A.M. (2004) *Governance* (Oxford: Polity).

Knill, C. (1998) 'European Policies: The Impact of National Administrative Traditions', *Journal of Public Policy*, 18(1): 1–28.

Knill, C. (1999) 'Explaining Cross-National Variance in Administrative Reform: Autonomous versus Instrumental Bureaucracies', *Journal of Public Policy*, 19(2): 113–39.

Knill, C. (2001) *The Europeanisation of National Administrations. Patterns of Institutional Change and Persistence* (Cambridge: Cambridge University Press).

Knill, C. (2004) 'Modes of Governance and their Evaluation', *TRAMES: A Journal of the Humanities and Social Sciences* 8(4): 352–71.

Knill, C. (2005) 'Introduction. Cross-National Policy Convergence: Concepts, Approaches and Explanatory Factors', *Journal of European Public Policy*, 12(5): 764–74.

Knill, C. (2006) 'Implementation', in J. Richardson (ed.), *European Union. Power and Policy-Making* (New York: Routledge).

Knill, C. (2008) *Europäische Umweltpolitik. Steuerungsprobleme und Regulierungsmuster im Mehrebenensystem* (Wiesbaden: VS).

Knill, C. and T. Balint (2008) 'Explaining Variation in Organizational Change: The Reform of Human Resource Management in the European Commission and the OECD', *Journal of European Public Policy*, 15(5): 669–90.

Knill, C., K. Holzinger and B. Arts (2008b) 'Conclusion', in K. Holzinger, C. Knill and B. Arts (eds), *Environmental Policy Convergence in Europe? The Impact of International Institutions and Trade* (Cambridge: Cambridge University Press).

Knill, C. and D. Lehmkuhl (1998) 'Integration by Globalization: The European Interest Representation of the Consumer Electronics Industry', *Current Politics and Economics in Europe* 8(2): 131–53.

Knill, C. and D. Lehmkuhl (2002a) 'The National Impact of European Union Regulatory Policy: Three Europeanization Mechanisms', *European Journal of Political Research*, 41(2): 255–80.

Knill, C. and D. Lehmkuhl (2002b) 'Private Actors and the State: Internationalization and Changing Patterns of Governance', *Governance*, 15(1): 41–63.

Knill, C. and A. Lenschow (1998) 'Compliance with Europe: The Implementation of EU Environmental Policy and Administrative Traditions in Britain and Germany', *Journal of European Public Policy*, 5(4): 597–616.

Knill, C. and A. Lenschow (eds) (2000) *Implementing EU Environmental Policy: New Directions and Old Problems* (Manchester: Manchester University Press).

Knill C. and A. Lenschow (2001) '"Seek and Ye Shall Find!" Linking Different Perspectives on Institutional Change', *Comparative Political Studies*, 34(2): 187–215.

Knill, C and A. Lenschow (2003) 'Modes of Regulation in the Governance of the European Union: Towards a Comprehensive Evaluation', in J. Jordana and D. Levi-Faur (eds), *The Politics of Regulation. Institutions and Regulatory Reforms for the Age of Governance* (Cheltenham: Edward Elgar).

Knill, C. and A. Lenschow (2005) 'Compliance, Communication and Competition: Patterns of EU Environmental Policy Making and Their Impact on Policy Convergence', *European Environment* 15(2): 114–28.

Knill, C. and D. Liefferink (2007) *Environmental Politics in the European Union. Policy-Making, Implementation and Patterns of Multi-Level Governance* (Manchester: Manchester University Press).

Knill, C., K. Schulze and J. Tosun (2010) 'Politikwandel und seine Messung in der vergleichenden Staatstätigkeitsforschung: Konzeptionelle Probleme und mögliche Alternativen', *Politische Vierteljahresschrift*, 51(3): 409–432.

Knill, C. and J. Tosun (2009) 'Harmonization, Competition, or Communication: How Does the EU Shape Environmental Policy Adoptions of Within and Beyond Its Borders?', *Journal of European Public Policy*, 16(6): 873–94.

Knill, C. and J. Tosun (2010) *Politikgestaltung in der Europäischen Union: Die Entstehung und Umsetzung der Dienstleitungsrichtlinie* (Baden-Baden: Nomos).

Knill, C., and J. Tosun (2011) 'Policy Making', in D. Caramani (ed.) *Comparative Politics* (Oxford: Oxford University Press).

Knill, C., J. Tosun and M.W. Bauer (2009) 'Neglected Faces of Europeanization: The Differential Impact of the EU on the Dismantling and Expansion of Domestic Policies', *Public Administration*, 87(3): 519–37.

Knill, C., J. Tosun and S. Heichel (2008a) 'Balancing Competitiveness and Conditionality: Environmental Policy-Making in Low-Regulating Countries', *Journal of European Public Policy*, 15(7): 1019–40.

Knoepfel, P., C. Larrue, F. Varone and M. Hill (2007) *Public Policy Analysis* (Bristol: The Polity Press).

Kobrin, S.J. (1997) 'The Architecture of Globalization: State Sovereignty in a Networked Global Economy', in J.H. Dunning (ed.), *Governments, Globalization, and International Business* (Oxford: Oxford University Press).

Kohler-Koch, B. and B. Rittberger (2006) 'Review Article: The "Governance Turn" in EU Studies', *Journal of Common Market Studies*, 44(1): 27–49.

König, T., Tsebelis, G. and M. Debus (eds) (2010) *Reform processes and policy change: veto players and decision-making in modern democracies* (New York: Springer).

Kooiman, J. (1993) *Modern Governance: New Government: Society Interactions* (London: Sage).

Kooiman, J., M. Bavinck, R. Chuenpagdee, R. Mahon and R. Pullin (2008) 'Interactive Governance and Governability: an Introduction', *The Journal of Transdisciplinary Environmental Studies*, 7(1): 1–20.

Kouzmin, A., E. Löffler, H. Klages and N. Korac-Kakabadse (1999) 'Benchmarking and Performance Measurement in Public Sectors', International *Journal of Public Sector Management*, 12(2): 121–44.

Krasner, S.D. (1983) 'Structural Causes and Regime Consequences: Regimes as Intervening Variables', in S.D. Krasner (ed.), *International Regimes* (Ithaca, NY: Cornell University Press).

Krasner, S.D. (1988) 'Sovereignty: An Institutional Perspective', *Comparative Political Studies*, 21(1): 66–94.

Kreppel, A. (2009) 'Executive-Legislative Relations and Legislative Agenda Setting in Italy: From Leggine to Decreti and Deleghe', *Bulletin of Italian Politics*, 1(2): 183–209.

Kreppel, A. (2011) 'Legislatures', in D. Caramani (ed.), *Comparative Politics* (Oxford: Oxford University Press).

Kriesi, H. (2011) 'Social Movements', in D. Caramani (ed.), *Comparative Politics* (Oxford: Oxford University Press).

Kübler, D. (2001) 'Understanding Policy Change with the Advocacy Coalition Framework: An Application to Swiss Drug Policy', *Journal of European Public Policy*, 8(4): 623–41.

La Palombara, J. (1964) *Italian Politics* (Princeton: Princeton University Press).

Laffont, J.J. and J. Tirole (1991) 'The Politics of Government Decision Making: A Theory of Regulatory Capture', *Quarterly Journal of Economics*, 106(4): 1089–127.

Lamartina, S. and A. Zaghini (2011) 'Increasing Public Expenditure: Wagner's Law in OECD Countries', *German Economic Review*, 12(2): 149–64.

Lambert, R. and J. Curtis (2008) 'Opposition to Multiculturalism among Québécois and English-Canadians', *Canadian Review of Sociology*, 20(2): 193–207.

Lascoumes, P. and P. Le Galès (2007) 'Introduction: Understanding Public Policy through its Instruments', *Governance*, 20(1): 1–21.

Lasswell, H.D. (1956) *The Decision Process: Seven Categories of Functional Analysis* (College Park: University of Maryland Press).

Laumann, E.O. and D. Knoke (1987) *The Organizational State. Social Choice in National Policy Domains* (Madison: University of Wisconsin Press).

Laws, D. and M.A. Hajer (2008) 'Policy in Practice', in: M. Moran, M. Rein and R.E. Goodin (eds), *The Oxford Handbook of Public Policy* (Oxford: Oxford University Press).

Lee, S. and S. McBride (2007) 'Introduction: Neo-Liberalism, State Power and Global Governance in the Twenty-First Century', in: D. Lee and S. McBride (eds), *Neo-Liberalism, State Power and Global Governance* (Dordrecht: Springer).

Leeke, M., C. Sear and O. Gay (2003) 'Introduction to Devolution in the UK', *House of Commons Research paper* 03/84 (London: House of Commons).

Lehmann, W. (2009) 'Lobbying the European Parliament', in D. Coen and J. Richardson (eds), *Lobbying the European Union, Institutions, Actor and Policy* (Oxford: Oxford University Press).

Lehmbruch, G. (1982) 'Introduction: Neo-corporatism in Comparative

Perspective', G. Lehmbruch and P.C. Schmitter (eds) *Patterns of Corporatist Policy-Making* (Beverly Hills: Sage).

Lehmbruch, G. and P.C. Schmitter (eds) (1982) *Patterns of Corporatist Policy-Making* (Beverly Hills: Sage).

Lehmkuhl, D. (2000) *Commercial Arbitration: A Case of Private Transnational Self-Governance?* (Bonn: Max-Planck Project Group Law, Politics and Economics).

Lehoucq, F., G. Negretto, F. Aparicio, B. Nacif and A. Benton (2008) 'Policymaking Under One-Party Hegemonic and Divided Government in Mexico', in E. Stein and M. Tommasi (eds), *Policymaking in Latin America: How Politics Shape Policies* (Washington, DC: Inter-American Development Bank).

Lenschow, A., D. Liefferink and S. Veenman (2005) 'When the Birds Sing. A Framework for Analysing Domestic Factors behind Policy Convergence', *Journal of European Public Policy*, 12(5): 797–816.

Leonard, L. (2007) *The Environmental Movement in Ireland* (Dordrecht: Springer).

Levi-Faur, D. (2002) 'Herding towards a New Convention. On Herds, Shepherds and Lost Sheep in the Liberalization of the Telecommunications and Electricity Industries', Paper presented at the workshop 'Theories of Regulation', Nuffield College, University of Oxford, May 25–26.

Levi-Faur, D. (ed.) (2012) *The Oxford Handbook of Governance* (Oxford: Oxford University Press).

Levintova, M. (2007) 'Russian Alcohol Policy in the Making', *Alcohol and Alcoholism*, 42(5): 500–5.

Lieberman, E.S. (2005) 'Nested Analysis as a Mixed-Method Strategy for Cross-National Research', *American Political Science Review*, 99(3): 435–52.

Liefferink, D. and M.S. Andersen (1998) 'Strategies of the "Green" Member States in EU Environmental Policy-Making', *Journal of European Public Policy*, 5(2): 254–70.

Lijphart, A. (1994) 'Democracies: Forms, Performance, and Constitutional Engineering', *European Journal of Political Research*, 25(1): 1–17.

Lijphart, A. (1999) *Patterns of Democracy: Government Forms and Performance in Thirty-Six Countries* (New Haven: Yale University Press).

Lindberg L.N. and S.A. Scheingold (1970) *Europe's Would-Be Polity* (Englewood Cliffs, NJ: Prentice-Hall).

Lindblom, C.E. (1959) 'The Science of Muddling through', *Public Administration Review*, 19(2): 79–88.

Lindblom, C.E. (1965) *The Intelligence of Democracy: Decision Process through Adjustment* (New York: Free Press).

Lindblom, C.E. (1979) 'Still Muddling, Not Yet Through', *Public Administration Review*, 39(6): 517–26.

Lindblom, C.E. and D.K. Cohen (1979) *Usable Knowledge* (New Haven: Yale University Press).

Linder, S.H. and B.G. Peters (1989) 'Instruments of Government: Perceptions and Contexts', *Journal of Public Policy*, 9(1): 35–58.

Lindquist, E., Mosher-Howe, K.N. and X. Liu (2010) 'Nanotechnology . . . What Is It Good For? (Absolutely Everything): A Problem Definition Approach', *Review of Policy Research*, 27(3): 255–71.

Lindvall, J. (2009) 'The Real but Limited Influence of Expert Ideas', *World Politics*, 61(4), 703–30.

Lippmann, W. (1964) *Public Opinion* (New Brunswick: Transaction Publishers).

Lipset, S.M. and S. Rokkan (1967) 'Cleavage Structures, Party Systems, and Voter Alignments: An Introduction', in S.M. Lipset and S. Rokkan (eds), *Party Systems and Voter Alignments* (New York: Free Press).

Lipsky, M. (1980) *Street-Level Bureaucracy. The Dilemmas of Individuals in the Public Service* (New York: Russell Sage Foundation).

Loughlin, J. (2011) 'Federal and Local Government Institutions', in D. Caramani (ed.), *Comparative Politics* (Oxford: Oxford University Press).

Lowi, T. (1964) 'American Business, Public Policy, Case Studies and Political Theory', *World Politics*, 16(4): 677–715.

Lowi, T. (1972) 'Four Systems of Policy, Politics, and Choice', *Public Administration*, 32(4): 298–310.

Lukes, S. (1974) *Power: A Radical View* (London: Macmillan Press).

Lütz, S. (2010) 'Governance in der politischen Ökonomie I: Maktro- und Mesoperspektiven', in A. Benz and N. Dose (eds), *Governance: Regieren in komplexen Regelsystemen – Eine Einführung* (Wiesbaden: VS).

Maddison, S. and R. Denniss (2009) *An Introduction to Australian Public Policy: Theory and Practice* (Cambridge: Cambridge University Press).

Mahon, R. and S. McBride (eds) (2008) *The OECD and Transnational Governance* (Vancouver: University of British Columbia Press).

Mahoney, J. (2000) 'Path Dependence in Historical Sociology', *Theory and Society*, 29(4): 507–48.

Mahoney, J. (2006) 'Analyzing Path Dependence: Lessons from the Social Sciences', in A. Wimmer and R. Kossler (eds), *Understanding Change* (London: Palgrave).

Mair, P. and C. Mudde (1998) 'The Party Family and Its Study', *Annual Review of Political Science*, 1(1): 211–29.

Majone, G. (1991) 'Cross-National Sources of Regulatory Policy Making in Europe and the United States', *Journal of Public Policy*, 11(1): 79–106.

Majone, G. (1994) 'The Rise of the Regulatory State in Europe', *West European Politics*, 17(3): 77–101.

Majone, G. (1996) *Regulating Europe* (London: Routledge).

Majone, G. (2008) 'Agenda Setting', in M. Moran, M. Rein and R.E. Goodin (eds), *The Oxford Handbook of Public Policy* (Oxford: Oxford University Press).

Maley, M. 2000. 'Too Many or Too Few? The Increase in Federal Ministerial Advisers 1972–1999', *Australian Journal of Public Administration*, 59(4): 48–53.

Maloney, W.A. and J.W. van Deth (eds) (2010) *Civil Society and Activism in Europe. Contextualizing Engagement and Political Orientations* (London: Routledge).

Manow, P. and S. Burkhart (2007) 'Government's Legislative Self-Restraint under Divided Government: Evidence from the German Case, 1976–2002', *Legislative Studies Quarterly*, 32(2): 167–91.

March, J.G. and J.P. Olsen (1984) 'The New Institutionalism: Organizational Factors in the Political Life', *American Political Science Review*, 78(3): 734–49.

March, J.G. and J.P. Olsen (1989) *Rediscovering Institutions: The Organizational Basics of Politics* (New York: Free Press).

March, J.G. and J.P. Olsen (1996) 'Institutional Perspectives on Political Institutions', *Governance*, 9(3): 247–64.

March, J.G. and J.P. Olsen (2008) 'Elaborating the "New Institutionalism", in R.A.W. Rhodes, S.A. Binder and B.A. Rockman (eds), *The Oxford Handbook of Political Institutions* (Oxford: Oxford University Press).

Marin, B. and R. Mayntz, (eds) (1991) *Policy Networks. Empirical Evidence and Theoretical Considerations* (Frankfurt am Main: Campus).

Marsh, D., M.J. Smith and D. Richards (2000) 'Bureaucrats, Politicians and Reform in Whitehall: Analysing the Bureau-Shaping Model', *British Journal of Political Science*, 30(3): 461–82.

Marston, G. and R. Watts (2003) 'Tampering with the Evidence: A Critical Appraisal of Evidence-Based Policy-Making', *Australian Review of Public Affairs*, 3(3): 143–63.

Martin, L.L. (2008) 'International Economic Institutions', in R.A.W. Rhodes, S.A. Binder and B.A. Rockman (eds), *The Oxford Handbook of Political Institutions* (Oxford: Oxford University Press).

Martin, L.L. and B.A. Simmons (1998) 'Theories and Empirical Studies of International Institutions', *International Organization*, 52(4): 729–57.

Martin, L.W. and G. Vanberg (2005) 'Coalition Policymaking and Legislative Review', *American Political Science Review*, 99(1): 93–106.

Matland, R. (1995) 'Synthesising the Implementation Literature: The Ambiguity-Conflict Model of Policy Implementation', *Journal of Public Administration Research and Theory*, 5(2): 145–74.

May, P.J. (2002) 'Social Regulation', in L.M. Salamon (ed.), *The Tools of Government, A Guide to the New Governance* (New York: Oxford University Press).

May, P.J. (2003) 'Policy Design and Implementation', in B.G. Peters and J. Pierre (eds), *Handbook of Public Administration* (Thousand Oaks: Sage).

Mayntz, R. (1979) 'Public Bureaucracies and Policy Implementation', *International Social Science Journal*, 31(4): 633–45.

Mayntz, R. (1993) 'Governing Failures and the Problems of Governability: Some Comments on a Theoretical Paradigm', in J. Kooiman (ed.), *Modern Governance: New Society Government Interactions* (London: Sage).

Mayntz, R. (2002) 'Common Goods and Governance', in A. Héritier (ed.), *Common Goods. Reinventing European and International Governance* (Lanham: Rowman & Littlefield).

Mayntz, R. (2010) 'Governance im modernen Staat', in A. Benz and N. Dose (eds), *Governance: Regieren in komplexen Regelsystemen – Eine Enführung* (Wiesbaden: VS).

Mayntz, R. and H.-U. Derlien (1989) 'Party Patronage and the Politicization of the West German Administrative Elite, 1970–1987: Towards Hybridization?', *Governance*, 2(4): 384–404.

Mayntz, R. and F.W. Scharpf (1995) 'Der Ansatz des akteurzentrierten Institutionalismus', in R. Mayntz and F.W. Scharpf (eds), *Gesellschaftliche Selbstregelung und politische Steuerung* (Frankfurt am Main: Campus).

Mazmanian, D. and P. Sabatier (1983) *Implementation and Public Policy* (Glenview: Scott).

McBeth, M.K., Shanahan, E.A., Arnell, R.J. and P.L. Hathaway (2007) 'The Intersection of Narrative Policy Analysis and Policy Change Theory', *Policy Studies Journal*, 35(1), 87–108.

McCarthy, N. and A. Meirowitz (2007) *Political Game Theory: An Introduction* (Cambridge: Cambridge University Press).

McCombs, M. (2004): *Setting the Agenda: The Mass Media and Public Opinion* (Polity Press: Oxford).

McCombs, M.E. and D.L. Shaw (1972) 'The Agenda-Setting Function of Mass Media', *Public Opinion Quarterly*, 36(2): 176–87.

McConnell, A. (2010) *Understanding Policy Success: Rethinking Public Policy* (Basingstoke: Palgrave Macmillan).

McCool, D. (1995) *Public Policy Theories, Models and Concepts: An Anthology* (Englewood Cliffs: Prentice Hall).

McCubbins, M. and T. Schwartz (1984) 'Congressional Oversight Overlooked: Police Patrols versus Fire Alarms', *American Journal of Political Science*, 28(1): 167–79.

McCubbins, M., R. Noll and B. Weingast (1987) 'Administrative Procedures as Instruments of Political Control', *Journal of Law, Economics & Organization*, 3(2): 243–77.

McDavid, J.C. and L.R.L. Hawthorn (2006) *Program Evaluation & Performance Measurement: An Introduction to Practice* (Thousand Oaks: Sage).

McLaughlin, M.W. (1987) 'Learning From Experience: Lessons From Policy Implementation', *Educational Evaluation and Policy Analysis*, 9(2): 171–78.

Meier, K.J. (1994) *The Politics of Sin* (Armonk, NY: M.E. Sharpe).

Meier, K.J. (2000) *Politics and the Bureaucracy: Policymaking in the Fourth Branch of Government* (New York: Harcourt College).

Meseguer Yebra, C. (2009) *Learning, Policy Making, and Market* (Cambridge: Cambridge University Press).

Mileur, J.M. (1992) 'The Politics of E.E. Schattschneider', *Political Science and Politics*, 25(2): 176–80.

Miller, L.R. (2004) *Democratic Efficiency: Inequality, Representation, and Public Policy Outputs in the United States and Worldwide* (Bloomington: Authors House).

Mitchell, A.D. and E. Sheargold (2009) 'Global Governance: The WTO's Contribution', *Alberta Law Review*, 46(4).

Moe, T.E. (1981) 'Toward a Broader View of Interest Groups', *The Journal of Politics*, 43: 531–43.

Mooney, C.Z. (1999) 'The Politics of Morality Policy: Symposium Editor's Introduction', *Policy Studies Journal*, 27(4): 675–80.

Mooney, C.Z. (ed.) (2001) *The Public Clash of Private Values: The Politics of Morality Policy* (Chatham: Chatham House).

Moran, M. (2005) *Politics and Governance in the UK* (Basingstoke: Palgrave Macmillan).

Moran, M., M. Rein, and R.E. Goodin (eds) (2008) *The Oxford Handbook of Public Policy* (Oxford: Oxford University Press).

Moravcsik, A. (1993) 'Preferences and Power in the European Community: a Liberal Intergovernmentalist Approach', *Journal of Common Market Studies*, 31(4): 473–524.

Mueller, D.C. (2003) *Public Choice III* (Cambridge: Cambridge University Press).

Mulgan, R. (1996) 'The Australian Senate as a House of Review', *Australian Journal of Political Science*, 31(2): 191–205.

Müller, W.C. (2011) 'Governments and Bureaucracies', in D. Caramani (ed.), *Comparative Politics* (Oxford: Oxford University Press).

Myles, J. and P. Pierson (2001) 'The comparative political economy of pension reform', in P. Pierson (ed.), *The New Politics of the Welfare State* (Oxford: Oxford University Press).

Mytelka L.K. and K. Smith (2002) 'Policy Learning and Innovation Theory: An Interactive and Co-Evolving Process', *Research Policy*, 31(8–9): 1467–79.

Nadakavukaren Schefer, K. (2010) *Social Regulation in the WTO: Trade Policy and International Legal Development* (Cheltenham: Edward Elgar).

Nagel, S.S. (ed.) (2001) *Handbook of Public Policy Evaluation* (Thousand Oaks, CA: Sage).

Newton, K. and J.W. van Deth (2010) *Foundations of Comparative Politics* (Cambridge: Cambridge University Press).

Niskanen, W.A. (1971) *Bureaucracy and Representative Government* (Chicago: Aldine-Atherton).

Noël, A. (2004) 'Introduction: Varieties in Capitalism, Varieties in Federalism', in A. Noël (ed.), *Federalism and Labour Market Policy: Comparing Different Governance and Employment Strategies* (Montreal: McGill-Queen's University Press).

Nollkaemper, A. (2009) 'The European Courts and the Security Council: Between Dedoublement Fonctionnel and Balancing of Values: Three Replies to Pasquale De Sena and Maria Chiara Vitucci', *European Journal of International Law*, 20(3): 862–70.

Norman, R. (2003) *Obedient Servants? Management Freedoms and Accountabilities in the New Zealand Public Sector* (Wellington: Victoria University Press).

North, D.C. (1990) *Institutions, Institutional Change and Economic Performance* (Cambridge: Cambridge University Press).

Nykiforuk, C.I.J., J. Eyles and H.S. Campbell (2008) 'Smoke-Free Spaces Over Time: A Policy Diffusion Study of Bylaw Development in Alberta and Ontario, Canada', *Health and Social Care in the Community*, (2008) 16(1): 64–74.

Oakshott, L. (2009) *Essential Quantitative Methods: For Business, Management and Finance* (Basingstoke: Palgrave Macmillan).

O'Connor, K. and L. J. Sabato (2009) *American Government: Roots and Reform* (New York: Longman).

OECD (2011) 'Health Data 2011', www.oecd.org/document/16/0,3343,en_2649_34631_2085200_1_1_1_1,00.html.

Oliver, T.R. (2006) 'The Politics of Public Health Policy', *Annual Review of Public Health*, 27: 195–233.

Olson, M. (1965) *The Logic of Collective Action: Public Goods and the Theory of Groups* (Cambridge, MA: Harvard University Press).

Ostrom, E. (1990) *Governing the Commons: The Evolution of Institutions for Collective Action* (Cambridge: Cambridge University Press).

O'Toole, L.J. Jr (2003) 'Interorganizational Relations in Implementation', in B.G. Peters and J. Pierre (eds), *Handbook of Public Administration* (Thousand Oaks: Sage).

O'Toole, L.J. Jr (2007) 'Governing Outputs and Outcomes of Governance Networks', in E. Sørensen and J. Torfing (eds), *Theories of Democratic Network Governance* (Basingstoke: Palgrave Macmillan).

O'Toole, L.J. Jr and K.J. Meier (1999) 'Modelling the Impact of Public Management: Implications of Structural Context', *Journal of Public Administration Research and Theory*, 9(4): 505–26.

Page, E.C. (2003) 'The Civil Servant as Legislator: Law Making in British Administration', *Public Administration*, 81(4): 651–79.

Page, E. and B. Jenkins (2005) *Policy Bureaucracy: Government with a Cast of Thousands* (Oxford: Oxford University Press).

Painter, M. (1991) 'Policy Diversity and Policy Learning in a Federation: The Case of Australian State Betting Laws', *Publius*, 21(1): 143–57.

Paquin, S. (2010) 'Federalism and Compliance with International Agreements: Belgium and Canada Compared', *Hague Journal of Diplomacy*, 5(1–2): 173–97.

Parkin, A.W. and J. Summers (2006) 'The Constitutional Framework', in D. Woodward, A. Parkin and J. Summers (eds), *Government, Politics, Power and Policy in Australia* (Frenchs Forest: Pearson Education Australia).

Parkinson, C.N. (1958) *Parkinson's Law or The Pursuit of Progress* (London: John Murray).

Patton, D. (2007) 'The Supreme Court and Morality Policy Adoption in the American States: The Impact of Constitutional Context', *Political Research Quarterly*, 60(3): 468–88.

Pawson, R. and N. Tilley (1997) *Realistic Evaluation* (London: Sage).

Pelizzo, R. and R. Stapenhurst (2008) 'Tools of Legislative Oversight', in R. Stapenhurst, R. Pelizzo, D.M. Olson, and L. Von Trapp (eds), *Legislative Oversight and Budgeting: A World Perspective* (Washington, DC: The World Bank).

Peltzman, S. (1976) 'Toward a More General Theory of Regulation', *Journal of Law and Economics*, 19(2): 211–40.

Penner, E., Blidook, K. and S. Soroka (2006) 'Legislative Priorities and Public Opinion: Representation of Partisan Agendas in the Canadian House of Commons', *Journal of European Public Policy*, 13(7): 1006–20.

Percival, G.L. (2009) 'Exploring the influence of local policy networks on the implementation of drug policy reform: The case of California's Substance Abuse and Crime Prevention Act', *Journal of Public Administration Research and Theory*, 19(49): 795–815.

Perry, H.W., Jr. (1991) *Deciding to Decide: Agenda Setting in the United States Supreme Court* (Cambridge: Harvard University Press).

Peters, B.G. (1996) 'Theory and Methodology', in H.A.G.M. Bekke, J.L. Perry and T.A.J. Toonen (eds), *Civil Service Systems in Comparative Perspective* (Bloomington: Indiana University Press).

Peters, B.G. (1998) *Globalization, Institutions and Governance* (Florence: The Robert Schuman Centre at the European University Institute).

Peters, B.G. (2004) 'Politicization in the United States', in P.B. Guy and J. Pierre (eds), *The Politicization of the Civil Service in Comparative Perspective* (London: Routledge).

Peters, B.G. (2010) *The Politics of Bureaucracy: An Introduction to Comparative Public Administration* (London: Routledge).

Peters, B.G. (2011) 'Approaches in Comparative Politics', in D. Caramani (ed.), *Comparative Politics* (Oxford: Oxford University Press).

Peters, B.G. and F.K.M. van Nispen (eds) (1998) *The Study of Policy Instruments* (Cheltenham: Edward Elgar).

Peters, B.G. and J. Pierre (1998) 'Governance without Government? Rethinking Public Administration', *Journal of Public Administration Research and Theory*, 8(2): 223–43.

Peters, B.G. and J. Pierre (eds) (2006) *Handbook of Public Policy* (Thousand Oaks, CA: Sage).

Pevehouse, N. and K. Warnke (2005) 'International Governmental Organizations', in P.F. Diehl and B. Frederking (eds), *The Politics of Global Governance* (Boulder: Lynne Rienner).

Pierre, J. and B.G. Peters (2000) *Governance, Politics and the State* (Basingstoke: Palgrave Macmillan).

Pierson, P. (1994) *Dismantling the Welfare State? Reagan, Thatcher, and the Politics of Retrenchment* (Cambridge: Cambridge University Press).

Pierson, P. (1996) 'The Path to European Integration: A Historical Institutionalist Analysis', *Comparative Political Studies*, 29(2): 123–63.

Pierson, P. (2000) 'Increasing Returns, Path Dependence, and the Study of Politics', *American Political Science Review*, 94(2): 251–67.

Pierson, P. (2004) *Politics in Time: History, Institutions, and Social Analysis* (Princeton: Princeton University Press).

Poel, D.H. (1976) 'The Diffusion of Legislation among the Canadian Provinces: A Statistical Analysis', *Canadian Journal of Political Science*, 9(4): 605–26.

Pollitt, C. (1986) 'Beyond the Managerial Model: The Case for Broadening Performance Assessment in Government and the Public Services', *Financial Accountability and Management*, 2(3): 155–70.

Pollitt C. (2006) 'Performance Management in Practice: A Comparative Study of Executive Agencies', *Journal of Public Administration Research and Theory*, 16(1): 25–44.

Pollitt, C. and G. Bouckaert (2000) *Public Management Reform: A Comparative Analysis* (Oxford: Oxford University Press).

Pollitt, C. and C. Talbot (eds) (2004) *Unbundled Government* (London: Routledge).

Pollitt, C., Talbot, C. and J. Caulfield (2004) *Agencies. How Governments do Things through Semi-Autonomous Organizations* (Basingstoke: Palgrave Macmillan).

Polsby, N.W. (1963) *Community Power and Political Theory* (New Haven: Yale University Press).

Powell, W.W. (1990) 'Neither Market Nor Hierarchy: Network Forms of Organization', *Research in Organizational Behavior*, 12(1): 295–336.

Pralle, S. (2006) *Branching Out and Digging In: Environmental Advocacy and Agenda Setting* (Washington, DC: Georgetown University Press).

Pressman, J.L. and A. Wildavsky (1973) *Implementation: How Great Expectations in Washington are Dashed in Oakland* (Berkeley: University of California Press).

Provan, K.G. and P.N. Kenis (2008) 'Modes of Network Governance: Structure, Management, and Effectiveness', *Journal of Public Administration Research and Theory*, 18(2), 229–52.

Puchala, D. and R. Hopkins (1983) 'International Regimes: Lessons from Inductive Analysis', in S.D. Krasner (ed.), *International Regimes* (Ithaca, NY: Cornell University Press).

Pülzl, H. and O. Treib (2007) 'Policy Implementation', in F. Fischer, G. Miller and M. Sidney (eds), *Handbook of Public Policy Analysis: Theory, Politics, and Methods* (Boca Raton: CRC Press).

Quinn, L.M. and R.S. Magill (1994) 'Politics versus Research in Social Policy', *Social Service Review*, 68(4): 503–20.

Raab, J. and P.N. Kenis (2009) 'Heading toward a Society of Networks: Empirical Developments and Theoretical Challenges,' *Journal of Management Inquiry*, 18(3), 198–210.

Radaelli, C.M. (1995) 'The Role of Knowledge in the Policy Process', *Journal of European Public Policy*, 2(2): 159–83.

Radaelli, C.M. (2000) 'Policy Transfer in the European Union: Institutional Isomorphism as a Source of Legitimacy', *Governance*, 13(1): 25–43.

Radaelli, C.M. (2004) 'The Diffusion of Regulatory Impact Assessment: Best Practice or Lesson-Drawing?', *European Journal of Political Research*, 43(5): 723–747.

Radaelli, C.M. (2005) 'Diffusion without Convergence: How Political Context Shapes the Adoption of Regulatory Impact Assessment', *Journal of European Public Policy*, 12(5): 924–43.

Radaelli C.M. (2009) 'Desperately Seeking Regulatory Impact Assessments. Diary of a Reflective Researcher', *Evaluation*, 15(1): 31–48.

Radnor, Z. and M. McGuire (2004) 'Performance Management in the Public Sector: Fact or Fiction?', *International Journal of Productivity and Performance Management*, 53(3): 245–60.

Ragin, C. (1987) *The Comparative Method: Moving Beyond Qualitative and Quantitative Strategies* (Berkeley: University of California Press).

Ragin, C. (2006) 'How to Lure Analytic Social Science out of the Doldrums: Some Lessons from Comparative Research', *International Sociology*, 21(5): 633–46.

Rajagopalan, N. and A. Rasheed (1995) 'Incremental Models of Policy Formulation and Non-incremental Changes: Critical Review and Synthesis', *British Journal of Management*, 6(4): 289–302.

Rasch, B.E. and G. Tsebelis (eds) (2010) *The Role of Governments in Legislative Agenda-Setting* (London: Routledge).

Reichard, C. (2003) 'Local Public Management Reforms in Germany', *Public Administration*, 81(2): 345–63.

Reinalda, B. (2009) *History of International Organizations: From 1815 to the Present Day* (Abingdon: Routledge).

Rhodes, R.A.W. (1996) 'The New Governance: Governing without Government', *Political Studies*, 44(4): 652–67.

Rhodes, R.A.W. (1997) *Understanding Governance. Policy Networks, Reflexivity and Accountability* (Buckingham: Open University Press).

Rhodes, R.A.W. and D. Marsh (1992) 'New Directions in the Study of Policy Networks', *European Journal of Political Research*, 21(1–2): 181–205.

Rhodes, R.A.W., S.A. Binder and B.A. Rockman (eds) (2008) *The Oxford Handbook of Political Institutions* (Oxford University Press: Oxford).

Richardson, J.J. (ed.) (1982) *Policy Styles in Western Europe* (London: Harper Collins Publishers).

Richardson, J.J. and A.G. Jordan (1983) 'Overcrowded Policymaking. Some British and European Reflections', *Policy Sciences*, 15(3): 247–68.

Richardson, J.J., G. Gustafsson and G. Jordan (1982) 'The Concept of Policy Style', in J.J. Richardson (ed.), *Policy Styles in Western Europe* (London: Allen & Unwin).

Riker, W. (1962) *The Theory of Political Coalitions* (New Haven: Yale University Press).

Riker, W. (1986) *The Art of Political Manipulation* (New Haven: Yale University Press).

Rittel, H.W.J. and M. Webber (1973) 'Dilemmas in a General Theory of Planning', *Policy Sciences*, 4(2): 155–69.

Robichau, R.W. and L.E. Lynn jr. (2009) 'The Implementation of Public Policy: Still the Missing Link', *Policy Studies Journal*, 37(1): 21–36.

Rochefort, D.A. and R.W. Cobb (1995) 'Problem Definition: An Emerging Perspective', in D.A. Rochefort and R.W. Cobb (eds), *Shaping the Policy Agenda: The Politics of Problem Definition* (Lawrence: University Press of Kansas).

Rodrik, D. (2000) 'How Far Will Economic Integration Go?', *Journal of Economic Perspectives*, 14(1): 177–86.

Rogers, E.M. (2003) *Diffusion of Innovations* (New York: Free Press).

Rogers, E.M., Dearing, J.W. and D. Bregman (1993) 'The Anatomy of Agenda-Setting Research', *Journal of Communication*, 43(2): 68–84.

Rogers, P.J., Petrosino, A., Huebner, T.A. and T.A. Hacsi (2000) 'Program Theory Evaluation: Practice, Promise, and Problems', in P.J. Rogers, T.A. Hacsi, A. Petrosino, and T.A. Huebner (eds), *Program Theory in Evaluation Challenges and Opportunities: New Directions for Evaluation*, No. 87 (San Francisco: Jossey-Bass).

Roller, E. (2005) *The Performance of Democracies: Political Institutions and Public Policies* (Oxford: Oxford University Press).

Ronit, K. and V. Schneider (1999) 'Global Governance through Private Organizations', *Governance*, 12(3): 243–66.

Room, G. (2012) *Complexity, Institutions and Public Policy: Agile Decision-making in a Turbulent World* (Cheltenham: Edward Elgar).

Rose, R. (1987) 'Steering the Ship of State. One Tiller but Two Pairs of Hands', *British Journal of Political Science*, 17(4) 409–53.

Rose, R. (1991) 'What is Lesson-Drawing?', *Journal of Public Policy*, 11(3): 3–30.

Rosefielde, S. (2011) 'China's Perplexing Foreign Trade Policy: Causes, Consequences, and Solutions', *American Foreign Policy Interests*, 33(1): 10–6.

Rosenau, J.N. and E.-O. Czempiel (eds) (1992) *Governance without Government: Order and Change in World Politics* (Cambridge: Cambridge University Press).

Rossi, P.H, M.W. Lipsey and H.E. Freeman (2004) *Evaluation: A Systematic Approach* (Thousand Oaks: Sage).

Roy, R.K. and A.T. Denzau (2003) *Fiscal Policy Convergence from Reagan to Blair: The Left Veers Right* (London: Routledge).

Rubin, A. and E.R. Babbie (2009) *Essential Research Methods for Social Work* (Pacific Grove: Brooks/Cole).

Rüdig, W. (1987) Outcomes of Nuclear Technology Policy: Do Varying Political Styles Make a Difference?', *Journal of Public Policy*, 7(4): 389–430.

Russell, M. (2001) 'What are Second Chambers for?', *Parliamentary Affairs*, 54(3): 442–58.

Sabatier, P.A. (1986) 'Top-Down and Bottom-Up Approaches to Implementation Research: a Critical Analysis and Suggested Synthesis', *Journal of Public Policy*, 6(1): 21–48.

Sabatier, P.A. (1988) 'An Advocacy Coalition Framework of Policy Change and the Role of Policy-Oriented Learning Therein', *Policy Sciences*, 21(2–3): 129–68.

Sabatier, P.A. and H.C. Jenkins-Smith (eds) (1993) *Policy Change and Learning: an Advocacy Coalition Approach* (Boulder: Westview Press).

Sabatier, P.A. and H.C. Jenkins-Smith (1999) 'The Advocacy Coalition Framework: An Assessment', in P. A. Sabatier (ed.), *Theories of the Policy Process* (Boulder: Westview Press).

Sabatier, P.A. and D.A. Mazmanian (1980) 'The Implementation of Public Policy: A Framework of Analysis', *Policy Studies Journal*, 8(4): 538–60.

Sabatier, P.A. and C.M. Weible (2007) 'The Advocacy Coalition Framework: Innovations and Clarifications', in P.A. Sabatier (ed.), *Theories of the Policy Process* (Boulder: Westview Press).

Sager, F. and C. Rissi (2011) 'The Limited Scope of Policy Appraisal in the Context of Referendum Democracy: the Case of Regulatory Impact Assessment in Switzerland', *Evaluation*, 17(2): 151–63.

Sala-i-Martin, X. (1996) 'Regional Cohesion: Evidence and Theories of Regional Growth and Convergence', *European Economic Review*, 40(6): 1325–52.

Salamon, L.M. (ed.) (2002) *The Tools of Government: A Guide to the New Governance* (Oxford: Oxford University Press).

Sanderson, I. (2002) 'Evaluation, Policy Learning and Evidence-Based Policy Making', *Public Administration*, 80(1): 1–22.

Sartori, G. (2005) *Parties and Party Systems: A Framework for Analysis* (Wivenhoe Park: ECPR Press).

Sausman, C. and R. Locke (2004) 'The British Civil Service: Examining the Question of Politicisation', in B.G. Peters and J. Pierre (eds), *Politicization of the Civil Service in Comparative Perspective* (London: Routledge).

Sbragia, A.M. (2000) 'Environmental Policy: From Excitement to Problem-Solving', in H. Wallace and W. Wallace (eds), *Policy-Making in the European Union* (Oxford: Oxford University Press).

Scartascini, C. (2008) 'Who's Who in the PMP: An Overview of Actors, Incentives, and the Roles They Play', in E. Stein and M. Tommasi (eds), *Policymaking in Latin America: How Politics Shapes Policies* (Washington, DC: Inter-American Development Bank).

Scharpf, F.W. (1988) 'The Joint Decision Trap. Lessons from German Federalism and European Integration', *Public Administration*, 66(3): 239–78.

Scharpf, F.W. (1996) 'Politische Optionen im vollendeten Binnenmarkt', in M. Jachtenfuchs and B. Kohler-Koch (eds), *Europäische Integration* (Opladen: Leske & Budrich).

Scharpf, F.W. (1997a) *Games Real Actors Play: Actor-Centered Institutionalism in Policy Research* (Boulder: Westview Press).

Scharpf, F.W. (1997b) 'Introduction. The Problem-Solving Capacity of Multi-Level Governance', *Journal of European Public Policy*, 4(4): 520–38.

Scharpf, F.W. (1999) Regieren in Europa. Effektiv und demokratisch? (Frankfurt am Main: Campus).

Schattschneider, E.E. (1960) *The Semisovereign People: A Realist's View of Democracy in America* (New York: Holt, Rinehart & Winston).

Schimmelfennig, F., and U. Sedelmeier (2004) 'Governance by Conditionality: EU Rule Transfer to the Candidate Countries of Central and Eastern Europe', *Journal of European Public Policy*, 11(4): 661–79.

Schmidt, M.G. (1995) 'Policy-Analyse', in A. Mohr (ed.), *Grundzüge der Politikwissenschaft* (München: Oldenbourg).

Schmidt, M.G. (1996) 'When Parties Matter: A Review of the Possibilities and Limits of Partisan Influence on Public Policy', *European Journal of Political Science*, 30(2): 155–83.

Schmidt, M.G. (1998) *Sozialpolitik in Deutschland. Historische Entwicklung und inter-nationaler Vergleich* (Opladen: Leske & Budrich).

Schmidt, M.G. (2002) 'Political Performance and Types of Democracy: Findings from Comparative Studies', *European Journal of Political Research*, 41(1): 147–63.

Schmidt, S.K. and R. Werle (1998) *Coordinating Technology. Studies in the International Standardization of Telecommunications* (Cambridge: MIT).

Schmidt, V. (2008) 'European Political Economy: Labor Out, State Back, In Firm to the Fore', *West European Politics*, 31(1–2): 302–20.

Schmitt, C. and P. Starke (2011) 'Explaining Convergence of OECD Welfare States: A Conditional Approach', *Journal of European Social Policy*, 21(2): 120–35.

Schmitter, P.C. (1977) 'Modes of Interest Intermediation and Models of Societal Change in Western Europe', *Comparative Political Studies*, 10(7): 7–38.

Schnapp, K.-U. (2000) 'Ministerial Bureaucracies as Stand-In Agenda Setters? A Comparative Description', *WZB Discussion Paper*, FS III 00–204.

Schneider, A. and H. Ingram (1990) 'Behavioral Assumptions of Policy Tools', *The Journal of Politics*, 52(2): 510–29.

Schneider, A. and H. Ingram (1997) Policy Design for Democracy (Lawrence: University of Kansas Press).

Schneider, V. (1992) 'The Structure of Policy Networks: A Comparison of the Chemicals Control and Telecommunications Policy Domains in Germany', *European Journal of Political Research*, 21(1–2): 109–29.

Schneider, V. (2006) 'Business in Policy Networks: Estimating the Relative Importance of Corporate Direct Lobbying and Representation by Trade Associations', in D. Coen and W. Grant (eds), *Business and Government: Methods and Practice* (Opladen: Barbara Budrich Publishers).

Schröter, E. (2004) 'The Politicization of the German Civil Service: A Three-Dimensional Portrait of the Federal Ministerial Bureaucracy', in J. Pierre and B.G. Peters (eds), *The Politicization of the Civil Service* (London: Routledge).

Scriven, M. (1967) 'The Methodology of Evaluation', in R.W. Tyler, R.M. Gagne and M. Scriven (eds), *Perspectives of Curriculum Evaluation* (Chicago: Rand McNally).

Scruggs, L.A. (1999) 'Institutions and Environmental Performance in Seventeen Western Democracies', *British Journal of Political Science*, 29(1): 1–31.

Seibel, Wolfgang (2001) 'Administrative Reforms', in: K. König and H. Siedentopf (eds), *Public Administration in Germany* (Baden-Baden: Nomos).

Selin, H. and S. D. vanDeveer (eds) (2009) *Changing Climates in North American Politics: Institutions, Policymaking, and Multilevel Governance* (MIT Press: Cambridge).

Shadish, W.R., T.D. Cook and D.T. Campbell (2001) *Experimental and Quasi-Experimental Designs for Generalized Causal Inference* (Belmont, CA: Wadsworth).

Shane, P. (2008) 'Analyzing Constitutions', in R.A.W. Rhodes, S.A. Binder and B.A. Rockman (eds), *The Oxford Handbook of Political Institutions* (Oxford: Oxford University Press).

Shapiro, S. (2011) 'The Evolution of Cost-Benefit Analysis in U.S. Regulatory Decisionmaking', in D. Levi-Faur (ed.), *Handbook on the Politics of Regulation* (Cheltenham: Edward Elgar).

Sheingate, A.D. (2000) 'Agricultural Retrenchment Revisited: Issue Definition and Venue Change in the United States and European Union', *Governance*, 13(3): 335–63.

Shepsle, K.A. (2008) 'Rational Choice Institutionalism', in R.A.W. Rhodes, S.A. Binder and B.A. Rockman (eds), *The Oxford Handbook of Political Institutions* (Oxford: Oxford University Press).

Shepsle, K.A. and B. Weingast (1987) 'The Institutional Foundations of Committee Power', *American Political Science Review*, 81(1): 85–104.

Shimkhada R., J.W. Peabody, S.A. Quimbo and O. Solon (2008) 'The Quality Improvement Demonstration Study: An Example of Evidence-Based Policy-Making in Practice', *Health Research Policy and Systems*, 6(5): 1–12.

Siaroff, A. (1999) 'Corporatism in 24 Industrial Democracies: Meaning and Measurement', *European Journal of Political Research*, 36(2): 175–205.

Simmons, B.A. and Z. Elkins (2004) 'The Globalization of Liberalization: Policy Diffusion in the International Political Economy', *American Political Science Review*, 98(1): 171–89.

Simmons, B.A. and L.L. Martin (2002) 'International Organizations and Institutions', in W. Carlsnaes, T. Risse and B.A. Simmons (eds), *Handbook of International Relations* (London: Sage).

Simon, H.A. (1955) 'A Behavioral Model of Rational Choice', *Quarterly Journal of Economics*, 69(1): 99–118.

Simon, H.A. (1957a) *Models of Man: Social and Rational* (New York: Wiley).

Sinclair, B. (2006): *Party Wars: Polarization and the Politics of National Policy Making* (University of Oklahoma Press: Norman).

Sinclair, T.J. (1999) 'Bond-Rating Agencies and Coordination in the Global Political Economy', in C.A. Cutler (ed.), *Private Authority and International Affairs* (Albany: State University of New York Press).

Skogstad, G. (ed.) (2011) *Policy Paradigms, Transnationalism, and Domestic Politics* (Toronto: University of Toronto Press).

Slovic, P., B. Fischhoff and S. Lichtenstein (1982) 'Facts Versus Fears: Understanding Perceived Risk', in D. Kahneman, P. Slovic and A. Tversky (eds), *Judgement Under Uncertainty: Heuristics and Biases* (Cambridge: Cambridge University Press).

Smith, K.B. (2002) 'Typologies, Taxonomies, and the Benefits of Policy Classification', *Policy Studies Journal*, 30(3): 379–95.

Smith, T.B. (1973) 'The Policy Implementation Process', *Policy Sciences*, 4(2): 197–209.

Snidal, D. and K. Abbott (2000) 'Hard and Soft Law in International Relations', *International Organization*, 54(3): 421–56.

Soroka, S. (2002) *Agenda-Setting Dynamics in Canada* (Vancouver: University of British Columbia Press).

Sprinz, D. (1999) 'Empirical-Quantitative Approaches to the Study of International

Environmental Policy', in S.S. Nagel (ed.), *Policy Analysis Methods* (Commack, NY: Nova Science), pp. 41–64.

Starke, P., H. Obinger and F. Castles (2008) 'Convergence towards where: In what Ways, if any, are Welfare States Becoming more Similar?', *Journal of European Public Policy*, 15(7): 975–1000.

Steinmo, S., K. Thelen and F. Longstreth (eds) (1992) *Structuring Politics: Historical Institutionalism in Comparative Analysis* (New York: Cambridge University Press).

Stephens, R. (2003) 'The Economic and Social Context for the Changes in Accident Compensation', *Victoria University of Wellington Law Review*, 34(2): 351–66.

Steunenberg, B. and D. Toshkov (2009) 'Comparing Transposition in the 27 Member States of the EU: The Impact of Discretion and Legal Fit', *Journal of European Public Policy*, 16(7): 951–70.

Stigler, G.J. (1971) 'The Theory of Economic Regulation', *Bell Journal of Economics and Management Science*, 2(1): 3–21.

Stone, D.A. (1988) *Policy Paradox and Political Reason* (Glenview: Scott, Foresman, and Company).

Stone, D.A. (1989) 'Causal Stories and the Formation of Policy Agendas', *Political Science Quarterly*, 104(2): 281–300.

Stone, D.L. (2001) 'Think Tanks, Global Lesson-Drawing and Networking Social Policy Ideas', *Global Social Policy*, 1(3): 338–60.

Stone, D.L. (2004) 'Transfer Agents and Global Networks in the "Transnationalisation" of Policy', *Journal of European Public Policy*, 11(3): 545–66.

Stone, D.L. (2008) 'Global Public Policy, Transnational Policy Communities and their Networks', *Policy Studies Journal*, 36(10): 19–38.

Stone Sweet, A. (2007) 'The Politics of Constitutional Review in France and Europe', *International Journal of Constitutional Law*, 5(1): 69–92.

Stone Sweet, A. (2011) 'Constitutions and Judicial Power', in D. Caramani (ed.), *Comparative Politics* (Oxford: Oxford University Press).

Strang, D. and J.W. Meyer (1993) 'Institutional Conditions for Diffusion', *Theory and Society*, 22(4): 487–511.

Streeck, W. (1982) 'Organizational Consequences of Neo-Corporatist Cooperation in West German Labor Unions', G. Lehmbruch and P.C. Schmitter (eds.) *Patterns of Corporatist Policy-Making* (Beverly Hills: Sage).

Streeck, W. (1994) 'Staat und Verbände: Neue Fragen. Neue Antworten?', in W. Streeck (ed.) *Staat und Verbände* (Opladen: Westdeutscher Verlag).

Streeck, W. and P.C. Schmitter (1981) *The Organisation of Business Interests: A Research Design to Study the Associative Business Action in Advanced Industrial Societies of Western Europe* (Berlin: Wissenschaftszentrum Berlin).

Streeck, W. and P.C. Schmitter (eds) (1985) *Private Interest Government: Beyond Market and State* (London: Sage).

Streeck, W. and K. Thelen (2005) 'Introduction: Institutional Change in Advanced Political Economies', in W. Streeck and K. Thelen (eds), *Beyond Continuity: Institutional Change in Advanced Political Economies* (Oxford: Oxford University Press).

Strøm, K. (1990) 'A Behavioral Theory of Competitive Political Parties', *American Journal of Political Science*, 34(2): 565–98.

Strøm, K. (1995) 'Parliamentary Government and Legislative Organisation', in H. Döring (ed.), *Parliaments and Majority Rule in Western Europe* (Frankfurt am Main: Campus).

Suleiman, E.N. (1974) *Politics, Power and Bureaucracy in France* (Princeton: Princeton University Press).

Summers, J. (2006) 'Parliament and Responsible Government', in D. Woodward, A. Parkin and J. Summers (eds), *Government, Politics, Power and Policy in Australia* (Frenchs Forest: Pearson Education Australia).

Sunstein, C. (2005) *Laws of Fear: Beyond the Precautionary Principle* (Cambridge: Cambridge University Press).

Tallberg, J. (2002) 'Paths to Compliance: Enforcement, Management, and the European Union', *International Organization*, 56(3): 609–43.

Tang, S.-Y. and C.-P. Tang (1999) 'Democratization and the Environment: Entrepreneurial Politics and Interest Representation in Taiwan', *China Quarterly*, 158: 350–66.

Taylor, D. and S. Balloch (2005) 'The Politics of Evaluation: An Overview', in S. Balloch and D. Taylor (eds), *The Politics of Evaluation* (Bristol: The Policy Press).

Teichman, J. (2004) 'The World Bank and Policy Reform in Mexico and Argentina', *Latin American Politics and Society*, 46(1): 39–74.

Tenbensel, T. (2003) 'Interest Groups', in R. Miller (ed.), *New Zealand Government and Politics* (Melbourne: Oxford University Press).

Thakur, R. (2006) *The United Nations, Peace and Security* (Cambridge: Cambridge University Press).

Thelen, K. (1999) 'Historical-Institutionalism and Comparative Politics', *Annual Review of Political Science*, 2: 369–404.

Thelen, K. and S. Steinmo (1992) 'Historical Institutionalism in Comparative Politics', in S. Steinmo, K. Thelen and F. Longstreth (eds), *Structuring Politics: Historical Institutionalism in Comparative Perspective* (Cambridge: Cambridge University Press).

Thompson, G., J. Frances, R. Levacic and J. Mitchell (eds) (1991) *Markets, Hierarchies, & Networks: The Coordination of Social Life* (London: Sage).

Thomson, R. (2009) 'Same Effects in Different Worlds: The Transposition of EU Directives', Journal of European Public Policy, 16(1): 1–18.

Tiernan, A. (2007) *Power without Responsibility? Ministerial Staffers in Australian Governments from Whitlam to Howard* (Sydney: UNSW Press).

Timmermans, A. and P. Scholten (2006) 'The Political Flow of Wisdom: Science Institutions as Policy Venues in the Netherlands', *Journal of European Public Policy*, 13(7): 1104–18.

Tömmel, I. and A. Verdun (eds) (2009) *Innovative Governance in the European Union: The Politics of Multilevel Policymaking* (Boulder: Lynn Rienner).

Torenvlied, R. (1996) 'Political Control of Implementation Agencies: Effects of Political Consensus on Agency Compliance', *Rationality and Society*, 8(1): 25–56.

Tosun, J. (2012) *Environmental Policy Change in Emerging Market Democracies: Central and Eastern Europe and Latin America Compared* (Toronto: University of Toronto Press).

Tosun, J. and C. Knill (2011) 'The Differential Impact of Economic Integration on Environmental Policy', in M. Jovanovic (ed.), *International Handbook on the Economics of Integration Volume III* (Cheltenham: Edward Elgar).

Treisman, D. (2000) 'Decentralization and Inflation: Commitment, Collective Action, or Continuity', *American Political Science Review*, 94(4): 837–57.

Trondal, J. (2010) *An Emergent European Executive Order* (Oxford: Oxford University Press).

True, J.L., Jones, B.D. and F.R. Baumgartner (2007) 'Punctuated Equilibrium Theory: Explaining Stability and Change in American Policymaking', in P.A. Sabatier (ed.), *Theories of the Policy Process* (Boulder: Westview Press).

Truman, D.B. (1951) *The Governmental Process: Political Interests and Public Opinion* (New York: Alfred A. Knopf).

Tsebelis, G. (1995) 'Veto Players and Law Production in Parliamentary Democracies', in H. Döring (ed.), *Parliaments and Majority Rule in Western Europe* (Frankfurt am Main: Campus).

Tsebelis, G. (2000) 'Veto Players and Institutional Analysis', *Governance*, 13(4): 441–74.

Tsebelis, G. (2002) *Veto Players. How Political Institutions Work* (Princeton: Princeton University Press).

Tsebelis, G. and E. Alémán (2005) 'The History of Conditional Agenda Setting in Latin America', *Latin American Research Review*, 40(2): 3–26.

Tullock, G. (1965) *The Politics of Bureaucracy* (Washington, DC: Public Affairs Press).

Turnpenny, J., M. Nilsson, D. Russel, A. Jordan, J. Hertin and B. Nykvist (2008) 'Why is integrating policy assessment so hard? a comparative analysis of the institutional capacities and constraints', *Journal of Environmental Planning and Management*, 51(6): 759–775.

Turnpenny, J., C.M. Radaelli, A. Jordan and K. Jacob (2009) 'The policy and politics of policy appraisal: emerging trends and new directions', *Journal of European Public Policy*, 16(4): 640–53.

Union of International Associations (2008) *Yearbook of International Organizations* (Brussels: Union of International Associations).

Vanberg, G. (1998) 'Abstract Judicial Review, Legislative Bargaining, and Policy Compromise', *Journal of Theoretical Politics*, 10(3): 299–326.

Van den Bossche, P. (2008): *The Law and Policy of the World Trade Organization: Text, Cases and Materials* (Cambridge University Press: Cambridge).

Van Meter, D.S. and C.E. Van Horn (1975) 'The Policy Implementation Process: A Conceptual Framework', *Administration and Society*, 6(4): 445–88.

Varone, F., S. Jacob and L. de Winter (2005) 'Polity, Politics and Policy Evaluation in Belgium', *Evaluation*, 11(3): 253–73.

Vatter, A. (2000) 'Consensus and Direct Democracy: Conceptual and Empirical Linkages', *European Journal of Political Research*, 38(2): 245–68.

Vatter, A. (2005) 'Bicameralism and Policy Performance: The Effects of Cameral Structure in Comparative Perspective', *Journal of Legislative Studies*, 11(2): 194–215.

Vedung, E. (1998) 'Policy Instruments: Typologies and Theories', in M.-L. Bemelmans-Videc, R.C. Rist and E. Vedung (eds), *Carrots, Sticks and Sermons* (New Brunswick/London: Transaction Publishers).

Vedung, E. (2000) *Public Policy and Program Evaluation* (New Brunswick, NJ: Transaction Publishers).

Verloo, M. (2001) 'Another Velvet Revolution? Gender Mainstreaming and the Politics of Implementation', *IWM Working Paper No. 5*: Vienna.

Vieth, R., H. Bischoff-Ferrari, B.J. Boucher, B. Dawson-Hughes, C.F. Garland, R.P. Heaney (2007) 'The Urgent Need to Recommend an Intake of Vitamin D that is Effective', *American Journal of Clinical Nutrition*, 85(3): 649–50.

Viñas, V. (2009) 'The European Union's Drive towards Public Policy Evaluation: The Case of Spain', *Evaluation*, 15(4): 459–72.

Vogel, D. (1986) *National Styles of Regulation: Environmental Policy in Great Britain and the U.S.* (Ithaca, NY: Cornell University Press).

Vogel, D. (1995) *Trading Up: Consumer and Environmental Regulation in the Global Economy* (Cambridge: Harvard University Press).

Vogel, D. and R. Kagan (eds) (2004) *Dynamics of Regulatory Change: How Globalization Affects National Regulatory Policies* (Berkeley: University of California Press).

Volden, C. (2006) 'States as Policy Laboratories: Emulating Success in the Children's Health Insurance Program', *American Journal of Politicsl Science*, 50(2): 294–312.

Volgy, T.J., Z. Šabič, P. Roter and A. Gerlak (2009) *Mapping the World Order: Participation in Regional and Global Organizations* (London: Blackwell).

Waarden, F. van (1992) 'Dimensions and Types of Policy Networks', *European Journal of Political Research*, 1(2): 219–34.

Waarden, F. van (1995) 'Persistence of National Policy Styles', in B. Unger and F. van Waarden (eds), *Convergence or Diversity?* (Aldershot: Avebury).

Wagner, A. (1893) *Grundlegung der politischen Ökonomie* (Leipzig: Winter).

Walgrave, S. and P. van Aelst (2006) 'The Contingency of the Mass Media's Political Agenda Setting Power. Toward A Preliminary Theory', *Journal of Communication*, 56(1): 88–109.

Walgrave, S., S. Soroka and M. Nuytemans (2008) 'The Mass Media's Political Agenda-Setting Power. A Longitudinal Analysis of Media, Parliament, and Government in Belgium (1993–2000)', *Comparative Political Studies*, 41(6): 814–36.

Ward, N., A. Donaldson and P. Lowe (2004) 'Policy Framing and Learning the Lessons from the UK's Foot and Mouth Disease Crisis', *Environment and Planning C*, 22(2): 291–306.

Wasieleski, D. (2001) 'Agenda-Building Theory: A Stakeholder Salience Approach for Determining Agenda Placement', *The Journal of Behavioral and Applied Management*, 2 (2): 113–30.

Watts, R.L. (1989) *Executive Federalism: A Comparative Analysis* (Kingston: Institute of Intergovernmental Relations, Queen's University).

Weale, A., Pridham, G., Cini, M., Konstadakopulos, D., Porter, M. and B. Flynn (2000) *Environmental Governance in Europe: An Ever Closer Ecological Union* (Oxford: Oxford University Press).

Weaver, R.K. (2008) 'Target Compliance: The Final Frontier of Policy Implementation', *Issues in Governance Studies*, 27(9): 1–11.

Weaver, R.K. and B.A. Rockman (1993) 'When and How Do Institutions Matter?', in R.K. Weaver and B.A. Rockman (eds), *Do Institutions Matter? Government Capabilities in the United States and Abroad* (Washington, DC: The Brookings Institution), pp. 445–61.

Weber, M. (1947) *The Theory of Social and Economic Organization* (New York: Free Press).

Weingast, B. (1996) 'Political Institutions: Rational Choice Perspectives', in R.E. Goodin (ed.), *A New Handbook of Political Science* (Oxford: Oxford University Press).

Weiss, C.H. (1995) 'Nothing as Practical as Good Theory: Exploring Theory-Based Evaluation for Comprehensive Community Initiatives for Children and Families', in J.P. Connell, A.C. Kubisch, L.B. Schorr and C.H. Weiss (eds), *New Approaches to Evaluating Community Initiatives: Volume 1, Concepts, Methods, and Contexts* (Washington, DC: Aspen Institute).

Weiss, C.H. (1997) 'Theory-Based Evaluation: Past, Present, and Future', *New Directions in Program Evaluation*, 1997(76): 41–55.

Weiss, L. (1998) *The Myth of the Powerless State* (Ithaca, NY: Cornell University Press).

Weiss, T.G. and S. Daws (eds) (2008) *The Oxford Handbook on the United Nations* (Oxford: Oxford University Press).

Wells, P. (2007) 'New Labour and Evidence Based Policy Making: 1997–2007', *People, Place and Policy Online*, 1(1): 22–9.

Werner, T. and G.K. Wilson (2008) 'Interest Groups', in D. Caramani (ed.), *Comparative Politics* (Oxford: Oxford University Press).

Wildavsky, A. (1964) *The Politics of the Budgetary Process* (Boston, MA: Little, Brown).

Wildavsky, A. (1979) *Speaking Truth to Power. The Art and Craft of Policy Analysis* (Boston: Little, Brown).

Wilensky, H.L. (1975) *The Welfare State and Equality. Structural and Ideological Roots of Public Expenditures* (Berkeley: University of California Press).

Willke, H. (1995) 'The Proactive State: The Role of National Enabling Policies in Global Socioeconomic Transformations', in H. Willke, C.P. Krück, and C. Thorn (eds), *Benevolent Conspiracies: The Role of Enabling Technologies in the Welfare State: The Cases of SDI, SEMATECH, and EUREKA* (Berlin: de Gruyter).

Wilson, J.Q. (1974) *Political Organizations* (Beverly Hills: Sage).

Wilson, J. Q. (1989) *Bureaucracy* (New York: Basic Books).

Wilson, J.Q. (1995) *Political Organizations* (Princeton: Princeton University Press).

Wilson, R. (2008) 'Policy Analysis as Policy Advice', in M. Moran, M. Rein and R.E. Goodin (eds), *The Oxford Handbook of Public Policy* (Oxford: Oxford University Press).

Windhoff-Héritier, A. (1980) *Politikimplementation: Ziel und Wirklichkeit politischer Entscheidungen* (Königstein: Anton Hain).

Windhoff-Héritier, A. (1987) *Policy-Analyse. Eine Einführung* (Frankfurt am Main: Campus).

Winter, S.C. (2003) 'Implementation Perspectives: Status and Reconsideration', in B.G. Peters and J. Pierre (eds), *Handbook of Public Administration* (Thousand Oaks, CA: Sage).

Wollmann, H. (2007) 'Policy Evaluation and Evaluation Research', in F. Fischer, G.J. Miller and M.S. Sidney (eds), *Handbook of Public Policy Analysis: Theory, Politics, and Methods* (Boca Raton: CRC Press).

Wood, B.D. and A. Doan (2003) 'The Politics of Problem Definition: Applying and Testing Threshold Models', *American Journal of Political Science*, 47(4): 640–53.

Wood, B.D. and A. Vedlitz (2007) 'Issue Definition, Information Processing, and the Politics of Global Warming', *American Journal of Political Science*, 51(3): 552–68.

Yang B.M., E.Y. Bae and J. Kim (2008) 'Economic Evaluation and Pharmaceutical Reimbursement Reform in South Korea's National Health Insurance', *Health Affairs*, 27(1):179–87.

Yin, R. (1994) *Case Study Research: Design and Methods* (Thousand Oaks: Sage).

Yothasamut J., S. Tantivess and Y. Teerawattananon (2009) 'Using Economic Evaluation in Policy Decision-Making in Asian Countries: Mission Impossible or Mission Probable?', *Value in Health*, 12(3): 26–30.

Young, O.R. (1994) *International Governance: Protecting the Environment in a Stateless Society* (Ithaca, NY: Cornell University Press).

Zahariadis, N. (1996) 'Selling British Rail. An Idea Whose Time Has Come?', *Comparative Political Studies*, 29(4): 400–22.

Zohlnhöfer, R. (2006) 'Vom Wirtschaftswunder zum kranken Mann Europas? Wirtschaftspolitik seit 1945', in M.G. Schmidt and R. Zohlnhöfer (eds), *Regieren in der Bundesrepublik Deutschland. Innen- und Außenpolitik seit 1949* (Wiesbaden: VS).

Zürn, M. (2004) 'Global Governance and Legitimacy Problems', *Government and Opposition*, 39(2): 260–87.

Zysman, J. (1994) 'How Institutions Create Historically Rooted Trajectories of Growth', *Industrial and Corporate Change*, 3(1): 243–83.

Index